Gender, Work & Population
in Sub-Saharan Africa

Titles on Geography,
Demography & Development
published by James Currey, London
& Heinemann, Portsmouth (N.H.)

The Impact of Structural Adjustment on the Population of Africa
ADERANTI ADEPOJU (ed.)

The Politics of Structural Adjustment in Nigeria
ADEBAYO O. OLUKOSHI (ed.)

Sex Roles, Population & Development in West Africa
CHRISTINE OPPONG (ed.)

Gender, Work & Population in Sub-Saharan Africa
ADERANTI ADEPOJU & CHRISTINE OPPONG (eds)

Gender, Work & Population in Sub-Saharan Africa

Edited by
Aderanti Adepoju
Christine Oppong

Published on behalf of
INTERNATIONAL LABOUR OFFICE
GENEVA
by
JAMES CURREY
LONDON
HEINEMANN
PORTSMOUTH (N.H.)

James Currey Ltd
54b Thornhill Square, Islington
London N1 1BE

Heinemann;
A Division of Reed Publishing (USA) Inc
361 Hanover Street
New Hampshire 03801

© International Labour Organisation 1994
First published 1994
1 2 3 4 5 98 97 96 95 94
A study prepared for the International Labour Office (ILO)
of the World Employment Programme with the financial support of the United Nations
Population Fund (UNFPA)

British Library Cataloguing in Publication Data

Gender, Work and Population in
Sub-Saharan Africa
    I. Adepoju, Aderanti II. Oppong,
Christine
    338.967
    ISBN 0-85255-407-9 (James Currey Paper)
           0-85255-408-7 (James Currey Cloth)
    ISBN 0-435-08953-6 (Heinemann Cloth)

Library of Congress Cataloging-in-Publication Data

Adepoju, Aderanti.
    Gender, work & population in sub-Saharan Africa / Aderanti
Adepoju, Christine Oppong.
        p. cm.
    Includes bibliographical references and index.
    ISBN 0-435-08953-6
    1. Women in rural development--Africa, Sub-Saharan. 2. Women-
-Employment--Africa, Sub-Saharan. 3. Work and family--Africa, Sub
-Saharan. 4. Fertility, Human--Africa, Sub-Saharan. I. Adepoju,
Aderanti. II. Title. III. Title: Gender, work and population in
sub-Saharan Africa.
HQ1240.5.A357A34 1994
305.42'0967--dc20   93-50628
                                                          CIP

Typeset in 10/11pt Plantin with Optima display by Colset Private Limited, Singapore
Printed and bound in Great Britain

Contents

Acknowledgements

This volume is the result of the combined efforts of many people, including the patient contributors; Mandy Eggleston, Heidi Najaf and Joan Robb, who processed words with skill and dedication beyond the call of duty; and the colleagues and others who kindly read and commented on earlier drafts and made suggestions, including Azita Berar-Awad, Ghazi Farooq, Catherine Hein, Eddy Lee, Lamine N'Diaye, Virginia Ofosu-Amaah, Ferdinand Rath, Peter Richards, Jag Sehgal and René Wéry.

The text is dedicated to those scholars and planners engaged in the tasks of collecting, analysing and using data for policy formulation and programming on issues connecting gender, population and development in a region where the basis for national and regional planning is notoriously lacking. It is hoped that it will be found especially useful in those interdisciplinary courses on population and development being held in regional training institutes.

Aderanti Adepoju
Christine Oppong

Preface

This volume is one of the publications emanating from a long and fruitful inter-agency collaboration in the labour and population field between the International Labour Office (ILO) and the United Nations Population Fund (UNFPA). It treats in an interdisciplinary manner a number of the gender issues, now at the forefront of national and international debates regarding women's roles in the spheres of production and reproduction. These issues are pertinent to both economic and population policy formulation and the design of programmes which are gender-aware and sensitive. They focus attention *inter alia* upon the availability and reliability of the economic and demographic databases and the gender-related concepts and methods used and required in collecting and analysing the information on which policies and programmes are based.

The essays included in this collection thus reflect several strands of thought and work which have been promoted in the context of an interdisciplinary programme focusing on gender, labour and population concerns at both national and workplace levels.

A theme is the need to improve modes of conceptualising, measuring, evaluating and documenting aspects of women's productive and reproductive roles and the ways in which these may interact and affect each other. Thus a concern of a number of the essays in this collection is to bring consideration of systems of familial roles and relationships more effectively into the framework used in collecting and analysing data needed for policy formulation and subsequent project design.

These essays are concerned both with the stereotypical forms of gender-blind data collection which have hampered the recording and addressing of women's productive activities and with the widespread overlapping for individuals of productive, procreative, domestic and socialising roles and the ways in which these are inextricably interlinked and interactive within overlapping systems of relationships.

Several of the essays included in this collection analyse comparative information from a number of countries. Others are case-studies from Botswana, Ghana, Swaziland and Zimbabwe. They highlight important lacunae in our understanding of economic-demographic interactions and processes at the micro level – processes which have a significant impact at national level on population and development outcomes.

They have been brought togerther *inter alia* to demonstrate to those involved in data collection, policy research, policy-making and programme design that more concerted efforts are required to document and analyse several critical dimensions of the diverse roles which women play in the processes of production and reproduction and how these are changing. A gender-aware and sensitive understanding of these processes is vital if programmes which will serve to promote and achieve the stated goals of national, social, economic and demographic policies are to be successfully designed and implemented.

René Wéry,
Acting Chief, Population Unit,
Migration and Population Branch,
Employment and Development Department,
International Labour Office, Geneva

1 Introduction

CHRISTINE OPPONG

This volume looks at various aspects of the culturally prescribed roles of women and men – that is, gender issues – and their relevance to a set of economic and population concerns, especially the recording of the economic and demographic facts upon which policies and plans are supposed to be based. The aspects of female and male roles considered include the extent to which domestic, conjugal and kin roles are overlapping and interlinked with occupational and parental roles. An important consideration is the extent to which the culturally distinct African forms of domestic organisation and systems of marriage, parenthood and kinship need to be taken into account when collecting, analysing and using economic and demographic data for policy-related purposes.

In this region women typically exhibit both the highest rates of economic activity and fertility and the highest levels of maternal and child mortality in the world. These economic and demographic facts are not, however, well recorded, nor are they as yet adequately addressed in population and development policies and programmes, though considerable progress has been made in the recent past.

Much labour is still family labour and most movable and immovable assets are still considered family property. Female family members produce and manage a large share of the goods and services, including agricultural products, with varying degrees of autonomy and self-reliance. These facts call into question the usefulness of manpower and agricultural surveys, which in the past have frequently labelled women as housewives or farmers' wives, omitting their energetic economic activities in homes and farms, which provide for the livelihood of dependent young and old, as well as themselves.

Accordingly, the major economic issue considered in this volume is the 'work' of women, and how it has been perceived, recorded and treated by statisticians, economists and policy-makers. Women's work has often been hidden in the tasks associated with domestic and conjugal roles, which has led to women's relative invisibility in the official labour statistics of many countries in the region. The reason for this admitted bias towards women's work, in contrast to men's work, is that in the past the economic activities of females have suffered even more from misconceptions, poor measurement and recording, and consequent neglect, than the work of men, since they have, as

1

noted, tended to be subsumed under women's roles as daughters, housewives and mothers.

The population focus includes aspects of reproduction in terms of the bearing, maintenance and rearing of the next generation. A pervasive concern is how these processes are being documented and regarded and how they are being affected by macro- and micro-level changes in women's and men's access to opportunities and resources at the domestic and community level. A topic of interest is ways in which women are spacing, timing, sharing and delegating child-bearing and child-care tasks in order to cope successfully over the life cycle as workers with simultaneous and often conflicting family responsibilities.

An underlying aim of this volume is thus to call the attention of economists, statisticians and demographers, as well as policy-makers working in the region, to a set of conceptual issues. These are related to the often inappropriate, stereotypical models of gender roles, in the processes of production and reproduction, which have hitherto underlain the collection of statistical data – the artefacts which are used in economic and demographic analyses and which consequently form the presumed basis upon which population policies and economic plans are based.

Accordingly, a number of conceptual problems are highlighted. The first is the fact that demographic and economic systems – including farming systems, the informal sector of small-scale, home-based production and processing, and the allocation of labour to different sectors of the labour force – can scarcely be understood within the African region if due attention is not paid to the changing and complex family systems of roles and relationships which underpin them and the multiple competing demands being made upon women's time and energy – as mothers, wives and kinswomen – by productive and reproductive responsibilities.

Attempts have been made to reach an understanding of the situation in Africa. Their limited success can be partly attributed to such oversight. Ingrid Palmer (1991) has recently stressed and discussed this point at length in the context of a consideration of gender issues in relation to national economic and population policies in the region.

Given the pervasiveness of family-based economic enterprises in the region, the assumption cannot be made that occupational roles can be studied meaningfully in isolation from familial roles. It is not simply that all workers have family responsibilities but that a large proportion of economic activity takes place in familial contexts and that a large proportion of productive resources, including land and labour, are still in the control of kin. This is particularly so for women, because they remain more enmeshed in traditional forms of economic activity – food production, processing and distribution – which typically occur on family farms and in the domestic domain. They are also likely to remain more under the control of and dependent upon relatives; they are especially dependent upon children and female relatives for assistance with both their productive and reproductive tasks. This is so for several reasons. One is the fact that male labour and land are generally controlled by men. Another is that women in the last resort are increasingly left holding and caring for the children, while they simultaneously continue their gruelling schedules of mainly manual labour. The latter applies not only in their capacity as mothers but also as grandmothers. Female-managed and maintained households are a rapidly growing household form in this region of the world as elsewhere.

The stress upon the above points might seem gratuitous, especially to any reader familiar with more than half a century of ethnographic analyses of African systems of kinship and marriage and traditional modes of organising production and reproduction in the region (see, for example, Lesthaeghe, 1989). But there is in fact a recent stream of evidence that gives cause for concern. This evidence comes from various reviews of the findings of the most ambitious, multi-country, comparative, economic and demographic surveys, as well as national data sets. It demonstrates that basic concepts underlying the collection and analysis of data – concepts such as household, parenthood and marriage – have often been poorly and stereotypically conceived and operationalised. What is more, women's work has frequently been so inadequately recorded that it is virtually impossible to make satisfactory correlations between variations in women's economic activities and demographic evidence regarding differences and changes in birth and death rates, etc. (e.g. Lloyd, 1990; Oppong, 1991).

An important and varying, yet systematically neglected, aspect of female and male roles within households and in family farming systems is the extent to which activities, interests, rights, duties, and decision-making are joint or separate – that is, shared or individually assumed. This applies to conjugal relations and to kinship – essentially the relative solidarity of sibling relationships. It is relevant to all aspects of family functioning, including property ownership and management, production and management of produce, domestic tasks, sexual relations, child-bearing and child-care (Oppong, 1982b).

Ethnographic accounts long ago demonstrated the differences between sibling and conjugal relationships in sub-Saharan Africa. On the one hand sibling relationships are solidary and unity is stressed. On the other hand conjugal roles are segregated and conjugal families are open groups with regard to basic family functioning (Oppong, 1992a). Substitutability of actors in familial roles (in both productive and reproductive activities and responsibilities) is universally typical. Thus marriages are potentially polygynous and wives often inherited or even rights in their domestic and sexual services shared during life. As far as parenting roles are concerned, substitution is evidenced by the continuing widespread prevalence of fostering of children by non-parental kin. This phenomenon is increasingly found relevant not only to the costs of child-rearing and family planning in the broadest sense, but to the allocation and spread of the benefits of child labour, and to the differential treatment, development and survival of children.

The primacy of the mother–child dyad is witnessed in the context of more complex domestic organisations, in which the most closely bonded units are mothers and their own children. All of these family features continue, to some extent, to be mirrored in traditional forms of economic organisation and have to be taken into account when economic and demographic decision-making is being analysed and considered (Oppong, 1992b).

This has led to a basic problem in the past design of data collection exercises and population policy strategies and development programmes relevant to household production and reproduction: at the micro level assumptions about the nature of family systems have been based upon an image of a stereotypical, functionally discrete, nuclear family unit, consisting of husband, wife and offspring, in which the nuclear or conjugal family is coterminous with the domestic group and simultaneously forms the unit for economic and demographic decision-making and related activities. Hence, for example, unfounded assumptions have been made that women's work is incompatible with high fertility and that women as wives are primarily unpaid family workers whose economic interests are congruent with those of their husbands.

The reality in sub-Saharan Africa is much more complex and varied – and also changing. Traditionally an array of effective mechanisms have been in place which have had the precise outcome of ensuring the security and continuity of descent groups and maximising the productive and reproductive energies of women as well as men, involving all family members from childhood to old age in these two inter-linked domains. This continues to be achieved to a diminishing degree.

The remaining twelve chapters in this volume focus attention on a variety of themes within this broad field of interest – highlighting aspects of female productive and reproductive roles and examining a variety of evidence from associated data sets of different kinds. These include national census statistics, labour force estimates, comparative data from World Fertility Surveys (WFS), Demographic and Health Surveys (DHS) and national surveys, and smaller-scale, special studies examining evidence on time use, role prescriptions, practices and beliefs. The first of these chapters gives the region-wide setting, the broad sweep of the population parameters.

Population Parameters

Chapter 2 by Aderanti Adepoju has as its subject the demographic facts which fashion population profiles in the region: the persistent high mortality and fertility and the widespread mobile search for means of survival, if not employment, in increasingly harsh economic environments. Special attention is paid to the situation of the female half of the population, noting the continuing gaps in literacy rates and schooling between the sexes and the comparatively limited access of women to various types of resource. Women's lives are to a large extent bounded by their activities and responsibilities as wives, mothers and food producers, processors and distributors, and they are seriously vulnerable to the physical dangers of unattended birth. It is noted that high parity and a high risk of maternal mortality greatly impair their health and life expectancy.

The traditional institutions that promote high levels of fertility and enable women to combine active and stressful reproduction and production throughout their lives are highlighted: early marriage, child-care delegation and fostering, and long spaces between births, maintained partly by extended breast-feeding. Children are their mothers' greatest assets – helping them in their work and giving a sense of present pleasure and future security.

The impact of change is discussed – the effects of education, of adopting modern methods of family planning, and of declines in traditional fertility levels. Aspects of these three interlinked changes in women's lives are documented, notably in Botswana, Ghana, Kenya and Zimbabwe.

Levels of maternal and infant mortality continue to be unfortunately high and are exacerbated whenever traditionally long birth intervals are no longer observed.

The impact of labour migration on women is explored – both female and male migration. During the past three decades the censuses have shown that women themselves are migrating to urban areas in greater and greater numbers in search of employment. At the same time large numbers become heads of households as husbands migrate in search of income.

Few countries are noted to be on the verge of fertility decline, and even the gains made in reducing infant mortality in the 1960s and 1970s have been eroded in the face of harsh economic conditions and policies in the 1990s.

The combination of deteriorating economic environments and performance and escalating population growth has resulted in traumatic increases in the numbers in poverty, and women and children are among the most vulnerable. The result of these changes has been increased female migration for work and growing numbers of women seeking both formal and informal sector employment.

Gender Biases: Asymmetry and Inefficiency

The next two chapters focus on women in agriculture. Chapter 3 by Ann Whitehead, a social anthropologist who has studied at first hand both the functioning of domestic groups in European and African societies and the processes of agricultural stagnation, development and change, highlights some of the implications of the prevalent gender stereotypes for economic planning. Her discussion proceeds within the context of the growing recognition that women are neglected human resources in development planning, the great historical and contemporary importance of female labour in sub-Saharan African farming, and the 20-year-long crisis in agricultural production.

She first describes women's work and women's active roles as family labourers and independent farmers. Then she notes the gaps in recording women's work in national statistics owing to unwarranted assumptions about the nature of the household and the domestic roles played by women within it (issues which are taken up again in detail in Chapters 4 to 6). Many development projects are observed to have been designed in such a way that women's planned role is often not one that they are able and willing to undertake. This fact raises the question of whether women's economic decision-making within the household enterprise has been adequately understood and whether the basis for modelling it has been established. This problem introduces the discussion of joint and separate conjugal interests within the farming household and also the question of the effects of the failure to consider women's economic decision-making on their maternal role activities and responsibilities. This leads to a consideration of maternal altruism, women's concern for their children, and how this affects their willingness to increase their labour inputs or their decisions about the sale of farm produce, etc. Finally the chapter deals with the implications of these considerations for economic policy and stresses the need for a rethinking of planning categories and methods of collecting statistics.

Safilios-Rothschild takes up these themes again in Chapter 4 and clearly spells out their importance for agricultural production. Women still remain to a large extent invisible for agricultural planners, since crucial data are either not collected or made available or not broken down by sex, or women are assumed to produce only food. Thus women have been seriously neglected at the national level in food security policies. They have also been neglected at the community and household level by extension agents. Agricultural researchers in varied contexts and farm types have documented how government extension workers, usually men, tend to assist men and neglect women farmers. Changes are, however, taking place as women increasingly appear in official statistics as the heads of households and studies are disseminated to policy-makers regarding women's management of farms and access to relevant resources and inputs. Moreover, increasing numbers of women are participating at all levels in agriculture-related work. Evaluations of agricultural projects are being carried out to see if women are being reached, and women's groups are being used to reach women farmers. Even so women are likely to need considerable assistance, both in terms of the actual delivery of agricultural resources, such as credit, and in terms of training in management, book-keeping, marketing and other skills.

As Safilios-Rothschild notes, in some situations there has of necessity been a gradual reorientation of policies and programmes towards women producers. In other cases neglect of women has led them to protest or withdraw their labour. Indeed, the crisis situation regarding agricultural production is itself conducive to greater openness on the part of policy-makers regarding appropriate remedies.

A very significant fact to which Safilios-Rothschild calls attention and which needs to be more widely disseminated is that several studies have proved that when production conditions are equal women farmers may be more productive than men.

Farm-level adaptations to reality, however, have not been matched by equivalent adaptations at the national policy-making level, and there is a lack of analysis of the separate impacts of policies on female and male farmers. As Safilios-Rothschild stresses, such neglect of gender issues in macro-economic policies has become increasingly serious following the adoption of structural adjustment policies. Ingrid Palmer (1991) has set out some of the issues that are considered most important to a gender analysis of structural adjustment in African agriculture, going beyond the sexual division of labour and the special constraints of female labour to consider the resource base of women's and men's respective management units or economic accounting units. The growing literature on African women in agriculture provides many examples of women's and men's separate as well as joint economic responsibility for different crops or fields. As Palmer has demonstrated, the picture is much more complex than the simple dichotomy of men's cash crops and women's food farming. However, there is a common underlying theme in the literature and that is the asymmetry of obligations and reciprocities in the allocation of household-level resources between women and men and this, like 'urban bias', is seen as a source of distortion and inefficiency.

Women's Work: Taking it into Account

Chapters 5 and 6 are concerned with the improvement of the databases on which national planning and policy formulation need to rest. Conventional labour force definitions have been heavily criticised for their tendency to omit much of the productive work that women do, which feeds and maintains them and members of their families. This is partly because of a broader failure to document what has in the past been called the 'informal sector' of production and service provision and partly because of the division between work inside and outside the home. The stereotype of the housewife doing housework in the home dies hard. Given the fact that waged and salaried employment occupies a small and diminishing segment of the African population, this is a major not a minor issue for planners and policy-makers.

First the issue of measuring and recording labour force participation in surveys and censuses is taken up and then the question of subsistence, mainly home-based production and processing. Chapter 7 then takes the example of one country, Ghana, and examines the treatment of statistical data over time and in the contemporary planning process.

The assessment of women's economic contribution to development became an important issue both nationally and internationally during the United Nations Decade for Women: Equality, Development and Peace 1975–85. Concern then became widespread about the persistent invisibility of much of women's economic activity at the macro level of national policy-making and accounting, while at the micro, household level women's contributions to family enterprises appear to be unpaid or unrewarded. Women's work is fully reflected neither in official labour force statistics nor in calculations of the gross national product.

It has become increasingly clear that the lack of information, both on the activities and on the monetary value of products and services produced by women, has aggravated the neglect of women and their work in national development planning – hence the emphasis on research and data collection as tools for policy development and planning.

Following the recommendations of international conferences during the United Nations Decade for Women, the United Nations and its specialised agencies have made a number of systematic efforts to recommend improvements in recording and accounting methods and to compile statistical indicators on women's situation globally. These include development of manuals on concepts and methods and the design of indicators (e.g. United Nations 1984a and b, 1990; Hussmans, Mehran and Verma, 1990) and revision of the system of national accounts, in particular the production boundary (United Nations, 1992). At the same time efforts have been made to produce and make available compilations of global statistical evidence, results of research and recommendations of statisticians, which provide useful training materials for national statisticians, planners and others (e.g. United Nations 1990, 1991; INSTRAW 1990).

A goal of these efforts is to encourage governments and other organisations to collect relevant information systematically by sex and to analyse the findings, to monitor progress and identify problem areas, and to use these data in planning and policy-making at the national and district levels.

A recent significant step forward in the tasks of conceptualising and recording economic activity occurred at the Fifteenth International Conference of Labour Statisticians held in Geneva in January 1993, when Statistics of Employment in the Informal Sector was the third item on the agenda.

Earlier, on the basis of their global review of evidence on female economic activities and how they are assessed and recorded, Dixon-Mueller and Anker (1988) have proposed several recommendations relevant to the needs of national planning and policy formulation exercises. The first is that economic indicators and other statistical data relating to population, development and human resource planning should be scrutinised closely in each country for possible sex biases resulting from the way economic and labour force concepts are defined and the way these data are collected. As they stress, a suitably revised system of data collection would not only measure women's contribution more accurately, but it would also facilitate the analysis of sex differentials in each sphere of activity, with the purpose of identifying problem areas and designing appropriate development policies and programmes. Through constructing an activity profile of agricultural households, for example, the full extent of each member's contributions can be measured and institutional barriers to improved productivity and earnings can be identified and addressed for women, men and children.

Their second recommendation is that there should be improved indicators reflecting the full extent of women's economic contribution and the gaps between women and men in their access to important economic resources, such indicators are necessary for successful development planning, and they can also help monitor the impact of macro-level economic, demographic and social changes, such as those consequent upon structural adjustment policies. The displacement or marginalisation of women in the labour force can be monitored, as can the intensified discrimination against girls or women in access to schooling, health care or other resources which may be occurring as resources diminish. At the same time planning needs and problem areas can be identified, including significant gaps between men and women in access to productive resources and employment opportunities. In addition, the impact of development projects on women and men, both negative and positive, can be assessed.

Another important result of producing better statistical indicators is that all the planners and agencies engaged in long-term economic policy-making and planning will come to realise that women are active participants in development and not simply beneficiaries.

An adequate database will also demonstrate the extent to which working women and their dependent children are among the poorest categories and their consequent need for better income-earning opportunities, training, tools and credit, etc. Lack of data may lead to the continuing invisibility of women working in the subsistence sector and in part-time, unprotected fields.

In Chapter 5, Richard Anker thus follows up his earlier work on this issue and examines the measurement of the labour force activities of women in the African region. He takes a detailed look at currently available estimates of female labour force participation in Africa and the reasons why there has been a very strong tendency to underestimate women's activities, examining published national estimates of female labour force participation. He then goes on to suggest ways these data could be improved in future surveys and censuses. His first conclusion concerns the paucity of labour force data in contrast with other regions of the world. Moreover, these data themselves consist largely of estimates, which are observed to be unstable over time and between surveys. Furthermore, different data sources are shown to give contrasting pictures of economic activity, and over a decade the ILO estimates themselves appear to change considerably. These findings lead Anker to express serious reservations as to the probable accuracy of the statistical record.

Research elsewhere has shown convincingly that reported female labour force participation rates are very sensitive to the way questionnaires are designed and questions are asked (e.g. Dixon-Mueller, 1985; Anker et al., 1988; Wainerman, 1991). Levels of participation can vary by as much as 60 per cent or more.

On the basis of the findings it seems clear that it would be helpful to test in African countries new methods of collecting data which have already been used elsewhere. Hopefully there will be opportunities in the 1990s for carrying out such tests and bringing about improvements in the ways data on women's labour force participation are collected in African countries.

In Chapter 6 Luisella Goldschmidt-Clermont discusses the issue of assessing the value of women's economic contributions in domestic and related activities. A number of time-use studies have shown the amounts of time allocated to such activities. Others have attempted to impute a monetary or material value to them. The author has elsewhere discussed studies of this kind and their policy relevance, in industrialised and developing regions (Goldschmidt-Clermont, 1982, 1983, 1987, 1990, 1992). After reviewing several illustrative examples, she goes on to examine the purposes for which such data may be collected.

First she points out that these data are required in order to monitor the economy, for what is missing in the existing statistics may amount to half or more of the labour actually expended by the population and 20–40 per cent of the goods and services actually consumed. Such data will show the balance between market- and household-based production and will help to monitor and understand the transfers which occur between them. Statistical data on households' non-market production are needed for monitoring changes in the allocation of 'extended' labour resources and for monitoring actual economic growth.

Since household production goes unrecorded, it also goes unconsidered in economic policy-making. Productive resources may only be allocated to market-oriented production, leaving those working in household production – mainly women – without the tools, training, credit and knowledge required to improve efficiency. If household working conditions were improved, labour might be released for other purposes. Information in this area is required for effective development policies. Similarly, the labour involved in domestic production needs to be documented for human resource planning and labour market policies. It is also needed to inform welfare policies, to establish household income comparisons, to measure standards of living, to promote appropriate legislation in connection with divorce settlements, inheritance, etc. Last but not least the author notes the relevance of such data to the formulation of population policies, since the economic value of children in household-based production is still very high in many countries, thus promoting high fertility. On the other hand, the intensity and severity of household labour demands may be connected with infant mortality and maternal morbidity, as for example the ill-effects upon pregnant women of carrying heavy loads of wood and water.

Goldschmidt-Clermont then goes on to describe methods which may be used to impute value to households' non-market output and to measure labour inputs.

Chapter 7 by Oti Boateng, Chief Government Statistician of Ghana, discusses the importance not only of providing better global statistics on economic and demographic issues, but also of producing detailed disaggregated data in order to permit improved analyses of women's situation and policy decisions more precisely focusing on women's needs. He thus reviews statistical data collection activities in Ghana, which have a century-old history, and examines collection and analysis of data on population issues. Finally he looks at the existing sex-specific data and their utilisation for policy decisions and implementation. The institutional and legal framework for statistical collection, analysis and use is also examined in a country with one of the best statistical records in the region.

Balancing Productive and Reproductive Roles

By now there is ample evidence that the ways in which women's work, however defined, is associated with child-bearing and levels of fertility and its regulation differ widely in different contexts according to an array of factors. Prominent among these is the extent to which productive and reproductive activities are simultaneously compatible.

In order to gain a more realistic picture of the potential and actual linkages between women's reproductive and subsequently socialising activity on the one hand and productive activities on the other, both types of activity need to be considered in detail and in parallel and their potential effects one upon the other. Thus, being pregnant is a different activity from breast-feeding in terms of a woman's strength, nutritional requirements and availability for work. Critical to the types of linkages found between women's economic activity and child-bearing and rearing are the range of forms each takes in a given socio-economic and cultural environment.

As Lloyd (1990) has argued and recently demonstrated, a creative approach to data analysis – and one might add collection – is called for in the study of work–fertility relationships. Many different issues need to be considered simultaneously, including the level of national and regional socio-economic development, the stage in the individual's life cycle and their time perspective (i.e. short-term or long-term), and the locus of control. Moreover, critical to any analysis are the characteristics of work, as well as the timing of births over the life cycle and the fact that levels of productive–reproductive role conflict will vary in different cultural and socio-economic contexts, according to the system of production and reproduction in which each is embedded. Furthermore, individual reactions to such potential conflicts and the demographic outcomes, including the impact on birth and death rates, will depend upon the psychic, social and material resources of the women concerned within their particular contexts of opportunities, values and available choices, and constraints of various kinds – including degree of control by elders and husbands (Oppong, 1983).

Given the many factors involved, the diversity of the traditional systems of production and reproduction, and the multiple causes of change, there is likely to be considerable variation observable at the individual level, even if in the macro perspective little observable demographic change appears to be taking place.

At the global level, studies have found that there is a consistent, strong and significant negative relationship between women's employment in professional and clerical (modern) occupations and completed fertility only in countries at the highest levels of development (United Nations, 1987). Such a strong negative relationship is not necessarily found in less affluent countries at lower levels of economic development, particularly African countries – in other words in contexts in which child-rearing is more cheaply and easily delegated and thus occupational–maternal role conflicts are minimised. Moreover, the low level of male incomes is likely to spur wives to earn. In addition, considerable numbers of women are raising children with only meagre or no benefit of male support.

Micro as well as macro evidence has upheld the contention that the most important ways in which modern sector work can affect fertility are through delaying age at marriage and through fertility regulation behaviour (e.g. United Nations, 1985). It is possible that no statistically observable relationship has been found between agricultural work and fertility, partly because of problems in measuring and defining economic activity. As already noted above, much of women's farming is not even officially documented.

Differences do exist in the records of female work rates according to life cycle, urban/rural residence and number of years of schooling. Rates often appear to increase with age through the reproductive years. Rural rates appear higher than urban rates in Africa, and more years of schooling are associated with higher recorded rates. This last, however, may be because lower levels of education are associated with more informal work, which is less likely to be reflected in official statistics. Given these problems of recording work, Lloyd (1990, p. 29) has recently warned that much of the lack of uniformity in the findings of previous empirical studies on the work–fertility connection can probably be attributed to differences in the definition and measurement of women's work in different countries. We might also mention here the systematic biases against recording 'informal sector activities', 'home-based production' and women's work on 'family farms', as discussed above.

In general, demographic data linked to information on female or male economic activities are lacking or based on estimates. No country has complete vital statistics and a published national census within ten years of a continuous population register. Some countries of the subregion suffer from an almost total lack of demographic data of all kinds. The sources of demographic data available include censuses, surveys and administrative records. The demographic surveys have included the World Fertility Surveys (WFS); the Westinghouse Demographic and Health Surveys (DHS); surveys undertaken in the context of the African Household Survey Capability Programme; socio-economic surveys which have a demographic component, such as the living standards measurement study of the World Bank; and *ad hoc* surveys. These multi-country surveys have at least included a limited amount of social and economic data as well as demographic variables, which increases their usefulness. The African countries which took part in the WFS all felt that the surveys had made an important contribution to knowledge of fertility. Indeed, fertility-related behaviour in the region has been better documented than migration or mortality.

Given the serious shortcomings of the multi-country surveys – with their focus on fertility (and health-related factors) at the expense of the measurement of other important variables – their potential explanatory power is limited. Women's economic activity rates are recognised as being a weak area in WFS work, and in the DHS only one West African country, Ghana, included a module on women's economic activity.

Chapter 8 makes use of this best data set from the DHS, which combines information on work and child-bearing and child location. In their chapter Blanc and Lloyd thus examine how women cope with the demands of work and child-bearing and child-rearing over the life cycle. They use a categorisation of work which is likely to be useful to future researchers. Economic activity is classified according to *type of occupation, location, mobility* and *type of remuneration*.

They deduce from their analysis – as have previous researchers describing how West African women juggle and cope with maternal, occupational and domestic activities and responsibilities – that women manage to combine cash work and child-bearing and rearing over the life cycle through child fostering and delegated child-care and a considerable amount of informal sector work, which can be combined with child-rearing. However, as reluctance to foster out small children grows, the costs of paid domestic help rise, and older siblings go to school, the costs of children to mothers are probably beginning to rise. In addition, the inadequacy of women's earnings to maintain dependants may mean greater dependence upon the fathers of their children, which may make inroads upon their autonomy and independence – a cost for women. Migration, urban housing costs, relatively meagre salary levels, and higher costs of food and transport are also likely to make rearing children more costly and reduce the demand for fostered children and their potential usefulness to employed mothers.

In Chapter 9 Robert Mazur and Marvellous Mhloyi look at the nature of the relationships between women's work and fertility in Zimbabwe. Their discussion is set within a historical framework of widespread dislocation of the population and rapid growth of the potential labour force seeking wage employment. Women's productive and reproductive roles are circumscribed by traditional expectations prescribing self-effacement and altruism in the familial context. Their power and status in maturity stem from grandmotherhood. At the same time, changes in the modern economy are affecting women's participation in agricultural and urban occupations. Their agricultural burdens are considerable and often shouldered alone, following male migration. Their off-farm activities are many and varied as they try to cope with the needs of dependent families. Urban employed women have multiple constraints to overcome, including husbands' fears, employers' discrimination, sex-segregated labour markets and lack of day care for children. More than a quarter of formal sector employment for women is domestic service and many are reduced to long hours of hard, unmechanised work in the informal sector, where they lack credit and suffer exploitation.

Significantly, the Zimbabwe Demographic and Health Survey (Zimbabwe, Central Statistical Office, 1989) indicated a marked decline in the previously high and stable fertility levels, leading to an estimated completed family size of 5.5, with urban women having an average of 4.1 births. Among the factors leading to change are trends towards delayed marriage among women with higher education. However, these are the women who also curtail breast-feeding, thus leading to potentially more closely spaced births. An important change since the 1984 Zimbabwe Reproductive Health Survey is the increased knowledge and use of modern contraceptives, especially by urban and educated women. Husbands' disapproval and lack of conjugal communication about family planning are among the documented obstacles to more widespread use.

An analysis of data on the fertility of women by type of occupation supports the hypothesis of greater incompatibility between formal sector work and child-bearing and rearing. Changes taking place in reproductive patterns are also clearly linked to the expansion of educational and health services to the previously excluded majority.

The subject of Chapter 10 by Aderanti Adepoju is the Swazi people, a small and ethnically homogeneous group with a considerable amount of male labour migration to South Africa. The population is young, rapidly growing, and characterised by high fertility, which is promoted and supported by an interlinked array of factors, including high levels of infant mortality. Traditional aspects of the family system persist, as documented in other countries in the region, including the widespread substitution of individuals in their conjugal, filial and parental roles through polygyny and fostering. This partly offsets the insecurity and crises prompted by the high levels of male absence and maternal and infant mortality.

The low sex ratio of males to females associated with male out-migration also has the corollary of a high proportion of female-headed households. In spite of this, women's roles are subject to constant and close scrutiny by husbands and in-laws. Respect, humility and submission are linked to legal minority status on the one hand, and heavy burdens of domestic and agricultural responsibility and activity on the other. Girls' and boys' opportunities to go to school are unequal, although the gap has been narrowing of late in spite of girls higher drop-out rates. One consequence of this is higher rates of male modern sector employment. Women remain typically in undocumented domestic and agricultural work, but their participation in wage employment is noted to be increasing.

The combination of high levels of fertility and of economic activity means that women are subject to widespread strain and role conflict, as they try to cope with the multiple and conflicting demands of babies and jobs, often without the legal, material, physical or psychological support of a husband.

Modern methods of birth spacing are increasingly widely used, despite the fact that they are considered 'unSwazi' and are forbidden by Swazi custom.

Chapters 8, 9 and 10 thus all examine the productive and reproductive roles of women, and to some extent men, in the context of household- and national-level strategies and resources. Changes at both levels are observed against a backcloth of comparative continuity in terms of gender and the sets of expectations associated with female roles.

Each chapter also depicts the uneasy contradictions in the expectations attached to female and male roles. Women in particular are seen to be simultaneously subject to conflicting prescriptions, as traditional role constraints persist and new demands are made upon them.

Family Welfare and Planning

Anthropologists have long noted the importance of the ready delegation of child-care to siblings and others for women's ability to make important contributions to subsistence economies. They have also documented the importance of traditional mechanisms of post-partum conjugal separation, whether within the same or different households, and sexual abstinence and prolonged breast-feeding for ensuring the spacing and stopping of births over the life cycle. The timing of births and child-care responsibilities is obviously an important factor in facilitating women's ability to balance productive and reproductive roles. Partial breast-feeding and early weaning on to solid foods has meanwhile been demonstrated to be associated with the mother's comparatively heavier involvement in subsistence activities. Women's participation in the subsistence economy thus not only has implications in terms of higher morbidity and mortality of infants, through the very early introduction of weaning foods to the newborn, but also has implications in terms of raising fertility, through cessation of full breast-feeding, shortening of the anovulatory period, and hence shorter birth intervals.

The post-partum sexual abstinence rule has played an important part in counteracting these tendencies towards higher mortality and shorter birth intervals. It also seems to be more widely prevalent in societies in which women are more actively engaged in subsistence activities. This underlines the fact that traditional mechanisms for spacing births are in place not only to protect the health and development of mother and child, as discussed below, but also to maintain the precarious balance between occupational/domestic and maternal role demands upon time and energy, to which the mother is constantly subject – a point which has been substantiated *inter alia* by detailed Yoruba field work (Adeokun, 1983). In the past decade, population scholars have built upon the earlier ethnographic work, demonstrating the importance of these spacing mechanisms and their erosion for fertility levels in sub-Saharan Africa (Page and Lesthaege, 1981; Lesthaege, 1989).

Contemporary case-studies of the infant feeding practices of working mothers in city environments have shown there are no simple direct associations between maternal employment, breast-feeding duration and use of feeding bottles, the modern mother substitute (Winikoff and Castle, 1988). These studies have rather shown the diversity and complexity of the changes that are taking place and the significance of several variables, including location of work, conditions of work – including maternity benefits and leave, and hours of work – child-care alternatives, job security and income effects. Separation of mother and baby because of work demands obviously affects the duration and intensity of breast-feeding, sometimes leading to the very early introduction of bottle-feeding. Continuation rates for breast-feeding depend upon such factors as ability to break up the working day by a home visit. It is not surprising in such contexts that educated and employed urban women are often observed to have shorter birth intervals than their rural counterparts.

In agricultural contexts the seasonality of labour demands on time and energy are also observed to have a serious impact upon women's ability to cope with the demands of pregnancy or lactation as well as farm work (Palmer, 1981). Periods of gruelling farm labour are associated with low birth-weights, early weaning, and thus short birth intervals and pressures towards higher levels of both infant mortality and fertility. These topics are in great need of detailed and serious study to see to what extent pressures on women's time at certain points in the agricultural cycle may lead to curtailment of breast-feeding and the consequent demographic effects, and what impact different types of agricultural innovation may have on these. Such potential changes need to be carefully studied in situations in which structural adjustment programmes are bringing about radical changes in the division of labour and resources in agriculture as incentives and relative prices change. Similarly, changes in land tenure and farming techniques may have a profound impact on women's farming work and ability to breast-feed (Oppong, 1991; Palmer, 1991).

African populations have hitherto shown considerable resistance to erosion of the post-partum taboo on sexual relations (Schoenmaeckers et al., 1981). The taboo does, however, require a high degree of social control within each local community and domestic and kin group, and can accordingly be quickly eroded if the pace of migration and escape from kin and community controls increases. It is an integral element in a system of social organisation – including polygyny, bride-wealth, localised lineage organisation, separation and distancing of spouses, and maintenance of control over land and labour by elders – which is fast breaking down in the face of social and spatial mobility and rapid urbanisation.

A decade ago, Mabogunje (1981) called attention to the fact that illiterate girls (largely still engaged in agriculture) remain subject to socialisation in traditional patterns of heterosexual relations and motherhood, and remain under the control of older kinswomen and affines, and are thus likely to maintain customary practices ensuring child spacing of three years or more. In contrast, highly educated women are likely to enjoy greater employment opportunities and access to modern family planning, as well as substitute foods and care for infants. This may not necessarily maintain traditionally long birth-spacing rhythms, but does make it possible to promote child survival and maternal health and stop at a certain family size. Evidence has shown that such women may adopt demographic and contraceptive innovations if their education and employment cause maternal–occupational role strain and conflict. Their parental aspirations for child 'quality' may also change, affected by possibilities and attitudes to child-care delegation, which are linked to changes in familial roles (e.g. Oppong and Abu, 1987).

More problematic, however, is the situation of young women who have just a few years of schooling and through this experience, and the migration for schooling and work often associated with it, have been removed from situations in which traditional norms and sanctions on sexual relations and behaviour prevail. This category of young women is the one most rapidly increasing both in absolute terms and in terms of proportion of the total female population. Thus, it is not surprising that rising levels of fertility are being observed and that the relationship between schooling and fertility often shows a U-shape rather than a straight negative relationship. Moreover, there is growing concern in most countries in the region regarding unsanctioned sexual intercourse and pregnancies among teenagers, including schoolgirls (Yeboah, 1993).

The last three chapters in this volume treat several interlinked themes all connected with aspects of family welfare and family planning and relevant to traditional and modern modes of child nursing, spacing and care in relation to women's work schedules. Chapter 11 by Yaw Ofosu thus considers breast-feeding and birth spacing. Chapter 12 by Katherine Abu takes a close look at factors affecting modern family planning in a northern Ghanaian town, and Chapter 13 by Benedicte Ingstad moves to Southern Africa and describes the roles played by grandmothers in Botswana in maintaining household viability.

In Chapter 11, Ofosu indicates the positive associations between mean duration of breast-feeding and post-partum amenorrhoea, demonstrating that lactational amenorrhoea makes an important contribution to the length of the birth interval among many women, except in those cases in which post-partum abstinence exceeds breast-feeding in duration. He warns that, given the important part played by prolonged breast-feeding and post-partum abstinence in traditional birth spacing in much of sub-Saharan Africa, these ongoing changes could have serious consequences, not only for the tempo of child-bearing but for infant survival, if appropriate policies are not put in place in good time. In cases in which shorter duration of breast-feeding is a consequence of the mother's labour force participation and the resulting separation of mother and baby, resources are required to promote the health of the child and maintain traditional child spacing patterns – that is, adequate bottle-feeding and modern contraception. Without these the survival of both mothers and children is at risk, as the calculations regarding the impact of short birth intervals on infant and maternal mortality levels attest.

There is some evidence among the most 'modernised' subpopulations that long inter-birth intervals are being maintained by modern means. Ofosu concludes as a result of his analysis that in West Africa the pace of change towards shorter durations of breast-feeding differs among different ethnic groups. This finding is meaningful if, like Lesthaege (1989), we realise that ethnicity stands for distinctive characteristics of the social organisation, including the sexual division of labour, and particular systems of kinship and marriage.

In Chapter 12 Katharine Abu addresses several critical research and programme issues, showing how small, informal qualitative studies can provide in-depth information on sensitive issues which are highly relevant to the development of communication strategies and the content of family welfare and family planning educational campaigns. She underlines the need for collecting information by a variety of methods simultaneously, as each method may reveal a different dimension of the underlying 'realities' and of people's conflicting attitudes and values. She clearly demonstrates the case for separate consideration of women's and men's points of view, situations and objectives. Although in some cases communication and consensus among husbands and wives may be possible, in many other cultural and socio-economic contexts female and male strategies and goals may be so conflicting as to prejudice the possibility of discussion or agreement. A basic consideration is that a wife only has one spouse at a time, while a man is always in a potentially polygynous conjugal situation.

Equally interesting is the contrast between the family planning attitudes and practices of people from two ethnic groups, in which the traditional values and practices associated with kinship, marriage, parenthood and domestic organisation differ considerably, affecting the ways in which both women and men perceive their reproductive behaviour and options.

Again the detailed contrast apparent between the views and actions of the materially impoverished and the secure, the illiterate and the literate, demonstrates the need to adapt communication strategies and messages sensitively according to the occupational niches of the people concerned. Change from the traditional values and practices surrounding procreation, child maintenance and child-care is seen to vary according to material and educational circumstances.

Chapter 13 focuses on the position of the maternal grandmother in changing Tswana society and particularly on her potentially important role with regard to the family planning practices of her daughters and the care of their children. In discussing family policies and their implication for demographic change in developing countries, attention has mostly been given to the role of the couple actually producing the children, and little to the role of other family or household members. This is in spite of an increasing awareness among planners, implementers and scientists of the importance of the grandparental generation in decision-making regarding sex and procreation in many developing countries.

Ingstad gives a brief outline of some of the main changes that have taken place in rural Botswana as a result of increased dependence on a money economy, especially through labour migration of men to South Africa. She emphasises two related consequences of this, the large (and probably increasing) number of households that are temporarily or permanently female-headed and the increasing number of children born out of wedlock and with no officially recognised father figure. These children most often grow up in their maternal grandparents'/grandmother's household, with or without the presence of their own mother. For these children, the maternal grandmother often becomes the most important care person, provider and decision-maker, thus also influencing profoundly their chances of survival. Several aspects of the roles of maternal grandmothers are discussed, including their potential and observed influence on the family planning decisions of their unmarried daughters, their influence on breast-feeding and nutrition, the ways in which they may encourage their daughters to continue nursing or make it possible for them to leave by taking over the care of the child, and their influence on the child's chances of survival through the quality of maintenance and care given.

Recognition of the maternal grandmother as an important provider of sustenance, care-giver and decision-maker in rural Botswana has implications for the planning and implementation of family welfare programmes, and underlines the fact that older women are an important target group for information and support services.

This, like several of the earlier chapters, provides an example of the kind of detailed analysis of economic, demographic and cultural data that is required if the pressures and constraints maintaining tradition and acting as spurs to innovation, in the area of work, family welfare and family responsibilities, are to be understood, and appropriate policies and programmes designed and implemented.

2 The Demographic Profile: Sustained High Mortality & Fertility & Migration for Employment ADERANTI ADEPOJU

The concern of African governments with current demographic crises encompasses a variety of issues, including the problem of rapid population growth and high fertility; high mortality, especially among infants and mothers; over-rapid urbanisation; population maldistribution, and teenage pregnancies. This chapter addresses the socio-economic environment that gives rise to and sustains high levels of fertility and mortality, and migration for employment. The emphasis is on gender issues, with special attention to the situation of the female half of the population in the region, including inequalities in access to resources in the modern world such as education and employment.

A typical African woman is probably the most underprivileged human being, illiterate, with limited access to resources. She not only faces discrimination and segregation, both in the organised labour market and in informal sector employment, but even has different legal rights as regards inheritance, land, credit, etc. At the moment, adult women get less education, lower pay – even when they work longer hours – and less access to professional training than men (Population Crisis Committee, 1988). Overall, 80 per cent of African women live and work in the rural areas under conditions that support and sustain high fertility and where the expected – sometimes actual – economic contribution of children is substantial.

Recognition is growing that there is a high social dividend to be gained from investing in women: better family nutrition, reduced fertility, lower infant mortality and lower population growth – gains that could accrue through educating women (Sadik, 1990a).

The Demographic Setting

The population of Africa, estimated at 513 million in 1983, increased rapidly to almost 648 million in 1990 and is expected to reach 813 million by the end of this century. The estimated rate of population growth in Africa, about 3 per cent per annum, stems from high fertility, with an average birth rate of 43 per thousand, and relatively high but declining mortality, about 13 per thousand in 1990 (Table 2.1).

Table 2.1 Population indicators for sub-Saharan Africa, 1990

| | Population in thousands | | Growth rate (%) 1990–95 | Government appraisal 1988[a] | Birth rate per 1000 1990 | Death rate per 1000 1990 | Life expectancy 1990 | Infant mortality per 1000 1990 | % Urban 1990 | Urban growth rate (%) 1990–95 | Fertility rate per woman 1990 |
	Mid-1990	2025									
World total	5 292 177	8 466 516	1.7		26	9	63	64	43	2.6	3.3
More developed regions[b]	1 205 192	1 352 086	0.5		13	9	74	12	72	0.8	1.9
Less developed regions[c]	4 086 985	7 114 429	2.1		29	9	61	71	33	3.6	3.7
Africa	647 518	1 580 984	3.0		43	13	53	96	34	4.9	5.1
East Africa[d]	194 822	523 024	3.2		47	15	51	106	22	6.4	6.6
Burundi	5 451	13 099	2.9	H	44	15	51	102	7	7.7	6.1
Ethiopia	46 743	112 268	2.7	H	46	21	43	142	12	5.2	6.3
Kenya	25 129	77 615	4.1	H	50	9	60	64	23	7.3	7.6
Madagascar	11 979	32 983	3.2	S	44	12	55	110	25	5.9	6.5
Malawi	8 427	22 804	3.3	H	51	18	48	138	14	7.0	6.9
Mauritius[e]	1 103	1 479	1.2	S	17	5	70	19	42	1.7	1.9
Mozambique	15 663	34 368	2.7	S	43	16	48	130	26	7.6	6.2
Rwanda	7 231	18 079	3.4	H	49	15	50	111	7	7.4	8.0
Somalia	7 554	18 903	2.4	S	46	18	46	121	36	4.4	6.5
Uganda	18 441	55 198	3.5	H	49	13	53	93	10	6.1	6.8
United Republic of Tanzania	27 328	84 783	3.7	H	49	12	54	96	32	7.9	7.0
Zambia	8 455	25 465	3.7	H	49	12	55	71	55	5.5	7.0
Zimbabwe	9 720	22 620	3.1		39	8	60	64	27	5.4	5.3
Central Africa[f]	69 563	179 645	2.0		44	14	52	98	39	4.9	6.0
Angola	10 020	24 730	2.8	S	46	18	46	127	28	5.4	6.3
Cameroon	11 245	26 177	2.7	H	41	14	52	86	49	5.0	5.7
Central African Rep.	2 912	6 814	2.5	H	43	18	47	122	46	4.2	5.8
Chad	5 678	13 244	2.5	S	43	17	47	122	33	5.8	5.8
Congo	1 994	4 963	2.8	L	43	15	50	65	42	4.3	5.8
Gabon	1 170	2 927	3.3	L	43	15	53	94	45	5.1	5.3
Zaïre	35 990	99 512	3.2	S	44	12	54	90	39	4.8	6.0

North Africa g	142 648	275 020	2.5		34	9	61	73	44	3.7	4.8
Algeria	25 363	50 590	2.9	H	36	7	64	60	44	4.1	5.2
Egypt	54 059	93 976	2.2	H	30	8	63	70	48	3.4	4.2
Libyan Arab Jamahiriya	4 544	12 846	3.6	S	43	8	63	68	70	4.7	6.7
Morocco	25 138	44 367	2.4	H	31	8	63	68	48	3.8	4.2
Sudan	25 195	59 594	2.9	S	43	14	51	99	22	4.6	6.3
Tunisia	8 168	13 283	1.0	H	26	6	67	47	54	2.7	3.4
Southern Africa	40 972	78 022	2.3		31	8	62	66	55	3.3	4.4
Botswana	1 285	3 363	3.5	H	44	9	60	58	23	7.0	5.9
Lesotho	1 773	4 272	2.8	H	39	10	58	89	20	6.2	5.6
Namibia	1 875	4 948	3.1		41	10	58	97	56	4.8	5.7
South Africa	35 248	63 232	2.1	H	29	8	62	62	58	3.1	4.2
West Africa h	199 511	525 271	3.3		47	14	51	102	33	5.5	6.7
Benin	4 740	12 987	3.2	S	49	17	48	101	41	5.9	6.9
Burkina Faso	9 006	22 677	2.8	S	46	17	49	126	9	5.9	6.4
Côte d'Ivoire	12 595	39 842	3.9	S	50	12	54	87	46	5.6	7.3
Ghana	15 020	37 031	3.1	H	42	11	56	81	33	4.3	6.2
Guinea	6 875	15 710	2.5	S	45	20	44	136	25	5.2	6.1
Liberia	2 553	7 240	3.3	H	44	12	56	79	44	5.1	6.4
Mali	9 361	24 141	3.0	S	48	19	46	159	19	4.7	6.6
Mauritania	2 024	4 962	2.8	S	45	17	48	116	42	5.7	6.4
Niger	7 109	18 940	3.1	H	50	18	46	124	19	6.5	7.0
Nigeria	133 016	301 312	3.5	H	48	14	52	96	35	5.7	6.8
Senegal	7 369	16 364	2.7	H	44	17	47	117	38	4.1	6.2
Seirra Leone	4 150	9 640	2.6	H	47	21	43	142	32	5.0	6.4
Togo	3 454	9 500	3.1	S	43	12	55	85	25	5.9	6.0

Notes : [a] Government appraisal of population growth: L = too low; S = satisfactory; H = too high.
[b] More developed regions comprise Northern America, Japan, all regions of Europe, Australia, New Zealand and the former Union of Soviet Socialist Republics.
[c] Less developed regions comprise all regions of Africa and Latin America, all regions of Asia excluding Japan, Melanesia, Micronesia and Polynesia.
[d] Including British Indian Ocean Territory and Seychelles.
[e] Including Agalesa, Rodrigues and St Brandon.
[f] Including São Tomé and Príncipe.
[g] Including Western Sahara.
[h] Including St Helena.

Source: Sadik, 1990a.

These rates, the highest in the world, are unlikely to decline substantially by the turn of the century. Even if the trends could be altered, the continent's population, because of the inbuilt momentum of a youthful age structure, would not only double within a generation but would also remain young. In 1990, about 45 per cent of the population of Africa was under the age of 15 while only 3 per cent was aged 65 or over. High, and in some cases rising, fertility and gradually declining mortality will reinforce this young age structure.

The diversity within the overall population geography of Africa requires, however, that generalisations should be qualified. Whereas high rates of population growth are experienced in West and East Africa (3.3 and 3.2 per cent, respectively), relatively low rates exist in Central Africa (2.0 per cent in 1990). However, the latter countries form a fairly small group and in time, given the extensive improvements in health standards that are occurring in most of them, especially Gabon, they may well catch up with the rest in this phenomenal growth process. Intra-regional and intra-country differences in growth rates are similarly very extensive (Adepoju and Clarke, 1985).

Africa has one of the lowest proportions of its population living in urban areas, 34 per cent in 1990, up from 27 per cent in 1983 (Table 2.1), but the rate of growth of the urban population is by far the highest among the regions of the world: 5 per cent per year during the 1960s, increasing to 7 per cent during the 1980–85 period, and dropping down to 5 per cent again by 1990. This rapid urban growth results from a combination of high natural increase and accelerated in-migration to towns. In 1980 about 133 million people lived in towns, but by the end of this century there may be 350 million urban dwellers, about 42 per cent of the total population. Even then Africa will still be one of the least urbanised regions of the world. There is, however, a remarkable variation between African regions, ranging from only 22 per cent in East Africa, 33 per cent in West Africa and 39 per cent in Central Africa to 44 per cent in North Africa and 55 per cent in Southern Africa (including the Republic of South Africa) in 1990 (Table 2.1). This is a substantial increase from the situation in 1983: 14 per cent in East Africa, 22 per cent in West Africa, 30 per cent in Central Africa, 42 per cent in North Africa and 46 per cent in Southern Africa (Adepoju and Clarke, 1985).

In spite of this high growth rate of the urban centres, Africa's rural population has been increasing steadily at close to 2 per cent per annum, making it the fastest growing of all the world regions except South Asia. This is in spite of the increasing exodus of youth from the rural areas in the prime of both productive and reproductive periods, and, in particular, the dislocating effects of out-migration on marriage patterns and family organisation in rural areas (Adepoju, 1988).

The average infant mortality rate for Africa of about 120 deaths per thousand live births in 1983 had declined slightly to 114 per thousand by 1988. In fact deaths among infants in the first year of life and among children up to the age of 5 account for about 50 per cent of all deaths in Africa (Sadik, 1989). By 1990, some progress had been made, with an estimated infant mortality rate of 96 deaths per thousand (Table 2.1). Substantial regional variations exist: East Africa, with an estimated infant mortality rate of 106 per thousand, tops the list, closely followed by West Africa (102 per thousand) and Central Africa (98 per thousand) (Table 2.1).

Children in Africa have the world's lowest life expectancy at birth, about 49 years for boys and 52 years for girls compared with 62 and 66 years respectively in Latin America and 69 and 77 years in North America. Overall, life expectancy in Africa was 14 years short of the Latin American average, 18 years short of the East Asian average and 25 years short of the North American average during 1980-85. Life expectancy was, with one or two exceptions, a full four years or more higher for females than males in 1987 (World Bank, 1989c). The estimated average life expectancy of 53 years in 1990 reflects slight improvements in health conditions, with North and Southern Africa recording the highest gains at 61 and 62 years, respectively.

Birth and death rates are also higher in Africa than in any other region of the world. The average number of children born to women in Africa exceeds six in several countries of the region; their counterparts in Latin America have four, with three in Asia and two in developed countries. Maternal mortality rates in Africa range from 16 to 110 deaths per thousand births. Prevailing rates are between 7 and 15 in developed countries (Sadik, 1990a). A crude death rate of 13 per thousand in 1990 (down from 16 per thousand in 1983) remains high, especially in East Africa (15 per thousand) and West and Central Africa (14 per thousand). Southern and North Africa recorded the lowest rates at 8 and 9 per thousand, respectively (Table 2.1).

Access to Education

Until recently the bias rooted in traditional sex roles limited the access of girls to formal education, especially beyond the primary level. In theory, girls are faced with the same education opportunity structure as boys. In practice, however, socio-cultural constraints still inhibit the education of girls beyond a certain level in various parts of the region and notably in Muslim areas.

The adult illiteracy rate (as a percentage of the population aged 15 and over) for sub-Saharan African countries was higher than for any other region of the world for both women (75 per cent) and men (54 per cent), in spite of the fact that since independence African governments have invested heavily in education, especially at the primary level. Consequently adult literacy has been increasing generally, and women have made important gains both in absolute levels of literacy and in female–male literacy ratios in most countries. Efforts to reduce female illiteracy are most evident among the youngest age group (Adepoju, 1991c).

In spite of the considerable efforts to introduce universal primary education, however, opportunities for education at any level still remain limited and educational opportunities for girls continue to lag behind those for boys. Efforts to bridge the gap in the 1960s brought improvements in school enrolment for girls: the percentage of girls aged 6–11 years enrolled in primary schools doubled (from 17 to 35 per cent) compared with an increase from 46 to 63 per cent for boys. The figures rose to 44 per cent for girls and 74 per cent for boys in the 1970s (Newman, 1984).

At the secondary level only 11 per cent of girls aged 12–17 years were enrolled in school in the 1980s. This had increased to 14 per cent by 1985. For boys, the corresponding proportions were 20 and 29 per cent respectively. At the tertiary level, the 1987 statistical year book published by the United Nations Educational, Scientific and Cultural Organisation (UNESCO) records a gross enrolment for females of 0.6 per cent of the 20–24 age group in 1980 and 0.8 per cent in 1985. Corresponding male enrolment was 2.1 per cent in 1980 and 2.7 per cent in 1985.

The extent to which females have access to literacy, education and vocational training programmes is an important indicator of current and potential female status in the sense that literacy and education are prerequisites for full participation in modern society. The relative access of males and females to these programmes can be measured in terms of literacy ratios, school enrolment, educational attainment, drop-out rates, and repeated years, etc., for males and females.

Mothers' education has been shown to be an important – perhaps the single most important – determinant of a family's health and nutrition. Indeed, women's education can be a reliable predictor of fertility: it has the strongest influence on women's control over their lives. Educated women tend to get married at older ages, and they are more likely to live in urban areas and work in the wage sector (Sadik, 1989). A few years' formal education has the potential to lower women's fertility: directly through increasing awareness of contraception and/or indirectly through raising the age at marriage, thereby reducing both the span of child-bearing years and the demand for children.

The African Woman's Productive and Reproductive Roles

In the traditional subsistence situation, early marriage is the norm for women, and a woman's life is closely oriented around her capacities to reproduce and provide for her family. Arduous involvement in child-bearing and rearing and the economic and domestic activities required for maintenance of children and grandchildren continues throughout life. The life cycle and plight of the average African woman were aptly described by a United Nations (1975) report thus:

> Before the age of 20, the [African] female carried a full load of adult responsibilities; by age 25 she might have given birth half a dozen times, by age 40 she might already be exhausted by illness, poor nutrition, child bearing and heavy work in the fields and at home; she dies early.

Those women who survive the period of maternal mortality tend on average to die at a relatively older age than their male counterparts. African women spend more or less all of their 30 years of reproductive life involved in the physical stresses of child-bearing and nursing. The large number of children they have and the high risk of maternal mortality greatly impair their health and life expectancy.

The early age of marriage and child-bearing among women, pregnancy wastage, and limited access to education, training and remunerated employment have severely constrained women's life chances and opportunities. The multiple demands and responsibilities of women's roles as child-bearers and rearers, workers inside and outside the home, and household managers are such that they often experience stress and conflict. In ideal circumstances, of course, their roles might complement each other. Child-care and fostering of children by non-parental kin enable women to balance their various activities.

The diverse patterns of participation of African women in economic activities reflect the varied cultural traditions, historical developments and political and ecological systems in the region. Certain characteristic and pervasive patterns are, however, either typical of developing countries in general or unique to the region but evident in spite of the poor quality of data on work, a topic on which later chapters focus attention. Thus, like women elsewhere in the developing world, they spend more of their time working than men (United Nations, 1991, p. 81). Indeed the gap between the hours worked by women and men is accounted to be greater in Africa than elsewhere in the world except for Asia and the Pacific regions. Studies have documented women as working 12–13 hours a week more than men and the prevalent economic and environmental crises have increased the working hours of the poorest women, as they struggle to maintain their families and provide them with the basic necessities of life, including food, fuel and water. At the same time men in the region do less domestic work than their counterparts in the developed world, so the double burden upon women is heavy.

The majority of women – 80 per cent – do agricultural work – planting, weeding, harvesting and processing – mainly of food crops to feed their families and sell in markets. A larger proportion of women workers are unpaid (on farms, etc.) and in self-employment than anywhere else in the world (United Nations, 1991, p. 86). Moreover, only in Africa have women's recorded economic participation rates declined as a result of the economic crises of the past two decades (United Nations, 1991, p. 86). Salesworkers predominate among African female formal sector workers, and fewer are in professional and clerical work than elsewhere. Moreover, as a recent ILO (1991) report has documented, female unemployment has apparently been rising since 1985 as a result of retrenchment policies, the reduced role of the public sector as a source of modern sector employment, and the declining performance of the retail trade sector.

It has been estimated that 2.5 million jobs have been lost by women in the past five years. Despite the considerable progress made in promoting formal education for girls and an increased awareness in most African countries of the inequities women face in the socio-economic and other spheres, women still seem to be more vulnerable than men as far as the labour market is concerned. In all occupational hierarchies they are clustered at the lower end. Many factors have been identified as hindering women from participating equally with their male counterparts, including lack of education and training; sex labelling of jobs, leading to sex-segregated labour markets; lack of crucial resources, including credit, land and machinery; lack of representation on decision-making bodies; and the continuous heavy burdens of unpaid domestic work, child-bearing and child-care, which restrict the time and energy available for income-earning.

Fertility Rates and Contraceptive Use

Women in sub-Saharan Africa are oriented towards motherhood. Traditionally a woman is expected to marry early and give birth to and rear (many) children; girls are socialised early in their lives into their key roles as mothers, housekeepers and producers. Indeed, a woman's status is measured largely by her capacity to reproduce and maintain children. Little girls learn early in life to look after babies and toddlers and to trade and farm like their mothers, sisters, aunts and grandmothers. Women manage to combine their dominant occupations, agriculture and trade, with child-rearing through the support of kin and the traditional birth-spacing practices described by Ofosu in Chapter 11. These cushion and diminish some of the strains and stresses of child-rearing.

Children are regarded as the real bond between husband and wife and their respective kin. Marriage as a social institution is justified by the birth of children. Among co-wives in polygynous marriages there is considerable competition as to who will bear the greatest number of children. Since children are perceived as sources of security, joy and esteem, infertility is regarded as a social stigma. It is prevalent in the Congo, Gabon, the Central African Republic, Cameroon, Angola, Zaïre and parts of Burkina Faso (Frank, 1983). Indeed the incidence of infertility is unusually high in Africa, especially in Central African countries. Estimates range from more than 20 per cent of women childless at the age of 45–49 in most of Central Africa to 12–20 per cent in East and parts of Central Africa.

Children are indeed their parents' – but especially their mothers' – most precious asset in Africa. The situation has been aptly described:

> [Children] provide desperately needed labour to assist in farm, home and market. They provide the links of kinship without which wives have no enduring rights in their marital homes or husband's assets, including land and thus security as well as economic status in old age. Without them conjugal links are tenuous and fragile. Without them daily laborious tasks cannot be completed. Without them a woman in virilocal marriage remains an outsider, marginal. Without them, a woman can never achieve full social or spiritual status. (Oppong, 1987a)

Not only do Africa's children contribute substantially to farming, cattle-rearing (herding), household chores and child-rearing but, 'as the frontier for fuel wood recedes and water and soil resources are depleted, the need for children to share the increased work burden intensifies' (World Bank, 1989c). The prevailing high fertility in Africa thus reflects the economic value of children, especially in rural areas. At the same time high mortality and socio-cultural factors shape the fertility aspirations and achievements of families.

One reason why fertility in Africa is high, and remains so, is that marriage occurs early and is almost universal (Arnold and Blanc, 1990). The age at marriage for women is lower in Africa than in any other region of the world, with about 50 per cent married by the age of 18 years; this is also true of the onset of child-bearing. Average age at marriage is 15.7 years in Sierra Leone, 18 years in Ghana, 16 years in Liberia, 17 years in Uganda, with a median age of 18.5 years in Kenya (Liberia, Bureau of Statistics, 1988; Ghana Statistical Service, 1989a; Arnold and Blanc, 1990).

In Liberia, where fertility has been more or less constant over the last 20 years, and may in fact be increasing slightly, women have an average of 6.5 births by the end of their child-bearing years. Their counterparts in Botswana would have 5 births, and 5.5 in Zimbabwe (Table 2.2). Fertility continues to be high in Ghana with an average of six children. In Uganda, where the high level of fertility has remained unchanged for the last 15 years, women have an average of seven births. Child-bearing begins early: 60 per cent of women have their first birth before the age of 20, and less than 3 per cent at 25 or older (Uganda, Ministry of Health, 1989; Zimbabwe, Central Statistical Office, 1989; Arnold and Blanc, 1990).

About 75 per cent of teenagers in Africa are mothers. Girls aged 15–20 years contribute between 10 and 15 per cent of Africa's overall fertility. This proportion reaches a high of 17 per cent in Mauritania, the Gambia, Burkina Faso and Niger. Indeed, Africa has the highest rate of births to very young mothers in the world: it is estimated that 40 per cent of teenage births are to women aged 17 or under. Comparable figures for Latin America, Asia and Europe are 39 per cent, 31 per cent and 22 per cent (Sadik, 1989). Early pregnancies have a serious impact on opportunities for education

Table 2.2 Statistics on fertility, mortality, and family planning: selected African countries

	Vital rates (last 5 years)		Knowledge and use of contraception (currently married women aged 15–49)		
	Total fertility rate[a]	Infant mortality/under-5 mortality (per 1000)	% Knowing any modern method[b]	% Currently using any method[c]	% Currently using any modern method[d]
Botswana, 1988	5.0	37/53	94	33	32
Burundi, 1987	7.0	75/152	64	7	1
Ghana, 1988	6.4	77/155	77	13	5
Kenya, 1989	6.7	60/89	91	27	18
Liberia, 1986	6.3	144/220	68	6	6
Mali, 1987	6.7	108/250	29	3	1
Ondo State, Nigeria, 1986–87	6.0	56/108	50	6	4
Senegal, 1986	6.6	85/191	63	5	2
Togo, 1988	6.2	83/158	81	12	3
Uganda, 1988–89	7.3	101/180	78	5	3
Zimbabwe, 1988–89	5.7	53/75	98	43	36

Notes: [a] Based on births to women aged 15–49 years in the five years preceding the survey.
[b] Excludes periodic abstinence, withdrawal and 'other' methods.
[c] Excludes prolonged abstinence.
[d] For births in five years preceding interview.
Source: DHS/Macro Systems, *Demographic and Health Survey Newsletter*, 1990, Colombia, p. 12.

and employment: a growing number of national governments in the region are becoming concerned about the negative impact of teenage pregnancy on girls' school attendance. Perhaps more importantly, they are damaging to their health and that of their children, and lead to repeated cycles of poverty and deprivation.

The Demographic and Health Survey (DHS) results for Kenya indicate that total fertility declined to 6.7 in 1989 (Table 2.2), from 7.7 in 1984 and 7.9 in 1977–78. This decline is partly attributed to an increased use of family planning: 27 per cent of married women currently use a contraceptive method, as opposed to 17 per cent in 1984. In Botswana, total fertility dropped from 7.1 in 1981 to 6.5 in 1984 and 5.0 in 1988. This trend is explained by increasing use of modern methods of contraception among women at all levels of education and a growing number of women achieving higher levels of education (Botswana, Central Statistics Office, 1989; Kenya, National Council for Population and Development, 1989).

While women in urban areas, especially the capital cities, have fewer children than women in rural areas, the most important differences in fertility levels are between educational groups. Thus in Uganda, as in Liberia, women with higher education have an average of five births compared with seven births for women with primary education. In Ghana, women with no education have on average 6.7 children compared with 3.6 for women with more than middle school education. In Botswana, women with no education have 6.0 children compared with 4.6 for those with full primary and secondary education or more. In Zimbabwe, women with no education have an average of seven births, those with some primary education six births, and those with secondary education or higher less than four births (Botswana, Central Statistics Office, 1989; Zimbabwe, Central Statistical Office, 1989).

Polygyny is still widely practised in rural areas and is also found in urban settings. In Uganda, 33 per cent of currently married women are in such unions (Uganda,

Ministry of Health, 1989). In Kenya, 23 per cent were in polygynous unions in 1989, a decline from 25 per cent in 1984 and 30 per cent in 1977–78 (Kenya, National Council for Population and Development, 1989). Where co-wives are constantly competing over the number of children (especially boys) they are capable of producing, asking women to practise family planning may be tantamount to asking them to forfeit a major source of future economic security or self-esteem (Wulf, 1985). According to Savane (1984), 'Polygamy, which is still widespread, encourages women to engage in a frantic race to have the most children in order to benefit from inheritance'.

To this factor must be added the fear of infant deaths, a legitimate fear where one-quarter of all children born die before their first birthday or soon after. Above all, the desire of men and the pressure exerted by their kin to perpetuate their names, ancestral spirits and descent lines through children is compelling.

The social forces supporting high fertility are thus still powerful. Having many offspring remains an ideal. They are the goal of marriage, and a measure of its success. Low levels of use of modern contraceptives are explained by the prevailing customs and values surrounding high fertility. Long durations of breast-feeding and long customary periods of post-partum sexual abstinence, in addition to secondary infertility and sterility, have in the past tended to depress fertility below its potential level. The effects of modernisation and urbanisation have, however, weakened these traditional constraints. At the same time, postponement of marriage and use of modern contraceptives are not yet firmly enough in place to substitute for these constraining mechanisms (Adepoju, 1991c).

Contraceptive *knowledge* is reasonably high in several countries (Table 2.2). Notable exceptions are Mali and Nigeria (Ondo State), where only 29 per cent and 50 per cent, respectively, of currently married women aged 15–49 years know of any modern method. Nearly all married women in Zimbabwe (98 per cent) possess such knowledge. In Botswana and Kenya the proportions exceed 90 per cent. Although the correlation between knowledge and current use of contraception is weak, over two-fifths of Zimbabwean women are current users, mostly of modern methods, followed by women in Botswana at 33 per cent. However, in the region as a whole only about 6 per cent or less of married women aged 15–49 currently use any modern method: 1 per cent in Mali and Burundi, 3 per cent in Uganda and Togo, and 5 per cent in Ghana. The exceptions are Botswana and Zimbabwe, as already mentioned, and Kenya, where the figure is 18 per cent (Arnold and Blanc, 1990; van de Walle and Foster, 1990).

The level of contraceptive use in Zimbabwe – 43 per cent of married women currently using some form of contraception in 1988 (Table 2.2), with 36 per cent having used one in the past, up from 38 per cent in 1984 – is the highest reported among sub-Saharan African countries. Almost all users – 96 per cent – rely on government-sponsored providers for contraceptive methods. This compares sharply with, for example, Uganda, where only 5 per cent of currently married women use any contraceptive method and only 22 per cent have ever used one (Uganda, Ministry of Health, 1989; Zimbabwe, Central Statistical Office, 1989).

The demand for family planning services in Africa is weak, even among the educated groups. Creating a demand for such services would involve fundamental changes in both norms and values, indeed in societal attitudes with respect to family size. The opposition of male partners poses a formidable barrier to the widespread use of family planning services by women in several parts of the region (Sadik, 1990a).

Religious and cultural factors constrain the successful implementation of family planning programmes in Africa. In Zaïre, officially a secular state, where 70 per cent are Christians and 60 per cent of all health facilities are run by church groups, which also control the educational institutions, the religious influence is quite strong. This is also the case in countries, such as Senegal and Mauritania, which are predominantly Muslim. However, religious opposition to family planning has perhaps weakened as a result of a series of sensitisation seminars and workshops for key religious leaders (Wulf, 1985).

Injectables and methods that require only occasional check-ups such as the IUD are increasingly preferred by rural women. This is in part because it frees them from daily usage and all the problems that this implies: forgetfulness; the fear of being castigated by mothers, mothers-in-law and co-wives who do not practise family planning, or of incurring the wrath of husbands who have not consented to their wives' practising family planning; and the lack of hygiene and privacy in rural areas.

Traditional African family values and practices promote child-bearing throughout the reproductive span. The cultural attitudes and social practices favouring large families are deep-rooted, and changes in these are only likely to occur as the systems supporting them change. To the average African, marriage is a social institution justified only by a quiverful of children. Indeed, the acquisition of a large number of wives and children confers considerable prestige on the male head. However, the traditional practice of birth spacing to promote maternal health and child development and to reduce conflicts between mothers' productive and reproductive roles does form a sound basis for the introduction of modern birth-spacing techniques.

To sum up, fertility remains high in sub-Saharan Africa: on average the total fertility rate exceeds six children per woman. Child-bearing begins in the teenage years and continues far into the later child-bearing years (Arnold and Blanc, 1990). In a recent study, van de Walle and Foster (1990) concluded that 'evidence for a sustained decline in completed family size is still weak everywhere in sub-Saharan Africa'. They also note that only in Botswana, Zimbabwe and Kenya, in that order, is the use of modern methods of contraception sufficient to account for a perceptible decline in fertility. These countries are also among those less affected by the economic crisis, with a more educated female population than other countries with comparable fertility data.

Infant, Maternal and Adult Mortality

Several studies, such as the Demographic and Health Surveys (DHS) and World Fertility Surveys (WFS), have shown that morbidity and mortality rates are high among children and mothers. The reasons commonly adduced for this include poor sanitation and nutritional status, limited health care facilities, poverty and high fertility (Azefor, 1981; Blacker et al., 1985).

The WFS results show that education of mothers has a favourable influence on infant survival (Hill, 1990). Blacker et al. (1985) concluded that many African populations, especially in West Africa, have relatively high mortality rates at ages 1–4 compared with infant and adult mortality. They also cautioned, however, that populations in close geographical proximity and with similar levels of mortality can exhibit very different mortality patterns.

There is a general consensus that infant and child mortality increases with parity; that the shorter the interval between births, the greater the risk of mortality; and that the nutritional status and health of both mother and child depend on adequate spacing between pregnancies (Karefa-Smart, 1986). These observations have been aptly summarised in the phrase 'too early, too many, too frequent and too late pregnancies', all of which pose serious threats to the health of the African mother and child.

Omran *et al.*'s (1987) extensive survey of the evidence from Africa confirmed that poor child spacing or short birth intervals, high parity, particularly 'grand multiparity' and large family size, and pregnancies that occur at risky maternal ages (under 20 or over 35 years) result in increased health risks.

Countries with more widespread knowledge and use of modern contraceptive methods and with a high proportion of educated women have relatively low infant mortality rates: 37 per thousand in Botswana and 53 per thousand in Zimbabwe, with under-5 mortality rates 53 per thousand and 75 per thousand, respectively (Table 2.2). Significantly, where the majority of women receive antenatal care, they are also more likely to have knowledge of, and actually to use, modern contraceptives.

Programmes to promote the health of mothers and children through antenatal, delivery and postnatal services, oral rehydration campaigns and extended immunisation campaigns have received outstanding co-operation from the governments and notable successes in Burkina Faso and parts of Ondo State in Nigeria (Hill, 1990). In general, however, progress has been slow owing to illiteracy, poverty and poor sanitation; the scarcity of medical personnel; the shortage of equipment and drugs; the inadequate health infrastructure, and a distribution of health services that does not correspond to population distribution (70 per cent or more of health institutions and medical personnel are located in the towns, where no more than 25 per cent of the region's population live). These difficulties have been compounded by the strains on the health services and the dwindling resources available to them consequent on the retrenchment policies of the structural adjustment programmes.

The complications of pregnancy and childbirth have profound effects on maternal mortality. One out of every 21 African women, or 4.8 per cent, dies as a result of pregnancy or childbirth. This compares unfavourably with 2.6 per cent and 1.1 per cent for women in South Asia and Latin America, respectively. Thus thousands of women die needlessly during or after childbirth. Additionally, the children die of causes that could have been avoided through preventive health measures: safe drinking water, better birth spacing, improved hygiene, immunisation, etc. (Karefa-Smart, 1986). Giorgis (1988) argues that:

> the high maternal mortality rate for African women [results from] the vulnerability of women during pregnancy and childbirth [to] years of malnutrition, disease, hard work and stress which makes the risk greater. For women, having too few children or too many children constitutes a risk. Women measure such risk in terms of their individual or collective experiences in their societies. The risk of child-bearing for example may be high, but for women the risk of infertility and sub-fertility may be much higher. This may mean loss of spousal loyalty, support, abandonment, and even divorce.

Teenage pregnancies constitute a particularly high health risk for both mothers and children. Furthermore, maternal mortality is increased and the health of women and children additionally jeopardised by certain traditional practices, including continuing widespread genital mutilation and dietary habits and customs that adversely impair the nutritional status of women during pregnancy and childbirth. The current health situation among women involves a tragic vicious circle, rooted in very early child-bearing and repeated and closely spaced births and pregnancies among older women – a scenario which poses formidable health problems to several millions of women in the region.

The structural adjustment programmes being implemented by more than 30 African countries have had a tremendous impact on the social services sectors, especially health and education. The cost-recovery strategy and the removal of subsidies in these sectors have resulted in rapidly rising costs, and poor underprivileged social groups have been severely affected. The level of nutrition has declined substantially, and indications are that infant mortality is on the increase, thus eroding the substantial gains in child survival of the previous decade. The same result has been produced by the sporadic droughts of the 1970s and 1980s in the Sahel, and epidemics in Ethiopia and Sudan, where the toll on children has been particularly severe. In addition, the unfortunate continuing prevalence of internecine strife in a number of countries adds to the death toll.

The most important widespread causes of death for under-5s include diarrhoea, respiratory tract infections, neonatal tetanus, prematurity, measles and malnutrition. A recent United Nations Children's Fund (UNICEF) study in Ghana shows, for instance, that the substantial gains achieved in reducing infant mortality in the 1960s and 1970s were reversed in the 1980s. In the late 1970s, the infant mortality rate was estimated at 86 deaths per thousand live births, down from 132 in 1960 and 107 in 1970. During the 1980s, however, the rate increased to between 107 and 120 deaths per thousand live births. Similarly the child mortality rate (among ages 1–4 years) declined gradually from 27 per thousand in 1960 to 15 per thousand in the late 1970s, but later increased to between 25 and 30 per thousand in the 1980s, especially in the 1983–84 period (UNICEF, 1988). As the report noted:

> The decreased production of food, coupled with the declining purchasing power of Ghanaians and the drastic increase in food prices had a most devastating effect on the nutritional status of Ghanaians, particularly pregnant and lactating mothers and preschool children. In addition, ... parasitic and infectious diseases related to poverty and underdevelopment like malaria, intestinal parasites, malnutrition, and scabies, continue to afflict a majority of Ghanaians. Diseases virtually eradicated by campaigns in the 1950s and 1960s began to reappear in the late 1970s as nutrition and health services declined. (UNICEF, 1988)

This observation would seem to apply to several African countries where the position of the vulnerable groups – children and (pregnant) women – has deteriorated considerably, as a result of adjustment policies which have led to economic cut-backs affecting their health and nutritional needs.

AIDS

The acquired immune deficiency syndrome (AIDS) epidemic is undoubtedly a major health hazard globally, with a profound impact at the individual, family and community levels. In Africa, Burundi, Côte d'Ivoire, Rwanda, the United Republic of Tanzania and Uganda appear to top the list as regards reported cases. Unlike the situation in developed countries, it is believed that the major cause of transmission of the human immunodeficiency virus (HIV) in Africa is through heterosexual intercourse and through the placenta from an infected mother to her unborn baby. Other causes include blood transfusion and drug abuse.

A general picture of the syndrome is gradually unfolding. According to Sadik (1990a):

> In a typical east or central African country, the disease is seen to be following a predictable 25–6 year course: starting with its emergence and spreading within the 'at risk' populations, with an annual infection rate rising steeply to a peak after 15 years and then gradually stabilizing at an infection rate of 2.2 per cent per year 10 years later when the numbers of additional cases infected equal the numbers of people dying from the disease. One model predicts that, in the continent as a whole, approximately 5 per cent of the adult population – that is one in 20 – will be infected with the disease by the year 2000.

The devastating effects of the spread of AIDS have captured the attention of policy-makers. In Uganda, for instance, sex education is beginning to be incorporated into school curricula for the first time, so that teenagers will be able to learn about AIDS, sexual relationships, health and family planning before they embark on their first sexual experience. Other countries have set up AIDS monitoring groups for anti-AIDS campaigns. Additionally, recent reports on the spread of HIV among infants and young people under the age of 15 have raised queries regarding routes of transmission other than sexual intercourse. In Zimbabwe, for instance, it is speculated that a full one-quarter of those infected with HIV are children while 60 per cent are youths under the age of 16. The demographic and economic consequences of the epidemic in the region will no doubt be profound.

Migration for Employment

The emphasis in female migration has shifted from women who accompany or join their husbands to women as autonomous migrants (Findley and Williams, 1990). Women may migrate in search of better opportunities, in response to natural disasters, or in flight from penury, war and internal strife. On the one hand, migration may give women access to, or strengthen, their economic independence and expose them to wider horizons and opportunities. On the other hand, it may be associated with serious vulnerability and exposure to economic and sexual exploitation. It is associated with profound changes in all of women's roles.

In analysing the phenomenon of autonomous female migration, especially in Botswana, Lesotho and Burkina Faso, where out-migration of adult males is quantitatively of prime importance, the changing sexual division of labour of those left behind and the decision strategy with respect to the timing are pertinent considerations. In the past women migrants have often been regarded not as free decision-makers but rather as followers of men, being dependent on the decision and act of migration of their husbands. This stereotype was based on survey findings which had a predominant category of 'joining husband' or 'to marry' as the major motivation for female migration.

Female migration has been conditioned, to a greater extent than male migration, by the structure of economic activities, socio-cultural factors defining sex roles, and the effect of education on the spatial and occupational mobility of women (Adepoju, 1983). The relative opportunity structure and the nature of employment for women in Africa in general are conditioned in part by their relative skills, the prevailing sex segregation and discrimination in the organised labour market, the perceived roles of women (and the associated constraints and sanctions) and the types of occupational structure.

In most parts of Africa, the structure of employment mostly requires men to work in plantation agriculture, industry, commerce and mechanised transportation. Thus, men tend to migrate alone, leaving their wives behind. The cultural factors that initially favoured the education of males over females have had the effect of confining women to the lower cadres of formal employment, given that employment in the organised labour market is highly correlated with education. Hence, the disadvantaged and least educated groups are confined largely to commerce and distributive trade (Adepoju, 1983; Stamp, 1989).

Education is closely correlated with migration, especially where this interacts with other socio-economic variables such as age, sex and occupation. Rapid urbanisation and the expansion of employment opportunities in both the formal and the informal urban sectors have, in combination, facilitated female migration to the towns. Education, a crucial agent for change, influences the aspirations of women and the range of opportunities available to them in the labour market. Over half of female migrants have at least some primary level schooling: for example, 57 per cent in Juba City, Sudan, and 54 per cent in Monrovia, Liberia (Findley and Williams, 1990). Widespread education among females means that women have, in recent years, greater opportunities for employment in the formal sector. Another result of the increasing proportion of educated women is the accelerated movement of young women into urban areas to seek further education and jobs. A full 40 per cent of female rural–urban migrants in Burkina Faso are aged 20–24 years. In Kenya, 38 per cent belong to that age group.

Tienda and Booth (1988) noted that male absenteeism, cash-cropping and declining land quality are pushing many more women out of rural areas. However, it is not just the poor quality of the land but the lack of access to it that is pushing rural women out of traditional agriculture – so far the major sector of employment. In Kenya, for instance, the land reform legislation denies independent access to land to women who are single heads of households and married women without sons (Selassie, 1986). In addition, the highly capitalised plantation agriculture has rendered many rural households landless.

The 1960, 1970 and 1980 rounds of censuses confirm that women in Africa are migrating to urban areas in greater numbers in search of wage employment. Two reasons have been advanced for this phenomenon: the deteriorating living and working conditions of women in rural areas and the instability of marriage. Thus, women in East Africa often migrate to urban areas in the expectation of greater autonomy. Single women in Uganda are able to improve their social position by increasing their autonomy through urban employment; the migration *per se* provides an alternative to their subordination in the villages (Tienda and Booth, 1988).

But female migration is not directed to urban areas alone: women sometimes accompany their husbands when they migrate to rural areas (Adepoju, 1984). Whatever the direction, recent empirical evidence tends to suggest that the very fact of migration tends to increase women's recorded participation in economic activities, and in particular the occupational mix among these migrants (Pittin, 1984).

West African women are unique in one respect: trading activities are their domain, a situation that has facilitated their visibility in both internal and international migration. Sudarkasa (1974–75) aptly documented this phenomenon among the Yoruba women of Nigeria and Benin. Women dominate short-distance rural-to-rural migrations, while men predominate in international and internal rural–urban migrations.

The explanation of female migration as autonomous rather than associational has so far focused on the vulnerable and insecure position of women, household structure and adaptation strategies, sex role constraints and marriage-related reasons, among others (Lim, 1988). But it is male-dominated rural out-migration that constitutes the dominant factor for households where women are either *de facto* heads, where male adults are temporarily absent, or *de jure* heads, where male adults are permanently absent (Makinwa-Adebusoye, 1988).

A large proportion of households are female-headed in Botswana, Lesotho and Swaziland: 45 per cent of rural households in Lesotho were headed by women in 1980 (Adepoju, 1988; Makinwa-Adebusoye, 1990), and the number is growing in Zambia and Kenya. In several parts of Zambia, for instance, between 39 and 50 per cent of rural households are female-headed (Safilios-Rothschild, 1988a).

In the Southern African countries (Botswana, Lesotho and Swaziland), where a significant number of the men migrate to work in the mines and plantations of South Africa for a contract period of two years (or less) at a time, returning home only periodically between contracts, the migrants often spend as long as 15–20 years in South Africa. The laws governing migration preclude women from moving with or subsequently joining their husbands. Female-headed households that are the offshoots of male out-migration are paradoxically among the poorest. In such cases, the men are not readily available for the arduous tasks of ploughing and planting; women, with or without the assistance of their children, find it increasingly difficult to adequately offset the labour contribution of their absentee husbands. This is especially the case when seasonal labour demand is at its peak (de Vletter, 1985; Makinwa-Adebusoye, 1990; Maro, 1990). Generally the remittances sent by migrants are irregular, and inadequate either to maintain household members or to hire labourers in sufficient numbers at peak periods to maintain output (Adepoju, 1988). The improverished rural economies, the difficulties of farming caused by the shortage of family labour, and the uncertain and inadequate remittances have literally pushed women to seek employment in the urban formal and informal sectors. This has, in the case of Lesotho and Botswana especially, resulted in female dominance in rural–urban migration.

In Lesotho, where 51 per cent of the adult males work in South Africa, the women left behind bear the key responsibility of farm production management, and increasingly have to make at least short-term decisions (Palmer, 1985b). As a result, considerable changes are taking place as regards family responsibilities, decision-making processes and the statuses and roles of women. This is particularly so with respect to the land tenure system: owners of land left uncultivated for up to two years normally lose title to such land. Increasingly, therefore, women have had to keep up cultivation in the absence of their husbands, some of whom visit home erratically. The day-to-day management of the farm is thus undertaken by migrants' wives, and few male kin offer any form of assistance, even with arranging for and supervising (male) hired labour (de Vletter, 1985; Adepoju, 1988; Ware and Lucas, 1988). Despite the relatively higher pay in South Africa, remittances are in any case often inadequate to cope with the high cost of hired labour. In the case of Botswana, Lesotho and

Swaziland, the women left behind sometimes purchase small farm equipment to reduce the burden of farming and cope with the labour shortage (de Vletter, 1985).

Refugees

The major causes of people becoming refugees in Africa include natural disaster, drought, ecological problems, internal conflicts and wars of liberation. Refugees include women, old people and children of rural background.

Information on the demographic characteristics of refugees, especially their age–sex composition, is based on a few generalisations from reports of the United Nations High Commissioner for Refugees, the news media, and various other sources. There appears to be a consensus that the majority of refugees are women and children. In general, between 40 and 60 per cent of refugees in Africa are children under the age of 15. These are the most needy among refugees and therefore of greatest concern to international and local relief agencies.

The predominance of women and children among refugees in Africa reflects both the major causes of exile and, indirectly, the young age structure of the African population. While the predominance of children reflects their share in the total population, the situation is exacerbated by the fact that in recent years armed conflicts have been the dominant cause of the refugees' flight. The children therefore escape while the men (and, in some cases, the women) are killed, imprisoned or stay behind to fight. In Chad, for instance, the combatants encourage their families to cross the border to Sudan and settle; they later visit their wives and children there. The situation of Zimbabwean and South African refugees is similar (Adepoju, 1989).

In general, female refugees are poor: in the process of flight, they lose what little possessions they have – land, cattle, etc. In refugee camps, many women are forced to take on additional responsibilities as heads of households and sole income-earners. Female refugees are predominantly of rural origin with the attendant characteristics of large family size, illiteracy, poor health, poverty and limited productive skills. These inadequacies come to a head in the refugee camps or settlements: only a few refugee women are able to engage in activities that rapidly promote their integration.

Women refugees are particularly vulnerable. They face multiple problems: the fact that they have abandoned their houses, insecurity, privation, the burden of looking after a family when the head of the family is not there, and many more. Shortage of water and prolonged drought often threaten the lives and health of female refugees and their children (Adepoju, 1989).

Concluding Remarks

Sub-Saharan Africa is a region of high fertility, which is sustained by the socio-cultural environment and the low level of development. The average completed family size of six children remains the ideal, and very few countries appear to be currently on the threshold of fertility decline. Some progress had been made in reducing mortality, especially among infants, in the 1960s and 1970s. However, recent economic recessions and the harsh adjustment policies adopted by several countries have had a serious impact on the health and nutritional status of mothers and children.

Consequently, the moderate gains made earlier in infant, childhood and maternal mortality seem to have been eroded. At the same time adult mortality may well increase as the AIDS epidemic intensifies.

The deteriorating economic environment and high rate of population growth in most African countries over the last two decades have combined to produce lower per capita incomes, and the number of people living below the poverty level has increased dramatically: women and children are the most vulnerable.

The stabilisation programmes, most visible in the education, health and employment sectors, have also intensified autonomous female migration. Women are increasingly drawn to the wage labour market (both formal and informal) as part of a survival strategy to augment meagre family incomes, as the chapter by Boateng on Ghana illustrates. Among the educated, migration of unaccompanied married women has taken firm root – a phenomenon that is both recent and uncommon in Africa's migratory scene. It illustrates the extent to which women alone are being compelled to shoulder the burdens of family maintenance and self-support.

3 Wives & Mothers: Female Farmers in Africa

ANN WHITEHEAD

The main focus of this chapter is the smallholder sector of agricultural production in sub-Saharan Africa.[1] The implications of some of the characteristics of women's work in this sector are discussed with respect to rural economic planning.[2] The discussion is situated in the context of three issues: first, the increasing recognition that women are a neglected human resource in development planning; second, the great historical and contemporary importance of female labour in sub-Saharan African farming; third, the 20-year-long crisis in agricultural production.[3]

The first section describes the role of women in smallholder production, adopting a broadly historical framework. The second section considers some of the problems of data collection which result in national statistics reflecting only very imperfectly the complex reality of contemporary women's work. The next section looks briefly at recent research findings on the effects of development projects on women.

The fact that many development projects are designed in such a way that women's planned role is not one they are able, or willing, to undertake raises the question of whether women's economic decision-making within the household enterprise has been adequately understood. In the section entitled 'The household: joint and separate interests' it is suggested that some of the basic features of women's labour allocation decisions are misunderstood because of inadequate conceptualisation of the particular combination of joint and separate interests within marriage in the African farming family. The next section looks at the extent to which women's concern for the welfare of their children affects their economic decision-making.

In the final section it is pointed out that many of the issues raised entail radical rethinking about planning categories and the collection of statistics. None of these problems is readily solvable, and all require high-level international co-operation and long-term planning. Nevertheless, if rational decisions about cost-effective ways of spending scarce national resources on African agriculture are going to be made, it is important to adopt an informed and critical stance on current categories and procedures. I pick out three particular areas in which sensitivity to conceptual problems would result in a greater visibility of women's work, a greater understanding of the basis of their economic decision-making, and greater precision in planning to harness their efforts to enhance agricultural production.

Women's Work in Agricultural Production in Sub-Saharan Africa[4]

One of the most common, everyday insights into the economic transformation undergone by tropical Africa in the last century or so is that it has created a twofold dichotomy in the rural division of labour. This dichotomy is on the one hand between subsistence and cash-cropping agriculture and on the other hand between women and men who inhabit, respectively, these sectors. This simple, dichotomous model, with its important gender component, derives from a set of stereotyped views about the characteristics of the farming systems of nineteenth-century Africa, and about contemporary women's work within rural production. Interwoven with an exaggeration of the division and competition between cash crop and subsistence crop sectors, and some misunderstanding of the nature of subsistence production, is an erroneous emphasis on Africa as a female farming area and on women's 'relegation to the subsistence sector' as the main consequence of the socio-economic changes of the twentieth century.

Female farming reconsidered

The idea of Africa as a female farming area was popularised by Ester Boserup (1970). She argued that sub-Saharan African farming systems, with their low-productivity techniques, could be described as female because of the importance of women's labour to them. More recent discussions (notably those by Guyer (1983), Wright (1983) and Richards (1983)) have argued her case. However, not all the farming systems at issue can be characterised as having been 'female' in any meaningful sense prior to the twentieth century. For many hundreds of years, and in environmentally and culturally significant areas, a substantial amount of farming work has been done by male farmers working with hoes.[5] Equally important, female farming systems, like their male counterparts, are based on a complex inter-relation of men's and women's work. The usefulness of labelling some of these farming systems as 'female' lies in the emphasis on the contribution of women's work to farming in contrast to the general view that agricultural field work is primarily a male province. In sub-Saharan Africa, it should not imply an absence of any male labour input into farming. Men's labour in the farming cycles of female farming areas is often critically important, as for example in land clearing. Several studies report women as having to purchase labour for this in their husbands' absence.[6]

The blanket characterisation of sub-Saharan African farming systems as female also serves to homogenise what is an area of considerable cultural and economic variety. In fact the integration of men's and women's work within farming systems varies markedly (see Guyer, 1980b, 1984a, b). As yet we have only a very imperfect understanding of how these differences may affect differences in the trajectory of economic change. An important element of Boserup's work is her argument that, during the twentieth century in sub-Saharan Africa, what she describes as modernisation has produced a dichotomous rural economy, in which male farmers are associated with a sector of enhanced productivity, which is producing for the market, while women are associated with an untransformed sector, in which they use traditional technology to produce for subsistence. The main impression given by Boserup's account is that the major economic changes in the sub-Saharan African countryside left women primarily doing the same tasks, but in a different setting, and with a consequently different contribution to the total rural economy. Subsequently, this idea of rural women being 'relegated to the subsistence sector' gained great ground. But in most parts of Africa this stereotyped view is only appropriate, if at all, to the early parts of this century. Recent historical scholarship suggests much more variety in the way local economies were incorporated into the world economy and gives us some idea of the greater complexity of local economic processes, especially since 1945. This much more complex view of the nature of rural economic change considerably undermines the idea of women being 'relegated to the subsistence sector'.

Labour migration and peasantisation
It is undeniable that male labour migration was an important feature of some rural areas during a large part of this century. The absence of men who are working elsewhere is still a critical characteristic of many African rural communities today. Obviously this has affected the viability and development of sub-Saharan African agriculture. One of the recurring focuses of early studies of rural economies was their cultural and social organisational capacity to adapt to the absence of men. Repeated findings of these early studies (which have been reassessed in Stichter (1985)) and of more recent work (e.g. Hay, 1976; Bukh, 1979) related to making use of women's hitherto 'under-utilised' labour[7] and changes in marriage relations.[8]

However, as Stichter (1985) pointed out, the effects of rural male labour migration have been far from uniform. In particular, the view that women's farming goes hand in hand with agricultural stagnation has undergone something of a shift. Stichter argues forcibly for the need to take into account differences in the agrarian situations within which the loss of labour occurs. The factors to be considered include the nature of the farming system and land rights, the degree of development of internal rural markets, cultural aspects of the sexual division of labour, the level, regularity and duration of wage-earning, and, most importantly, the degree, kind and pace of commoditisation of the rural economy itself. One of the main problems with many earlier perspectives on labour migration was that they ignored the way that commercial development in the agrarian economy itself was taking place side by side with the feminisation of food production and male labour migration. In some areas, though not of course all, male labour migration, plus the development of internal food markets, stimulated women to begin commercial production of agricultural crops. So, for example, women in Kenya are reported as producing maize for the market as early as 1918 (Kitching, 1980).

Recent work in agrarian and agricultural history has also given us a much greater understanding of the transformations that have taken place this century in the rural production systems of sub-Saharan Africa. Colonial rule ushered in, or hastened, increased household production for sale alongside a continued strategy of providing a proportion of household food requirements. Freund's admirable synthesis (1984) demonstrates that dualistic theories of African agriculture, according to which there is 'a conspicuous division between large-scale relatively capital intensive production of a narrow range of export crops, and a labour intensive peasant sector which provides the bulk of the population's food requirements' (Lochfie, 1975), are inadequate. Discussing this view, Tabatabai (1986) argued that early colonial policies were in many respects discriminatory: agricultural export crops were promoted with investment and improved techniques and agronomic practices at the expense of food production. Nevertheless, subsequent colonial and post-colonial policies, plus the important investment strategies of indigenous farmers themselves, have resulted in a much more varied pattern of agricultural development. An important consequence of the development of internal markets for food was the increasing production of food as cash crops, in addition to the cash crops produced for export. This lends support to Tabatabai's assertion that cash-cropping is not coterminous with the modern sector: 'There are innumerable examples of countries and regions within them, where the bulk of export crops are produced, along with food crops, by smallholders using equally primitive technologies' (1986). One might add that food production itself is by no means confined to 'backward' smallholder production, especially in countries such as Kenya, Zambia and Zimbabwe.

The final point to make is that the over-simple view derived from Boserup does not take into account the development of rural socio-economic differentiation and its effects on women. The smallholder sector has experienced cumulative agricultural innovation and intensification in the last 50 years, and this has produced considerably increased incomes for some households. The inter-relation between labour migration, investment in agriculture and increased commodity production has been the subject of much academic research, although relatively little of it has examined the effects on women (see Young, 1977; Kitching, 1980; Berger and Robertson, 1986; Bujra, 1986). Nevertheless, it is clear that socio-economic differentiation has produced considerable differences in women's trajectories, as it has in men's. Polarisation is increasingly apparent between those women who have benefited from increased rural incomes and those who have been marginalised as a consequence of the changed distribution of rural resources. Some women have benefited either as commercial farmers in their own right or as wives of successful commercial farmers, and there have also been improved opportunities for trade and other forms of production (e.g. beer brewing). Simultaneously, however, a stratum of rural households has developed which absolutely lacks the resources to meet consumption needs. One of its main characteristics is that it includes a growing number of female-headed households. There is now a large literature which stresses both labour migration and the effects of socio-economic differentiation in the countryside as causes of this growth of poor female-headed households (Cliffe, 1976; Kossoudji and Mueller, 1983; Safilios-Rothschild, 1985b). Although female-headed households in sub-Saharan Africa are relatively under-researched, it is known that they occupy more than one socio-economic category, and that they are not all among the rural poor. Nevertheless they often lack the resources to farm, and in some places are an important pool of casual labour (see Youssef and Hetler (1984) for a major review of all the available evidence).

Women's dual economic roles in the smallholder family
The growing incidence of female-headed households raises another important issue. For many rural women the type of household to which they belong, together with the nature of their economic resources, responsibilities and rights within that household, plays an important part in determining the characteristics of their economic activities. Empirical rural African studies since the 1940s (and earlier) have found, in an impressive number of cases, that, while wives are economically always important members of their domestic groups, they typically have multiple economic activities within them. Women household members, together with other 'dependants', may contribute to the household's agricultural production or other enterprises as unremunerated family labour; in addition they may have separate access to land and other resources and may work independently, either farming or engaging in other income-producing activities. The balance between the amount of time spent on this

dependent work for other household members and the independent work differs markedly from one society to another. There are often strict limits on the amount of work a husband may demand of his wife. Indeed, the combination of dependent and independent work must be seen in the context of a complex set of rights that household members have in relation to assets and labour, as well as to income and subsistence.[9] One of the important characteristics of the system of household allocation and distribution is that rarely, if ever, is it based on a simple notion of the sharing between household members of what are held as joint resources and funds (see Goody, 1976; Guyer, 1981; Oppong, 1982a; Whitehead, 1984).

In a north-east Ghanaian farming system with which I am familiar, that of the Kusasi people, the economic interdependence of husband and wife is set within two forms of household property/labour complex. Household organisation can be quite complex, with co-residing married men, who might be polygynous. Each household has a definite head and he directs the work of men and women on the household fields; these produce much of the staple crop (kept in a single granary) but also crops for sale for income to meet other needs of household members. In addition to these compound farms, adult men and women can have the use of land for 'private' farms, the product of which is owned by the individual farmer. But the disposal of farm products and the extent of private farming that men and women do is mediated by sex differences in the responsibility for family provision. Men are responsible for staple provision and women for 'soup ingredients'. Men farm more land than women and can call on their wives' labour. Women do not use their husbands' labour in the same way, and farm small fields. In addition, men use their greater income in far more varied and individualistic ways than women, who are particularly constrained in this regard by cultural values associated with motherhood.

The roots of these kinds of contemporary arrangement lie in the economic and social obligations that existed between men and women in the nineteenth century prior to transformation. At that time, sub-Saharan African societies lay on a wide continuum between closed economies, based on kinship collectivities, producing entirely for self-provisioning and internal markets, and complex forms of pre-industrial state, in which socio-economic differentiation, usually involving slavery and considerable production for exchange, had developed. In all these societies, domestic and conjugal relations, plus kinship relations in the widest sense, were important economically.

Within these systems of social relations, women's resource rights varied, both from society to society and according to women's socio-economic status within a particular society. However, men and women rarely had equal access to resources. Women's rights in the pre-commodity economy were based on their position within the kinship structure and the household, but they were often much more limited than men's. In bride-wealth societies, for example, men often had sole or greatest rights over livestock. Nevertheless, women did have access to some kinds of resource, especially land, and these were not merged with those of their husband to form a single fund,[10] nor were wives seen as fully economically dependent upon their husbands. This socially valued interdependence between men and women was particularly apparent in relation to their mutual responsibilities as parents. Associated in part with polygyny, there was often a much greater degree of separation of the interests of the mother-children group from those of the father than exists, for example, in the European kinship system. Here, too, there were few mutually defined responsibilities for children; instead one finds further interdependence, with the responsibilities divided between husband and wife, as father and mother (see, for example, Longhurst, 1977). In some cases, especially where women had access to substantial land to farm, it was mothers who had the major responsibility for feeding children. However, this was by no means universal (see, for example, Guyer, 1980a; Poewe, 1981; Longhurst, 1982). Finally, it should be re-emphasised that husbands could often claim their wives' labour for agricultural or other economic activities from which they did not share the proceeds. In this respect wives were in the same position as many other household members.

One of the major consequences of the economic changes of this century has been the radical alteration of the inter-relationship between these different components of women's domestic economic role. What the myth of 'relegation to the subsistence sector' also conceals, therefore, is the important set of contradictory pressures which have been set up in relation to women's different economic activities. In general, it has become difficult for women to pursue their independent farming, but all the more important for them to do so.

The pressure on women's independent farming derives from a number of factors. Women's initial comparative lack of overall resources has been critical in determining their ability to respond to new economic opportunities (see Hay, 1976; Pala, 1979; Kitching, 1980; Clark, 1981; Whitehead, 1984). Contemporary studies find women complaining of lack of land and capital and document the disadvantaged position of women within the new market and state-codified systems of land allocation (Pala, 1978; Muntemba, 1982; Caplan, 1984; WIN, 1985). Resettlement or irrigation schemes entailing large changes in land use seem most often to have serious adverse effects on women. Some rural women also have labour problems, not only because the men are away and they cannot afford to hire labour, but also because they are less able to mobilise wide-ranging social relations in the rural areas, including political links, for exchange work parties (Whitehead, 1984; Pottier, 1985b).

At the same time the increased cash production of the male smallholder has meant increased demands for wives to work as family labourers, but in many cases the system of intra-household distribution has not changed to take account of the changed character of the work that women are doing. One effect of production for sale is that what once circulated within the family as goods now comes in as money to the husband. Norms about the sharing of money are rarely the same as norms about the sharing of, for example, food. Distribution of income within the family thus becomes a field of intense dispute (e.g. Monsted, 1976). While women are doing more work for their husbands, the kinds of transactions that take place within many sub-Saharan African families remain predicated on women continuing to fulfil their responsibilities, especially for their children, by independent work. Numerous studies have pointed out that the domestic economic separation, together with an obligation to do unremunerated labour, is a situation of potential conflict between husbands and wives (Roberts, 1979, 1985; Whitehead, 1981a, b; Dwyer, 1983; Carney, 1988). Although this has been apparent in studies since the 1930s, the problem has become particularly severe with the world recession.

Contemporary rural women's economic activities
The working lives of contemporary rural African women exhibit an enormous diversity (see Table 3.1). While quite a large number of women combine both independent work and work for others, it should be noted that at different ends of the socio-economic spectrum women may emerge as working entirely for others (poor women)

Table 3.1 Typical categories of rural women's contemporary economic activity

	Independent farming	Labour for others
In smallholder production (producing for self-consumption and for sale)	On own account as smallholders' wives On own account as female heads of household	Unremunerated 'family labour' Labour remunerated in kind or cash for husbands and neighbours
In commercial production (producing for sale)	Own-account farmers, as wives Own-account farmers, as female heads of household Unremunerated 'family labour'	Managers for absent husbands Casual or permanent wage labour

or working entirely on their own (female heads of households engaged in commercial production).

In general, in the commercial farm sector, women work in all the categories of employment. Although there are not many studies of female commercial farmers, what there is suggests that only in some cases are rural households developing joint resource-holding (see Hill, 1963; Kitching, 1980; Cheater, 1981; Wright, 1983). Agricultural female wage labour is a very neglected area of study (see Feldman, 1981), but recent studies suggest that as well as being under-reported it is often seasonal and poorly paid (e.g. Sender and Smith, 1987; Evans and Young, 1988). Among female-headed households in the commercial sector there are probably a few independent, successful, commercial female farmers, but by and large female-headed households in commercial farming areas belong to the poorest category. These women work as casually or permanently employed wage labour, and own small plots of land. In male-headed households the richer women work in a combination of capacities in which they co-operate with their husbands' enterprises; they may also work as unremunerated family labour, as well as having independent enterprises of their own. In some cases they play an important role as farm managers for absentee husbands. The poorer women combine farming small plots of their own with work for their husbands and work for others, if it is available.

By far the highest proportion of women's labour input is in the smallholder sector, however. Although smallholder households produce directly a proportion of their required consumption goods, the balance between crops grown for sale and self-provisioning varies. Smallholders also vary in levels of productivity, techniques used, the sexual division of labour and reliance on female labour. In some cases smallholders employ casual and other wage labour for their cash-cropping activities. Characteristically, women in the smallholder sector have several sets of economic activities, and their independent farming may make an important contribution to family food production. They also provide a substantial proportion of the labour input in cash-cropping, often on their husbands' fields. While they work largely with unimproved techniques and inputs on their food crops, they may well be working with modernised inputs in the cash sector (Wright, 1983). They also retain a very substantial responsibility for a wide variety of domestic tasks, including essential processing of raw commodities to render them edible. It is also reported that the loss of the social security system provided by the more collective forms of responsibility in the pre-commodity kinship system means that many poor women are increasingly to be found working for their neighbours in return for food rather than for wages (Guyer, 1981; Pottier, 1985a).

Despite the considerable diversity of contemporary rural women's work in sub-Saharan Africa, both planners and academics would be hard put to get any sense of this diversity from most national statistics. It is almost impossible from macro-statistics to apportion women to the different categories of economic activity outlined.

The Recording of Women's Work in National Statistics

Persistent inaccuracy and inadequacy in statistics and data about the nature and importance of women's work in the rural sector are a profound stumbling-block to agricultural planning. One of the most widespread findings is of an enormous gap between the work that micro-studies and case-studies report women as doing and their work as recorded in macro-statistics about employment and agriculture. Africa escapes neither the general and global problems of sex discrimination in statistics (Oakley and Oakley, 1978; Nissell, n.d.) nor the sources of inadequate recording of Third World women's work, on which there now exists a substantial and increasingly sophisticated literature (see IBRD, 1979; ICRW, 1980; Benería, 1981, 1982; Dixon, 1982; Anker, 1983; Boulding, 1983; United Nations, 1984a; Pittin, 1985; Dixon-Mueller and Anker, 1988). Given the widespread nature of these problems it is not surprising, therefore, to find that much of rural African women's work is invisible at the macro level. Although there are some exceptions (for example the national series of Kenyan agricultural statistics), many tropical African countries have little macro-statistical material which yields any information about rural women's work on which to base planning decisions. This section will examine some of the reasons for women's invisibility in African national economic statistics, concentrating on technical issues relating to data collection and cultural stereotypes.[11]

The issue of the representation of women in Third World agricultural statistics has been taken up extensively by Dixon-Mueller in a series of publications, including studies for the ILO (Dixon, 1982; Dixon-Mueller, 1985; Dixon-Mueller and Anker, 1988). One thing she does is to compare national-level statistics commonly collected in census and labour-force-type surveys of employment, economic activity rates and occupation according to ILO conventions on labour force participation data, and statistics collected through farm and agricultural censuses, which are collected according to other conventions, often those of the Food and Agriculture Organisation (FAO). Farm censuses always produce a greater enumerated agricultural workforce: 'For unpaid females farm censuses sometimes identify as many as two to ten times the number of agricultural workers as do other sources' (Dixon-Mueller, 1985, p. 113).

More workers, especially women, are reported in farm censuses because the modes of collecting data are much more in tune with the nature of Third World rural work patterns. Farm censuses, which are often deliberately carried out during the busiest farming seasons, include 'a person who performs any agricultural work on the holding during the specified time period regardless of his work or whether he is paid to do it'. Moreover, their definitions of agricultural work include activities performed close to home, which might be recorded as housework or subsistence production according to the more restricted labour participation definitions. She shows, therefore, how international standards can be biased towards urban and developed countries' notions of employment and production. They are particularly not designed for enumerating self-employment, seasonal and casual work, or work which has a shifting and fluid pattern according to its intermeshing with other responsibilities – in short, for women's work.

In seeking to test the likelihood that a particular method of enumerating economic activity will record women's work accurately the following questions (taken from Dixon-Mueller, 1985) seem critical:

1 What is the time period of reference?

2 Is only the primary or main occupation or economic activity to be recorded?

3 Does the category 'production of economic goods and services' include production for own consumption?

4 By what criteria do unpaid family workers enter the employment category?

5 What amount of time must be spent on an activity during the reference period for the person to be recorded as economically active?

In addition to the technical problems of data collection, other problems contribute to the invisibility of rural African women's work. One such problem is who provides the information on household members. A male (presumed) head of household is not necessarily the most appropriate person to give information about other members of the domestic group. In sub-Saharan Africa, where, as outlined above, economic separation characterises relations between husbands and wives, it is particularly important to interview household members separately. The nature of wives' economic activities may not be known to the household head, and pervasive male cultural assumptions about the unimportance of women's work, shared by interviewer and respondent, may lead to systematic under-reporting. Equally important, however, may be the way in which cultural values lead women themselves not to recognise what they do as work. Vernacular translations of the term 'farming', for example, may exclude culturally specific categories of women's work which are objectively part of the agricultural labour processes. In some farming systems, for example, women's contribution to planting is given little acknowledgement. Another problem is that, because of the absence of a separate linguistic term to describe them, a whole series of activities (e.g. small livestock and poultry management; vegetable-growing; harvesting gathered tree products, such as sheanuts) may be effectively screened out when questions focus on more commercial notions of farming. Although this is true for both men and women, as Dixon-Mueller (1985) says, 'Because male interviewers and male and female respondents alike frequently consider many of the things women do as "housework" regardless of their intrinsic nature, tasks that for men are labelled economic activity may not be so for women.'

The problem of what actually is 'work' for women is particularly apparent in the recording of family labour. Because family labour is quintessentially part of the obligations of a wife and mother, it is often culturally evaluated not as 'work' but as a continuation of a woman's other social roles within the family. Social science conventions may then reproduce this judgement. In addition, the work that women do as family labourers is often what is called subsistence production, i.e. production for own consumption – as many commentators have emphasised, a category of economic activity poorly enumerated in national statistics. However, when we look behind the mechanisms by which some work reaches categories of enumeration, and some does not, we might find, I suggest, a more complex situation. It is difficult to measure women's work because it is bound up with their social roles within the family, and evaluations as to what constitutes 'domestic work' and what constitutes economic activity are difficult. At a more general level, enumeration is inadequate because the nature of domestic, household or subsistence production seems poorly understood. In order to examine this issue more carefully, I should like to consider the effects of development projects on women's work.

Development Intervention and Women's Work

There is a growing and increasingly sophisticated and comprehensive literature in which development projects have been evaluated in relation to their impact on women.[12] Much of this work suggests that the outcome of development interventions in rural areas has been unpredictable, if not negative, for example in its effects on rural productivity, because planners have ignored women's work. These studies suggest that it is difficult to predict how far rural women will be willing to increase their work intensity and that some projects have the unintended and presumably unwelcome effect of making women worse off. They report simple failure to apprehend the extent of women's work in agricultural production as not uncommon. Sometimes male farmers are targeted for inputs and extension work on crops which only their wives grow. There is also a widespread neglect of the significance to the farm household, as an integrated domestic economy, of a whole range of women's (and men's) activities. As a result, proposed new practices and crops may make these other economic activities – for example, food crop production or subsistence activities – much more difficult or unrewarding to do, with serious and unintended effects on household well-being. This is of course one corollary of the absence of data on these kinds of activity in national macro-statistics.

However, a more complex planning problem requires emphasis. There appears to be a critical lack of fit between the conceptual model of the socio-economic structure of the family farm enterprise which is enshrined in development projects and the complex and particular forms of social relations in actually existing types of sub-Saharan African household and farming enterprise. The planners' model is based on the idea of the conjugally based household as an economic enterprise in which the members work together. The husband/father is regarded as managing the resources on behalf of other members, and those others, conceptualised as his dependants, provide labour under his direction. This is shown in the way in which projects target inputs, and especially in the frequent requirement of a family labour input from household members (especially wives) other than the putative male head (see, for example, Hanger and Moris, 1973). However, as argued earlier, one of the most noteworthy characteristics of sub-Saharan African domestic organisation is that conjugal and household relations are emphatically not of this kind.

The difference between what is planned for and rural reality has important consequences, which can be illustrated in a well-known example – that of the largely unsuccessful attempt to introduce irrigated rice production in the Gambia, described by Dey (1981, 1982). In addition to other difficulties, problems stemmed from the 'male dominant', 'domestic sharing' model that was employed. An initial assumption was made that the men were the rice growers and that they had full control over the resources required to do so. Incentive packages included cheap credits, inputs and assured markets for male farmers. It was in fact the women who traditionally grew rice, both for household consumption and for exchange, within a complex set of rights and obligations between husbands and wives in relation to domestic provisioning. It was the common lands to which women had secured usufructuary rights that the scheme was proposing to develop for irrigated rice production. Backed by project officials, men established exclusive rights to these lands, pushing the women rice farmers out to inferior, scattered plots on which to continue cultivating traditional rice varieties. All access to inputs, labour and finance was mediated through husbands. Women became notably reluctant to participate as unpaid family labour (their planned role) and husbands had to pay them for working on the irrigated rice fields. Dey attributes the disappointingly low levels of improved rice production largely to these misunderstandings. Her findings are similar to those in a study of Mwea – an irrigated rice settlement project in Kenya (Hanger and Moris, 1973).

It is hardly surprising, therefore, that the most widely reported finding of the evaluation studies on development projects is that husbands and wives increasingly compete for the changed and/or enhanced rewards that an increased, or changed, labour allocation may bring (Conti, 1979; Carney, 1988). As mentioned earlier, existing intra-household distributional mechanisms do not automatically lead to sharing (let alone equitable sharing) when household product is in the form of money income. This, together with the enhanced use of women's labour in the form of 'family labour', means that wives have difficulty in getting access to income commensurate with their labour input. These negative effects on women's welfare and the resulting conflict between husbands and wives have mainly become apparent when women's failure to co-operate in the desired manner has actually undermined the outcome of planned change (Hanger and Moris, 1973; Dey, 1981, 1982).

Problems of market models for non-market economies and for women's work
One of the nagging questions must be why economic planners persist in making some of these mistakes. Traditional views about the role of women in the family may be influential. So, too, may political issues to do with the role of peasant labour in the national economy, especially in relation to the need to feed non-farming populations and to earn foreign exchange. Another important reason lies in the ways of conceptualising economic activities that are enshrined within mainstream economic planning. These have important limitations when it comes to analysing economic processes which are non-market in form.[13]

This point becomes apparent if we return to the way many project designs make assumptions about the availability of women's labour as family labour. This family labour is economically planned for on the basis that it does not need to be directly remunerated. As we have seen, the requirement that wives should provide family labour may be in effect a cultural innovation which has not necessarily been part of wives' customary obligations to their farmer husbands. Moreover, it is clearly inappropriate to assume that there will be no cost to the male farmer of using the labour of his wives and children. Some male heads of household have had to pay in cash for their wives' labour, or they have had to concede benefits in kind or in reciprocated labour (Dey, 1982). These costs are not properly accounted for in predicting the economic viability of particular production changes. One reason why women are written in as family labour is because they are often not thought to do much productive work. They may be getting fuel and water, grinding grain or cooking, but in so far as these are part of *domestic work* this is not thought of as productive labour. In many project plans, women's labour is assumed to have a low opportunity cost. This assessment rests on three assumptions: first, that women are not doing independent farming that produces goods for sale on the market; second, that there is no economic cost to the farm family of diverting her labour away from the work she already does; third, that women's other tasks can be done in some other way or forgone. Various problems arise as one attempts to move, conceptually, across the interface between the non-market and the market.

In the first place there is the problem of pricing women's labour. Assessing the value of labour which is not priced through being waged, or through producing money income, has to be done by imputation. Both of the common ways of imputing value to women's work provide unrealistic assessments of its likely true economic value in the economic conditions we are considering. A second method is to impute against opportunity cost, that is, on the basis of the wage that could be earned if that activity is forgone. However, apart from the fact that the idea of opportunity cost is misleading if there is little or no employment available, rural women's earnings in tropical Africa are often themselves artificially low.

Second, there is the perennial problem of where the line is drawn between productive and non-productive activity, and how subsistence production should be categorised.[14] Although it is still not uncommon to see the term 'productive employment' excluding growing food for self-consumption, most recent discussions of sub-Saharan African household production agree that values must be assigned to some non-market production (and the value of food production is almost always to be included). The question for planning purposes is which non-monetised activities should be assigned a value in individual and household income. This is particularly important in relation to planning for women and household production, since, within the range of non-monetary tasks that women do, some are more likely to be comparable with monetised production than others. Thus the value of her food growing may be more relevant to a woman's decision-making about harvesting a cash crop than the labour she expends on child-care.

The third point is, however, the most important one for this chapter. One of the major points thrown up by considering the market/non-market interface is the extent to which women's labour in sub-Saharan African farm families requires a different theory of allocation. Many of the planning interventions analysed above depend on the ability of the household head to persuade his wife to work on the market crops. Clearly, then, in devising strategies to raise smallholder market surplus, understanding the factors which affect a husband's ability to do this may be critical for project success. The assumption that women will provide family labour is based on an assumption that market work, which produces an income, must be preferred to household work, which does not, and on the assumption that the family labour model is the main form of the sexual division of labour and that this constitutes an unproblematic way of allocating women and men to various tasks within the farm enterprise. Such assumptions ignore the complex combination of joint and separate economic interests which are such an important feature of the African farm family.

The Household: Joint and Separate Interests

It was of course precisely the problems associated with the market/non-market interface that the new household economics sought to account for in modelling consumer choice in Western societies. The essence of this approach is that the household, not the individual, is the basic analytical unit and that time as well as money is a critical item in allocation decisions. The household is both a production and consumption unit, and within the household time is allocated to the non-market production of consumption goods. Attempting to model a theory of economic decision-making in which time is allocated for activities which meet consumption needs, as well as for income-generating activities for the purchase of consumption goods, is a potentially important step for examining the conditions of smallholder production in sub-Saharan Africa.

Relatively little application of new household economics has been made to Africa. A recent study by Low (1986), however, points out that conventional neo-classical models of the farm household are particularly inappropriate to the rural Southern African situation because they do not allow an explicit analysis of non-market production, while 'Household economics is particularly suitable for the analysis of non-market production at the household level' (p. 17). Low argues that peasant farmers in Swaziland failed to use improved techniques and inputs sufficiently to increase their income from marketed production because, first, the new techniques were used to reduce the time needed for non-market production to meet household consumption needs and, second, migrant wage employment is a preferred household income generator because it gives greater returns.

Low's (1986) analysis leans heavily on comparative advantage: in the reason he gives for male labour migration, for example – that for some household members there is a comparative advantage in wage employment compared with farm household production – and in his assumptions about the rationale behind the allocation of tasks in the non-market sphere within the household. Such arguments necessarily rest on theories of maximisation, enshrining concepts of interest. He thus assumes that individual household members act out of self-interest to maximise their and/or their households' utilities. But his analysis also assumes that individual interests are bound together to produce a common household interest.

It is for this reason that his discussion of the ways in which the 'farm household' allocates members' time rationally between the different sectors, and according to comparative advantage, rarely refers to the sex of the household members. In general, as Folbre (1986) points out, it is potentially inconsistent to suggest that individuals who are entirely selfish in the market (where there are no interdependent utilities) are entirely selfless within the family (where a joint utility is assumed). She suggests that some new household economists solve this 'intrinsically difficult problem' by assuming that within the family 'altruism' prevails. Concepts of interest and altruism, with their inevitable baggage of morality, are thus embedded within much economic modelling.

As this chapter has shown, African farm families do not fit in with this model. Moreover, several authors have questioned the value of the concept of the multifunctional bounded household in the African context (Guyer, 1981). The fluidity of residential groupings, the propensity of households to change composition and, in some cases, the absence of linguistic terms to describe them all suggest caution. In part the separation of resource streams within the domestic group means that exchange, and not necessarily sharing, may take place within the household, while kinship relations outside the domestic group may entail sharing, altruism and reciprocity. So the sharing/non-sharing boundary is not coterminous with the inside household/outside household boundary.

Altruism, Interests and Gender

There has been for some years (albeit largely from disciplinary perspectives other than economics) a minority view which strongly criticises the concept of the household as a unit. Rapp *et al.* (1977), Guyer (1981), Harris (1981) and Whitehead (1981b), among others, have pointed out that the view that the household is a consumption unit – often based on the idea that it is a set of people living together, who agree to share resources because they eat together – has an ideological character. In relation to Africa, such writers have mainly explored the implications of the demonstrable economic separation between husband and wife. One important theme is the way in which intra-household allocational forms lead to inequalities in consumption and in the distribution of goods and services (see Guyer, 1981; Dwyer, 1983). A good deal of this discussion is empirical in character, but there is some work which explores the ways in which sex differences in the notion of needs provide the cultural under-pinning for some of this inequality, as well as the household as a site of gender power. Nevertheless, in examining situations in which husbands seem able to control and consume a greater share of the 'household' resources, there is little discussion of just how far this implies that men are acting out of unbridled self-interest. The model of the household as a set of joint interests is thus abandoned, but there is little discussion of whether the household should instead be regarded as a set of wholly separate individual interests. This question is posed even more sharply in those analyses which interpret African marriage as a means of making women work harder for men's benefit. A number of writers argue that with the sub-Saharan African sexual division of labour, in the context of the non-pooling household, marriage is primarily a labour relation. Roberts (1983, 1984, 1985), for example, argues that marriage has always constituted a major way of recruiting women to African farming, but that its impor-tance in providing labour for the family farm is increasing as other family bonds (espe-cially those of sons to fathers) become lessened with the effects of more commercial production and wage labour. With this I would agree, but it is necessary to ask what the implications of this view are for wider theorising of economic behaviour within the household. In particular, when the separateness of the interests of husbands and wives is stressed, is there any potential for theorising a joint interest between them?

In this initial wave of attempts to 'deconstruct the household', one thing which has been ignored is the roles that husbands and wives have as parents. Parenting is generally understood as the most common source of altruistic behaviour. In models and theories which treat the household as a unit, parenting is assumed to create interdependence, common goals and a need for sharing. The feminist writings, on the other hand, imply (correctly) that this cannot be taken for granted – that common parenthood cannot be seen as automatically creating common interests. Once again, however, the question of how parenting affects behaviour, and how far the fact of parenting must modify hypotheses about self-interest as the mainspring of behaviour, is insufficiently examined.

Maternal altruism
In discussing forms of intra-household distribution in northern Ghana (Whitehead, 1981a), the idea of maternal altruism was introduced. This was said to be a set of values which leads men's and women's behaviour in the household/family to be different. The essential feature of this ideology is the construction of the mother's

responsibility for feeding her children and for their well-being. This ideology, it was suggested, leads Kusasi women to sell groundnuts to feed their children, while their own consumption levels are low. Men are more likely to spend on their own consumption.

Many societies enjoin altruistic behaviour on mothers. The issue is not one of individual variation (i.e. of how good a wife or mother a woman is) but of culturally prescribed ways of being a good mother. Maternal altruism is a culturally constructed ideology which operates as a brake on women's self-interest. One possibility is that motherhood creates a special set of interests for women such that their fortunes become bound up with the fortunes of the family. In north-east Ghana, for example, I argued that women's interests are actually much more bound up with the common granary than men's, so that in giving their unremunerated labour they are acting in their own interests, in the interests of their children, and in the interests of the household as a whole, including its male members. The general point to be drawn from all this is that self-interest and altruism are not gender-neutral concepts and that the failure to consider the sex of the human subjects whom economic theorists consider as acting out of self-interest *or* altruism, is a serious limitation. Nevertheless, this earlier work was wrong if it implied that men are always motivated by self-interest. Rather, notions of self-interest and of altruism are culture-bound, and one of the culturally specific characteristics may be that they are 'gendered' – that is, men and women may be socialised into being self-interested and altruistic in different ways and to different degrees. Folbre (1986) emphasises that in general socialisation encourages women to be more altruistic than men: 'Perhaps women's position in and commitment to families helps explain why women often seem less motivated by "economic" concerns than men.' At the kernel of women's economic decision-making may be socialisation into an altruism which means that women do not act out of self-interest, but are equally liable to take into account the interests of others.

Why do women work harder?
This can be illuminated by briefly looking again at some points raised in the earlier discussions. One of the potential dilemmas that a rural woman faces is that, because as a wife she has more than one set of economic responsibilities and activities, she may be faced with a choice between increasing her labour input to her own independent farming or increasing her labour input to her husband's crop. An important issue that emerged was that it seemed easier for a woman to have control over the disposal of income or product from her own farming than over that produced on her husband's fields. A number of studies found women reluctant to increase their role as family labourers, largely because the rewards do not compensate them for the reduction in income and welfare from their independent farming. However, research evidence suggests that women's refusal to work as family labourers is by no means universal. In some cases they are found to have increased the time spent working on household cash crops. This is the implication of the overall historical change of this century, and it is also apparent when we consider a study by Palmer (1985a) in which she looks at what happens to women in resettlement schemes.

She looks at two schemes in Burkina Faso (when it was Upper Volta) (Cloud, 1976; Conti, 1979) and one in Nigeria (Spiro, 1984, 1985). In all three cases the projects paid insufficient attention to women's independent food production and other sources of income. Their main input was envisaged as family labour. So the form of farming economy that was planned had disadvantages for the 'farmers' wives'. However, there were critical differences in women's response in the two countries. In Burkina Faso women's lack of co-operation was instrumental in making both schemes relatively unsuccessful. In the Nigerian scheme women were staying in the resettlement areas and co-operating to some extent with the project and their husbands.

How are we to understand the decision of the Nigerian women farmers to increase their unremunerated labour? Since we do not know what the women involved thought were the issues, we can only make a series of educated guesses. In arriving at these we must assume that the basis of women's decision-making is more complex than simply maximising their self-interest. This complexity comes from two main directions.

First, we need to recognise that other interests may be at stake apart from simple economic ones. One thing that I have consistently underemphasised so far is the non-economic implications of work as family labour. In fact women lose independence and autonomy when they increase their work as family labourers as well as control over the income from what they produce. Few studies have tried to examine whether this is something women take into account when deciding about their work roles. In the long term a woman's role in economic decision-making may be cumulatively diminished as her role in the family approximates more and more to that of a simple family labourer. In this regard the great difficulty some rural women have in securing any property rights when their husband dies, as against his kin, is important. Many women may also be reluctant to lose the possibility of providing themselves with an independent safety net if the overall economic prosperity of the household diminishes.

Second, we need to take into account that women may need to act in the interests of their children, as well as of themselves. The welfare of children is rarely determined solely by their mothers' economic roles and responsibilities. Although Trip (1981) found that in a poor area in northern Ghana children's well-being was bound up with their mother's income but not correlated with their father's economic success, by and large children are likely to have some claims on their father's resources.

Bearing these two points in mind, we can re-examine the differences in the cases discussed by Palmer. Unfortunately we are hampered by the lack of stringent economic data in the base studies. Data on returns to labour are either absent or not sufficiently comprehensive, and little emphasis is placed on the changes in farm productivity entailed in each particular package. If better economic data were available, significant differences in the cases discussed might well emerge. In the Burkina Faso schemes, the impression is of projects trying to tackle the poverty of poor farmers who were likely to remain poor. The male heads of household found it difficult to make a success of farming under the conditions of the project. The total amount of income or food available to the household as a consequence of the project was very small. In considerable contrast to the Nigerian case, the resettlement package was funded at a very high level, and the projected income levels for the resettled households were very attractive by rural standards.

In the Nigerian case, the total level of capital resources, the nature of the inputs, and the level of projected changes in agrarian output were such that household incomes were likely to increase. In this case, there were at least three possible ways in which women might benefit or feel they were benefiting, so as to want to work harder as family labourers. They could be benefiting directly through receiving a better standard of living as a consequence of the improved household income. Second, they might not be benefiting personally but their children's welfare might be improved. Finally, they might perceive long-term benefits to themselves or their children in working in a household that looked as if it had better economic prospects. This latter case suggests that a woman's own welfare or that of her children may be sufficiently linked into the success of the market production part of the household farming enterprise for her to be prepared to intensify her work efforts on her husband's crops. One of the central issues to emerge, then, in relation to planning for changes in women's work, is what are women's 'interests' and how do they relate to their position in the household?

Implications for Economic Planning and Broad Policy Themes

The discussion in this chapter may seem difficult to relate constructively to the imperatives faced by economic planners. I have identified some conceptual and theoretical problems relating to the prediction of economic behaviour in the non-market sphere, and especially to women's economic decision-making. These may seem so deeply rooted that, faced with the need to go on planning in the here and now, the only alternatives seem to be either to do nothing or to continue with the old models, which are at least familiar and their shortcomings understood.

Two factors suggest that we cannot go on as before. First, there is growing evidence of an agricultural crisis in the majority (though not all) of the countries of sub-Saharan Africa. Economists have traditionally seen their competence as restricted to market phenomena, but this approach needs urgent revision in the light of the present food crisis.

In the bargaining and debates about the most rational allocation of scarce economic resources, the agricultural planners face difficulties that derive from the characteristics of the agricultural sector which I have highlighted in this paper: namely the predominance of smallholder farming, which combines non-market and market production and which makes extensive use of women's labour. If scarce national resources are going to be diverted to the agricultural sector, the ability to make decisions about the cost-effectiveness of different strategies will depend on being able to predict their effects on women's work patterns and on the balance between self-provisioning and market production in general in the smallholder food-producing sector.

The second factor is a more general argument about women's role in national economic activity. In relation to farming, as in so many other areas of economic activity, national planners cannot afford to neglect women as a category of human resource. But planners will be able to take proper account of women only if sex difference is a category around which planning data are organised. Some of the important areas for which data are needed have been spelt out by Dixon-Mueller and Anker (1988).

My exposition in this chapter suggests three main areas for discussion and action.

Data collection

The first of these is the most well-developed theme in the literature, namely the importance of adequate conventional conceptualisation and categorisation for collecting data about women's work in farming. Similar issues are also raised by my suggestion that economic analysis of smallholder production, in which a high proportion of the labour input comes from women, is constrained by the dominance of economic concepts which relate to the market sector. Hence the importance of collecting data relating to the interface between non-market and market production. It is important here to look at the misrecorded and misunderstood productive economic activity of women which goes on in agriculture and in the self-provisioning sector under the label of domestic activities. All this is related to women's roles as mothers, because the culturally prescribed modes of being a mother are linked to their work characteristics in important ways.

This kind of change is not easy to enact. The current conventional classifications are international ones. Moreover, they are based on assumptions, both about the relevance of economic models and about the kinds of model that are appropriate, that pervade the whole national and international planning process. Nevertheless, the debate is going on at the international level and there are moves to codify changes. These include work carried out by the International Labour Office, including that presented and referred to in Chapters 5 and 6, and the attempts by the United Nations Economic and Social Affairs Statistical Office, in association with the International Research and Training Institute for the Advancement of Women (INSTRAW), to develop statistics and indicators on the status of women in the developing world.

The status of women's labour
The second area I have highlighted is the need to be much more sensitive to the status of women's labour in human resource planning. The paper has pointed out how critical the attempt to mobilise women as family labourers has been, in circumstances where modes of sharing in the household do not assume a common economic enterprise between household members. This exposes the fact that, put crudely, family labourers do not necessarily behave as wage labourers. What determines their work intensity is a complex of factors associated with the social relations of the family, including the way in which women, and men, as part of a particular culture and society, interpret the responsibilities of motherhood.

The single dominant theme of this discussion is the imperative of seeking ways to analyse and model women's work when performed as family labourers. Such economic modelling is not very far advanced. Most of the attempts fall within the new household economics school, but this model has paid insufficient attention to the separate interests and separate budgets of household members in its initial premisses, as well as to the conceptualisation of interpersonal power as an aspect of labour allocation decisions. The primitive nature of attempts to model women's decisions in relation to their work as family labourers does not mean that it is impossible at the planning stage to review critically the model of women's work that is being adopted. Are women being assumed to be available as family labour? Has any effort gone into devising institutional forms which ensure that the changed income will be available to women? How does this planned-for family labour fit in with the current work practices and obligations of women, especially in the sphere of responsibility for their children? The point here is that the term 'family labour' should never be seen as unproblematic. Behind its bland and apparently inoffensive face lies all the seething and unpredictable discontent of changing domestic labour relations. Wives' labour is clearly subject to a different set of constraints and incentives from any other work relation. The control that is exercised is direct, and interpersonal, and may involve elements of male–female coercion. A large number of potential factors have been hypothesised which might affect the ability of male household heads to influence their wives, but few of these have been empirically examined (Whitehead, 1981b).

Modelling motherhood

The final area I have emphasised is the importance of the gender-specific constraints and incentives that derive from women's responsibilities for their children. I have argued that, in addition to having problems with conceptualising the household and the sexual division of labour, economic planners also have problems conceptualising the economic effects of motherhood. My exposition highlights recent discussions of the ways in which ideas about altruism and self-interest are central to many varieties of economic thought.

Notes

1. The author is grateful to Alison Evans, Maureen Mackintosh, Megan Vaughan, Gavin Williams and anonymous readers for comments on earlier drafts of this chapter and for many clarifying discussions about the issues it raises.
2. This chapter will mainly exclude discussions of Southern Africa, where the political and economic effects of apartheid have created a specific regional form of some of the problems discussed here.
3. For general discussions of this crisis see World Bank, (1981, 1983), Berry (1984), *IDS Bulletin* (1985), Rose (1985) and Tabatabai (1986).
4. The issues in this section are explored more fully in Whitehead (1986).
5. Descriptions of contemporary 'male' farming areas of the West African savannah are to be found in Bryson (1980), Whitehead (1981a) and Richards (1983). More generally see Guyer (1983) and Pottier (1985a).
6. In considering the interdependence of men's and women's work in the sexual division of labour, Whitehead (1981b) points out that it is important to distinguish farming operations in which men's and women's input occurs in different crop spheres, so that the sexual division of labour is 'sex-segregated', from those where men and women work in sequence on the same crops – a sex-sequential division of labour. The effects of changes in male and female labour supply will be different in the two cases.
7. Guyer (1983) throws doubt on the socio-economic causes of some of these crop changes.
8. Phillips (1953) contains a number of studies which are interesting from this point of view.
9. The micro-economics of resource-holding within African rural households are complex and very varied. While the complete merging of the economic resources of husband and wife is uncommon, any implication in this description of its opposite – namely of complete economic separation – is to be strenuously avoided.
10. This characteristic of African domestic structures has been linked to a whole series of other aspects of their kinship structures by Goody (1976).
11. These issues have recently been fully discussed in Dixon-Mueller and Anker (1988).
12. This section is based on the following sources: Vail and White (1977), Conti (1979), Dixon (1980), Bryson (1981), Dey (1981), Spiro (1984, 1985), Burfisher and Horenstein (1985), Jackson (1985), Jones (1986), Carney (1988), Johnson (1988) and von Bulow and Sorensen (1988).
13. This also applies to men's domestic production, but because it is a smaller proportion of their total economic activity it is less significant in relation to men's work than to women's.
14. For a comprehensive discussion see Goldschmidt-Clermont (1982, 1987).

4
Agricultural Policies & Women Producers

CONSTANTINA SAFILIOS-ROTHSCHILD

Up to very recently agricultural policies and programmes in Africa have been formulated on the assumption that men are the farmers and their wives unpaid farm workers. Although everybody has been verbally acknowledging that women do most of the agricultural work, the prevailing image is of the male farmer as the decision-maker. The 'invisibility' of women farmers from agricultural planning and programmes has been well documented, even in countries such as Lesotho in which almost three-quarters of all rural households are female-headed (Safilios-Rothschild, 1985a).

In the 1980s, however, a major change took place in smallholder agriculture in many sub-Saharan African countries. Both 'pull' and 'push' factors were responsible for men's disengagement from smallholder agriculture and for women's taking over of the farm management role. The important pull factor was the increasing availability of profitable non-farm employment for men near or away from villages. The important push factor was the decreasing size of family landholdings as a consequence of the very rapid population growth and the splitting of smallholdings among sons (Safilios-Rothschild, 1990). As a result, smallholder agriculture has been transformed to 'feminised' agriculture in entire districts or provinces of many countries. In Eastern and Central Province in Kenya, for example, the combination of pull and push factors has been responsible for a very high degree of 'feminisation' of smallholder agriculture, in some districts up to 90 per cent of farms being managed by women (Safilios-Rothschild, 1988a). In Zambia, too, in some districts of Luapula and Northern Province, the proportion of women farm managers varies from 50 to 75 per cent (Safilios-Rothschild, 1985b).

Reasons for the Invisibility of Women Farmers

Despite this trend toward feminisation of smallholder agriculture, women remain 'invisible' from agricultural planning because of a number of synergistic factors.

The first is that crucial data about women producers are not collected or are not made available to agricultural planners and policy-makers. This is due to the fact that at present the collection and/or the analysis and presentation of most types of agricultural data is still not sex-segregated. Thus, in most African countries national statistics do not exist on such basic issues as:

1 The amount of land cultivated (but not necessarily owned) by men and women, by province and district.

2 The types of crops men and women cultivate, the amounts they produce, and the amounts of different crops they market in formal and informal markets.

3 The type and number of livestock owned by men and women.

4 The agricultural tasks performed by men and women.

5 Men and women farmers' access to agricultural extension, training, inputs, credit, technology and organisational membership in agricultural co-operatives and farmers' organisations (Safilios-Rothschild, 1983).

The lack of such sex-segregated agricultural statistics is responsible for the fact that information crucial to planners, such as who the full-time farmers are, is lacking.

Furthermore, many of the crucial issues for agricultural planning and programmes require a complementary set of agricultural statistics and research findings from in-depth studies. Questions such as who makes the important agricultural decisions cannot be settled without the findings from in-depth studies that are successful in breaking through the cultural barriers that make it difficult for wives to report that their husbands do not fulfil the cultural ideal of the major agricultural decision-maker. In-depth research studies conducted in villages in four different districts in Kenya, for example, show that women make key agricultural decisions about the family plots, as well as about their own plots, when the husbands are not full-time farmers, and especially when they work far from the community (Safilios-Rothschild, 1988b; and in World Bank, 1989b).

Moreover, evidence indicating that women make key agricultural decisions about their own plots will not necessarily have a significant impact on agricultural policies because, in the absence of relevant statistics, the stereotypical belief persists that women's plots are insignificantly small and that women's agricultural production does not enter the market but is consumed by the household. Whenever data are available from community studies, however, they indicate that women's plots often represent one-third to a half or even more of the total family holding. In fact, in some rural communities it has been found that, in the majority of households, women's plots represent half or more of the family holding or even the entire holding (Safilios-Rothschild, 1988b; and in World Bank, 1989b).

With a few notable exceptions (e.g. in Zambia), farming systems research has not so far successfully integrated gender issues and has not provided sex-segregated data. But even the sparsely available sex-segregated agricultural data often remain marginal and practically invisible to agricultural planners and policy-makers. This lack of relevant sex-segregated agricultural data permits sex role stereotypes, according to which the farmers are the men, to persist, with serious policy implications. For how can agricultural policies ensure that women farmers are reached by extension services and credit as long as the belief lingers that men make all major agricultural decisions?

The second major reason for women farmers' remaining invisible is the persisting idea of the farm household as a homogeneous unit headed by a man and encompassing one productive unit towards which all members contribute their resources. This concept and its impact on modes of agricultural data collection are largely responsible for the lack of sex-segregated agricultural statistics and in-depth data. The reality of two (or more, according to the number of wives in a household) productive sub-systems within farm households, the one more or less controlled by the man and the other(s) by the wife or wives, has not yet been entirely accepted by researchers, statisticians and policy analysts. Despite the fact that more than sufficient research and project evidence has been accumulated regarding the existence of this duality or plurality of productive subsystems, there is considerable resistance to their recognition. This is probably because it goes against the grain of cherished Western values and beliefs about an idealised conjugal family. In addition, accepting this complexity in the conceptualisation of the farm household signifies acceptance of the fact that women as well as men (in the same household) are farmers and that they both need to be separately reached by agricultural services and resources. This new conceptualisation of the household or domestic organisation requires, therefore, a drastic reorientation in agricultural policies and institutions.

Another important factor that reinforces African women farmers' invisibility is the fact that they cultivate but do not own the land. Land ownership titles are regularly used to define who is a farmer. The fact that in most cases men hold the land ownership titles reinforces the stereotypical image of the men as the farmers and the women as their assistants. Women's access both to agricultural services and resources and to organisational membership in agricultural co-operatives and farmers' organisations is handicapped because they do not own land. Agricultural policies still regard farmers with land ownership titles as the exclusive target for agricultural services and resources. Thus, within the Training and Visiting agricultural extension programme in Kenya most selected contact farmers are titled landowners and agricultural credit cannot even be obtained without such title. Furthermore, in many countries such as Kenya and Zambia, although the law itself does not impose such limitations, the by-laws of co-operative societies (especially marketing societies) have tended to require that farmers must have land ownership titles in order to be admitted as members. In this way, women farmers have been completely marginalised from the mainstream agricultural system.

In all African countries, there are powerful and pervasive sex stratification systems that ensure male superiority in terms of decision-making power as well as in terms of control of valued resources. These sex stratification systems are supported by laws and policies that spell out and legitimise men's dominant status and are justified by religious, traditional, moral and/or pseudo-scientific ideologies and beliefs (Safilios-Rothschild, 1982). These stereotypes, reinforced by the lack of factual information regarding women farmers, are widely held by professionals and policy-makers alike.

The case of Lesotho provides a good illustration of the power of sex role stereotypes. Although it is well known that the majority of men, especially from villages in the mountainous areas, are absent from the country, and estimates show that 60–70 per cent of rural households are female-headed, agricultural policies and institutions have not taken these facts into consideration. This has been achieved by means of sex-stereotyped beliefs that underline women's dependence on the absent men and minimise their role in agriculture, particularly the widespread belief that men come back from South Africa in time to perform such traditionally male agricultural tasks as ploughing and planting. In fact research data show that men coming home for one or two months' leave rarely perform these tasks (ILO, 1979). It is also believed that, despite the long absence of their husbands, wives are not able to make important agricultural decisions because men make them from afar or when they came back on leave (Safilios-Rothschild, 1985a). Again, the available research shows that wives over 25 years old who are the *de facto* heads of farm households make most important agricultural decisions, although some long-term decisions, especially those regarding cattle, may be made by husbands or jointly (Gordon, 1981).

These stereotypes regarding women farmers have serious consequences for agricultural planning and programmes. Two of the most widespread such stereotypes are that men cultivate cash crops while women cultivate food crops and that women farmers are subsistence farmers. Official statistics in some countries such as Ghana have, however, shown that one-third of farmers producing cash crops such as cocoa, rice and sugar cane and one-quarter of farmers producing tobacco, coconut and oil palm are women (Ewusi, 1978). An evaluation study of the Northern Integrated Development Project in Sierra Leone found that the majority of farmers cultivate cash crops and that women tend to be willing to sell a greater proportion of their agricultural output and to reinvest a greater proportion of their income in agriculture than male farmers (Karimu and Richards, 1980). In addition, in-depth studies have shown that women producers market half or more of some of the crops they produce (Safilios-Rothschild, 1988a, b).

The Consequences for Agricultural Policies of Women Farmers' Invisibility

Let us now examine the significance of the invisibility of women farmers for major agricultural policies such as:
1 Food security policies.
2 Pricing policies.
3 Extension policies.
4 Agricultural credit policies.
5 Agricultural research policies.

Food security policies
Although much attention has been paid recently to food security, the significant contributions of women farmers have not been taken into consideration. This is partly due to the fact that the concern with food security is greater at the national level than at the household level, since the former can have consequences for the balance of payments. Furthermore, the concern with food security has not helped increase awareness of the crucial role played by women farmers because food security at the national level (but not at the household level) may be achieved by predominantly male commercial farmers, as has been the case in Zambia, Zimbabwe and Malawi. Thus, the key role played by women in achieving food security, at the national as well as at the household level, by growing alternative food crops to the main staple (maize or rice), such as cassava, sorghum and millet, which in some areas (e.g. Luapula and Northern Province in Zambia) constitute the basic staple food, by selling food surpluses in local markets, and by spending a great proportion of their income on buying the food they need, has been largely neglected.

Although it is well known that informal markets are very important for all agricultural produce, and especially for crops that are not officially priced, agricultural planners and policy-makers have relied almost exclusively on the official marketing statistics provided by marketing co-operatives and marketing parastatals. These official markets, however, are only responsible for buying cash crops (especially exportable cash crops such as coffee, tea and cotton) and those food crops that are considered the basis for food security and protected by official producer prices such as hybrid maize. Until now, it is mostly male farmers who have sold cash crops and officially priced food crops to co-operatives and marketing parastatals. Women farmers, whether they cultivate the same crops as men or other crops such as millet, sorghum, cassava, groundnuts, sunflower, vegetables, fruits, etc., sell their produce in local markets, because they are not co-operative members. Research studies conducted in several rural communities in Kenya show that practically all women market varying proportions of their food crops, and that often bananas, potatoes, beans and other vegetables serve more as cash crops than as food crops since more than half of what is produced is marketed (Safilios-Rothschild, 1988a). The distinction between food crops and cash crops is thus not very meaningful. Clearly, women play a very important role in food security at the village and regional level by selling vegetables, fruit, staples, chicken, goats, sheep and fish in informal markets.

Pricing policies
While the role of women in food security is slowly beginning to be recognised, gender issues are not yet considered within the context of important macro-economic policies in the agricultural sector. In Kenya, for example, where agricultural pricing policies have been found to create incentives for increased agricultural production and to promote smallholder production, the impact of these policies on men and women smallholders has not been separately examined. These pricing policies have favoured increased producer incomes and investments in cash crops (coffee, tea and sugar cane) and staple cereals such as maize, wheat and rice but not in drought crops such as millet, sorghum and peas, oilseeds like groundnuts, castor beans, sesame and sunflower, or other pulses such as beans (Jabara, 1984). Since women smallholders most often cultivate beans, peas, groundnuts and sunflower in addition to maize, it can be assumed that they have benefited much less from agricultural pricing policies than male smallholders, who mainly grow coffee and tea. In addition, women in Kenya grow vegetables and fruits that they use more as cash than as food crops and that are not controlled by pricing policies. In Zambia the impact of pricing policies favouring traditional staples and tubers, particularly sorghum (priced almost as high as maize), which are mostly cultivated by women smallholders, was never studied (Safilios-Rothschild, 1985a).

The present economic theoretical framework classifies the production of women farmers under 'non-tradables', that is, products that are not affected by macro-economic policies such as pricing policies, currency devaluation and market liberalisation. It has been shown, however, that the marketing behaviour of African women farmers is significantly influenced by prices in that they produce and sell more of a particular food crop when the price is high (Henn, 1983). Furthermore, some women farmers (the percentage varying by country, province and district) produce export cash crops. Finally, in countries which import food crops, all women farmers produce 'tradables' since they produce food crops. These food crops are either the same as those that are imported or other food crops that can be substituted for the more desirable food crops when they become too expensive as a result of currency devaluation.

This neglect of gender issues in macro-economic policies has become increasingly serious as structural adjustment packages have been adopted in different countries. As a result, the analysis of the sex-differentiated impact of structural adjustment in the agricultural sector is either inadequate, stereotyped and misleading, or ideologically grounded. In any case, it cannot provide policy-makers with the information they need to design corrective measures to alleviate the negative impact of agricultural policies on some categories of women farmers.

Extension policies
Extension policies have not included and benefited women farmers for a number of interacting and mutually reinforcing reasons.
1 In many sub-Saharan African countries the definition of 'farmer', based on export cash crops or on improved maize cultivation, has excluded the majority of all smallholders, and particularly women. In Luapula Province in Zambia, for example, it was found that a farmer was defined as someone who cultivated hybrid maize. Thus, only men who cultivated at least 2–4 hectares of hybrid maize and who sold it to co-operatives were defined as farmers; such men represented only about 1–2 per cent of the farmers in the area, but they had exclusive access to extension and credit facilities. Practically all women, regardless of the amount of land and the type of crop they cultivated, were labelled 'subsistence' farmers and left outside the context of agricultural institutions. In fact, many of these women cultivated 2 hectares of local maize, cassava, sorghum or finger millet, local beans, groundnuts or vegetables in *dambos*, selling much of their produce at the local markets. In view of the prevailing scarcity of extension personnel and of means of transport, it was not judged to be crucial for women, who were viewed as subsistence farmers, to be reached with extension information (International Fund for Agricultural Development, 1986). Research findings from Kenya show that women who are known to market their surplus locally or who cultivate relatively large plots are more often selected as contact farmers than those who market less produce (Safilios-Rothschild, in World Bank, 1989b).
2 A persisting belief, to a considerable extent reinforced by the 'women in development' literature, that women farmers can be effectively reached only by women extension workers has considerably curtailed women farmers' access to extension. Studies undertaken by the FAO in five sub-Saharan African countries have shown, however, that women extension workers encounter a number of structural difficulties, partly due to their multiple roles, that complicate field posting. Only in one country (Sierra Leone) have women expressed a preference for women extension workers, while the majority of women have voiced a lack of confidence in women extension workers, who they think are less knowledgeable about agriculture than men (Gill, 1987). Furthermore, a recent US Agency for International Development (USAID) evaluation of agricultural programmes (Carloni, 1987) and an evaluation of the performance of agricultural extension workers in Kenya (Safilios-Rothschild in World Bank, 1989b) with regard to reaching women farmers showed that women extension workers do not reach more women farmers than male workers. However, the organisation of women farmers into groups greatly increases the probability of being reached by male extension workers, even in areas with strong taboos regarding male–female interactions.
3 The continuing emphasis on providing information on home economics as well as agricultural information to women farmers through women home economists,

partially retrained in agriculture, probably represents the most serious barrier to women's access to extension, especially in countries in which a separate women's extension unit is created. The consequence of this trend is that the women extension workers, who are expected to provide advice not only on crop production, livestock and fisheries but also on topics such as nutrition, family planning, sanitation and health, often receive only a short agricultural training. Furthermore, in countries that have created a separate women's extension unit, women farmers are served by a small number of women extension workers since governments cannot afford to finance a women's unit of adequate size (Safilios-Rothschild, 1990).

Agricultural credit policies
Agricultural credit policies are the least adapted of all policies to the reality of feminisation of smallholder agriculture. This is at least partly due to the fact that in many countries credit policies do not favour smallholders at all, men or women. But, in all cases, women farmers are in a less favourable position than men because they do not have land ownership titles to act as collateral and because they cannot become members of co-operatives (largely because they do not have land titles), through which agricultural credit is often channelled. Thus, even when women are the only farmers in the household, they do not have access to agricultural credit, while the men can receive credit and use it for non-agricultural activities (Safilios-Rothschild, 1987).

In several countries, small women's projects have been set up, but these have had little impact, simply providing a few women farmers with small agricultural loans. Evaluations have shown that women in fact receive larger amounts of credit from mainstream gender-responsive credit schemes that cover both men and women smallholders than from small credit schemes targeted only at women (Lycette and Self, 1984).

It seems, therefore, that if women farmers are to be reached the basis for agricultural loans must be changed from land ownership to full-time engagement in agriculture and past agricultural performance. In addition, credit should be linked directly to savings by making systematic and mandatory savings the cornerstone of agricultural credit (Safilios-Rothschild, 1990). There is considerable evidence that women smallholders have a much greater propensity than men to save, both as individuals and as group members.

Agricultural research policies
Agricultural research policies have hitherto focused mainly on cash crops and on producing high-yield varieties for food crops without taking into consideration other criteria such as taste and labour requirements. These high-yield varieties, though often praised, can create serious labour bottlenecks which threaten household food security and bring about intra-household conflicts because the bottlenecks impede women's food production and income generation (Chabala and Nguiru, 1986).

In order to help increase agricultural productivity, agricultural research policies need to place an emphasis on the development of agronomic solutions for existing labour bottlenecks. Such solutions may include the development of crop mixes and new varieties with different maturity cycles, which would spread labour requirements more evenly over a longer period, and of varieties with a shorter maturity period, which would help solve the productivity problems of women farmers in many countries (particularly in the Sahel). Such varieties would help increase agricultural productivity in areas in which, because women must work in their husbands' fields before they can work in their own, they are obliged to plant and weed later than the optimal time, with negative consequences for yields (Safilios-Rothschild, 1990).

Decreasing the Invisibility of Women Farmers

On the more positive side, recent experiences indicate that the following factors help decrease the invisibility and marginalisation of women producers and facilitate the rationalisation of agricultural policies and programmes by targeting them on full-time women farmers.

1 *The documentation of a high percentage of female-headed households, de jure and de facto, in the official statistics of the country.* As long as only isolated in-depth research studies document the existence of a high percentage of women farm managers because a high percentage of them are *de facto* heads of household, there will be little impact on agricultural policies. This is true for Kenya, where a number of studies (Rukandema, 1980; Rukandema *et al.*, 1981; Safilios-Rothschild, 1988a; and in World Bank, 1989b) show a very high percentage (40–90 per cent) of women farm managers but the official statistics still show a low percentage (27.3 per cent), including only *de jure* female-headed farm households (Central Bureau of Statistics, 1981).

In Zambia, on the other hand, the high percentage of female-headed rural households was documented in the 1980 Population Census and the 1982–83 and 1983–84 Farm Surveys. This was because the statistics included *de facto* female-headed households created either through the husband's migration for a year or more or through polygyny. The latter type of female-headed household, seldom referred to in development literature, the autonomous polygynous household, is the separate household of a second, third or fourth, etc., wife and her children, who lives in a separate hut, has her own land to cultivate, and makes all the agricultural decisions about her land. These definitions of female-headed households adopted by the Zambia Population Census helped portray more accurately the high incidence (39–50 per cent) of female-headed rural households in several districts of Luapula, Northern, Eastern and Western Provinces (Safilios-Rothschild, 1985b). However, the Zambian experience also showed that the collection of such data is not sufficient. It is necessary to analyse these data and present them to agricultural policy-makers in conjunction with factual information regarding the access female heads of farm households have to agricultural services and resources. This was done by a special policy project undertaken in Zambia, which analysed and presented the data through seminars for senior agricultural planners and policy-makers. In these seminars, the high percentage of female-headed farm households was juxtaposed with existing data from ministries, development banks, research and evaluation studies showing women farmers' inadequate access to all types of agricultural services and resources. The policy-makers attending these seminars were asked to formulate recommendations regarding the changes in agricultural policies that were needed to increase women smallholders' access to agricultural services and resources (Safilios-Rothschild, 1985b).

2 *Considerable pressure, in many donor countries, particularly the United States, Canada, the Netherlands and the Scandinavian countries, to take gender issues into consideration in development.* This new intellectual and political environment is

responsible for the fact that women specialists have been increasingly hired both as permanent staff and as consultants in agriculture-related projects and programmes; that women producers have been increasingly included in the target group of agricultural projects (especially those financed by these countries); that women specialists now participate in agricultural preparation and evaluation missions; and that funds have been made available for policy seminars regarding women producers and for research studies that will help delineate the basic principles of the dual agricultural enterprise and economy existing within African rural households. This is an extremely important development that is beginning to influence the planning and policies of international agricultural organisations as well as of national government planning and agricultural ministries.

3 *The availability of funds for special evaluation missions within the context of large agricultural projects, to examine the extent to which the methodologies used are effective in reaching women farmers and to recommend more effective methodologies.*

4 *The widespread organisation of women farmers into groups.* In countries such as Burkina Faso, Ghana, Lesotho, Kenya, Mali, Nigeria, Senegal, Sierra Leone, Zimbabwe, and some provinces in Zambia, in which women are highly organised, the reorientation of agricultural policies and the implementation of agricultural programmes aiming to reach women producers are facilitated by the existence of these groups. The utilisation of women's groups is both efficient and cost-effective in terms of scarce manpower resources. It also helps overcome socio-cultural difficulties over male–female contacts, encountered in some areas, by enhancing male extension workers' ability to reach women farmers.

Even when the women's groups do not have collective agricultural production as a goal and even when they suffer from organisational problems, they represent a valuable grassroots organisation that can be used for the effective delivery of agricultural services to women producers. It has been shown that line agencies can successfully link into existing women's groups not only for the delivery of agricultural extension, training and inputs but also for afforestation, enviromental protection (e.g. against soil erosion), testing of farm implements, farm trials, and the dissemination and maintenance of technology (Harrison, 1987).

5 *A gradual adjustment, in some countries, of agricultural policies and programmes to the existing gender reality in smallholder agriculture.* In some cases, the necessity to reorient agricultural services to women farmers has become obvious to implementation agents. A good example comes from Kenya, where the agricultural extension programme gradually adjusted successfully to the fact that the majority of smallholders were women. When the Training and Visiting programme was first adopted in 1982–83, the selection of contact farmers was made according to the traditional criterion of land ownership and, with the exception of some widows, all contact farmers were men. Gradually, however, the extension agents began to realise that this criterion was not appropriate, since most of the men selected were not involved in farming and were seldom present at the bi-monthly extension visits. Their wives, on the other hand, were always present at the extension visits and were eager to learn since they were the full-time farmers. Since most of the extension agents' meaningful contacts with farmers were with women, they gradually began to replace the initially selected contact farmers with women full-time farmers and women's groups. In Makuyu District, Central Province, for example, they adopted full-time farming rather than land ownership as the criterion for selection of contact farmers, with a resulting majority of women contact farmers (Safilios-Rothschild, in World Bank, 1989b).

6 *The implementation difficulties encountered by agricultural programmes based on the assumption that there is only one farming system in the household, controlled by the husband.* The increasing availability of social impact evaluations of large agricultural programmes has shown that many implementation difficulties are due to the faulty assumptions on which they are based, a fact that has helped increase awareness about the separate existence of women producers. In Senegal, for example, when the settlement project in the Terres Neuves region did not accommodate women's traditional rights to individual land, it encountered a strong protest by the active women's group threatening to 'withdraw all the women from the project area, if provisions were not made to clear women's fields'. As a result, the project was obliged to accommodate the separate needs of women (World Bank, 1984a). In Gambia, similarly, as Whitehead has already noted above, an agricultural project that introduced irrigated paddy production ignored the importance of women's long-established rights to swamps for rice cultivation and to control over the resulting income. The project developed irrigation schemes largely controlled by men, mostly from swamps previously cultivated by women. Thus, women's land rights were eroded and their ability to earn income curtailed. This serious deterioration in their status led them to withdraw their labour from the project, with a resulting overall decrease in rice production. Similar project experiences are accumulating, and are helping to underline the existence of gender-specific farming systems within the household and the need to reorient agricultural institutions so as to serve both men and women farmers.

7 *The failure of agricultural policies and programmes to increase agricultural production and to ensure food security in many African countries, which is creating an atmosphere within which policy-makers and donors alike have been willing to re-examine their assumptions and strategies.* Within this atmosphere of re-examination of agricultural strategies, there is more willingness to discuss women producers as very important actors in agricultural production who have not yet benefited from agricultural interventions but who have the potential to increase significantly their contributions to food security and agricultural growth.

WOMEN'S WORK:
TAKING IT INTO ACCOUNT

5 Measuring Women's Participation in the African Labour Force

RICHARD ANKER

Issues related to 'women in development' are now at the top of policy and research agendas. Policy-makers are increasingly realising that development, social and population objectives cannot be attained unless the crucial role women play in economic development is recognised and taken into account. Researchers are increasingly realising that the special needs and constraints faced by women such as those resulting from cultural and social norms need to be taken into consideration if behaviour is to be understood and useful policy suggestions made.

In order to assess and affect women's role in development, it is necessary to have accurate data on how women are integrated into the development process taking place in their country. It is not a question of ascertaining *whether* women are contributing to development but of ascertaining *how* women are contributing to development. This situation is particularly critical as regards labour force statistics, where there has been in recent years an outcry against the current state of affairs where women's labour force participation is greatly under-reported in official government statistics.

This need to recognise and measure women's contributions to development was emphasised throughout the United Nations Decade for Women from 1975 to 1985 as well as at the beginning- and end-of-decade conferences in Mexico City and Nairobi. There have been repeated appeals for statistics which more accurately reflect the true extent of women's labour force activity.

At its 71st Session in 1985, the International Labour Conference, in a resolution on equal opportunities and equal treatment of men and women in employment, said:

> As existing statistics often fail to reflect accurately women's participation in the labour force, efforts should be made to improve statistical data collection and analysis so as to reflect more fully the contribution of women to productive activities and other aspects of their employment.
>
> The ILO should contribute to the collection of improved data ... by reviewing and evaluating the use of new concepts and definitions for measuring labour force participation. (ILO, 1985)

The forward-looking strategies of the World Conference to Review and Appraise the Achievements of the United Nations Decade for Women, held in Nairobi in 1985, also called for improved data collection:

Timely and reliable statistics on the situation of women have an important role to play in the elimination of stereotypes and the movement towards full equality. Governments should help collect statistics and make periodic assessment in identifying stereotypes and inequalities. (United Nations, 1986)

The Governing Council of the United Nations Fund for Population Activities (UNFPA), at its 35th Session in June 1988, stressed the need to collect accurate and meaningful statistical data on women and 'noted with satisfaction' UNFPA's efforts in this area (UNFPA, 1988b). Nafis Sadik, UNFPA's executive director, has indicated that:

data collection and analysis should be more gender-specific and gender-sensitive than it has been in the past. Much methodological and empirical work is needed to better quantify the contribution of women to national income accounts and to population welfare in general. (UNFPA, 1988d)

The present chapter takes a detailed look at currently available estimates of female labour force participation in Africa and the reasons for its very strong tendency to be underestimated. In doing so, it draws upon published national estimates of female labour force participation in Africa. The discussion then goes on to suggest ways that these data could be improved in future labour force surveys and population censuses. Results from methodological surveys conducted in India and Egypt, with which the author has been associated, are drawn upon here.

Estimates of Female Labour Force Participation in Africa and Around the World

Official estimates of the female and male labour force are typically drawn from population censuses and national labour force surveys. It is important to note that such estimates for sub-Saharan African countries are far from complete, as only about 60 per cent have official labour force estimates by age and sex and only about 30 per cent have estimates of the labour force by occupation or industry based on a national survey or census reported in the ILO's *Yearbook of Labour Statistics*. This relative paucity of labour force data contrasts sharply with the situation in other regions of the developing world (Table 5.1).

Table 5.1 Number and percentage of developing countries reporting national labour force data by age, sex, occupation and industry, by region of world[a]

Region	Labour force by age and sex	Industrial classification (ISIC) by sex	Occupational classification (ISCO) by sex
Africa (sub-Sahara) ($N = 36$)	22 (61%)	12 (33%)	11 (31%)
North Africa and Middle East ($N = 17$)	10 (59%)	13 (76%)	12 (71%)
Asia[b] ($N = 21$)	15 (71%)	15 (71%)	15 (71%)
Latin America ($N = 23$)	22 (96%)	20 (87%)	18 (78%)
Total ($N = 97$)	69 (71%)	60 (62%)	56 (58%)

Notes: ISIC: International Standard Industrial Classification.
ISCO: International Standard Classification of Occupations.
[a] Includes all developing countries with 1 million or more population in 1985 with relevant labour force data (since 1970) reported in source.
[b] Includes Fiji.
Source: ILO: *Yearbook of Labour Statistics* (various years).

In an effort to fill in the gaps in national estimates, the ILO has attempted to compile 'labour force data which has been standardised, so far as possible, in particular as regards concept, scope, coverage and age classification to improve national comparability' (ILO, 1973).

Using estimates compiled by the ILO, it is possible to observe how these estimates of female labour force participation for sub-Saharan Africa differ from those for other regions in the developing world (Fig. 5.1). Notice that estimated rates for men are similar around the world, as indicated by the small difference between the highest and lowest reported regional rates (top two lines in Fig. 5.1). For women, on the other hand, there are tremendous regional differences. Sub-Saharan Africa has, according to these estimates, medium to high female activity rates, with about 60 per cent of adult African women estimated to be in the labour force. This overall rate for sub-Saharan Africa is similar to that estimated for South East Asia; it is lower than that for China but higher than that for the other major developing regions.

When these estimates for sub-Saharan Africa are disaggregated into estimates for each of its four major subregions (Table 5.2), we find considerable variation in the labour force participation rate for women aged 30–34 years. Rates are much higher in East Africa (71.0 per cent) than in West Africa (57.1 per cent), Central Africa (52.9 per cent) or Southern Africa (45.6 per cent).

When the estimates are disaggregated further into country estimates of female labour force participation within an African subregion such as West Africa, we again find great variation (Table 5.2). Three countries have an estimated rate of over 90 per cent, five have a rate between 60 and 69 per cent, five have a rate between 40 and 59 per cent, and three have a rate below 35 per cent.

There is also considerable instability in reported female labour force estimates in Africa, as reflected in different surveys. To illustrate this, we have brought together in Table 5.3 different estimates of labour force participation for women aged 15–44 years for countries where such data are available from official national censuses or surveys and from a World Fertility Survey inquiry as well as from the ILO. One cannot but be struck by the variability in these estimates for each country. Even within the ILO's own estimates (made in essence ten years apart based on what were, at the time, felt to be the best currently available data), one observes large differences.

In the face of this evidence on estimated female labour force participation rates in sub-Saharan Africa, one must of necessity be extremely sceptical about its accuracy, especially since women are known to play a major role in agriculture in Africa (and the vast majority of Africa's labour force is engaged in agriculture).

Possible Reasons for Inaccuracy in Female Labour Force Participation Rates

Is it possible to explain why female labour force participation rates tend to be under-reported and why they seem to vary so much from one inquiry to another? In the light of answers to these two questions, is it possible to suggest ways in which female labour force data could be collected and presented so as to correct for these problems? These questions are taken up in the present and subsequent sections.

Three possible reasons for the marked tendency of female participation in the labour force to be under-reported in population censuses and labour force surveys were

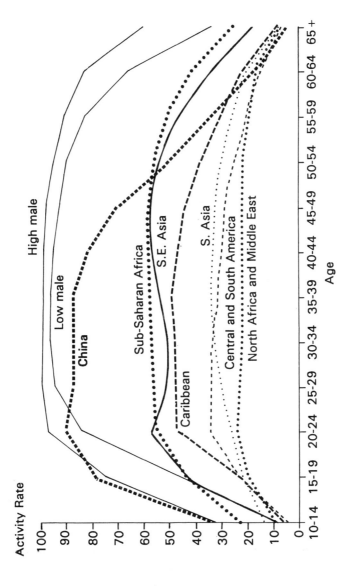

Fig. 5.1 *Female and male activity rates by age and region based on ILO estimates, 1980. 'High male' and 'low male' lines represent the regions with the highest and lowest male activity rates for each age category.* **Source:** ILO, 1986a, Vol. V, Table 2.

Table 5.2 Female labour force participation rates for women aged 30–34 years based on ILO estimates, sub-Saharan Africa, 1980

Sub-Saharan Africa	60.7
East Africa	71.0
Central Africa	52.9
Southern Africa	45.6
West Africa	57.1
Benin	97.3
Burkina Faso	90.9
Cape Verde	34.0
Côte d'Ivoire	58.3
Gambia	68.7
Ghana	60.8
Guinea	67.7
Guinea-Bissau	67.6
Liberia	46.5
Mali	17.0
Mauritania	21.2
Niger	92.6
Nigeria	53.1
Senegal	65.5
Sierra Leone	46.2
Togo	54.4

Note: The rate for sub-Saharan Africa is 62.1 per cent when South Africa is excluded from the calculation.
Source: ILO, 1986a.

Table 5.3 Female labour force participation rates for selected countries from various sources

Country	World Fertility Survey (WFS)[a]	Official national data[b]	ILO estimates[c]	
			1975	1980
Cameroon	69	47	66	45
Ghana	89	62	63	53
Kenya	13	NA	47	64
Lesotho	22	35	82	68
Senegal	74	64	57	60
Sudan	34	21	11	20

Notes: 1. Restricted to sub-Saharan countries with rates reported for WFS in Allsopp (1982).
2. Age groups were: 15–50 (and married) for WFS; 15–44 for ILO estimates; 15–44 for official estimates.
3. Years of estimates were: 1974–79 for WFS; 1975 and 1980 for ILO estimates; 1982, 1970, 1976, 1985 and 1973 for official estimates for Cameroon, Ghana, Lesotho, Senegal and Sudan, respectively. NA Not available.
Sources: [a] Allsopp, 1982.
[b] ILO: *Yearbook of Labour Statistics* (various years).
[c] ILO, 1977, for 1975 estimates; ILO, 1986a, for 1980 estimates.

identified and investigated in detail in earlier work by the author. This included an in-depth review of the relevant research literature (Anker, 1983) and methodological or 'methods test' field studies carried out jointly by the ILO and the Operations Research Group (ORG) in rural areas of India (Anker, *et al.*, 1987, 1988) and by the ILO and the Central Agency for Public Mobilization and Statistics (CAPMAS) in Egypt (Anker and Anker, 1988, 1989; Anker, 1990), where approximately 1600 and 1000 rural households were interviewed, respectively. The measurement issues specifically investigated in these studies were:

1 Which type of questionnaire provides more accurate data on female labour force activity: a keyword questionnaire (which includes a series of detailed follow-up keyword questions) or a simplified time-use schedule (in which information is collected on each of 13 important economic activities)?

2 Does the sex of the interviewer affect the reporting of female labour force participation?

3 Are the responses provided by (usually male) proxy-respondents different from those of women who respond on their own behalf (self-respondents)?

Results from both the Egyptian and the Indian surveys indicate quite clearly that reported female labour force participation rates are very sensitive to the way in which a questionnaire is designed and questions asked. Also, the broader and more encompassing the definition of labour force participation that is used, the more important it is to ask clearly and specifically what women have been doing. Both men and women are basically willing to provide reasonably accurate information about women's labour force activity. The main problem is that they often do not understand the concept of labour force activity as defined in international recommendations and as requested through ambiguous survey questions. This should hardly be surprising, since even labour force statisticians often do not agree on what constitutes labour force activity! In Fiji, for example, a person had to tend more than ten chickens to be considered a labour force participant (Blacker, 1978). In a study on national practices in 70 developing countries which investigated whether the value of various subsistence activities was included in national income (and thus whether the activities should be considered as labour force activities), it was found that 71 per cent of developing countries included the imputed value of forestry activities, 39 per cent food-processing, 50 per cent handicrafts, and 7 per cent water-carrying (Blades, 1975).

We found in the Indian (and Egyptian) methods test studies we conducted that 16 (16)[1] per cent of sample rural women were reported to have performed labour force activities for more than the minimum time (47 hours in the past season in India and 130 hours in Egypt) in response to a keyword question that enquired about a woman's 'main activity'; this rate became 41 (27) per cent when a question about 'secondary activity' was also asked, and 48 (29) per cent when a question about 'work' was asked. These rates compare with 88 (54) per cent when respondents were asked specifically about the performance of 13 labour force activities from a list of activities which included farming, animal care, wage employment, petty trading, etc. (Anker and Anker, 1988; Anker et al., 1988). There were also enormous differences in responses to the same questions when only activities which involve monetary transactions (i.e. wage/salary employment plus work in family-owned enterprises where products are sold) were considered. Reported female labour force activity rates for market-oriented activities went from 7 (14) to 18 (22) and 24 (23) when questions on 'main activity', 'secondary activity' and 'work' were asked, as compared with 32 (30) per cent when an activity/time-use schedule was used.

Tabulation of results from the Egyptian and Indian studies by the sex of respondents and interviewers indicates that male biases (that is, husbands under-reporting their wives' activity or the insensitivity of male as opposed to female interviewers) were not major causes of the under-reporting of female labour force activity in these studies – although male proxy-respondents in Egypt did significantly under-report the performance of wage/salary activities by women in the past year as compared with female self-respondents (about 10 per cent as compared with about 17 per cent).

There are, of course, other factors that may constitute important reasons for the under-reporting of women's labour force participation, such as:

1 *Length of reference period and timing of a survey/census, given the seasonal nature of many labour force activities.*

There are two main labour force concepts in common usage: the 'current labour force', which provides a snapshot of the labour force for a short reference period (such as the past week), and the 'usual labour force', which provides an estimate of people attached to the labour force for a long reference period (such as the past season or past year).

In the 1971 Indonesian census, for example, women comprised 41 per cent of the labour force based on a 'last cropping season' reference period compared with 32 per cent based on a 'previous week' reference period (World Bank, 1980). In the 1940 Peruvian census, women comprised only 14 per cent of the agricultural labour force based on 'present' occupation (using the past week reference period) as compared with 31 per cent based on 'usual' occupation (Durand, 1975).

In sub-Saharan Africa, where agricultural activity is very seasonal, estimates of the current labour force are obviously going to be sensitive to the time of year a survey/census is conducted. It is clear that sub-Saharan African countries should either use a long reference period or, if a one-week reference period is used, conduct surveys several times during the year.

2 *Use of a minimum number of hours criterion, that is, a person must have engaged in labour force activity for at least a certain number of hours in the reference period to be included in the labour force.*

For wage/salary labour and for work performed in enterprises (including family-owned enterprises) where products are sold, there is, for all intents and purposes, no minimum work-time criterion for estimating the current labour force included in the international recommendations.[2]

For people who were unpaid family workers (i.e. worked as an unpaid family helper in a family farm or enterprise other than one where products are sold), previous international recommendations (1954 and 1966) included a provision that work needed to be done for more than one-third of normal working time – usually taken to be 15 hours in the reference week.[3] This provision was dropped in the 1982 international recommendations and replaced by a provision that activities involving the production or processing of primary products for own or household consumption needed to 'comprise an important contribution to total consumption of the household' for these to be considered as a labour force activity (ILO, 1982). Unfortunately, since the new 'important contribution criterion' is difficult to define and measure, most countries continue to rely on the earlier one-third rule. Since women are more likely than men to be engaged in family-based labour force activities, women are more likely than men to be excluded from the labour force by this continued use of a minimum work-time criterion. This could be an important factor in reducing female labour force estimates in areas of the world such as sub-Saharan Africa where agricultural activities are subject to major peaks and troughs in activity throughout the year.

3 *Basing labour force estimates on the performance of one main labour force activity.*

Labour force estimates are almost always based on the performance of one major activity. This is partly because unemployment is defined as the complete absence of employment during a short reference period such as one week; thus the performance of any labour force activity qualifies a person for inclusion in the labour force. Yet for women the performance of many different work activities is a way of life. Most women cannot afford the luxury of performing only one (or even two) labour force activities.

All this causes two major problems for measuring women's labour force participation. First, many censuses/labour force surveys rely on a question about a person's 'main activity'. This turns out to be a disastrously poor question for measuring women's labour force participation. Both because of the 'housewife' stereotype and because of the extremely long hours all women put into housework and child-care, housework is often seen as their 'main activity'; even if they do labour force activities as well, the labour force activities they engage in may be for fewer hours. Second, even women reported to have engaged in a labour force activity are often seen by statisticians as marginal labour force participants, because they are only given 'credit' for the time they spend in one (or sometimes two) labour force activities.

It is clear that information needs to be collected on all of the labour force activities a woman performs, if her economic contribution is to be completely measured and recognised. This obviously implies that labour force questionnaires should not be based on overly simple questions and concepts such as 'main activity' or 'main occupation'.

4 *Ineffective training and sensitisation of interviewers to the difficulties involved in the collection of accurate information on female labour force activity, and in particular to the need to avoid the trap of stereotyping a woman as an inactive 'housewife'.*

There is relatively little direct evidence on the effect of training and sensitisation of interviewers on the reporting of female labour force activity – although there is reason to believe that these do have a significant influence. Some evidence is provided by the methodological labour force studies conducted in Argentina and Paraguay by Catalina Wainerman (1988), where labour force information was collected for over 1000 men and women in both rural and urban areas of each country using two different interviewer training sessions. One set of interviewers attended a two-hour training session, while the second set attended four training sessions held over a two-day period. Though the results were confounded by the use of different questionnaires by the two sets of interviewers, Wainerman still felt justified in concluding that interviewer training had an important effect on the reporting of female labour force activity.

A second example comes from Egypt, where reported adult female labour force participation rates rose from about 5 per cent to 12 per cent between the 1982 and 1983 national labour force surveys – implying an increase of approximately 1.5 million female labour force participants. This change can be traced largely to a conscious effort on the part of the Egyptian statistical office (CAPMAS) to increase the enumeration of female labour force participants through improved training and increased sensitisation of interviewers to the need to collect information on women's labour force activity, particularly activities done on the family farm (Anker and Anker, 1989).

That improved training and increased sensitisation are important should not be surprising, since the 'housewife' stereotype for women and the 'worker' stereotype for men are both very strong throughout the world. Despite this, it would be dangerous to rely on training and sensitisation as a panacea for improving the measurement of women's labour force participation.

Potential Usefulness of Methods Test Studies in Improving Female Labour Force Data in Africa

A number of suggestions put forward in this chapter are based on the results of methodological surveys carried out in India and Egypt, for which the author was partly responsible. Many readers must have been curious about these methodological studies or 'methods tests'. How are they structured? And would it be useful to do one in sub-Saharan Africa?

'Methods tests' are studies designed to compare systematically results obtained from different approaches to the collection of survey data. They provide statistically valid evidence on the best approaches to the collection of data; they can thus provide information on how to collect reliable data that avoids, for example, gender and other biases.

Methods test surveys typically use balanced sample designs where several groups comprised of equal numbers of randomly chosen people (or households) are each subjected to one preselected approach to data collection. In the ILO/CAPMAS Egyptian study, for example, where 96 households were interviewed in each sample village, equal numbers of sample households were interviewed using each of two types of questionnaire (time-use/activity schedule; keyword questionnaire), two types of respondent (self-respondent; proxy-respondent) and two types of interviewer (male; female). This prescribed balanced study design, which is shown schematically for one sample village in Fig. 5.2, resulted in eight cells of equal size:

1 Keyword questionnaire, male interviewer, self-respondent.
2 Keyword, male, proxy.
3 Keyword, female, self.
4 Keyword, female, proxy;
5 Time-use schedule, male, self.
6 Time-use, male, proxy.
7 Time-use, female, self.
8 Time-use, female, proxy.

This balanced study design allows the data analyst to compare results for elements within any one of the three main treatment factor sets without considering the effects of the other treatment factors (as long as one is not concerned with interactions between factor sets).

As already observed, female labour force data for sub-Saharan Africa are far from complete and far from accurate. To help correct this situation, insights from methods test surveys would be very useful, especially since government statistical offices (in Africa as elsewhere) are conservative when it comes to altering data gathering, analysis and reporting procedures. They rightly worry about comparability of results over time; about the cost and time required to collect data and report results; about sample sizes and accuracy of results for population subgroups; and about their ability to collect accurate and detailed information in large national inquiries where training and supervision are often inadequate. For these and other reasons, government statistical offices are cautious about accepting new ideas and new approaches. Methods test studies can help convince and guide them by providing insights based on statistically valid results drawn from their own country setting.

It is, of course, possible to use the results from methods test studies in other countries, such as from the Egyptian and Indian studies described above. We feel confident

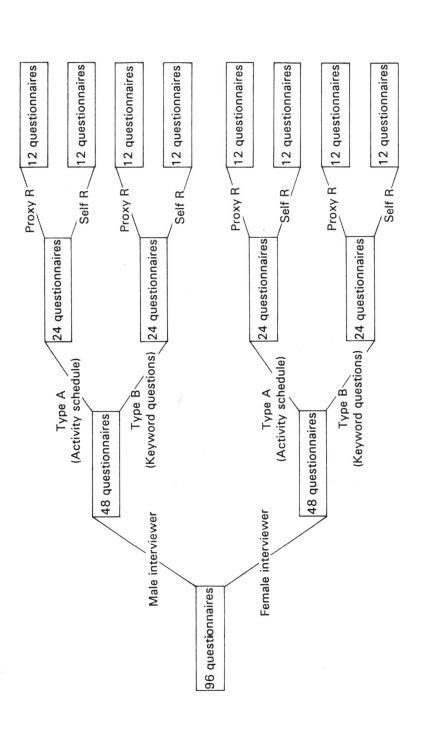

Fig. 5.2 *Schematic representation of study design for one sample village from ILO/CAPMAS Egyptian methods test survey.* **Source**: Anker and Anker, 1988.

that findings from these studies can be generalised as regards the need to be absolutely clear about how labour force activity is defined (and consequently the usefulness of reporting results for several labour force definitions) and the need to use explicit questions or schedules which mention specific labour force activities. It is nevertheless an empirical question as to how important these factors are in Africa. Furthermore, the results of the Egyptian and Indian studies differed somewhat in that (female) self-respondents and (mostly male) proxy-respondents provided similar responses in India but different ones in Egypt. These particular results are thus clearly not generalisable to African countries.

In addition, of course, there are a number of important measurement issues which we did not directly address in the Egyptian and Indian methods tests – issues such as the importance of extensive training and sensitisation of interviewers; whether asking first about activities performed in the past week results in different responses as compared with asking first about activities performed in the past year; whether similar problems arise when obtaining information about urban-type non-agricultural labour force activities (especially informal sector activities) as with rural-based farm and animal-related activities; whether results are sensitive to the time of year when information is gathered even when a one-year reference period is used, etc. New methods test studies in African countries should therefore prove extremely valuable for guiding statistical offices on how best to collect data on the size of the female labour force.

Conclusions

As indicated in this and other chapters, there is considerable awareness among both policy-makers and scholars that the available statistics on female labour force participation in the Third World are often inaccurate, in that they under-report the level of women's labour force activity.

In Africa the situation is particularly difficult. Many African countries do not have official labour force estimates by age and sex, and only a distinct minority have data by occupation or industry. Partly for these reasons, official and unofficial estimates of the female labour force in Africa are highly suspect and in many instances hardly believable. It is well known from qualitative studies as well as from well-conducted surveys that African women play a major role in agriculture.

But how can this situation be remedied? This chapter has made a number of practical suggestions based on the available research literature and results from two specially designed methodological surveys in India and Egypt. While using these suggestions should make it possible to collect much more accurate female labour force data in sub-Saharan Africa than is done at present, there is also a need to undertake fresh methodological studies in sub-Saharan Africa in order to ascertain whether there are important differences in the situation there as compared with that found in other regions of the developing world.

Notes

1. Percentages in brackets refer to the Egyptian study.
2. While there is usually a minimum work-time criterion of one hour in the reference week, this is so

low that for all practical purposes it is equivalent to no criterion at all. In the Egyptian survey, for example, less than 1 per cent of sample rural women were excluded from the labour force because they worked less than one hour in the reference week.

3. This discussion is concerned with measurement of the current labour force based on a short reference period such as the past week. For measuring the usual labour force, which is based on a long reference period such as last year or last season, there are no international recommendations on minimum work-time, although a majority work-time criterion is often used (e.g. for at least half of the days or weeks in the reference period; see Mehran (1986)). The implications of using such a criterion for measuring the usual labour force are obviously similar to those discussed in the text above for the current labour force.

6 Assessing Women's Economic Contributions in Domestic & Related Activities

LUISELLA GOLDSCHMIDT-CLERMONT

This chapter deals with the economic valuation of households' productive activities which fall outside the scope of official statistics (national product and labour statistics). These activities, for own consumption, are outside the 'production boundary' as defined by the 1968 *System of national accounts* (United Nations Statistical Office, 1968). They include:

1 Domestic activities (preparation of meals, upkeep of dwelling and surroundings, care of clothing, care of dependent household members, food preservation, water-fetching, fuel collection).

2 Repairs of own equipment (household equipment, dwelling, vehicles).

3 Processing of primary commodities for own use (food preservation, making cloth or furniture, etc.) by households who do not produce the primary commodities.

4 Production of other commodities for own use (clothes, shoes, etc.) by households who do not sell them on the market.

5 Production of primary products for own use (backyard vegetable gardening, raising chickens, etc.).

'Domestic and related activities', 'non-market household activities', 'non-market household production' and 'non-market household labour' are used interchangeably in this paper to refer to the above activities.

Several time-use studies document the time devoted to such activities in African countries. However, time-use data are generally not comparable to other statistical data and do not therefore permit economic valuations. Only a very limited number of studies have collected data specifically for economic purposes. These studies are presented in some detail in an earlier publication (Goldschmidt-Clermont, 1987, pp. 73–108). They illustrate how important it is to collect such data if one is to understand the economics of household production for own consumption, consumption levels in poor households, the interface between the market and non-market sectors of the economy and, in particular, the distribution of labour between·market-oriented and non-market activities.

Dahl, for example, found that in Botswana in 1974–75, gathering represented

7 per cent of gross output for own consumption of traditional farmers and only 2 per cent for intermediate farmers (Dahl, 1979, Table 1.12.2, p. 1/6), while Mueller, also studying Botswana in 1974–75, found that:

> Opportunities for wage labour are quite limited in Botswana, particularly for women and children . . . Autarchical modes of production imply that asset-poor households often use family labour to a point where marginal returns from work are very low . . . In Botswana the marginal productivity of work time in rural self-employment is very low. People with small holdings of productive assets may be forced by their poverty to pursue some work which adds only minimally to income. (Mueller, 1984, pp. 335–336, 357)

Henn, studying Southern Cameroon during the period 1964–74, made the following findings:

> The principal male and female adult labourers in the contemporary peasant families of Southern Cameroon devote nearly half their combined labour time to subsistence production, a third to cash-earning activities, and about a quarter to domestic labour. On this basis [labour hours], the typical peasant wife provides a labour contribution to family welfare which is 45 per cent greater than that made by her husband [i.e. 51 and 35 hours per week respectively in 1964] . . .
>
> In 1974, out of the 52 hours of women's weekly labour, 20 were spent on domestic labour. The woman's domestic labour consists of over two hours daily in preparing the main evening meal and one half hour warming its leftovers for the next day's breakfast (750 hours per year). Water carrying, clothes and dish washing, and marketing for family consumption needs take up at least 250 more hours per year. Childcare is integrated into all other activities. Older children may help with domestic labour but this does not reduce the principal female's labour times below the conservative figures used here.
>
> Commodity production has a higher return per labour hour than subsistence production. Technical and social constraints prevent the wholesale switch from subsistence to commodity-producing activities which these differing relative returns would theoretically stimulate . . .
>
> The social relations of patriarchal subsistence still exert a major impact on male and female economic decisions concerning the allocation of their total labour time. Women are constrained by the historically received social definition of their 'obligations' to husband and children – obligations which both make their labour days half again as long as the husband's and restrict the portion they can devote to cash-earning activities to only 19 per cent . . .
>
> Both the rising opportunity costs and the crucial importance of women's food producing labour to family welfare have the effect of limiting the rural woman's ability to switch out of subsistence and concentrate her labour on activities which bring the highest cash return. For men, on the other hand, the lesser importance of their subsistence activities allows a great deal of flexibility in the time and effort which can be devoted to alternative cash-earning activities. These 'constraints' to rational economic choice, and the overburdening of one family economic agent while the other is 'underemployed', are contemporary effects of the patriarchal subsistence social relations of production . . .
>
> Men work only 35 hours a week on all tasks. Peasant women, in contrast, spend 51 hours a week working. It is clear that men *dispose* of sufficient potential labour to help their wives in food production. The fact that, even with rising returns to commodity food production and falling returns to cocoa, men have not yet shown much of a tendency to work with their wives, speaks to the power of the traditional social relations. These relations are gradually changing, but their remaining influence is still strong. Younger husbands may support their wives' efforts by clearing all their fields and financing their marketing ventures. Men who go further, however, and actually help in the field not only subject themselves to ridicule by the older male villagers, but may be accused of sorcery. (Henn, 1978, Table IV.1, p. 165; pp. 167, 169, 176, 219–20)

Time-use is but one perspective from which to assess the economic significance of domestic activities. There are others. A French study performed in Southern Cameroon, for instance (SEDES, 1966, p. 112, quoted by Henn, 1978, pp. 165, 169, 241), shows that the 440 kilograms of firewood per person used to prepare evening meals each year mean that an average woman carries home at least 2 tonnes annually.

In spite of such scattered illustrations of women's economic activity in the household, overall valuations of domestic and related activities for African countries are entirely lacking. In order to remedy this lack, it is necessary to clarify the purposes for which the data are needed, then to outline appropriate measurement methodologies, and finally to start field work.

Purposes for Which Data on Domestic and Related Activities are Needed

The methodology adopted for economic measurements should be as closely linked as possible to the uses for which the data are required. This study therefore starts by looking at the potential uses of data on non-market household activities.

Monitoring the economy

Labour market statistics provide data on the allocation of labour resources within the population; national accounts describe the outcome of economic activity. These sets of statistics do not, however, provide a comprehensive picture of the population's productive activity, as they account mostly for market-oriented activity. Indeed, except for own-account production of primary commodities and negligible amounts of manufacturing, the bulk of production for own consumption is not accounted for in official statistics. According to research studies, what is missing in the statistics amounts to about half the labour actually expended by the population and 20–40 per cent of the goods and services actually consumed. The first purpose of collecting data on non-market household activities is therefore *to fill a statistical gap and to produce 'extended labour' statistics and 'extended production' accounts.*

Quantitative data are needed for an understanding of the relationships between market production and household production, and of the transfers of production that occur between them. In present statistics, the effects of these transfers are misleading: growth appears greater than it actually is when production is transferred from households to the market, and vice versa when the transfer is in the opposite direction. Statistical data on non-market household production are therefore required *for monitoring changes in the allocation of (extended) labour resources and for monitoring actual economic growth.*

Economic planning

The absence of quantitative data on household production for own consumption prevents it from being adequately taken into consideration in economic planning. Particularly in developing economies, market-oriented production is given priority as regards the assignment of productive resources (labour, land, improved technology, technical training, loans) because it is more conspicuously 'economic'. Such practices directly affect working conditions in the household by increasing the workload of unpaid household members, sometimes with consequences for their health. In the long run, they also affect the functioning of the monetised sectors of the economy, which are dependent on the satisfactory performance of vital household activities. Data are therefore needed *to ensure that non-market household production is allocated productive resources commensurate with its economic significance.*

Development policy
Labour productivity varies from one activity to another. How productivity in non-market household production compares with productivity in market-oriented activities is unknown. In order to improve working conditions in the household and, perhaps, to release labour for other purposes, data are needed *to identify the least productive activities and to introduce more satisfactory technologies.*

Labour policy
Labour market statistics are designed to describe the labour involved, or susceptible of being involved, in market-oriented activities. Because the emphasis is on employment, statistical definitions do not adequately reflect the involvement of the population in non-market household activities.

The allocation and availability of labour resources are therefore incompletely documented by present statistics. Data on labour expended in non-market household production are required *for the formulation of labour market policies and for labour resources planning.*

Welfare policy
'Domestic and related activities, in poor households, are not a matter of boosting household welfare and consumption but represent the margin allowing for survival. Women in developing countries must devote long hours to back-bending work each and every day, and there are few, if any, days which do not require these tasks to be performed' (Anker, Preface to Goldschmidt-Clermont, 1987, p.v). Measurements of income inequalities at the household level are often limited to inequalities in monetary income; they usually neglect income in kind generated by non-market household activities. The latter may, in some circumstances and particularly in developing countries, contribute a sizeable share of households' extended consumption (Henn, 1978; Acharya and Bennett, 1981; Evers, 1981a, b); for income comparisons, this income in kind should thus be combined with monetary income (the concept of 'extended income'). Standard of living measurements should, in addition, account for the number of labour hours (forgone leisure) invested in securing extended income; as proposed by Kusnic and Da Vanzo (1980), income measures should be standardised at a common (mean) number of labour hours. Data on the value of non-market household production and on the corresponding unpaid labour inputs are therefore required in order *to establish household income comparisons, to measure standard of living, and to formulate welfare policies.*

Legal policy
The *Nairobi forward-looking strategies* (United Nations, 1986) stress the impact of incomplete measurement of women's economic contributions on several aspects of women's status. Among women's unrecorded economic activities, non-market household work and, in particular, domestic activities occupy a significant proportion of

their labour time; however, in several countries the law does not acknowledge the income in kind thus generated as a contribution to household income and consumption. As a result, women's juridical and economic status is negatively affected: when a marriage ends, for instance, widowed or divorced women often face financial hardship. In order to remedy this situation, it is necessary to measure the amount of work required (e.g. the number of hours worked) and the value of non-market output. Data on the amount of labour expended and the value of domestic services are needed *to promote appropriate legislation and to assist courts in the financial settlement of divorces, cases of wrongful death, inheritance, etc.*

Social policy
The contribution made by domestic activities to the functioning of the monetised sectors of the economy is also not fully recognised: unpaid workers who perform domestic activities are often not entitled to social benefits in their own right. Recognition of the indirect contribution these activities make to the functioning of the economy is needed *to ensure that unpaid household workers are granted the social status and social benefits enjoyed by other workers.*

Population policy
The economic value of children, particularly in non-market household production, and its impact on high fertility levels is recognised. However, because women's productive and reproductive roles are closely intertwined and because so little is known about the economic value of domestic activities, individuals (women themselves) and planners tend to overlook the importance of the domestic role; they tend to see women's role in the household merely as a matter of biological reproduction and compliance with socially determined supportive roles. Quantitative data are needed in order to grasp, at the household level, the complete picture of the biological, social and economic roles simultaneously filled by women and of their combined impact on fertility (Oppong and Abu, 1987). The data collected for the purposes enumerated above are therefore relevant *for the formulation of population policies.*

Methodologies for Measuring Domestic and Related Activities

Valuing household output: the general procedure
For use in economic and social policy formulation, the imputed value of households' non-market output has to be determined by methods compatible with national accounting procedures. The general procedure in national accounting when estimating total value added is to measure the amount of output in physical units, to value it at market prices, and to deduct the value of intermediate goods and services used in the production process (i.e. intermediate consumption). This procedure is used in particular for imputing value to non-market outputs such as agricultural product consumed by the producer, but it can be applied to all non-market household output.

One relevant example of the application of such a procedure is afforded by the Rural Income Distribution Survey, carried out in Botswana in 1974–75. The survey was designed for measuring, among other things, the contributions of various sources of income to total household income, and the statistical distribution of income among households in the rural areas (Botswana, Central Statistics Office and Ministry of Finance and Development Planning, 1976, pp. 7–8).

Data on the volume of production (crops, cattle, game, fish, wild food, firewood, building materials, etc.) were collected from a representative sample of 1800 households surveyed once a month over one year (pp. vi and 19). Production for own consumption was valued at producers' selling prices averaged over the 12-month survey period (Central Statistics Office price lists, supplemented by special surveys, e.g. for edible wild plants). Expenses incurred in the production process were deducted for determining value added (pp. 48; 56–59; 62–65; 201–210; 271–273; 291).

Income data were collected both for market-oriented activities and for non-market activities (i.e. household production for own consumption). Data were collected for crop and animal husbandry, hunting, fishing, firewood collection and gathering edible wild plants (pp. 206–210 and 232–236). (They are unfortunately not shown separately in the final publication.)

This general procedure for measuring and valuing non-market household output is reviewed in more detail in paragraphs 1 to 3 below.

1 Measurements of the amount of household output have to be done by activity. The following are examples of the sorts of measurement which have been utilised in valuations:

a Meal preparation: the frequency and content of various types of meal prepared at home; sometimes information is also collected on the origin of food and its level of processing, the number of people consuming the meals, etc.

b Food preservation: the amount of fruit, vegetables, fish, etc., preserved by various methods.

c Care of dependent household members: the number of children of various ages cared for at home (part-time or full-time) and the kind of care given (physical care, general supervision, training in special skills, etc.); the number and characteristics of people receiving special care at home (elderly, handicapped, ill people) and the kind of care given.

d Upkeep of dwelling and its surroundings: the surfaces swept and cleaned on a routine basis; the kind and frequency of repairs and maintenance of a periodic kind (remudding or replastering floors and walls, repairing household equipment, etc.).

e Care of clothing: the frequency and amount of laundering, mending, etc.

f Manufacturing for household consumption: the number of clothes home-made, by type (sewn, knitted or woven; skirts, dresses, trousers, socks, pullovers or other; for children, women or men); amount and type of furniture produced at home; amount of soap made; number of baskets woven, etc.

Guidance on how to carry out such measurements can be derived from several studies performed in both industrialised and developing countries.

2 Once measured in physical units, household output is assigned an imputed value (gross output value) on the basis of market prices for goods or services equivalent to those produced in the household. The following are examples of prices which have been used for calculating the imputed gross output value of household production:

a Price of various types of foods or of meals available commercially, comparable in content and quality to the home-prepared ones.

b Price of processed, semi-processed or commercially preserved foods.

c Price of wild food, fuel, home-delivered water.

d Price paid for laundering performed away from home.

e Price of market-produced goods (ready-made clothes, soap, furniture, etc.).

National accounting offers guidance on the problems raised by price determination. The experience gained in value imputations for agricultural subsistence production (prices differing between areas, seasons, rural and urban markets) is applicable to other non-market goods.

3 Once gross output value has been calculated, intermediate consumption has to be deducted in order to obtain value added. This is a standard procedure in national accounting, which we need not discuss here in detail. For some activities in rural areas, the value of intermediate consumption may, however, be negligible; gross output value is then used instead of value added.

In industrialised economies, market penetration is great and market substitutes that yield values for the imputations are readily available. This is not the case to the same extent in developing countries, but imputations based on the prices of equivalent market products have been used for the valuation of some domestic or related activities in Nepal (Acharya and Bennett, 1981), Pakistan (Alauddin, 1980), Botswana (Dahl, 1979) and Indonesia (Evers, 1981a, b).

Valuing household output: alternative procedures

The general procedure described above is the preferable one when it can be applied. In some areas and for some household products, however, market substitutes may not be available; the price imputation required by the general procedure is therefore not possible. Alternative approaches must then be devised for the valuation of these particular household products.

In valuing water-carrying in Lesotho, for instance, Feachem *et al.* (1978) take as a starting point the cost of constructing a water supply. In valuing food-processing in Nigeria, Prest and Stewart (1953) value crops in their most processed form. Another alternative procedure is the imputation of returns to labour in other activities; it is examined in some detail in the following paragraphs.

When value added cannot be derived directly from the price of a market product, an alternative possibility is to impute to the corresponding labour time the value of returns to labour in reference activities: subsistence activities (Blades, 1975, p. 63) or other household activities for which returns can be readily determined. The latter method was used by Cabanero (1978) in the Philippines to compute the contribution of children to household production. She calculated the hourly rate of returns to labour from the value of the goods they produce at home for household consumption and for sale (farm tools, furniture, woodwork and woodcraft, repairs, home-sewn clothes, embroidery, woven materials, food-processing, washing clothes for others) and utilised this rate for valuing all home production, including child-care and housework. (Her results are worth noting: children's returns to labour in home production are higher than their market wages for all income classes, holding age constant.)

There are preliminary indications that returns to labour vary widely from one activity to another within domestic activities (Goldschmidt-Clermont, 1983) and within subsistence activities (Nag *et al.*, 1978). It is therefore advisable to use average returns in as many reference activities as possible for the imputation, rather than selecting exceptionally high or low values.

This method (i.e. returns to labour) can also be used as a short cut in situations where measurements of the amount of household output are not available, while time-use data are already available. Returns to labour in the various household activities can be calculated on a representative sample of households and imputed to the time-use data.

Attention is drawn to the difference in data requirements of the two major methods presented here. Value added calculated by the general procedure does not require any time-use data. The returns to labour method requires the measurement of the amount of household output and its valuation at market prices (as in the general procedure) for the reference activities only, and, in addition, time-use data for all activities.

Measuring labour inputs into domestic and related activities
Non-market household labour is excluded from labour statistics for conventional reasons (alignment with national accounts definitions) and not because of obstacles to measurement pertaining to its nature. For use in labour policy formulation, measurements of non-market household labour have to be integrated with labour market statistics into the concept of 'extended labour'. They therefore have to be made either in terms of number of persons or in terms of number of hours worked.

Statistical measurements of labour inputs in market-oriented activities are mostly expressed in *number of persons*. Research studies estimating the number of persons involved in non-market household production usually take as a starting point the number of full-time housewives, or the number of households (with one person per household supposedly devoted full-time to these activities), or the number of married women. Time-use studies demonstrate that such estimates are based on a conceptual oversimplification of the actual situation. (Full-time housewives are not necessarily the only members of a household to participate in these activities, nor do all households have a full-time housewife, and so on.) Although such rough estimates are interesting because they provide orders of magnitude, they are unlikely to be of much use in monitoring developments or formulating policies.

Labour statistics also give *number of hours worked* in market-oriented activities as an auxiliary set of data; these data are derived from industrial surveys. Time-use studies give hours worked in both market-oriented and non-market activities; they are derived from household surveys. Because these sets of data are derived from different sources, their compatibility raises problems: estimates of hours worked in the market differ. Comparisons of hours worked in market-oriented and non-market activities can therefore be achieved only on the basis of time-use studies (household surveys) and not of labour statistics.

Numerous household-level studies of time use have been performed both in developing and in industrialised countries. As a result, the amount of labour expended in non-market household production is better documented in the sociological and anthropological literature than is the output of these activities in the economic literature.

Household-level measurements of time use provide more precise data on amount of work done than measurements in terms of number of persons. In addition, they depict the distribution (pattern) of labour inputs over the day and the week, an important feature for the study of households' non-market activities and for labour resources planning.

When a detailed analytical breakdown of household activities is required, a problem may arise in connection with activities simultaneously performed (like mending clothes while taking care of children); this problem is usually solved by distinguishing between primary and secondary activities.

It has been pointed out that time measurements only give a limited description of labour input. They do not, for instance, give any information about the physical effort required for the performance of a task – a shortcoming particularly noticeable in areas where advanced technologies are not generally available and where the physical effort expended per unit time of work may vary greatly from one task to another.

The Collection of Data on Non-Market Household Activities

Questions relating to survey planning, sampling, anthropological observation, etc., are not elaborated here, as they are not specific to the field under consideration; recommendations, literature and experiences are available from specialised publications.

Numerous economic assessments of non-market household activities have been performed in a variety of cultural, economic and social settings. (For a discussion of some 120 economic assessments see Goldschmidt-Clermont (1982, 1987)). On the basis of these studies, a lot of experience has been gained relating to data collection methodology and data sources specific to non-market activities. Time-use measurements, in particular, have been carried out for some 60 years now and constitute an active form of research in sociology, anthropology and home economics. The abundant literature on time-use research (methodology and results) and the experience of those involved provides a solid base for measuring the amount of labour expended in non-market household production.

Data sources
Commonly used data sources are:
1 Official statistics (census and national survey data on household composition, dwelling characteristics, consumer expenditures, prices, wages, etc.).
2 Special studies conducted for business, policy or other purposes; nutrition and food studies; trade bulletins, price lists, etc.
3 Special household surveys conducted to collect data on time use, the volume of household production, and household expenditures; in some surveys, questions are also added on the motivations for household production (forgone expense, quality preferences, conformity with social expectations, personal satisfaction, lack of alternatives, etc.).
4 Anthropological studies using participant observation or key informant interviews, and covering a satisfactory number of representative households; such studies are sometimes combined with special household surveys.

Miscellaneous problems
In national accounting and labour statistics, conventional rules define the 'production boundary', that is, the boundary defining which activities are to be considered 'economic', and therefore registered, and which activities are not. At the household level, output and time use are more easily recorded as perceived by households, which may be different from the statistical conventions.

If the data collected at the household level are to be used for macro-economic estimates (comparisons with gross national product, etc.), provision must be made for statistical distinctions at the data collection stage.

The *coverage and categorisation of households' non-market activities* differ from one study to another. These differences in part reflect differences in purpose: studies concerned with women's problems, for instance, generally concentrate on domestic activities and neglect other non-market activities. The differences also reflect the lack of co-ordination and the absence of common definitions in this field. For instance, some studies include care of children in the domestic activities package, while others do not; some restrict measurement to food preparation, care of clothing and cleaning the dwelling, while others also include care of household animals or upkeep of the dwelling surroundings. Such differences hinder the comparability of results from different studies.

A similar problem arises in relation to the coverage of persons. Insufficient coverage of *persons participating in households' non-market production* sometimes hinders the interpretation of results. For instance, some studies aiming to describe the homemaker's workload do not collect data on the contribution other household members make (without remuneration) to the performance of domestic activities.

A related problem arises in the handling of *domestic servants*. Because the latter are accounted for in labour market statistics and their services are included in national accounts aggregates, studies of households' non-market production often omit to record them. One consequence of this omission is that differences in non-market output between households remain unexplained. The labour inputs of domestic servants should be measured alongside those of household members; their services should be included in the valuation of non-market production as intermediate consumption of services. Adjustments should be made, at the macro-economic level, to avoid double counting.

Goods and services received as gifts from other households are usually omitted, because households' non-market production is defined as production for own consumption. This definition should probably be considered only a first approximation and should therefore undergo some revision. In order to interpret differences in workload or consumption between households, *gifts and exchanges* should be accounted for both in the originating and in the consuming household.

The valuation of household output requires the *selection of market products equivalent to those produced by households.* This selection can be done on the basis of available objective comparisons (performed by public or private organisations) or on the basis of households' judgements expressed in the special surveys mentioned above. In some cases, the availability of several market substitutes raises problems of choice. In other cases, the only substitutes available are paid domestic services; the valuation has then to be based on returns to labour in other activities.

The Next Steps Forward

Interest in households' production for own consumption continues to grow both in international bodies (United Nations, 1986, 1992; United Nations Economic and Social Council, 1987; United Nations Statistical Commission and Economic Commission for Europe, 1987) and in academic institutions.

Imaginative efforts have been deployed in all parts of the world in order to meet the problems raised by the imputation of monetary values to productive activities whose characteristic is precisely the absence of monetary transactions: labour inputs are unremunerated and the product, consumed by household members, is not sold.

Unfortunately, various methodologies are used for these valuations and their results are therefore not fully comparable. Even now, further economic assessments of household activities are being planned without co-ordination and sometimes using unsatisfactory measurement methods.

Given the state of the art, the performance of economic valuations of non-market household activities requires two distinct sets of action: one at the national level, the other at the international level.

National-level action

At country level, several steps need to be followed in a determined order, on the assumption that means for performing valuations are limited and that the valuations should be useful for the largest possible range of purposes.

1 Examination of which part of households' non-market production is, in practice, recorded in the national accounts and in labour market statistics. (National practice may differ from international recommendations.)

2 Identification, listing and categorisation of unrecorded activities.

3 Review of the purposes for which a valuation of unrecorded activities is wanted, distinguishing between immediate (primary) purposes and additional purposes (of potential interest or that might come up at a later time).

4 Determination of data requirements and adoption of valuation method(s), in accordance with international guidelines.

5 Review of possible data sources in order to elicit already available data. Some sources may yield sufficiently precise and directly usable data, while others may only yield orders of magnitude, useful for giving general orientations. Listing of missing data.

6 Examination of data collection possibilities in relation to data needs and means available. Costs and means will to a large extent determine whether observations will have to be made using a limited number of case-studies, or whether a household survey can be carried out.

7 Carrying out of case-studies to test valuation methods and to identify the parameters bearing on the nature, amount and value of household activities: family size and composition, availability of substitute goods and services, urban or rural environment, etc. This step provides household-level measurements that are useful *per se* in policy formulation and provides information on parameters that is essential for cutting down to a minimum the size of a household survey.

8 Macro-level estimates, based on the data provided by a special household survey. Satellite accounts (production, consumption and labour accounts) are then constructed, showing the respective contributions of market activities, recorded non-market activities and unrecorded non-market activities to extended production, extended consumption and extended labour.

To conclude, household-level valuations are useful for both macro- and micro-level purposes. They are particularly useful when amount of output and amount of labour input are measured simultaneously. If, in addition, labour expended in market-oriented activities is also measured, the macro-economic assessment of labour allocation between market and non-market activities becomes possible. *Household-level valuations of non-market output combined with total time measurements* thus provide data for many of the purposes envisaged at the beginning of this paper.

International-level action

As a result of the conventional production boundary used in national accounting, some of the activities contributing to a population's consumption are recorded in production and labour statistics, while others, similar in nature, are not. Consideration of how to overcome these statistical gaps is now on the agenda of several statistical bodies (United Nations Statistical Commission and Economic Commission for Europe, 1987; United Nations Statistical Commission and ILO, 1987). These gaps affect policy formulation in several fields; it is therefore urgent that progress be made in the economic measurement of activities heretofore unrecorded.[1]

Notes

1. Interested readers are referred to the author's related writings (Goldschmidt-Clermont, 1990, 1992). These discuss *inter alia* the fact that the revised version of the United Nations *System of national accounts* acknowledges the economic contribution made by domestic activities and recommends that households' non-market production be recorded in a special 'satellite account' within the national accounts system.

7 Gender-sensitive Statistics & the Planning Process

E. OTI BOATENG

During the past decade and a half, several international conferences have emphasised the need to generate more sex-specific and gender-sensitive statistics. This concern stems from the need to determine accurately the contribution of women to development and the fact that many of the existing data do not adequately measure their contribution. The challenge, therefore, is not only to provide global statistics but, more importantly, to produce detailed disaggregated data that will permit better analysis and much more focused policy decisions on women. Such disaggregated data give better insight into the various socio-demographic and economic factors which interact to affect population and development outcomes.

This chapter reviews the collection of statistical data in Ghana and examines the extent to which gender issues, including recording of women's economic activities have been addressed in data collection, analysis and dissemination. It also examines Ghana's 1969 population policy with respect to its data collection and analysis component and its impact on the education, employment and fertility of women.

Recent trends in the development of statistics in Ghana are examined, including institutional strengthening and the way in which such developments facilitate the generation of sex-specific statistics. The promulgation of the Statistical Service Law in 1985, the establishment of a National Committee of Producers and Users of Statistics in 1988, the strengthening of links between the Ghana Statistical Service and the National Council on Women and Development, and, finally, the establishment of the National Development Planning Commission all illustrate the building of an enduring statistical capability that is able to respond to the country's complex data needs. The utilisation of existing sex-specific data for policy decisions and implementation is also discussed.

Specific surveys such as the Ghana Living Standards Survey (1988, 1989) (Ghana Statistical Service, 1989d) and Ghana's National Industrial Census (1987) (Ghana Statistical Service, 1989c), as well as the experience of the country's Structural Adjustment Programme and its concomitant Social Dimensions of Adjustment project, are looked at with a view to demonstrating the efforts being made to integrate gender factors into statistical data generation in the country. Improvements in the publication of statistics exemplified in several recent publications of the Ghana Statistical Service are also highlighted. Finally, existing mechanisms for the dissemination of statistical information in Ghana are discussed, and a set of recommendations given for the more effective development of gender-sensitive statistics, which have the potential to serve as the basis of gender-sensitive population and development planning.

The Basic Data Sources

Ghana has a long history of statistical data collection. Data from three major sources, namely, censuses, sample surveys and administrative records, have for a long time provided the basis for development planning and decision-making in the country. These sources of data are complementary, and analyses and policy decisions frequently make use of more than one source.

Officially, population censuses have been carried out in Ghana since 1891. Before that time, however, several traditional rulers in the country used to conduct periodic counts of the population in each of the towns and villages under their jurisdiction. A simple method was usually adopted where heads of families were required to put in a calabash or similar receptacle a grain or a cowrie for each member of the family, the sex of a person being determined by the type of object. A reasonable count of the population by sex was then obtained by adding the locality totals obtained by counting the contents of the calabashes.

Under the British colonial administration, six population censuses were undertaken. Censuses were conducted every ten years from 1891 until 1941, the last being interrupted by the Second World War. The next census was carried out in 1948. Independent Ghana has witnessed three very successful censuses in 1960, 1970 and 1984, which were planned on a more scientific basis than the previous ones.

Sample surveys have been carried out in the country since the early 1930s. Examples of some of the early surveys are the survey of a Gold Coast village carried out by W.H. Beckett between 1932 and 1935; the Ashanti Survey carried out by Fortes, Steel and Ady in 1945; and the survey of juvenile delinquency in the Gold Coast carried out by G. Tooth between 1946 and 1948 (see UNESCO, 1956, pp. 53–99). Since the beginning of the 1960s, several sample surveys have been carried out to obtain detailed statistical information on particular subjects as well as important data to supplement the census information.

The administrative records maintained by government ministries, parastatals, private firms, universities and research institutions have also provided additional sources of statistical information. Vital registration was introduced in Ghana by the colonial administration as far back as 1888 under the Cemeteries Ordinance of that year. Since that date, several ordinances have introduced changes into the system; by 1926, registration of births, deaths and burials was extended to Africans. Further improvements were introduced by the Births and Deaths Registration Legislative Act (Act 301) of 1965 and the NLC Decree 285 of 1968, which made the registration of births and deaths compulsory. Through its Centre for Health Statistics, the Ministry of Health collects and compiles health data. The Ministry of Education keeps statistical records on enrolment at all levels of the educational system, while the Department of Labour keeps employment and unemployment records. In addition, small-scale studies and other studies using anthropological and other non-traditional methods of data collection have been available to supplement statistical information from the three major sources (Ardayfio-Schandorf and Kwafo-Akoto, 1990).

The population censuses conducted over the years have provided considerable statistical information both for planning the country's social and economic development and for formulating, implementing and evaluating realistic population policies. They have also been a major source of information on women as well as men. All the censuses have produced tabulations for both sexes, while the three most recent ones have also provided detailed small area statistics for localities such as the enumeration area or the local council area. The censuses have also provided the basic data for studies of trends in respect of the size, structure, spatial distribution and other related characteristics of the nation's human resources, which are essential in carrying out the restructuring of the social and economic system of the country. Finally, the censuses have provided the scientific sampling frame for many surveys conducted to generate additional sex-specific data.

The sample surveys have provided a relatively inexpensive but efficient mechanism for generating data during inter-censual periods as well as detailed statistical information on specific topics. In addition to supplementing the census information, some sample surveys have been conducted to check on the quality of the census data. The sample surveys have yielded a wealth of information on important development issues, most of which is available separately for each sex.

Administrative records have also been useful for planning purposes. They have provided a framework for identifying basic needs and for monitoring and evaluating programmes. They have also provided the basis for social indicators necessary for measuring standards of living and assessing the performance of various sectors of the economy. Some administrative records such as vital statistics are traditionally compiled by sex and can therefore be easily utilised for analysis on gender issues. Although there are some inadequacies in the data found in administrative records, in many cases data are collected at such regular intervals and presented in such detail as to make them ideal for planning and sectoral decision-making. Taken together, the pool of statistical information from the population censuses, sample surveys and administrative records has made possible a more effective formulation and implementation of programmes designed to improve the welfare of the people.

Separate statistics on women have been collected and compiled from time to time in recent years but they have tended to focus on the reproductive rather than the productive roles of women. This may be partly attributed to the absence of a clear-cut policy on women in development which could translate into basic data collection strategies. With the recent upsurge of demand for sex-specific data, following several international conferences in the past decade, it can be hoped that more conscious and concerted efforts will be made to collect, analyse and utilise more comprehensive data sets to promote further societal development planning. The ultimate goal should be to have all statistics relating to people as statistical units disaggregated and presented by sex, and not biased in terms of focus and content. This calls, among other·things, for improved measurement of women's labour force participation and economic activity as well as men's and of better data on men's values and behaviour in respect of procreation as well as women's.

Ghana's Population Policy

In 1969, Ghana formulated a population policy aimed at improving the quality of the human resources and the standard of living of the population. The policy, which was framed as an organic part of social and economic planning and development activity, recognised the importance of data collection and analysis for its successful implementation.

The crucial importance of data collection and analysis in the formulation of appropriate development policies was emphasised in several areas of the policy (Government of Ghana, 1969). The third basic principle states that

> specific and quantitative population goals will be established on the basis of reliable demographic data and the determination of demographic trends. In order to achieve this goal, the policy further recommends that steps should be taken to strengthen the statistical, research and analytical facilities and capabilities of Government and of public and private educational and scientific organisations.

The above recommendation reflects the recognition by government of the need for reliable demographic data, to be used not only as the basis for setting specific and quantitative population goals but also to determine demographic trends. It was also recognised that the government's statistical services needed to be expanded to facilitate the conduct of periodic inter-censual sample surveys, essential for the projection of current trends as well as for the estimation of the size, distribution, economic activities and other characteristics of the population.

The policy also stipulated that the Central Bureau of Statistics (now the Statistical Service) was to take steps to co-ordinate and monitor all population research in order to ensure integration of effort, prevent wasteful duplication, and develop a pool of information well suited to aid the analysis and support of planning and administration.

The reduction of mortality and fertility, which constitutes an important aspect of population policy and programmes, is highlighted in the second basic principle of the policy. The effective implementation of this basic principle requires the collection and analysis of vital statistics on the population.

The policy document explicitly promotes fertility regulation and also places great emphasis on the education of women and their employment outside the home. Thus, to assist in the safe and effective control of fertility, the fourth basic principle of the policy states that 'the Government will encourage and itself undertake programmes to provide information, advice and assistance for couples wishing to space or limit their reproduction'. In this connection, vigorous and practical steps were to be taken to distribute as widely as possible reliable information on the various means of contraception and to make birth control advice and services readily available to all couples wishing to make use of them. Studies of legal and administrative structures and policies were also to be undertaken to determine ways in which they might be reoriented to reduce pro-natalist influences and promote lower fertility.

At the same time, in an effort to make the best use of human resources in the country, the fifth basic principle of the policy explicitly states that 'ways will be sought to encourage and promote wider productive and gainful employment for women; to increase the proportion of girls entering and completing school; to develop a wider range of non-domestic roles for women'. It was assumed that such employment would benefit both individual women, by improving real incomes, and the economy as a whole, and would also have a dampening effect on family size. Similarly, it was apparently imagined that the expansion of educational opportunities for girls would have the dual effect of increasing their social, vocational and technical skills and at the same time permitting the country to benefit from the expected inverse relationship between education and fertility.

The sixth basic principle of the policy, which focuses on migration, is 'to guide and regulate the flow of internal migration, influence spatial distribution in the interest of development progress, and reduce the scale and rate of immigration in the interest of national welfare'. In this connection, both the office of the Principal Immigration Officer and the Migration Section of the Statistical Service were to be strengthened to permit the development and analysis of relevant statistical information on migration. In addition, it was envisaged that government would provide support for research on the subject.

In the seventh and final basic principle of the policy, it was envisaged that provision would be made to establish and maintain regular contact with population programmes throughout the world and to participate in a two-way flow of information and sharing of experience of population activities. This two-way exchange of information necessarily involves the collection and analysis of population data.

The above review demonstrates that the question of the collection and analysis of population data was specifically addressed in the Ghana Population Policy of 1969, as well as issues relating to the fertility, employment and education of women. It also indicates that the successful implementation of the population policy will require both females and males to be fully represented in the collection and analysis of reliable data on the population and on population-related activities. Such data are also essential to facilitate the effective integration of women and population factors into national development planning and programmes.

Impact of the Population Policy

Following the introduction of the Ghana Population Policy of 1969, considerable progress has been made in establishing and promoting census and survey programmes in the country. The post-independence population censuses of 1960, 1970 and 1984 were organised in accordance with the principles and procedures recommended by the United Nations and thus have all the essential features of a modern population census. These censuses have provided data on the total size of the population and have generated a large stock of sex-segregated statistical information for planning the social and economic development of the country and for the formulation, implementation and evaluation of the national population policy. In addition, in-depth analyses of the census data have been undertaken to establish trends relating to the size, structure, spatial distribution and other characteristics of the population, as envisaged in the population policy. As an integral part of these censuses, post-enumeration enquiries were designed, essentially to check coverage and content errors of the censuses but also to obtain additional information not catered for in the main censuses.

Population growth, fertility and other population characteristics
On the basis of the available demographic data, long-, medium- and short-term demographic goals were formulated in 1975 for implementation under the National

Family Planning Programme. As a long-term goal, the rate of population growth, which was estimated to be 2.7 per cent per annum at the time, was to be decreased to 1.7 per cent by the year 2000. The projected decline in the growth rate of the population would still have meant a doubling of the country's total population of 8.6 million in 1970 by the year 2000.

In the medium term, 1975–85, no significant decline in the rate of natural increase was expected to occur. The crude death rate was expected to decline faster than the birth rate. It was nevertheless anticipated that the birth rate would show some downward movement due to the positive socio-economic changes and increased efforts of the National Family Planning Programme. The available data suggest, however, that efforts to reduce the rate of population growth achieved minimal results. Between 1970 and 1984, the rate of growth of Ghana's population stood at 2.6 per cent per annum.

According to the policy, fertility levels were also too high in relation to economic growth and family well-being. Poor maternal and child health, inadequate spacing between births, and high frequency of induced abortions were among the negative consequences of high fertility. Measures were therefore to be instituted to reduce the total fertility rate (TFR) from about seven children at the time to four by the turn of the century. Policy measures were also to be taken to influence the preference of the population for large families.

Results from periodic surveys carried out by the Statistical Service indicate only a slight decline in the TFR, from 7.2 in 1960–64 to 6.5 in 1975–79, as observed in the Ghana Demographic and Health Survey (GDHS) conducted in 1988. Analysis of desired family size among all married and fecund women shows a mean of 6 children in 1979–80 (Ghana Fertility Survey) and a mean of 5.5 children in 1989 (GDHS). Although there seems to be a slight decline in desired family size, the existing level indicates that high fertility intentions still persist within the population and reflects the need to strengthen efforts at reducing such high fertility desires.

In the absence of reliable vital statistics, information on mortality has mainly been derived from population censuses and demographic sample surveys. The available data do show a decline. According to the 1960 and 1971 post-enumeration census surveys, infant mortality rates were 126 and 87 per thousand live births, respectively, while the estimates obtained in the GDHS were 100, 86 and 77 per thousand live births for the periods 1973–77, 1978–82 and 1983–87, respectively.

A closer look at the age structure of the population for 1984 reveals that 45 per cent were under the age of 15, 51 per cent between 15 and 64, and 4 per cent aged 65 years and over. This structure implies a high youthful dependency ratio of 88 per cent, while the total dependency ratio is 96 per cent. This heavy burden on the economically active population limits their ability to save, thus lowering investment, which is what forms the basis for employment generation for the growing army of job-seekers. The very young population also implies the allocation of more and more resources to provide educational and health facilities.

The sex distribution of the population indicates that there have been more females than males in the country since 1970. The sex ratio (ratio of males to females), which stood at 102 per cent in 1960, declined to 99 per cent in 1970 and 97 per cent in 1984. This may be attributed both to the mass out-migration of aliens in the period 1960–70 and to Ghanaian out-migration in 1970–84, both involving more men than women. Only the Brong Ahafo Region, with a sex ratio of 104 per cent, and Western Region, with a ratio of 103 per cent, recorded fewer females than males in 1984, mainly due to the influx of men from other regions to engage in agricultural activities.

Population density increased along with the rapid population growth, from 28 people per square kilometre in 1960 to 36 in 1970 and 52 in 1984. The rate of increase in population density was very uneven, however, with some regions and areas attracting large populations while others lost heavily. In 1984 regional densities ranged from a high of 441 people per square kilometre in the Greater Accra Region to a low of 31 in the Northern Region. At the same time some localities in the Greater Accra Region had a density of more than 4000 people per square kilometre while large localities such as Bole, Damango, Salaga and Tumu had densities of less than 10.

The proportion of urban population in the country increased from 23 per cent in 1960 to 29 per cent in 1970 and 32 per cent in 1984. The urban population thus grew at around 4.8 per cent per annum during the 1960s and at 3.4 per cent during the period 1970–84. One striking feature here is the fall in the relative share of urban males within the 15–44 age group, from 52 per cent in 1970 to 48 per cent in 1984, while that of females within the same group increased from 48 per cent to 52 per cent.

In general, internal migration takes place in all directions, but contrary to popular belief the most dominant is urban–urban, not rural–urban migration. This is demonstrated by the results of the 1984 Population Census and the Ghana Living Standards Survey (GLSS), where rural–urban migration came fourth (16 per cent) after urban–urban (34 per cent), urban–rural (22 per cent) and rural–rural migration. Analysis of intra- and inter-regional migration indicates that in 1984 there were 110 men to every 100 women inter-regional migrants, but only about 64 men to every 100 women intra-regional migrants.

The more urbanised areas, such as the regional capitals and industrial centres, continue to receive a more than proportionate share of migrants. The implication here is that these more urbanised areas are likely to face greater housing problems, although they are comparatively well off as regards other social services and amenities such as drinkable water and electricity. Furthermore, given the sex and age of migrants, there exists a dearth of productive labour in the rural areas, where the primary agricultural sector, which forms the mainstay of the economy, is situated. There is thus a need to re-examine programmes aimed at adjusting the spatial distribution of the population.

Education
Although Western-type education was introduced into the country more than a century ago with the passing of the first Educational Ordinance in 1852, it was only on the threshold of independence that concentrated efforts were made to make education available to the masses. Under the Accelerated Development Plan of 1951, there was a tremendous increase in enrolment at all levels of education, especially at the primary level. Efforts were also initiated to encourage girls, and those from remote rural areas, to take advantage of the educational facilities being made available.

There have been significant improvements in school attendance since the 1960s. The proportion of the population aged 6 years and over who had ever attended school increased from a low of 27 per cent in 1960 to 43 per cent in 1970 and 57 per cent in 1984. Whereas the proportion of ever-attending males increased from 37 per cent in 1960 to 53 per cent in 1970 and 65 per cent in 1984, the corresponding proportion for females increased from a low of 17 per cent in 1960 to 34 per cent in 1970 and 48 per cent in 1984. In other words, the gap between males and females is closing.

Even though there has been an improvement in school attendance over time, progress was greater in the first decade after independence. The growth rate of past school attendance during the 1960s was 5.3 per cent per annum for males and 9.1 per cent for females, as against 5.1 per cent for males and 7.4 per cent for females between 1970 and 1984. The growth rate of enrolment in primary and middle schools actually declined, but was to some extent compensated for by increases in secondary school enrolment.

Nor have improvements in school attendance been uniform throughout the country. The rate of increase has been faster for urban than rural dwellers, while the male–female gap is wider in rural than in urban areas. Significant differences also exist among the regions, in addition to a sharp north–south differential. Whereas in 1984 only 13 per cent of urban males and 26 per cent of urban females in Greater Accra Region had never attended school, the Northern Region recorded rates of 55 per cent for males and 77 per cent for females in urban areas. In the rural areas the rates were 35 per cent for Greater Accra males and 56 per cent for females, as against 86 per cent for Northern males and 94 per cent for females. In the south, the Eastern Region had the lowest rates of any rural area: 25 per cent for males and 44 per cent for females. In the past the gaps between the regions and the sexes were even wider.

When one considers the school age group of 6–14 years, the 1984 data indicate that only 66 per cent of urban male children and 53 per cent of female children were reported as currently attending school. The corresponding rates in the rural areas were much lower, at 51 per cent for males and 40 per cent for females. It is clear that much more still needs to be done if the objective of universal primary education is to be achieved. Among the 10–14 age group enrolment was only 78 per cent for urban males and 68 per cent for females, with lower rates for the rural areas of 73 per cent for males and 63 per cent for females.

The elementary school population aged 6–14 years was estimated at 2.4 million in 1990 and projected to be 2.9 million in 1995 and 3.5 million in the year 2000, as against 2.1 million reported in 1984. This substantial increase in such a short period has great implications for the provision of teachers, classrooms and other requisite facilities to ensure that the quality of education is maintained. Finally, even though the objective of educating a greater proportion of girls is gradually being realised, greater efforts are still needed to bring female education to a level that will have a significant impact on fertility and national development as a whole.

Economic activity
As mentioned earlier, the need to promote women's employment and education was specially stressed in the 1969 Ghana Population Policy. This view was re-echoed seven years later in the World Population Plan of Action (1976), which recommended 'the full integration of women into the development process particularly by means of their greater participation in educational, social and political opportunities'.

The labour force of Ghana grew from 2.7 million in 1960 to 5.5 million in 1984. While the rate of growth of the total population was 2.6 per cent per annum, the adult population aged 15–64 years grew at a higher rate of 2.8 per cent between 1970 and 1984. The female labour force had a phenomenal annual growth rate of 4.8 per cent compared with the male rate of 2.8 per cent. Also, for the first time, the female economically active population exceeded the male by a margin of about 5 per cent. The female percentage of the economically active population increased from 37 per cent in 1960 to 51 per cent in 1984 (Table 7.1). During the same period, the percentage of homemakers who were female declined from 98 per cent to 90 per cent. In an effort to cope with the worsening economic conditions during the 1970s, most female homemakers were forced into economically remunerative activities to supplement the household income. Furthermore, with increasing numbers of women taking advantage of education in the 1950s and 1960s, larger cohorts of educated women entered the labour market (Table 7.2), a process which was also facilitated by the exodus of men and the tacit encouragement of female employment by government and private enterprises.

The employed population constituted 97 per cent of the economically active population in 1984 as against 94 per cent in 1970. The distribution of employed persons by sex and major industries indicates that agriculture absorbed almost two-thirds of the men and 56 per cent of women in 1984 (Table 7.3). The next most important industry for female employment was wholesale and retail trade and restaurants, absorbing 24 per cent in 1984 and 26 per cent in 1970. For men, the sector of community, social and personal services had the next highest concentration of employees, at 13 per cent in 1984 and 16 per cent in 1970. Female participation in manufacturing was 14 per cent in 1984 and 15 per cent in 1970. The data again show that petty trading and preparation of food for the market are dominated by women.

The occupational composition of employed people reveals a pattern similar to that of the industrial. Agriculture constitutes the mainstay of the economy, with about two-thirds of men and more than half of women engaged in agricultural activities (Table 7.4). For men, production and related workers, transport equipment operators and labourers constitute the next most important group, absorbing 19 per cent in 1984 and 23 per cent in 1970. For women, the next largest occupation was sales workers, accounting for 24 per cent in 1984 and 26 per cent in 1970. Professional, technical and related workers showed a stable proportion of around 5 per cent for men in 1970 and 1984, but for women there was an increase from 2 per cent in 1970 to almost 3 per cent in 1984. Indeed, female employment in professional, technical, administrative and managerial categories increased by 281 per cent from 28,679 in 1970 to 80,543 in 1984. At the same time, the annual rate of growth in the number of women employed by central government and public boards increased to 7.4 and 9.2 per cent, respectively, between 1970 and 1984 (Table 7.5). Thus, not only have women become predominant in the total labour force, they have also considerably increased their share of 'white-collar' employment.

The recorded unemployment rate, which was stable at 6 per cent in 1960 and 1970, dropped considerably to 3 per cent in 1984. Whereas the rate for women was slightly lower than 3 per cent, that for men was slightly higher. Urban unemployment was about four times higher than the rural rate in 1984. Moreover, over two-thirds of the unemployed were in the 15–24 age group, with a higher proportion of women than men. In the 25–44 age group, however, the unemployment rate was higher for men.

More than two-thirds of the total working population were self-employed in 1984. Sixty-three per cent of working men as against 76 per cent of women were reported as self-employed (Table 7.5). While the proportion of self-employed in the labour force increased for both men and women between 1970 and 1984, employees showed

Table 7.1 Percentage distribution of selected occupations of employed persons aged 15+ by sex and type of school attended, Ghana, 1984

Occupation	Sex	Number	As percentage of all occupations	No schooling	Primary	Middle	Secondary	Commercial/ technical	Teacher training	University
All occupations	Total	5 422 480	100.0	55.13	8.51	30.12	3.21	1.50	1.6	0.47
	M	2 637 029	48.63							
	F	2 785 451	51.37							
	Sex ratio	94.7		67.00	82.75	151.76	290.78	213.58	182.49	662.78
Professional, technical and related workers	Total		4.09	0.46	0.61	5.09	24.38	14.88	88.68	65.67
	Sex ratio	180.3		132.88	152.02	126.24	256.76	467.21	168.67	597.84
Administrative and managerial workers	Total		0.30	0.04	0.07	0.26	2.69	1.79	0.82	15.16
	Sex ratio	1029.9		640.74	586.81	1177.14	1161.03	1464.95	489.97	1006.08
Clerical and related workers	Total		2.35	0.07	0.16	3.73	22.75	26.09	2.01	7.17
	Sex ratio	235.5		931.99	541.03	301.77	243.41	102.39	455.25	493.12
Sales workers	Total		13.83	14.29	14.38	13.84	11.00	12.07	1.40	2.77
	Sex ratio	12.4		7.55	5.98	18.23	105.89	49.95	93.99	627.27
Service workers	Total		2.41	1.61	1.64	3.72	5.23	5.46	0.74	1.20
	Sex ratio	187.9		301.45	92.42	149.75	210.85	115.24	250.39	352.28
Agriculture, animal husbandry, forestry workers and hunters	Total		60.65	70.78	68.07	49.34	20.23	16.34	4.85	5.71
	Sex ratio	111.3		88.01	103.09	198.15	921.45	604.23	946.03	3025.00
Production and related workers, transport equipment operators and labourers	Total		16.36	12.75	15.08	24.01	13.73	23.37	1.49	2.33
	Sex ratio	123.0		53.09	131.75	254.36	370.81	595.89	203.86	715.00

Source: 1984 Population Census of Ghana, 'Demographic and economic characteristics', Total Country (Ghana Statistical Service, 1987a).

Table 7.2 Percentage distribution of economically active persons[a] aged 15+ by sex and type of school attended, Ghana, 1970 and 1984

Census year	Sex	Total	No schooling	Primary	Middle	Secondary	Commercial/technical	Teacher training	University
1984	T	100.0	55.1	8.5	30.1	3.2	1.5	1.1	0.5
	M	100.0	45.4	7.9	37.3	4.9	2.1	1.4	0.8
	F	100.0	64.3	9.1	23.3	1.6	0.9	0.7	0.1
1970	T	100.0	72.2	7.9	16.2	1.6	0.7	1.0	0.4
	M	100.0	63.5	8.2	22.8	2.5	1.1	1.3	0.6
	F	100.0	82.7	7.4	8.3	0.5	0.3	0.6	0.1

Note: [a] The unemployed are excluded from this distribution.
Sources: Ghana, Census Office: *Economic characteristics: 1970 Population Census of Ghana*, Vol. IV (unpublished), and *1984 Populations Census of Ghana*. 'Demographic and economic characteristics', Total Country (Ghana Statistical Service, 1987a).

Table 7.3 Distribution of employed persons aged 15+ by sex and major industries, Ghana, 1970 and 1984

Industry	Sex	Number		Percentage	
		1970	1984	1970	1984
All industries	T	3 133 047	5 422 480	100.0	100.0
	M	1 717 928	2 637 029	100.0	100.0
	F	1 415 119	2 785 451	100.0	100.0
Agriculture, hunting, forestry and fishing	T	1 786 710	3 310 967	57.0	61.1
	M	1 015 113	1 750 024	59.1	66.4
	F	771 597	1 560 943	54.5	56.0
Mining and quarrying	T	30 986	26 828	1.0	0.5
	M	28 640	24 906	1.7	0.9
	F	2 346	1 922	0.2	0.1
Manufacturing	T	380 415	588 418	12.1	10.9
	M	166 911	198 430	9.7	7.5
	F	213 504	389 988	15.1	14.0
Electricity, water and gas	T	12 205	15 437	0.4	0.3
	M	11 758	14 033	0.7	0.5
	F	447	1 404	0.0	0.1
Construction	T	73 564	64 686	2.3	1.2
	M	70 936	60 692	4.1	2.3
	F	2 628	3 994	0.2	0.1
Wholesale and retail trade, restaurants	T	435 972	792 147	13.9	14.6
	M	67 078	111 540	3.9	4.2
	F	368 894	680 607	26.1	24.4
Transport, storage and communication	T	84 301	122 806	2.7	2.3
	M	82 033	117 806	4.8	4.5
	F	2 268	5 000	0.2	0.2
Finance, insurance and real estate	T	9 370	27 475	0.3	0.5
	M	7 522	19 933	0.4	0.8
	F	1 848	7 542	0.1	0.3
Community, social and personal services	T	319 524	473 716	10.2	8.7
	M	267 937	339 665	15.6	12.9
	F	51 587	134 051	3.6	4.8

Sources: Ghana, Census Office: *Economic characteristics: 1970 Population Census of Ghana*, Vol. IV (unpublished), and *1984 Population Census of Ghana*, 'Demographic and economic characteristics', Total Country (Ghana Statistical Service, 1987a).

a decrease for men and overall constituted less than one-fifth of the total working force. There were substantially more male employees than females. The proportions of unpaid family workers were more stable, but remained predominantly female and in agriculture.

With respect to the quality of the labour force, it can be observed that, over the years, it is becoming increasingly educated. While 64 per cent of the male and 83 per cent of the female labour force had never attended school in 1970, the respective figures for 1984 were 45 per cent and 64 per cent (Table 7.2). However, even in 1984 the majority of agricultural and related workers had never been to school, and the labour force is still not highly educated. Furthermore, females still have a long way

Table 7.4 Distribution of employed persons aged 15+ by sex and major occupations, Ghana, 1970 and 1984

Occupation	Sex	Number		Percentage	
		1970	1984	1970	1984
All occupations	T	3 133 047	5 422 480	100.0	100.0
	M	1 717 928	2 637 029	100.0	100.0
	F	1 415 119	2 785 451	100.0	100.0
Professional, technical and related workers	T	119 675	221 704	3.8	4.1
	M	91 582	142 598	5.3	5.4
	F	28 093	79 106	2.0	2.8
Administrative and managerial workers	T	11 323	16 246	0.4	0.3
	M	10 737	14 809	0.6	0.6
	F	586	1 437	0.0	0.1
Clerical and related workers	T	86 366	127 575	2.7	2.4
	M	73 008	89 551	4.2	3.4
	F	13 358	38 024	0.9	1.4
Sales workers	T	413 510	750 179	13.2	13.8
	M	50 369	82 721	2.9	3.1
	F	363 141	667 458	25.7	24.0
Service workers	T	90 164	130 736	2.9	2.4
	M	69 189	85 317	4.0	3.2
	F	20 975	45 419	1.5	1.6
Agricultural, animal husbandry and forestry workers and hunters	T	1 798 256	3 288 808	57.4	60.7
	M	1 026 530	1 732 610	59.8	65.7
	F	771 726	1 556 198	54.5	55.9
Production and related workers, transport equipment operators and labourers	T	613 753	887 232	19.6	16.4
	M	396 513	489 423	23.1	18.6
	F	217 240	397 809	15.4	14.2

Sources: Ghana, Census Office: *Economic characteristics: 1970 Population Census of Ghana*, Vol. IV (unpublished), and *1984 Population Census of Ghana*, 'Demographic and economic characteristic', Total Country (Ghana Statistical Service, 1987a).

to go as regards educational and employment opportunities. With a large part of the labour force that has either never attended school or has had only primary and middle school education, the task of introducing innovations and improvement will be difficult, especially in the agricultural sector, which absorbs the largest contingent of the labour force.

Tables 7.6 and 7.7 give labour force projections until the year 2000, which may be used as a basis for employment planning.

Institutional Strengthening

The office of the Government Statistician was created in 1948 by the Statistics Ordinance (Cap. 251) to collect, compile and publish statistical data on Ghana. After independence, the office was transformed into the Central Bureau of Statistics by the Statistics Act of 1961. Throughout the 1950s and 1960s the country was very well served with statistical data. However, the production of statistics was severely affected in the 1970s by the decline in the economy, coupled with the exodus of experienced

Table 7.5 Distribution of employed persons aged 15+ by employment status and sex, Ghana, 1970 and 1984

Employment status	1970			1984			Percentage change			% Annual growth rate		
	Total	Male	Female	Total	Male	Female	Total	Male	Female	Total	Male	Female
Employees	693 802 (22.1)	601 361 (35.0)	92 441 (6.5)	876 902 (16.2)	670 177 (25.4)	206 726 (7.4)	26.4	11.4	123.6	1.7	0.8	5.7
Central government	249 344	215 501	33 843	310 658	214 888	95 770	24.6	−0.3	183.0	1.6	0.0	7.4
Public boards	121 073	109 580	11 493	241 640	199 628	42 012	99.6	82.2	265.5	4.9	4.3	9.2
Co-operative enterprises	6 427	6 094	333	2 374	1 677	697	−63.1	−72.5	109.3	−7.1	−9.2	5.3
Private enterprises	316 958	270 186	46 772	319 590	251 862	67 728	0.8	−6.8	44.8	0.1	−0.5	2.6
International organisations	–	–	–	2 640	2 122	518	–	–	–	–	–	–
Self-employed	1 964 845 (62.7)	918 736 (53.5)	1 046 109 (73.9)	3 777 675 (69.7)	1 650 617 (62.6)	2 127 058 (76.4)	92.3	79.7	103.3	4.7	4.2	5.1
With employees	147 686	99 208	48 478	256 505	153 372	103 133	73.7	54.6	112.7	3.9	3.1	5.4
Without employees	1 817 159	819 528	997 631	3 521 170	1 497 245	2 023 925	93.8	82.7	102.9	4.7	4.3	5.1
Unpaid family workers	410 839 (13.1)	136 477 (7.9)	274 362 (19.4)	679 422 (12.5)	248 075 (9.4)	431 347 (15.5)	65.4	81.8	57.2	3.6	4.3	3.2
Others	63 531 (2.0)	61 354 (3.6)	2 207 (0.2)	88 481 (1.6)	68 160 (2.6)	20 321 (0.7)	39.3	11.1	820.8	2.4	0.8	15.9
Total in employment	3 133 047 (100.0)	1 717 928 (100.0)	1 415 119 (100.0)	5 422 480 (100.0)	2 637 029 (100.0)	2 785 451 (100.0)	73.1	53.5	96.8	3.9	3.1	4.8

Sources: Ghana, Census Office: *Economic characteristics: 1970 Population Census of Ghana*, Vol. IV (unpublished), and *1984 Population Census of Ghana*, 'Demographic and economic characteristics', Total Country (Ghana Statistical Service, 1987a).

Table 7.6 Projected labour force participation rates by age group and sex, Ghana, 1985–2000

Age group	1985		1990		1995		2000	
	Male	Female	Male	Female	Male	Female	Male	Female
15–19	42.8	53.7	42.9	54.0	43.0	54.0	43.0	54.0
20–24	83.0	85.5	83.1	85.5	83.2	85.5	83.2	85.5
25–29	96.3	90.9	96.4	93.4	96.6	94.7	96.6	94.7
30–34	97.7	92.0	97.7	94.0	97.8	95.1	97.8	95.1
35–39	98.3	92.7	98.4	94.6	98.5	95.6	98.5	95.6
40–44	98.4	93.2	98.5	94.8	98.6	95.7	98.6	95.7
45–49	98.4	93.5	98.6	95.1	98.7	96.0	98.7	96.0
50–54	97.6	92.3	97.8	93.9	97.9	94.8	97.9	94.8
55–59	96.3	90.8	96.6	92.7	96.7	93.8	96.7	93.8
60–64	94.3	86.6	94.8	88.8	95.1	90.2	95.1	90.2
65+	84.0	65.3	85.6	68.5	86.6	70.6	86.6	70.6

Source: Unpublished projections by Ghana Statistical Service, Accra.

Table 7.7 Projected labour force by age group and sex, Ghana, 1985–2000

Age group	1985		1990		1995		2000	
	Male	Female	Male	Female	Male	Female	Male	Female
15–19	273 135	348 814	320 505	407 181	378 458	475 565	443 232	555 35
20–24	441 145	467 979	513 400	541 561	603 103	629 972	711 465	736 391
25–29	422 978	417 514	492 884	497 790	575 706	585 098	676 737	680 780
30–34	360 316	357 453	413 436	417 291	482 685	491 230	563 060	570 145
35–39	304 464	307 711	346 546	354 916	399 327	410 762	466 726	478 175
40–44	249 932	255 128	290 951	300 892	331 922	344 438	382 407	395 035
45–49	213 223	217 667	236 543	245 956	276 046	289 304	314 806	329 128
50–54	168 554	172 764	195 532	205 672	217 640	231 614	254 528	270 709
55–59	135 627	139 947	150 382	160 216	175 378	190 793	195 677	213 743
60–64	106 768	110 302	114 406	122 384	128 239	140 480	151 022	166 589
65+	182 926	157 081	192 441	178 405	206 257	201 210	226 475	225 594
Total	2 859 068	2 952 360	3 267 026	3 432 264	3 774 761	3 990 466	4 386 135	4 621 645

Source: Unpublished projections by Ghana Statistical Service, Accra.

and trained personnel, including statisticians, to other countries. The strengthening of statistical, research and analytical capabilities envisaged in the population policy was also affected, as was the Central Bureau of Statistics' co-ordinating and monitoring role as regards population research. During the 1980s, however, considerable efforts have been made to rebuild and further strengthen the statistical capability of the country.

The 1979 Constitution of the Third Republic made provision for the establishment of a Statistical Service to operate under a Statistical Service Board. In December 1985, the government enacted the Statistical Service Law (PNDCL 135), which established the Statistical Service as part of Ghana's public services. As part of Ghana's Economic Recovery Programme launched in 1983, the government strengthened the Statistical Service through the provision of high-level manpower, vehicles and other facilities essential for efficient statistical work. This support enabled the Service to conduct successfully the 1984 Population Census of Ghana and to update its regular statistical publications. In addition, several statistical projects have been undertaken in recent years, including the Ghana Living Standards Survey (GLSS), the Ghana Demographic and Health Survey (GDHS) and the Ghana Industrial Census, some of which are discussed later.

The Statistical Service has now been restructured to improve its capacity to cope with its expanded activities. Some existing sections have been merged into new divisions, while additional divisions have been created to reflect its increased functions. The Policy Planning and Co-ordination Division, for example, has been created to study the data needs of various users in the country and recommend appropriate statistical policies. It is also expected to co-ordinate all statistical activities in the country, including those of government departments, and to ensure that all other statistical units conform to the accepted statistical standards necessary to maintain comparability and quality of data.

An Analytical Studies and Development Division has also been established to deal with data analysis, methodological development and implementation of new methodologies, and to strengthen the capabilities of the Service as it adapts and utilises new methodologies. A permanent Sample Survey Section has also been established to conduct sample surveys and review survey activities. The professional staff in this section have provided a core of trainers to assist in questionnaire development and the training of survey field staff.

In furtherance of the co-ordination role of the Statistical Service as envisaged in the country's population policy, a National Committee of Users and Producers of Statistics (NACPUS) was established in 1988 to identify user needs and co-ordinate the production of statistics. This committee, under the chairmanship of the Government Statistician, provides a forum for healthy interaction between users and producers of statistics in Ghana. Fourteen sectoral working groups, including a Gender-Specific Statistics Working Group, have now been set up under NACPUS to evaluate the production and utilisation of statistics in the respective sectors. The Gender-Specific Statistics Working Group, embracing representatives of the National Council on Women and Development and other women's groups in the country, is expected to emphasise the importance of improving the production and dissemination of basic data on women's activities. Other working groups under NACPUS include Agricultural, Industrial, Trade, Financial, Population and Demographic, Judicial and Crime, Culture and Tourism, Health and Education Statistics.

The Statistical Service recognises that the ability to produce reliable, timely and gender-sensitive statistics depends, to a large extent, on the availability of highly trained and experienced personnel. As a result, steps have been taken to recruit an increased number of graduates to improve efficiency further. Side by side with staff recruitment, a comprehensive staff training programme, involving regular in-service training, training in local institutions of higher education and external training, has been introduced for both graduate and non-graduate staff to upgrade their skills. The training programme, which covers a wide range of subjects and procedures, is geared towards strengthening the human resource capability for collection, processing, analysis and dissemination of statistical information. In this connection, important strides have been made in the analysis of the 1984 Population Census data. The expansion in the statistical system recommended in the third basic principle of Ghana's population policy has thus been initiated in the Statistical Service.

The National Development Planning Commission

To further improve the integration of population issues with development planning, the government has established a National Development Planning Commission (NDPC) to provide for the continuous formulation and review of national development plans. The National Development Planning Commission Law provides for the establishment of a secretariat as the executive agency of the NDPC. It establishes and details the functions of:

1 Planning, Programming and Budgeting Units in each sectoral ministry.
2 Regional Co-ordinating, Monitoring and Evaluation Committees and Units.
3 District Planning Authorities and Development Planning Budgeting Units.

The Law also requires a District Development Plan to be prepared with the full participation of the local communities. It provides for a local public hearing at which the district plan is explained to people and at which they may submit written or oral opinions for submission to the NDPC concurrently with the draft plan. This calls for district-based population data for planning at the district level.

Thus, for the first time in the history of Ghana, development plans are being formulated and implemented at the district level. This will give a new impetus to plan implementation, monitoring and evaluation in the country. It will also give an empirical demonstration of a feedback interaction between the population and the plan at the local level. The Statistical Service has already initiated steps to strengthen its regional and district offices to enable it to cope effectively with the expected increase in demand for gender-sensitive statistics at both the regional and the district levels. The NDPC will be expected to co-ordinate population policy issues and related gender-sensitive activities in the country.

Policy Utilisation of Existing Sex-Specific Data

Since independence, population data collection has provided the country with statistical information for planning the social and economic development of the nation. In addition to population size by sex, age and geographical distribution, the censuses collect data on birthplace, nationality, school attendance, type of economic activity, occupation, industry and employment status. Community-level information relating to source of water supply, availability of schools and the nearest health facility are also collected. Rural and urban development schemes have benefited immensely from the accumulation of population census data. The data are disaggregated by locality and by urban and rural components, thus facilitating the computation of the rates of growth of the rural and urban populations as well as the national population, and providing the basis for projecting the national, urban and rural populations.

Statistics on literacy and educational attainment have been used in assessing and evaluating the effectiveness of the educational system. Educational policies, geared towards the integration of the successive stages, have been aided by projections of attendance at all education levels and estimates of the needs of the system in terms of the supply of teachers and equipment as well as the construction of new schools, colleges and universities. It is worthy of note that current educational reforms have utilised demographic data and administrative records quite extensively for the planning of the junior secondary school system. At the planning stages, decisions to establish new structures, train additional teachers and provide new educational materials were based on the size of the target population, comprising children aged 6–12 years. The existing population statistics were supplemented by the results of the population-based school-mapping study conducted by the Ministry of Education.

Ghana's labour policies have also benefited a great deal from the collection and analysis of data on economic activity. The determination of the size of the economically active population has been a valuable instrument for measuring participation rates by age and sex, and for gauging the extent and composition of human resources available in the country. Furthermore, data on employment status, occupation and industry have provided invaluable information by sex for assessing the utilisation of human resources and for formulating policies and programmes for their development, as recommended by the population policy and other national policy documents.

The expansion in population data collection has also facilitated the planning of health services. Estimations of populations at risk and determinations of total population, age and sex structure, and geographical distribution of the population have been valuable in the planning of general medical services and in the setting of targets for numbers of doctors, health personnel, hospital beds and other health facilities. The planning of maternity and child health care services has benefited from data on fertility, stillbirths, maternal mortality, infant and child mortality, and morbidity in mothers and children.

Programmes to control and eradicate certain diseases which are sex- or age group-specific have also utilised information about the age and sex structure of the population. Furthermore, programmes specifically designed to combat degenerative disease and handicaps in old age have assumed greater importance in the country because of the increased life expectancy.

Because demographic characteristics play such an important role as indicators of health levels, demographic data have been utilised in the health sector not only for planning but also for evaluating progress made in the implementation of health programmes, as illustrated by the evaluation of the primary health care programme conducted in 1985. Half-way to the target date for achieving the objectives set out by the Ministry of Health, an evaluation of the programme revealed, among other things, that:

1 10 per cent of the population were fully immunised against tuberculosis, diphtheria, tetanus and measles.
2 64 per cent of the population had a health care/first aid facility available within one hour of travel.
3 83 per cent of villages had no trained community health workers.
4 42 per cent of villages had trained traditional birth attendants.
This is a classic demonstration of the use of population-related data for evaluating policy implementation.

Demand for food in Ghana, as in other countries in Africa, has been determined more by the size of the population than by growth in incomes. The structure of the population generates different patterns of demand for various food items. In this connection, detailed statistics are needed on a continuous basis to effect progressive adjustments to the food production plans. Agricultural censuses have been conducted in addition to annual agricultural surveys to collect and analyse data on size and composition of urban and rural populations, agricultural and farm populations by sex, employment in agriculture, problems related to the seasonal nature of farm activities, part-time employment and underemployment. The policy of government at the macro level has been to achieve a rate of increase in the supply of food which is high enough to sustain the rate of increase in the population. Food production thus needs to increase faster than the population so that increasing future demand can be met.

The existing sex-specific statistics have provided important inputs in the formulation of the government's new Medium-Term Agricultural Development Programme. The programme, which covers the period 1991–2000, explicitly recognises that 'any agricultural development strategy must address the gender issue'. The programme therefore has the objective of bringing services physically closer to women, involving them in the formulation and management of programmes that affect them, and making women (individually or in groups) the contact point in order to deliver services directly to the beneficiaries and receive feedback.

Under the programme, the government will encourage the establishment of small-scale agricultural processing by promoting women's groups to achieve economies of scale, secure group credit and expand market output. This recognition of the gender dimension of agricultural production is essential to ensure sustained agricultural growth and development.

Another important area where population data collection and analysis have featured prominently is the assessment of the performance of the entire economy. Data on the per capita gross national product (GNP) and other population-based development indicators are used to gauge the extent to which living standards and welfare have improved. Finally, the fact that reliable and timely data are available is helpful in the country's negotiations with external bodies.

The Statistical Service now places greater emphasis on data analysis and interpretation to enable users to derive more benefit from the data. Such analysis and interpretation of data are also intended to improve the analytical capability and upgrade the professional skills of the staff. Under the ongoing Ghana Living Standards Survey (GLSS) project, the Service has set up a Socio-Economic Analysis Unit to undertake statistical analysis. Some analysis of the 1970 and 1984 censuses, as well as of the Ghana Demographic and Health Survey (GDHS) results, has been carried out by professional staff of the Service.

The Statistical Service now publishes a number of reports which serve as sources of information for the evaluation of programmes initiated under the population and other national policies. The census reports, for example, give information about the demographic, social and economic characteristics of the population, while the *Quarterly Digest of Statistics* contains summary statistical information on socio-economic trends in areas such as employment and earnings, prices, education and other population characteristics, which facilitate the determination of policy relating to gender.

Data Collection Under the Structural Adjustment Programme

The Ghana Living Standards Survey
In 1987, the government launched the Structural Adjustment Programme, aimed at sustaining the high rate of growth of the economy and creating an efficient, well-integrated and growth-oriented economy. In this connection, the Ghana Living tandards Survey (GLSS) was launched in September 1987 to focus on the social dimensions of the adjustment. The GLSS, which is a nationwide household survey,

is meant to measure and monitor changes in the living standards of the population on a continuous basis. It is also meant to assist in the design of appropriate policies to improve the welfare of the population, especially that of vulnerable groups, including women and children, who are adversely affected by the adjustment process. The survey was originally scheduled for two years, but it has been extended for a further four years under the Social Dimensions of Adjustment (SDA) project. Two years of data have been collected and the third year survey, embracing consumption and expenditure, was completed in 1992, while community level data, collected in conjunction with the survey, will also be analysed and published in 1993.[1]

The survey results have been used to improve the national accounts estimates and in the determination of national minimum wages. The results have also made it possible to establish a baseline poverty profile for the country, which provides a framework for future discussion of poverty alleviation in Ghana (see Boateng *et al.*, 1990). The GLSS has provided additional data essential for the construction of a Social Accounting Matrix (SAM), initiated by the Statistical Service, to enable the country to organise macro-economic data, including national accounts, at various levels of disaggregation.

The results of the first year of the GLSS indicated that rural women have more children than urban women on average and that fertility increases with age up to the age of 40–49. The data also show that a high percentage (88 per cent) of mothers had had antenatal consultations during their last pregnancy. Out of 2388 women interviewed, 80 per cent had previously given birth. The mean number of births to the women in the sample was four. Breast-feeding was found to be widespread, with mothers breast-feeding their children for an average of 17 months. The duration of breast-feeding decreases, however, with urbanisation.

Data on morbidity show that more than a third (36 per cent) of household members interviewed reported having been ill or injured during the four weeks prior to the survey, the proportion being highest among those under 5 years and over 50. The average number of days of illness or injury during the four-week period was about eight. Morbidity among females was found to be generally higher than among males except in the 0–5 age group.

It was found that the mean height and weight of boys are on average greater than those of girls. 'Wasting' (i.e. weight-for-height below a standard limit) was found to be predominant among children aged 16 to 18 months while 'stunting' (i.e. height-for-age below a standard limit) was more pronounced among children aged between 16 and 60 months. The results, which show that 7.6 per cent of the children were wasted while as many as 31 per cent were stunted, compare very well with the 1988 Ghana Demographic and Health Survey (GDHS) results. The data indicate little or no variation in the level of wasting and stunting between the sexes, but some differences were observed for variables such as age, type of birth, region of enumeration, mother's level of education, and whether or not the child was ill with diarrhoea.

The level of wasting appeared to be normally distributed with age, while stunting generally increased with increasing age, thus strengthening the evidence that long-term nutritional deficiencies have a cumulative impact on linear growth. The data further showed that, while there is no clear relationship between wasting and expenditure level, stunting decreases with rising expenditure levels. Whereas about 38 per cent of those in the poorest first quintile were stunted, about 21 per cent of those in the fifth quintile exhibited stunted growth. The problem of wasting and stunting is much more serious in the savannah zone (i.e. Northern, Upper East and Upper West Regions) than in other parts of the country. The data from the second year of the GLSS reveal that about a third (31 per cent) of the children were stunted, which conforms with the results obtained in both the GDHS and the first year of the GLSS. On the other hand, only 2.9 per cent of the children under consideration were wasted. This indicates an improvement in children's nutritional status when compared with the results of the two previous surveys.

The GLSS results also show that a large percentage (68.7 per cent) of households in the country use firewood for cooking, with the rest using mainly charcoal. In the rural areas, 92 per cent of households use firewood, while in Accra 81 per cent use charcoal. The government has started to develop liquefied petroleum gas as a cooking fuel, in order to combat deforestation and the concomitant environmental degradation. This development is also expected to have a significant positive impact on women through the reduction of time spent on cooking and related activities, which could be utilised for other productive ventures to improve their income and welfare.

The results confirm that literacy rates are higher for males than for females and much lower in the rural areas than in the urban areas. The results further indicate that a majority of the poorest 20 per cent of the population live in rural areas and that non-cocoa farming households with uneducated heads account for a large proportion of the poor.

The results of the GLSS clearly support the strategy of poverty alleviation programmes and projects aimed at improving the access of the poor and vulnerable, including women, to employment opportunities and income generation assets, in addition to increasing the productivity of both their physical and their human assets. Under the SDA project, the GLSS data will be used to conduct several analyses, including studies on the role of women under structural adjustment, to guide policy decisions in the various sectors.

The National Industrial Census
As part of the government's Industrial Sector Adjustment Programme under the country's Economic Recovery Programme, the Statistical Service conducted a two-phase National Industrial Census in 1987 and 1988. The results of the census show that 83 per cent of all industrial establishments are concentrated in the Greater Accra, Ashanti, Eastern and Western Regions, with Greater Accra Region accounting for 31 per cent and Ashanti Region for 30 per cent. Of the total number of people working in industrial establishments, 83 per cent live in the above-mentioned four regions, with Greater Accra Region accounting for 35 per cent, Ashanti Region for 24 per cent, Western Region for 14 per cent and Eastern Region for 10 per cent. The location of industrial establishments undoubtedly influences the spatial distribution of the population. In the country's population policy, it was specifically stated that 'The Government will adopt policies . . . to influence spatial distribution in the interest of development progress.' But, more than 20 years after the implementation of the policy, establishments in the industrial sector are still concentrated in only four out of the ten regions of the country.

The census results further show that only 21 per cent of those working in industrial establishments are women. The proportion of women ranges from 24 per cent in manufacturing to 10 per cent in mining and quarrying and 8 per cent in electricity and water. Female participation was found to be high in such activities as salt production, fish preservation, the manufacture of bakery products, oil extraction, the manufacture of clothes and the brewing of malt liquor. The female–male ratio was 0.9 in salt production, 1.3 in fish preservation and 0.5 in the fats and oil industry. In nearly all cases where the female–male ratio was high, however, the women were found to be own-account small-scale producers, operating mostly under co-operatives or an association type of ownership and classified as belonging to the informal sector.

Analysis, Publication and Dissemination of Population Census Results

The Preliminary Report on the 1984 Population Census, which contains a summary analysis of the provisional results and accounts of the conduct of the census, was published in December 1984. Under the expanded census publications programme of the Statistical Service, a total of 31 volumes are being issued on the 1984 Population Census. Under the programme, a conscious effort has been made to make the publications more gender-sensitive and to respond to data needs at the national, regional and local levels. The population data in the *Gazetteer*, published in February 1987 in two volumes, have for the first time been disaggregated by sex. In addition, the *Gazetteer* provides basic information on each of the 56,170 localities enumerated in the census in alphabetical order of locality.

A series of 11 volumes on the demographic and economic characteristics, one for each of the ten administrative regions of Ghana and another for the whole country, was also published in December 1987. Almost all the tables contained in these volumes are disaggregated by sex, including tables showing population by five-year age groups, single year of age, region, urban or rural residence, birthplace, school attendance, education, industry, occupation and employment status, and number of households by size and sex of head of household. This is also the first time in the country's census history that such information has been published separately for each region.

A further series of ten special Reports on Localities by Local Authorities was also published in June 1989 for the regions. These publications focus on the local authorities in the regions and provide information on population by sex, community-level facilities such as education, health and water supply, and number of houses in each locality.

The publication of the 1984 Population Census reports have thus provided a wealth of readily available sex-specific information for research, planning and decision-making at the national, regional, district and locality levels. The publications are also expected to assist in the government's decentralisation programme. In particular, the information is expected to assist the district assemblies in the preparation of their composite budgets and plans.

The Statistical Service has also carried out analyses of the results of the 1984 Population Census of Ghana in five subject areas: evaluation, migration, economic activities, education and housing.

A permanent Population Census Analysis Section has been set up within the Statistical Service to help bridge the gap between population data collection and analysis. Furthermore, in an effort to strengthen the capability of the Statistical Service to undertake demographic analysis, the United Nations Population Fund

(UNFPA) has sponsored a project to carry out a comprehensive analysis of the results of the various censuses and surveys conducted in the country, and to publish and disseminate the results. Under the project, a special study of the socio-economic effects of migration in Ghana has also been undertaken.

Mechanisms for data dissemination
The utility of any statistical data depends, among other things, on the extent of dissemination of the data. The Statistical Service recognises that users need to know what type of statistical information is available before they can make use of it. The Statistical Service has, over the years, been disseminating statistical information, including population data, through its publications. Among these publications are the various advanced and final reports on population censuses and household surveys conducted in the country. The Service has also established a customer computer service to assist those needing specific statistical information on the population. This service has proved very popular with users. The dissemination of statistical information through the medium of floppy discs and Bernoulli boxes has also begun on a limited scale. The Statistical Service hopes to look into the application of compact disc technology soon. Networking is also a possibility, but the Service will be guided by extreme caution in this area, on account of the confidentiality of the information it collects. The Statistical Service has also been participating in Trade and Industry Fairs organised throughout the country to publicise its activities.

Media publicity, in the form of press releases, press conferences, and radio and TV discussion programmes as well as articles in the newspapers, is also used to disseminate statistical information. Seminars and workshops provide additional means of data dissemination. Since 1987, Statistics Day has been celebrated on 18 November each year in line with the Economic Community of West African States (ECOWAS) declaration about the importance of creating an awareness among the public of the crucial role of statistics in nation-building. The first celebration of African Statistics Day in November 1989 also provided a good opportunity for the launching of three publications of the Statistical Service, namely, the *Ghana Demographic and Health Survey report* published in September 1989, the *Ghana Directory of Industrial Establishments* published in July 1989, and the *Ghana Living Standards Survey: first year report* published in October 1989 (Ghana Statistical Service, 1989a, c, d). These avenues for the dissemination of statistical information are to be further developed in the future.

The Statistical Service also recognises the importance of having strong links with sector ministries, universities, research institutions and other internal and external bodies in the area of statistical data collection, analysis and dissemination. In particular, the Service co-operates closely with the National Council on Women and Development in an effort to improve the collection, analysis and dissemination of gender-specific statistics. Great efforts will continue to be made to strengthen these links further. To this end, the Statistical Service intends to establish a composite database, using results from the censuses and other household surveys conducted in the country. Collaboration with research organisations at home and abroad has resulted in studies such as that appearing here in Chapter 8.

Conclusion

In discussing statistical data collection activities in Ghana, this chapter has shown that a considerable amount of sex-specific statistical data has been collected and utilised for planning and policy decisions. At the same time the rebuilding of the institutional foundations and consequent improvement in statistical capability have further facilitated the production of statistics. A lot more effort is, however, needed if the objective of integrating gender-sensitive statistics in national development is to be properly achieved.

In the supreme quest to improve the welfare of the people, care must be taken not to mask the contributions and needs of both sexes in the development process. This implies conscious and systematic collection of sex-segregated statistical information which, *inter alia*, takes account of sex in the classification of households by socio-economic group. Such statistical information is essential for a better understanding of the ways in which the various groups in the population are being influenced by changing socio-economic conditions and for more effective targeting of policies and programmes towards these groups.

In conclusion, it is emphasised that:

1 Gender-sensitive statistics need to be integrated in national planning, research and information systems.

2 National policies should require all statistics relating to people as statistical units to be compiled and presented by sex.

3 Improved guidelines on the collection, analysis and dissemination of data on both women and men need to be developed.

4 In the collection of data on women and men, priority should be given to both their productive and their reproductive roles.

5 Compilation of administrative records needs to be reviewed and improved to enhance their coverage, frequency of presentation and gender-sensitivity.

6 Composite databases of sex-specific statistics are required to assist research and policy decisions on gender, population and development issues.

7 Closer co-operation between statistics-producing agencies and users needs to be fostered to ensure optimal production and utilisation of gender-sensitive statistics.

Notes

1. A report entitled 'Rural Communities in Ghana' is available from the Statistical Office.
2. ECOWAS adopted 18 November as Statistics Day in the sub-region. In 1989 OAU and ECA adopted the ECOWAS 18 November as African Statistics Day.

BALANCING
PRODUCTIVE & REPRODUCTIVE ROLES

8

Women's Work, Child-Bearing & Child-Rearing over the Life Cycle in Ghana

ANN K. BLANC & C.B. LLOYD

The ways in which women's paid employment interacts with child-bearing in developing countries vary widely, even within groups engaged in apparently similar occupations (Mason, 1984; United Nations, 1985, 1987; Dixon-Mueller, 1989; Lloyd, 1990). In the poorest countries, women are usually able to sustain relatively high rates of child-bearing, even when participating in modern sector employment, because of the availability of extended family support and relatively cheap domestic labour. On the other hand, in many countries that have achieved moderate levels of development, women working in the modern sector have significantly smaller families than other women. Indeed, even women in traditional informal sector employment may find it difficult to raise more than a few children while working.

Although development has been associated historically with a steady growth in women's participation in the paid labour force and a long-term decline in fertility, there are many exceptions to this general pattern, which are documented in a comparative analysis of World Fertility Survey (WFS) data (United Nations, 1985, 1987). One explanation for these cross-country differences that is receiving increasing attention in the literature is differences in child-care practices and beliefs. A variety of strategies for caring for children in developing countries have been documented in recent studies (Mason and Palan, 1981; Joekes, 1983; Oppong and Abu, 1987; Bledsoe and Isiugo-Abanihe, 1989). These appear to be influenced by four sets of factors:

1 Gender roles.
2 The availability of unskilled domestic labour.
3 Family systems.
4 Beliefs about the socialisation of the young.

The extent of women's participation in paid work and the type of work they perform (including whether they work in the formal or the informal sector) are influenced by their access to land and capital, their skills and experience, the structure of the labour market for women, and the cash rewards of market work (Standing, 1978; Ware, 1988). Occupational and educational discrimination often restrict women's work opportunities in the formal sector to selected occupations and industries. As a result, in the course of socio-economic development, as the maintenance of the family depends increasingly on access to the cash economy, women face a smaller range of opportunities than men within the diversifying labour market and these are found largely in the informal sector (Boserup, 1970), where pay is low and unsteady and social security is not available. In some settings, this may mean women are confined to their homes, but it may also mean long hours away from home, either self-employed or working for employers who provide little in the way of job protection or social support. The limited opportunities for women that such a system provides make girls a readily available source of child-care for their siblings and older women a readily available source of child-care for their grandchildren, not to mention the opportunities for cash available to women as domestic servants in the homes of others.

In many high-fertility settings, extended kinship networks and complex households provide a relatively secure institutional setting for the rearing of the young, which is not excessively vulnerable to the death, migration or outside employment of a parent. The extent to which women have access to child-rearing support therefore depends on residential arrangements and the social organisation of family life. Co-residence with extended family members, such as parents, siblings and grandparents, seems likely to increase the probability of child-care being shared by other family members. The living arrangements of spouses is a further dimension of household structure which may be associated with child-care alternatives. Customs regarding the co-residence of husbands and wives, age differences between spouses, marital dissolution, the prevalence of polygyny, and the practice of widow inheritance affect the extent to which fathers are available to care for or take responsibility for the care of their children, as well as the general circumstances under which women live (Abu, 1983; Hagan, 1983; Awusabo-Asare, 1988).

In West Africa (and a few other parts of the world), a widely used alternative to providing care within the household is child fostering (Goody, 1976; Ainsworth, 1989; Page, 1989). In a setting in which kin ties are strong and encompass a wide range of responsibilities and rights, the practice of child fostering is thought to reflect the belief that the costs and benefits of child-rearing are appropriately shared among kin groups (Fiawoo, 1976; Goody, 1976; Isiugo-Abanihe, 1985; Oppong and Abu, 1987). Further, parents are not viewed as necessarily the most desirable disciplinarians of their own children. Especially in a society where formal education is not universal, child fostering is a mechanism for the socialisation of children (Goody, 1976).

In this chapter we examine women's child-rearing strategies in relation to employment and family size in Ghana, a country where high rates of cash employment for women are known to coexist with high fertility. Our framework emphasises the ways in which women make choices regarding these three critical elements of their lives over their reproductive years. While women of child-bearing age in Ghana are clearly confronted with a variety of choices regarding fertility, employment and child-rearing, they are also constrained by many factors beyond their control, including poverty, gender roles, labour market opportunities, the specific family to which they belong, the availability of family planning services, and social norms relating to child-bearing and child-rearing. The specific choices available as well as those actually chosen will vary over the life cycle. We examine occupational characteristics, work patterns, household composition, fertility and child-care arrangements among women over the course of their reproductive years. We view these elements as interacting with one another to form patterns which reflect a balancing of roles as women respond to shifting responsibilities over the life cycle. Because child fostering is a flexible social institution designed to meet the needs of children and their parents at various phases of their development, we explore its determinants in some depth in the second part of the chapter. We conclude with a discussion of the implications of our findings for changes in fertility and women's employment, and the relationship between them. Further, we identify possible avenues through which the burden of child-care may be shifting in Ghana and the likely consequences for women over the life cycle.

The Data

The data for this analysis come from the 1988 Ghana Demographic and Health Survey (GDHS).[1] In addition to the core questionnaire, which was designed to collect data on fertility, family planning and maternal and child health, the GDHS questionnaire incorporated a special module on women's employment. The module included detailed questions on women's current work, such as occupation, hours worked per day, travel time to work, regularity of work, earnings, control over earnings, and child-care arrangements while working. Information was also collected on employment before marriage and between births.

One important decision made during the development of the employment module was to limit the type of productive work recorded to *work for cash, other than on a family farm or in a family business*. There were two reasons for this decision (see Mason and Blanc, 1985). First, in many developing countries, particularly in rural areas, the distinction between housework and productive work may be unclear, especially if particular productive tasks are defined as part of women's normal domestic responsibilities. To the extent that this is true, sample surveys are likely to underenumerate women's participation in productive roles, as Anker has discussed at length in Chapter 5, unless these surveys collect detailed time-use data or spend considerable time educating respondents as to what to consider part of 'housework' and what part of 'employment'. Neither of these alternatives seemed feasible in the GDHS since the employment module was a short supplement to the core questionnaire and not the main focus of the survey. The second reason for including only cash employment was that the empirical evidence available indicates that it is work for money which is typically related to fertility, and the purpose of the women's employment module was not to measure women's productive activities *per se* but to collect information which would help to explain fertility and related behaviour.

The GDHS also provides data on household composition, residential arrangements and migration, as well as standard background variables. The GDHS data set contains a complete live-birth history for each respondent, the residence status of each living child, each woman's marital status, and information on the co-residence of ever-married women with parents and spouse. The household data include information on whether the natural parents of children under the age of 15 are present in the household, as well as data on the age and sex of all household members. Because the oldest women interviewed were 49, our analysis of the woman's life cycle is limited to the years between 15 and 49.

These data present new opportunities for the analysis of employment and childbearing because they combine information on living arrangements and residence of children with data on women's employment and fertility. None the less, limitations remain, including the incomplete nature of the information on child-care (the whereabouts of children living away from their mothers is not known), the under-reporting of women's paid employment, and the lack of information on economic circumstances and resource flows between family members.

The Context: Recent Trends in Ghana

Ghana achieved independence in 1957. In the early post-independence years, the country experienced dramatic improvements in educational enrolment, particularly for girls, and continued migration to urban areas. Steady economic growth was achieved until the early 1970s (Ghana, Central Bureau of Statistics, 1983). From 1972 through until the early 1980s, the economy experienced a progressive decline for a variety of reasons, with per capita real income falling substantially (Ghana Statistical Service, 1989a; Glewwe and Twum-Baah, 1989). At the time of the WFS survey in 1979–80, the economic situation was extremely poor, following extensive out-migration of workers to neighbouring Nigeria and Côte d'Ivoire (Tabatabai, 1986), a dramatic decline in real wages, and rapid inflation. In 1983, the government launched an Economic Recovery Programme, whose impact was initially slowed by the repatriation of as many as 1.2 million Ghanaians from Nigeria alone (Tabatabai, 1986). From 1984 until the time of the GDHS in 1988, economic conditions improved steadily from their low point in the early 1980s. Since 1985, when real output regained its 1980 level, growth in real output has been steady at 5.8 per cent a year and inflation rates have fallen (Glewwe and Twum-Baah, 1989).

Recent changes in women's socio-economic circumstances
In reviewing recent demographic trends and other changes in women's circumstances, we will focus on events in the 1980s as framed by the two national fertility surveys, the WFS in 1979–80 and the GDHS in 1988 (Ghana, Central Bureau of Statistics, 1983; Ghana Statistical Service, 1989a). During the decade, relatively little appeared to change for women. The steady growth in the urban population apparent in earlier years did not continue in the 1980s – roughly one-third of the women interviewed in each survey were urban residents – while the rate of improvement in education for women slowed noticeably.

Women in Ghana are well known for their high rates of economic activity. A comparative study of women's work rates for 38 developing countries participating in the WFS programme (12 of which were in Africa) found women's recorded economic activity – defined to include non-cash and family work[2] – to be highest in Ghana (United Nations, 1985). For ever-married women aged 25–49, the proportion working was 92 per cent. Work rates in other countries where similarly broad definitions were applied were lower, ranging from roughly 80 per cent in Côte d'Ivoire (a close neighbour) to 11 per cent in Jordan. For practical purposes, it can be assumed that all but a minority of women in Ghana participate in productive activity other than 'housework'. As previously noted, for the GDHS it was felt that it would be more appropriate to measure the activities of only those women who worked for cash in non-family activities. Table 8.1 presents a comparison of the proportion of women aged 15–49 working for cash and not for their families by occupation from the 1979–80 WFS and the 1988 GDHS. The overall rate of participation in non-family cash work is high – roughly 51–54 per cent. The only noticeable change is a decrease of almost 8 per cent in women working in agriculture. This recorded decline in agricultural employment is probably the result of misinterpretations of the GDHS work question. Women were asked: 'Are you currently doing any work for money, other than on a farm or business run by your family?' It is likely that some women may as a result have thought that farm work should be excluded.[3] For this reason, we have to assume that non-family agricultural workers earning cash were at least slightly undercounted in 1988.[4]

Table 8.1 Percentage distribution of women aged 15–49 by occupation, Ghana, 1979–88

	WFS 1979–80	GDHS 1988
Non-family cash work	54.4	50.7
Professional/technical	2.7	2.8
Clerical	1.3	1.2
Sales	24.5	26.4
Self-employed agriculture	15.1	8.9
Agricultural employees	2.0	0.4
Private household	0.2	0.1
Other service	1.3	1.6
Skilled production	7.1	8.8
Unskilled production	0.3	0.4
Family or non-cash	45.6	49.3
All women	100.0	100.0
Number of women	6 125	4 488

Source: WFS and GDHS standard recode files.

Recent changes in child-bearing and child-rearing

The total fertility rate (based on the five years before the survey) remained virtually unchanged during the 1980s: in 1979–80 it was estimated at 6.46 births per woman (United Nations, 1987), and, in 1988, at 6.43 births per woman (Ghana Statistical Service, 1989a). The proportion of recent births that were wanted remains high: 91 per cent in 1979–80 and 90 per cent in 1988 (Bongaarts, 1990). Among currently married women, the proportion using modern methods of contraception is very low, and virtually unchanged between the two surveys: 5.5 per cent of currently married women reported current use of a modern method in 1979–80 and 5.2 per cent in 1988 (United Nations, 1989; Ghana Statistical Service, 1989a). There has been a slight rise in age at first marriage and a very slight decrease in the prevalence of polygyny among younger women. The average duration of breast-feeding is prolonged (20 months in the GDHS) and there is no evidence that there has been any change in this pattern. Thus, all the intermediate factors influencing fertility trends have been relatively stable over this period.

Child-bearing is not necessarily synonymous with child-rearing in Ghana, where children often live away from one or other of their parents or even both of their parents for periods of their childhood. The practice of child fostering is well documented in Ghana in demographic (Isiugo-Abanihe, 1985; Page, 1989) and anthropological sources (e.g. Oppong, 1973; Goody, 1976; Oppong and Abu, 1987). Five types of child fostering have been identified: kinship fostering, crisis fostering, apprentice fostering, educational fostering and domestic fostering (Goody, 1976). Kinship fostering, probably the most common, involves sending children to live with relatives. Crisis fostering is the result of an event that dissolves the nuclear family, such as death, divorce, separation or economic hardship. Apprentice and educational fostering entail sending children to either kin or non-kin who are expected to provide assistance in acquiring formal or Koranic education or the learning of a trade. This type of fostering may also be used to strengthen economic, political or social alliances. Domestic fostering reflects the practice of sending children, especially girls, to provide domestic services, including child-care, in the households of others. Child fostering can occur if parents migrate, leaving their children behind, or if children are sent away from either of their parents to live elsewhere. Thus a woman's child-rearing responsibilities may at any point include the care of children who are not her own but at the same time may exclude the care of some of her own children who are living elsewhere.

Data on child fostering are available for several points in time in Ghana. Although they are not strictly comparable, they can be used to draw conclusions about possible trends in the institution of fostering over time. Data from the WFS household survey provide estimates of the proportion of children residing in households where their mothers were not resident (Page, 1989). Included among these children would be the children of women over the age of 49 and children whose mothers were dead – two groups of children for whom data on separation from the mother are not available from the GDHS. None the less, these differences are not sufficient to explain the sharply lower proportions of the youngest children (aged 0–4) fostered in the GDHS compared with the WFS (see Table 8.2).[5] Similar declines for the youngest group are also apparent if data from the 1971 census on absence from both parents (Isiugo-Abanihe, 1985) are compared with the GDHS household data, in which absence from both parents is also recorded (Table 8.2).[6] These comparisons present strong evidence of a decline in fostering at the youngest ages, a decline that cannot be explained solely by the economic downturn in the late 1970s or early 1980s. While the reasons for this trend are not known, its consequences are likely to be an increase in the costs of children to mothers.

The proportions fostered in the other age groups are slightly lower at the time of the GDHS than recorded in the WFS, but this can be largely explained by the inclusion of orphaned children and the children of older mothers in the WFS estimate. When the fostering estimates from the GDHS household data are compared with estimates from the 1971 census (Isiugo-Abanihe, 1985), the prevalence of fostering among children aged 6–10 appears to have declined as well, but the possibility that the rates from the 1971 census have been overestimated makes it impossible to be sure. It is very unlikely that fostering rates for older children have declined.[7]

On average, girls are slightly more likely to be fostered away than boys, whether fostering is defined in terms of absence from mother or absence from both parents. The percentage of children living away from one or both parents increases steadily with the age of the children. While girls and boys experience similar rates of parental absence below 10, the rates for girls are notably higher in the 10–14 age group, possibly because of the greater tendency to foster out girls as domestic servants and child-minders.

Shifts in Work and Child-Care Arrangements over the Life Cycle

As already indicated, fertility remains high in Ghana. Women aged 45–49 in the GDHS survey reported an average of 7.3 children ever born per woman in 1988 (see Table 8.3). This translates into 5.6 living children for women in this age group. At any moment in time, however, women of reproductive age are likely to have fewer children for whom direct care is required. This is because younger women are still building their families while older women are likely to have some children who are already grown up. If we look at the variation in the mean number of children under 15 over a women's reproductive years, we see that a woman's child-rearing responsibilities grow by roughly one child every five years until her mid-thirties. From her mid-thirties until

Table 8.2 Trends in child fostering, Ghana, 1971–88 (%)

Children	Household data 1971[a]	Household data 1979–80[b]	Household data 1988	Women 15–49 1988
Residing away from mother				
0–4				
Total		12.4		4.2
Male		11.8		4.0
Female		13.2		4.4
5–9				
Total		24.5		18.2
Male		23.3		17.2
Female		25.9		19.2
10–14				
Total		33.3		29.3
Male		31.2		26.4
Female		35.1		32.5
Residing away from both parents				
0–5				
Total	14.5		7.4	
Male	13.1		6.8	
Female	15.3		8.0	
6–10				
Total	23.7		17.6	
Male	20.4		16.1	
Female	26.2		19.1	
Groups of fostered children included				
Living mother aged 15–49				
With father		X		X
Without father	X	X	X	X
Living mother >49				
With father		X		
Without father	X	X	X	
Dead mother				
With father		X		
Without father	X	X	X	

Notes: [a] These figures may possibly be an overestimate because 19 per cent of the cases were ambiguous when a child's father was not the household head.

[b] Page provides estimates of child fostering by region. National estimates were derived from a weighted average of the regional estimates, using the proportion of women in the sample residing in each region. If some fostered children do not reside in the same region as their mother, these estimates will be biased.

X indicates that fostered children with the characteristics indicated in the left hand column were included in the data.

Sources: 1971: Isiugo-Abanihe, 1985.
1979–80: Page, 1989.
1988 household and individual data: GDHS standard recode file.

her mid-forties, the number of living children continues to grow by roughly one child every five years, but the number of dependent children (defined as those under 15) declines, falling to 2.1 for women aged 45–49. The levels and patterns of child-care responsibilities have shown no change during the 1980s, as can be seen from a comparison of the GDHS and WFS data. Women's responsibilities reach a peak during their thirties and then fall back by the end of their reproductive years to the levels experienced in their late twenties.

Table 8.3 Fertility and child-care responsibilities of all women aged 15–49 over the life cycle, Ghana, WFS and GDHS

Women by age	Mean CEB		Mean living children		Mean children under 15		Mean resident children under 15	
	WFS	GDHS	WFS	GDHS	WFS	GDHS	WFS	GDHS
15–19	0.2	0.2	0.2	0.2	0.2	0.2	NA	0.2
20–24	1.4	1.3	1.2	1.1	1.2	1.1	NA	1.0
25–29	2.7	2.7	2.4	2.3	2.4	2.3	NA	1.9
30–34	4.0	4.2	3.5	3.5	3.3	3.3	NA	2.8
35–39	5.4	5.5	4.6	4.6	3.4	3.5	NA	2.9
40–44	6.1	6.6	5.1	5.4	3.0	2.9	NA	2.5
45–49	6.7	7.3	5.4	5.6	2.2	2.1	NA	1.7

Notes: CEB = Children ever born. NA = Not available.
Sources: GDHS and WFS standard recode files.

Employment patterns

Working women in Ghana are concentrated in three broad occupational categories: sales, skilled production and agriculture are the only categories containing more than 5 per cent of reproductive aged women (see Table 8.1). An examination of the more detailed 100-category occupational coding reveals a similar concentration of women within each of these groups. Working proprietors in wholesale and retail trade account for 98 per cent of the sales categories. Food and beverage processors and tailors and dressmakers make up 85 per cent of the skilled production category, two-thirds of whom work at home. Among the agricultural group, 96 per cent are identified as farmers or farm managers.

Because of the extreme concentration of women within a few occupational groups, we decided to combine information on occupation and location of work into new occupational groupings in order to discriminate between working women more clearly in terms of their circumstances. The resulting groups are defined as follows:

1 *Modern cash*, including professional, technical and related workers, administrative and managerial workers, clerical and related workers, as well as sales supervisors and buyers, technical salesworkers, commercial travellers and manufacturers' agents.

2 *Traditional cash at home*, including all other sales workers, service workers and all skilled and unskilled production workers working at home.

3 *Traditional cash travelling*, including salesworkers as well as beverage processors and tailors who sell what they can by walking from place to place in a circumscribed area.

4 *Traditional cash away*, including women in all the occupations listed above under category (2) who travel from their homes to a workplace or a market-place.

5 *Agriculture*, including self-employed as well as agricultural employees.

Less than 6 per cent of modern cash workers and only 2 per cent of agricultural workers work at home, so there was no need to distinguish women in terms of location of work in these categories. Categories (6) and (7) include all women not working for cash in rural and urban areas, respectively. A large majority of these women are likely to be working in family farms or businesses but some are exclusively engaged in housework. The rural non-cash category also includes those cash workers who were inadvertently excluded from the agricultural category.

Table 8.4 Occupational characteristics of women aged 15–49 according to revised grouping,[a] Ghana, GDHS

Occupation	Distribution	Mean years of education	Mean hourly wage (cedis)	Mean hours per day	% Working most of time	% Controlling own earnings (all women)
Modern cash	4.3	5.8	64.7	6.6 (7.6)[b]	94.8	93.8
Traditional cash						
Home	15.0	4.3	42.6	7.1	60.0	93.4
Travelling	3.0	5.2	45.8	5.9	57.9	90.2
Away	18.9	4.5	51.4	6.8 (8.1)[b]	65.8	92.6
Agriculture	9.3	3.1	23.2	5.5 (6.8)[b]	70.9	86.2
Rural non-cash	35.3	3.7	–	–	–	–
Urban non-cash	14.2	5.4	–	–	–	–
Total	100.0					

Notes: – = Not applicable.
[a] For definition, see text, p. 119.
[b] Including travel time to work.

The distribution of women according to this unconventional occupational grouping is presented in Table 8.4. Roughly 37 per cent of all women are found in the traditional cash sector, fairly evenly divided between those working at home and those working away, with a small percentage (3 per cent) working as they walk from place to place. Mean years of education are highest among women in the modern cash sector, as we would expect, but they are also relatively high among traditional travelling workers and urban women who do not participate in non-family cash work. The least educated women are in agriculture and in rural non-cash work.

The GDHS collected data on various dimensions of current work including earnings, daily hours, travel time to work, intensity of work and control over earnings. Table 8.4 presents data on how these characteristics vary across our new occupational groups. The average hourly wage varies from 23 cedis in agriculture to roughly 65 cedis for modern cash workers.[8] The lower wage in agriculture partly reflects the larger percentage of seasonal workers in that sector (19 per cent). Among traditional cash workers, wages rise with distance from the home. Among salesworkers, those who travel furthest from the home come in contact with the largest markets, and thus are able to manage larger inventories if they have small shops or stalls at the market-place where they work. Taking women working in traditional cash work away from home as an example, these wages would imply that a woman working full-time all year could cover roughly 25–30 per cent of the average household's expenditure in Ghana in 1988.[9] However, as Chapter 6 by Goldschmidt-Clermont emphasises, much of women's economic contribution to the maintenance of family members remains unacknowledged and unassessed.

Mean hours worked per day vary from 7.1 in traditional cash work at home to 5.5 in agriculture. If travel time to work is included, the range is wider – from 5.9 to 8.1 hours per day – and the levels are higher. Virtually all modern cash workers work most of the time (roughly 95 per cent). The proportion working most of the time varies from 58 per cent to 71 per cent in the traditional occupational groups. In all occupations, a large majority of women decide how the money they earn will be used, with percentages ranging from 86 per cent in agriculture to roughly 94 per cent in modern cash work. This statistic attests to the remarkable autonomy of working women in Ghana.

Table 8.5 Variations in occupational distribution of women aged 15–49 by background characteristics, Ghana, GDHS (%)

| | | Cash | | | | Non-cash | |
| | | Traditional cash | | | | | |
	Modern	Home	Travelling	Away	Agriculture	Rural	Urban
Age							
15–19	0.2	6.2	3.1	10.2	2.5	48.2	29.5
20–24	3.6	13.8	2.4	18.3	5.9	38.6	17.3
25–29	7.2	14.3	3.4	21.3	9.6	33.5	10.7
30–34	6.6	18.3	2.5	22.3	11.7	31.7	7.0
35–39	5.5	22.5	3.6	20.5	12.5	25.0	8.3
40–44	4.4	18.8	3.9	19.7	14.4	29.9	8.9
45–49	3.3	19.3	2.2	22.4	18.2	28.2	6.4
Region							
Western	4.1	15.7	1.3	21.6	13.1	35.1	9.0
Central	3.0	16.4	2.8	17.3	25.1	25.9	9.5
Greater Accra	7.4	20.0	6.0	29.9	1.8	1.8	33.1
Eastern	4.7	14.3	3.2	18.5	9.6	38.9	10.8
Volta	4.0	10.1	2.4	12.3	7.3	51.0	12.9
Ashanti	5.0	15.7	2.9	19.2	3.1	37.4	16.7
Brong-Ahafo	3.4	11.1	2.2	10.1	16.7	45.9	10.7
Northern and Upper	1.8	15.6	2.0	20.3	4.9	49.3	6.1
Education							
None	0.6	15.1	2.4	17.8	13.2	42.4	8.6
Primary	0.6	17.7	3.2	20.9	8.9	35.9	12.8
Middle	4.6	15.0	3.7	20.0	6.9	31.3	18.4
Middle +	31.3	8.4	2.4	14.6	0.9	15.5	26.9
Total of all women	4.3	15.0	3.0	18.9	9.3	35.3	14.2

Source: GDHS standard recode file.

However, this autonomy may be seriously constrained by women's earning power in relation to household needs.

Table 8.5 presents data on women's occupations by various background characteristics including age, region and education. The most striking feature of the occupational distribution is the steady increase, with increasing age, in the proportion of women in non-family cash work, in both urban and rural areas. This reflects women's increasing self-reliance: as they get older and their children mature, they take on cash work, mostly on their own account. In the absence of any trend in the occupational distribution over time, these differences across the age groups can safely be interpreted as reflecting life-cycle phenomena. Among women over the age of 30, the proportion in sales remains fairly steady; however, the smaller percentage of older women in the modern cash sector may reflect the process of urbanisation and economic development that occurred earlier. The proportion of women in non-family cash work is surprisingly similar across the education groups but their occupational distribution is not. The percentage of women with a middle school or higher education in non-family cash work is 58 per cent. It is 49 per cent among women with no education. However, the majority of the most highly educated working women are in the modern cash sector, whereas the overwhelming majority of women with middle school education or less are found in the traditional cash or agriculture sectors.

Child-care responsibilities and living arrangements

While data from the GDHS do not permit a direct calculation of women's net child-rearing responsibilities at any point in time, it is possible to look at the proportion of children living away from their mother in relation to the presence of children in her household who have no resident parents. As most of these households include at least one older adult woman in addition to the respondent, however, it is possible that some of these resident fostered children are not the direct responsibility of the women interviewed in the sample. In Table 8.3 we can see that the mean number of children under 15 who are resident with their mother is roughly half a child less than the total number in this age group for all women over the age of 25. Rates of fostering increase dramatically from ages 15 to 25 as the numbers of children and the average age of children increase, but after the mid-twenties the rates stay roughly the same. Drawing on data on the composition of the households (presented in Table 8.6) in which the women reside, we can examine the variation in the average number of children without resident parents in a woman's household over the life cycle in comparison with the variation in the number of her own children resident with her. This provides a crude measure of net child-rearing responsibilities (see Fig. 8.1). It is striking how complementary the patterns of fostering in and out appear to be over the life cycle: the mean number of children per woman fostered into the household is greatest among the oldest and youngest women, while during the years of their own peak child-rearing responsibilities women have fewer fostered-in children on average and have more children of their own fostered out.

The prevalence of child fostering varies by ethnic group, but within each the proportion of mothers with dependent children (under 15) with at least one child away from home is greatest for women over 30 when the child-rearing burden is at its peak (see Table 8.7). Among women aged 30–39, the prevalence of fostering varies from a low of 20 per cent among other Ghanaians to 48 per cent among the Ga-Adangbes. Among this ethnic group separate residence of spouses and separate residence of female and male kin are traditional patterns which still affect the composition of many domestic groups. These data provide a useful background to the anthropological literature on child fostering in Ghana, which often concentrates on a relatively small sample for one ethnic group.

The prevalence of fostering also varies by marital status. Among the ever-married group, the formerly married mothers have the highest rates of child fostering at every age, rising to 43 per cent among women aged 30–39. Within the married group, however, there are no clear patterns that differentiate mothers in polygynous unions from those in monogamous unions or those who live with their husbands from those who do not. Never-married mothers are primarily younger women with a few children at most. Among them fostering can only be measured for the 20–29 age group, and here the figure is similar (24 per cent) to that for other women at that age.

Child fostering as an institution thus provides a mechanism for the redistribution of some of a woman's child-rearing responsibilities over the life cycle. Co-residence with parents provides another such mechanism. Table 8.8 shows the distribution of women of different ages according to marital and residential status. For our purposes here residential status relates to co-residence with husband and/or with parents (either the woman's own parents or her husband's). Obviously, the possibility of living with parents depends on their being alive, so the proportion of women living with parents declines steadily with age. On average, however, roughly a quarter of a

Table 8.6 Percentage distribution of usual household residents in households in which women aged 15–49 reside (excluding respondents themselves), Ghana, GDHS

	15–19	20–24	25–29	30–34	35–39	40–44	45–49	Total
Children without parents in household[a]	7.7	6.6	6.4	4.2	4.3	4.6	7.6	6.1
Less than 6	2.3	1.8	1.7	0.8	0.9	1.3	2.2	1.6
6–10	3.3	2.6	2.7	2.0	1.7	2.0	3.5	2.6
11–14	2.1	2.2	2.0	1.4	1.7	1.3	1.9	1.9
Children with at least one parent in household[b]	41.0	43.0	53.2	59.8	56.5	52.0	44.2	49.3
Less than 6	17.6	25.9	31.8	28.9	24.7	19.9	16.5	24.2
6–10	13.6	10.1	15.5	20.4	19.5	18.8	15.9	15.6
11–14	9.8	7.0	5.9	10.5	12.3	13.3	11.8	9.5
Other females 15 +	27.4	25.2	17.4	15.0	15.9	17.7	20.8	20.7
Males 15 +	23.9	25.3	23.0	21.0	23.2	25.6	27.4	23.9
Total	100.0	100.0	100.0	100.0	100.0	100.0	100.0	100.0
Mean number of household residents[c]	6.4	5.7	5.2	5.9	6.2	6.3	5.9	5.9
Number of household residents	6 184	5 496	4 974	4 201	3 628	2 537	2 371	29 391
Number of women	970	970	952	708	585	401	400	4 986

Notes: [a] Neither parent is a usual resident of the household.
[b] At least one parent is a usual resident of the household.
[c] Excluding respondents themselves.
Source: GDHS household data.

Mean number of children

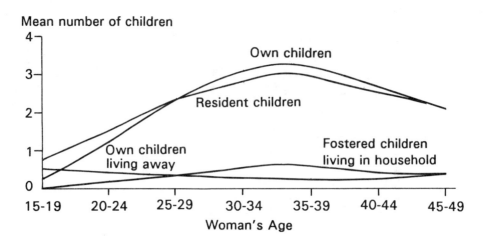

Fig. 8.1 *Mean number of children aged 0–15 per woman by residence of child and woman's age, Ghana, GDHS.*

woman's reproductive years after her first marriage are spent living with parents in a variety of marital circumstances.[10] Roughly 40 per cent of those years are spent in the absence of a husband, either because wives do not co-reside with their husbands, or because of marital disruption. The proportion of women divorced, widowed and separated rises steadily with age, with most of the older women in this group residing away from parents. Thus, residential flexibility both for children and for mothers allows women the possibility of a variety of child-rearing arrangements, but that flexibility grows more limited with time due to the death of parents and spouses and the increased incidence of divorce and polygny.

Child-Care Arrangements for Working Women

Ghanaian women are able to sustain a high level of economic activity despite high rates of child-bearing; indeed, their rates of economic activity in the non-family cash sector rise sharply over the life cycle as their need for income increases along with the number of dependent children. The residential flexibility of mothers and children, as discussed above, provides one possible societal mechanism through which the conflicts over time arising from women's multiple roles can be alleviated. For many of the occupations women pursue in Ghana, however, child-care and work may be reasonably compatible. Because occupations differ in the demands they place on women, we would expect the propensity of women to foster out children to vary according to their occupation, as would their choice of other home-based child-care arrangements.

Data on the prevalence of fostering by women's age and occupation appear in Table 8.7. The most striking feature of these data is the small differences between occupations and between cash and non-cash workers in the prevalence of fostering. While overall rates are slightly lower for those not working for cash, non-cash workers have among the highest rates of fostering during the peak child-rearing years in the

Table 8.7 Percentage distribution of women with dependent children (under 15) with at least one child away, by occupation, ethnicity, marital status and age, Ghana

	Age group			Total
	20–29	30–39	40–49	20–49
Occupation				
Modern cash	25	32	32[a]	29
Traditional cash				
Home	23	34	30	28
Travelling	26	33	30	28
Away	25	37	38	32
Agricultural	16	40	38	31
Rural non-cash	20	37	32	26
Urban non-cash	19	41	28	26
Ethnicity				
Akan	21	36	31	27
Ga-Adangbe	32	48	44	37
Ewe	22	39	43	31
Guan	21	47[a]	43	36
Mole-Dagbani	18	34	22	24
Other Ghanaian	14	20	25	18
Other African	25	46	52	36
Marital status				
Never married	24	00[a]	–	15
Formerly married	26	43	40	34
Monogamous				
With husband	23	34	34	28
Without husband	15	39	29	22
Polygynous				
With husband	23	41	30	32
Without husband	23	35	34	30

Note: [a] Fewer than 20 cases.
Source: GDHS.

thirties, when access to cash may be particularly important for the proper rearing of children.

The GDHS collected information on specific child-care arrangements during working hours from all women who were defined as working and who had at least one resident child under 6. By including fostering as a child-care category, all working women with a living child under 6 can be included in the information on child-care. Table 8.9 presents the proportion of women using different types of child-care while working, according to occupation, education and marital status. The categories of child-care while working include:

1 The woman herself.
2 Members of her family (husband, children or other relatives).
3 School or other institutional child-care.
4 Fostering.
5 Other, including neighbours, friends, servants and others.

It is not known how women handled the question when they had more than one child under 6. It was assumed that child-care arrangements would be the same for all children. In the case of fostering, there were 72 cases where women fostered out one

Table 8.8 Percentage distribution of women aged 15–49 by marital and residential status according to current age, and synthetic cohort estimates of the number of years and percentage distribution of years between age 15 and 49 spent in each status, Ghana, GDHS

| Age | Never married | Currently married | | | | Formerly married | | Total |
| | | Living with husband | | Not living with husband | | | | |
		With parents	Without parents	With parents	Without parents	With parents	Without parents	
15–19	73.7	4.4	5.8	6.6	3.8	1.8	2.2	100.0
20–24	22.7	12.7	25.1	16.6	13.8	4.1	5.0	100.0
25–29	4.6	15.4	43.5	13.2	14.7	2.5	6.1	100.0
30–34	1.7	12.5	49.1	10.3	15.8	4.2	6.3	100.0
35–39	1.1	10.5	51.2	8.9	17.7	3.2	7.3	100.0
40–44	1.9	8.3	54.3	5.3	16.3	3.6	10.2	100.0
45–49	1.9	5.2	50.0	5.5	16.4	2.7	18.3	100.0
Percentage distribution across all age groups	15.7	9.9	39.9	9.5	14.1	3.2	7.9	100.0
Number of years (15–49)	5.5	3.5	14.0	3.3	4.9	1.1	2.8	35.0
Number of women	909	465	1 607	465	592	139	296	4 473

Source: GDHS standard recode file.

Table 8.9   Percentage distribution of working mothers with at least one living child under 6 by child-care arrangements, occupation, education and marital status, Ghana, GDHS

	Herself	Family[a]	School[b]	Fostered[c]	Other[d]
Occupation					
Modern cash	29.0	31.7	19.6	9.3	10.2
Traditional cash					
Home	63.9	22.7	3.6	7.7	2.3
Travelling	30.5	53.7	7.3	6.3	1.2
Away	40.2	41.3	6.6	9.9	2.0
Agriculture	51.5	38.1	4.7	4.3	1.3
Education					
None	49.8	40.4	2.8	5.3	1.7
Primary	50.4	35.9	4.1	7.3	2.0
Middle	48.3	30.6	7.8	10.5	3.6
Middle +	32.7	31.8	20.9	9.1	5.4
Marital status					
Never married	41.4	31.0	6.9	17.2	3.4
Married with husband and parents	50.7	37.3	5.5	5.5	1.0
Married with husband, no parents	41.9	38.2	7.7	10.2	2.0
Married with parents, no husband	42.8	44.3	1.5	8.8	2.5
Married, no husband or parents	51.2	32.6	6.9	5.9	3.4
Formerly married, with parents	47.2	35.9	11.3	5.7	–
Formerly married, no parents	51.6	21.6	6.5	18.3	2.2

Notes: [a] Husband, children and other relatives.
       [b] School and other institutional care.
       [c] For women with more than one child, they are grouped under fostered if *one* of their children is fostered.
       [d] Neighbours, friends, servants, other.
Source: GDHS standard recode file.

child and had another at home using one of the other types of arrangement. This group of women was coded in the fostered group.

The most striking fact to emerge from the table is the apparent compatibility of work and child-rearing even when children are very young. Even in the modern cash sector and among the most educated women, roughly 30 per cent of women report caring for their children while they work. For all groups but modern cash workers, the most educated women, never-married women and formerly married women not living with their parents, more than 80 per cent of child-care is undertaken by the woman herself or her family. Residence with parents is an important source of child-care for formerly married women and married women not currently residing with their husband. School and institutional care and other non-family arrangements, which are likely to be expensive, are only significant among the most modern and educated women. Fostering as a child-care arrangement for very young children is used most by modern cash workers, traditional cash workers who travel to work, and more educated women, as well as by never-married women, formerly married women not living with their parents, and married women living with their husband but not their parents. This suggests that grandparents play an important role in the early rearing and socialisation of children, regardless of their residential location (Date-Bah, 1986), and this role continues to be important (although maybe less so than in the past), even among the most modern women.

Micro-studies have shown that fostering norms and practices vary with ethnicity, education, residence, age and family size as well as occupation (e.g. Oppong and Abu, 1987). Multi-variate analysis of the GDHS data – estimating separate models for each of three age groups of children, including these factors and using logistic regression – supports several of these findings (Blanc and Lloyd, 1990). Thus, the number of children a woman has and their ages have been shown to be clearly associated with fostering. In general, the more children a woman has in a particular age group, the more likely she is to foster out a child in that age group. Among women with at least one child under 6, for example, each additional child in that age group approximately doubles the probability of fostering. In addition, the probability of fostering out a child in a given age group is lowered by the existence of children in other age groups. Having a living child older than 6 reduces the probability of fostering out a child under 6. This effect is greatest with siblings aged 11–14. Conversely, having a living child under age 6 reduces the probability of fostering out a child aged 11–14. These results are consistent with the notion that older siblings serve as caretakers for their younger brothers and sisters.

Never-married and formerly married women are two to three times more likely to foster out a child under 6 than monogamously married women. Some of the children fostered out by never-married and formerly married women may fall into the category of 'crisis fostering'. In many West African cultures tradition dictates that children born out of wedlock and children whose parents separate or divorce be sent to either the mother's or the father's kin for rearing (Fiawoo, 1976; Goody, 1976). This practice is partly an effort to retain and strengthen children's kinship ties but may also be motivated by the practical difficulties of single mothers attempting to raise children alone. Formerly married women are also somewhat more likely than married women to foster out older children. Women in polygynous unions also appear more likely to foster out a young child than women in monogamous unions, but the reasons for this are not immediately clear. In addition, as expected, an ever-married woman who is living with her parents or her husband's parents is less likely to foster out a child than other women.

The effect of having recently migrated is also a positive and statistically significant factor. One form of child fostering does not involve sending the child away; rather, the mother herself leaves the child with others and migrates in order to continue schooling or training or to find employment. This form of fostering may be particularly prevalent among rural women who migrate to urban areas and may be related to difficulties in securing adequate housing in urban areas and the desire to maintain ties with relatives in rural areas (e.g. Isiugo-Abanihe, 1985).

The rate of fostering appears to be approximately equal for urban and rural women when other factors are controlled, although the reasons for fostering out children may differ between the two groups. Women classified as visitors are also more likely to have children absent than rural or urban residents.

Neither employment status nor level of education appears to have a strong effect on the likelihood of fostering. As already mentioned, women who work in modern or traditional cash occupations are slightly more likely to foster out children than women in non-cash occupations, but none of these effects is statistically significant.

The pattern of effects among self-employed women working in agriculture is somewhat puzzling. The relationship between working in agriculture on a self-employed basis and fostering out is positive and significant for the oldest age group of children. This may reflect the practice of fostering out children, especially girls, to provide domestic labour for relatives and others. The pattern of effects for different age groups of women reflects the age pattern described earlier: that is, women are most likely to foster out children when they are in the middle of their reproductive years and least likely to foster at the beginning and end of the reproductive years.

Significant differences between ethnic groups in the likelihood of fostering are found for all three age groups of children. The Ga-Adangbe are significantly more likely to foster out children than the Akan, the largest ethnic group. The Ewe and Guan also appear to be more likely to foster than the Akan, although the differences are not as large and are not statistically significant.

Overall, the results of the statistical models support the view that fostering is a resilient institution that continues to support child-rearing in both traditional and modern settings. Education, modern sector employment and urban residence cannot account for variations among women in the practice of fostering. Marital status, migrant status, and the number and age distribution of own children are among the most important factors explaining variations in fostering, which appears to be practised by all categories of women, educated and uneducated, urban and rural, in response to shifts in life circumstances. When a change in marital status or place of residence, or the addition of a child, increases the demands of child-rearing, women seem to use fostering as a means of adjusting to their changed circumstances.

Conclusions

On the surface, our findings paint a picture of remarkable harmony between women's productive and reproductive roles in Ghana. Extended kin networks and child fostering are long-established institutions which ideally provide a sophisticated social security system for child-care and socialisation. They help women smooth out the demands of child-rearing over their life cycles. They are flexible institutions that can be used to meet the needs of the very poor as well as those of the upwardly mobile or better off, and child fostering as an institution has the potential to enhance children's opportunities. The majority of mothers in Ghana appear able to care for their young children while working – possibly a reflection of the type of work they do, and the fact that they work primarily in the informal sector. Furthermore, as their child-rearing responsibilities grow with age, Ghanaian women are able to shift from family work to cash work, in order to try and meet the growing cash demands of more and older children.

However, to the extent that the spread of education, new economic opportunities and child-care aspirations have already increased women's reluctance to foster out very young children, the costs of children to some mothers are probably beginning to rise (as indicated by the downward trend in very young fostering shown in Table 8.2). Furthermore, economic growth is likely to be accompanied by a resumption in the growth of school enrolment and a growing dependence of families on access to employment in the cash economy, both because of their increased demand for market goods and services and because of inevitable reductions in the contribution made by children to the maintenance of the household. While their strong tradition of autonomy and independence gives Ghanaian women control over the allocation of their earnings, their earnings alone may become increasingly inadequate to meet their own and their children's needs. This could result in greater dependence on the earnings of men for child support.

Another important consequence of economic and demographic growth in Ghana is the increasing urbanisation of the population. While urbanisation brings with it greater access to education opportunities and paid employment, it also results in kin dispersal because of migration and increased housing costs. Both factors are likely to increase the costs of child-rearing and to stretch the capacity of the institution of child fostering by increasing the supply of children to be fostered and reducing the demand. Evidence of stress and of conflict between maternal and working roles, among teachers, nurses and factory workers, has been accumulating in both rural and urban areas of Ghana for some time (Oppong, 1977). The system of fostering cannot halt the inevitable rise in the costs of rearing children. Its ability to continue to spread these costs widely and recapture some of the returns will depend on the maintenance of strong family ties.

Women in Ghana face a difficult future. Their traditional autonomy is being undermined by the growing importance of the cash economy and their rising aspirations for their children. On the other hand, children (both their own and those of others) have traditionally been a source of status, strength and support. Women have no reliable alternative sources of support in an economy in which only 4 per cent of women are employed in the modern cash sector.

Acknowledgements

We gratefully acknowledge the assistance of Rebecca Appiah, Director of the GDHS, in the interpretation of our findings and the computing assistance of Trevor Croft and Jonathon Sampson. The authors share equal responsibility for this work. A version of this paper has appeared as *Women's childrearing strategies in relation to fertility and employment in Ghana* in the Population Council Working Paper series, No. 16, 1990.

Notes

1. The GDHS was carried out by the Ghana Statistical Service between February and June 1988. The sample is nationally representative (and self-weighting), consisting of 4 406 households in which 4 488 women aged 15–49 were successfully interviewed (Ghana Statistical Service, 1989a).

2. The women's work question in the WFS in Ghana was worded as follows: 'As you know, many women work – I mean, aside from doing their own housework. Some take up jobs for which they are paid in cash or kind. Others sell things, or have some business or work on the family farm. Are you at the present time working for pay or profit?' The emphasis on 'pay or profit' at the end of the question might suggest that non-cash work would go unreported but the actual data show relatively large numbers of women (768 or 16.3 per cent of working women) working for payments in kind or unpaid. Others were working for cash but for a family member or on a family farm. Thus, despite the use of the words 'pay or profit', the Ghana WFS appears to have captured essentially all of women's work activity, as intended in the WFS model core questionnaire. This was worded as follows: 'As you know, many women work – I mean aside from doing their own housework. Some take up jobs for which they are paid in cash or kind. Others sell things or have a small business or work on the family farm. Are you doing any such work at the present time?'

3. The interviewers' instructions were very clear on what was intended by this question. 'What' we are interested in here is employment in which a woman earns money *independently* of her family's control, i.e. in which she herself earns money rather than contributing to a common family economic enterprise, and in which she works free of direction of family members.' However, Rebecca Appiah recollected confusion on the part of some supervisors as to the intention and interpretation of this question.

4. We made a comparison of the proportion of women reported by the WFS and GDHS to be working in agriculture on a self-employed basis and found the pattern of under-reporting of self-employed agriculture work to be very uneven between regions in the GDHS, suggesting the possibility of differences in the handling of the questionnaires in different regions. The proportions were as follows:

Region	WFS	GDHS
Western	14.7	13.1
Central	30.6	25.1
Greater Accra	1.6	1.8
Eastern	13.8	9.6
Volta	20.5	7.3
Ashanti	15.1	3.1
Brong-Ahafo	36.8	16.7
Northern and Upper	4.3	4.9

Sources: WFS standard recode and Table 8.5.

5. At these ages, very few children would have mothers over the age of 49. Some children's mothers would be dead, but this is unlikely to explain more than two percentage points of the difference observed. In the GDHS data, 7.4 per cent of the children aged 0–5 in the household were away from both parents and 5.3 per cent of the same age children of women aged 15–49 were away from their mothers. Because fostering to fathers is relatively unusual at young ages (most young fostered children are raised by grandparents (Fiawoo, 1976)), the major difference between these two estimates is the extent of maternal orphanhood.

6. Even if Isiugo-Abanihe's estimates for 1971 are assumed to be inflated by as much as 20 per cent (see notes to Table 8.2), a decline of four to five percentage points is apparent.

7. One factor influencing absence from parents at this age is attendance at secondary boarding schools.

8. Women were free to report earnings in any way they preferred, i.e. hourly, daily, weekly, monthly or annually. They also provided information on the average hours worked on a typical day of work and about whether they worked most of the time, part-time, seasonally or irregularly. To calculate hourly wages for women reporting weekly, monthly or annual earnings, we needed information on average working days per week, per month and per year. At the suggestion of Rebecca Appiah, we assumed that modern cash workers worked a five-day week and all others a six-day week. When daily hours were not reported, we assumed them to be eight. For seasonal workers, we divided the estimated hourly wage in half to take account of the fact that the availability of work is limited to certain times of the year.

9. This is based on an assumed 6.8 hours per day (Table 8.4), six days a week and 50 weeks a year. It assumes an average household size of seven and per capita household expenditure of 55,645 cedis per year, based on data from the 1988 Living Standards and Measurement Survey (LSMS) in Ghana (Boateng *et al.*, 1990).

10. This is based on a synthetic cohort estimate of the number of years spent in each type of marital and living arrangement, using the assumption that the average woman would divide her time between statuses over the life cycle in the same proportions as women of different ages in 1988.

9

Women's Work & Fertility in Zimbabwe: Ending Underdevelopment with Change

ROBERT E. MAZUR & MARVELLOUS MHLOYI

The main objective of this chapter is to improve understanding of the nature of the relationships between women's work and fertility in contemporary Zimbabwe. Having achieved independence in 1980, Zimbabweans find themselves in an era of rapid social and economic change. Yet it is essential first to examine both the general and the historically specific processes which have contributed to the peculiar articulation of underdevelopment and development in Zimbabwe and which provide the framework for understanding women's existing position in the larger socio-economic structure as well as, ultimately, the prospects for transformation and change. In turn, the meaning of contemporary patterns of fertility and the nature of change in the intermediate future are principally derived from this framework.

The available evidence concerning the structure of the economy and the nature of economic activity is first examined, with an emphasis on women's complex patterns of involvement. After a brief look at demographic trends in Zimbabwe, the relationship between women's economic activities and status and fertility patterns and differentials in Zimbabwe is compared with that observed in other societies. The prospects for change in fertility patterns and the extent to which these are linked to possible changes in women's roles and status will form the speculative but substantiated conclusion.

Underdevelopment, Work and Gender

Underdevelopment of the economy

The enduring characteristics of Zimbabwe's bifurcated economy as a 'labour reserve' articulated with a capital-intensive 'modern sector' originated nearly a century ago in the form of British-sponsored conquest and settlement. The division of land administered by the European settlers required the forcible relocation of tens of thousands of African households to the poorest half of the land and preserved the most fertile land for the minority European farmers (Palmer, 1977, p. 238). The semi-proletarianised 'labour reserve' character of the former was reinforced through the imposition of various taxes and discriminatory pricing policies, principally embodied in the 1931 Ma Control Act and its 1934 amendment, which prevented commercial competition in agriculture by Africans. Legal restrictions permitted African men to earn cash for payment of taxes and for consumer needs almost exclusively through 'temporary' migration to work on the Europeans' farms and mines, and in the expanding urban commercial and industrial sector (Arrighi, 1973), though wages were insufficient to support a family that did not retain an agricultural base. In the decades prior to independence, estimates of the extent of out-migration among adult men were consistently around 50–75 per cent, though among male heads of households the rates of absence at any given time were somewhat lower (Mitchell, 1969; Garbett, 1975; Government of Zimbabwe (GOZ), 1984; Mazur, 1986). Cycles of return and repeat migration have been thoroughly institutionalised.

Access to the modern sector was similarly regulated, with migrant workers' urban residence always conditional upon formal employment (the 1936 Native Registration Act) and with mobility restricted through discriminatory legislation (the 1943 Industrial Conciliation Act) to protect the position of European workers. Stabilisation of the migrant workforce became important during the phase of import substitution industrialisation, stimulated by curtailment of core countries' exports during the Second World War. Multinational corporations' roles have expanded greatly during the last four decades and they now occupy dominant positions in nearly all sectors of the modern economy (Clarke, 1980). Stabilisation entailed compulsory work, the creation of separate peri-urban townships, minimum wages and subsidised food for urban workers (Shopo, 1985). None the less, few Africans received a wage sufficient to support a family above poverty level.

Extreme differentiation between European and African farming households was mediated by the state's creation of a small middle class of African freehold farmers (the 1930 Land Apportionment Act). Ultimately, however, nearly all of the state's subsidies were directed to European farmers, who achieved a consistent export capacity with a variety of agricultural crops (Shopo, 1985). Such results must be tempered with the recognition of widespread chronic malnutrition and high rates of morbidity and mortality in the labour reserves, which have become greatly 'overpopulated' in the context of technological stagnation, neglect of capital investment and environmental deterioration (Gilmurray et al., 1978; Shopo, 1985).

At the time of independence, Zimbabwe's government demonstrated its understanding of the underlying population dynamics and how they related to its development history:

> The most urgent problems confronting the country are the resettlement of large numbers of people who had been displaced and regrouped in 'protective villages' [during the war of national liberation] and the reconstruction of essential infrastructure such as roads, health establishments and schools that had been destroyed throughout the country. Primary health care is described as the cornerstone of the Government's socio-economic development policy. Imbalances in the provision of services will be redressed by increased facilities in rural areas, and maternal health services will be established. Health care is provided free for those with very low incomes [those earning less than $150 per month, the vast majority of the population]. The Government considers the rate of fertility to be too high and desires partial intervention to control it. To resettle returning refugees, internal rural displaced persons and urban squatters, a program of rural development is being planned which will resettle entire communities in rural areas. In those new rural growth points, Government services will be expanded and the growth of industry will be encouraged. The level of immigration is significant and is to be reduced in the future. (United Nations, 1986b, pp. 48–49)

In this official policy statement, as well as that articulated by Zimbabwe's President, it is evident that 'Zimbabwe seriously takes into account population issues and their relationship to socio-economic development' (Mugabe, 1985, p. 179). While the high rate of population growth is identified, the specific role of fertility policies is placed within a broad perspective on the inter-relationship between population and development issues.

The independent Zimbabwean government has begun to address some of the structural problems in the economy through increased producer prices, infrastructure development and expanded services in the labour reserves (now euphemistically termed 'communal areas'), and a programme of household resettlement from the reserves on to land purchased from European farmers (Munslow, 1985; GOZ, 1986, p. 28). The latter had provided for approximately 55,000 families by 1990, with only 2000 resettled in 1990 (Palmer, 1990; *Africa Confidential*, 1991a, p. 5); a variety of internal and external forces have contributed to this being significantly less than the 162,000 families originally planned by 1983 (Munslow, 1985). The greatly increased volume of crops marketed by African farmers has been widely heralded, indicating recovery from the devastating effects of the liberation struggle in the late 1970s and the drought in the early 1980s (GOZ, 1986, p. 25). None the less, the overwhelming pressures on the still inadequately developed communal areas, the relatively slow pace of resettlement, and the almost prohibitive costs of developing significant growth points are resulting in a continued exodus from rural areas to the main urban centres. There are an estimated 1.2 million homeless people in Zimbabwe's towns and cities (*Facts and Reports*), 1991a, p. 10).

When we view Zimbabwe's national development from the perspective of world system analysis, Zimbabwe is involved in the process of associated dependent development (Cardoso and Faletto, 1979), albeit less comprehensively than more commonly cited examples such as Brazil, the Republic of Korea, South Africa and Taiwan, China. This is conveyed by noting that Zimbabwe's gross domestic product in 1985 was derived from a diversity of sources: agriculture (16 per cent), mining (8 per cent), manufacturing (22 per cent), infrastructure and producer services (20 per cent), and non-material activities (34 per cent), the latter representing government expenditures (GOZ, 1986, p. 5). Its exports are primarily agricultural and mineral raw materials and its imports are primarily intermediate and capital goods. More than two-thirds of the capital in strategic sectors of the economy is foreign-owned, and Zimbabwe's debt service ratio has risen dramatically in the post-independence period to constitute 28 per cent of its foreign exchange earnings (Clarke, 1980; GOZ, 1986, p. 4; Knight, 1990, p. 203).

The impact of underdevelopment on economic activities
While Zimbabwe's population has increased more than 30 per cent since the 1982 Census of Population, the latter remains the principal source of comprehensive data on population and labour force structure. The population of working age (15 years and over) in 1982 was estimated to be 3.91 million, with women constituting 52 per cent of the total. The economically active population consisted of 1.45 million people, 27 per cent of whom were women (GOZ, 1985a, pp. 100–106). As defined, this consisted of the producers of economic goods and services; the economically active population, that is the labour force, included employed workers, the self-employed, unpaid family workers, and those who were unemployed and seeking work. It

excluded housewives, students and those who were fully disabled. While this approach is more comprehensive than most usually applied in Africa and elsewhere in the developing world (Boulding, 1983; Cutrufelli, 1983, p. 87), there is still likely to be under-reporting of women's economic activities due to a combination of cultural and definitional reasons. A definition of labour force broadened to include those in the communal farming areas, many of whom were producing some crops for the market, included an additional 1.04 million people, 56 per cent of whom were women. Subsequent discussion of the labour force excludes the communal farmers, as detailed information about them is currently unavailable, but their substantial contribution to the national economic product is gaining increasing recognition (GOZ, 1986, p. 25).

Labour force participation rates for men aged 20–59 in urban areas ranged from 82 to 94 per cent according to specific age group, including participation in the informal sector. In the rural areas, but excluding the communal farmers, male labour force participation rates were 48–63 per cent. Overall, it was estimated that 84 per cent of adult men were employed and 16 per cent unemployed. Approximately 44 per cent of the adult urban population were women. Urban women's recorded labour force participation rates ranged from 37 to 43 per cent, and they constituted 26 per cent of the documented adult urban labour force. Women represented 28 per cent of the officially recorded labour force in the rural areas, though many work unofficially as farm labourers when their husbands' bosses so require. Among the female economically active population, an estimated 27 per cent were considered unemployed. Recognising that only the middle and upper classes can 'afford' to be unemployed (Boulding, 1983, p. 290), in other words, that all adolescents and adults must engage regularly in some activity that keeps them alive, any official quantification of the labour force and the unemployed must be viewed cautiously. As can be noted from a comparison of 1984 and 1988 survey data, the definition of labour force participation is different. While work for cash or kind during the past month was considered in 1984, only current work for cash was considered in 1988, with a consequent recorded decline in labour force participation of 1 per cent. This inconsistency in what is considered work reflects society's perception of women's activities and, by implication, their status.

The principal post-independence problem remains that of creating new viable jobs and opportunities for diverse economic activities in a way that effectively transforms the inherited economic structure. The number of commercial farm workers – particularly women – has declined by at least 30 per cent (Shopo, 1985, p. 64; Kazembe, 1986, p. 384), owing at least in part to legislation establishing realistic minimum wages, in marked contrast to the pre-independence situation. The expansion of the government sector to provide health and educational services that were denied the majority population before 1980 and the limited amount of new foreign investment have resulted in a very limited expansion of formal sector jobs.

The modest growth in wage employment has been inadequate. The unemployed population has grown from 250,000 to 1.25 million in the last ten years (*Africa Confidential*, 1991c, p. 6). At present, formal sector jobs are obtained by less than 10 per cent of the estimated 250,000–300,000 annual school leavers (GOZ, 1983a, pp. 71–72, 1986, pp. 6, 48; Knight, 1990, p. 203; Morna, 1990, p. 64; *Africa Confidential*, 1991b, p. 5). Estimates of the number of new jobs needed do not take into account further likely rural–urban migration. Thus, growth in wage employment is expected to satisfy the needs of only a small proportion of the labour force. As a result, people engaged in economic activities in the urban 'informal sector' constitute a large and increasing proportion of the labour force (Davies and Sanders, 1987). It is anticipated that the current five-year Structural Adjustment Programme (SAP) will result in a reduction of the civil service by 20–25 per cent (25,000–30,000 jobs) and of private sector employment by 10 per cent (20,000 jobs) (*Facts and Reports*, 1991b, p. 17). It has been estimated that US$3.75 billion is required to provide jobs simply for the new entrants into the labour force – which is equivalent to 75 per cent of the GDP (*Facts and Reports*, 1991c, p. 16).

Impact on women's economic roles and status
As in most African countries cultural prescriptions associated with gender stipulate that a woman in Zimbabwe has major reproductive, productive and domestic roles to play: to reproduce and extend the familial line, to facilitate economic production and to feed the family. Women perform all food-related tasks, taking responsibility for the seed from its germination through to its appearance at the family table. The surplus sold to the Grain Marketing Board is the man's preserve.

Women are also expected to supplement the family economy by engaging in non-agricultural activities. They are not expected to buy cattle, but keeping small live-stock such as goats and sheep is common (Kazembe, 1986). Implicit in all this is the expected role of women, which precludes acquisition of wealth for themselves, but instead insists that they reinvest all their profits in caring for and maintaining the family – perceived as the 'essence of womanhood'. These practices are highly institutionalised; they are derived from the cultural practice of bride-wealth payment, according to which a woman's labour is a man's 'possession'; land use rights are also vested in the man (Kazembe, 1986). Whenever there are religious festivals women are expected to brew the beer, prepare the food and ululate while the men perform the rituals – men's traditional prerogative. There was very little value placed on female participation in economic activities outside the home in either the pre-colonial or the colonial period (Kazembe, 1986, p. 379).

After completing her child-bearing, a woman traditionally assumes another familial role, that of guiding (socialising) her daughter-in-law and making important decisions, including those relating to the rearing and feeding of the grandchildren, particularly the termination of breast-feeding to facilitate a subsequent pregnancy.

Despite the pervasive power of cultural prescriptions regarding women's roles, it is vital to look at the complex nature of development in Zimbabwe's history, and in particular the implications for women. Indeed, a historical overview of Zimbabwe's underdevelopment is essential because 'to understand the role of rural women, we have to first look at the determinants of agricultural production and the division of labour by sex. Similarly, to understand changes in agricultural production and household allocation of labour, we have to understand the changing demands of the world economy' (ILO, 1984, p. 10).

The creation and manipulation of the migrant labour system has produced a significant degree of structural differentiation of Zimbabwe's dependent economy that affects the very nature of work (ILO, 1984, pp. 29–33; Mazur, 1986). Gender differences in constraints and opportunities are pronounced, again reflecting the purposes of those who institutionalised the migrant labour system (Seidman, 1981). Yet differentiation of socio-economic positions and characteristics among women is equally noteworthy (Cutrufelli, 1983, pp. 115–116). Thus, it is necessary to examine the nature of changes affecting women that are occurring in peasant farming and commercial farming, and in the urban informal and formal sectors. To date, no study exists that adequately describes these structural differences in women's socio-economic position, let alone analyses their implications for understanding patterns of fertility in Zimbabwe.

Zimbabwean women are acutely conscious of the tremendous variety of social and economic problems that face them, many derived directly or indirectly from manipulative colonial regulations, policies and institutions. What follows is a summary of the problems discussed by the Zimbabwe Women's Bureau (1981), Muchena (1982a, b, 1984), Weiss (1986) and Batezat et al. (1988). Necessarily of primary concern is the fact that Zimbabwean women traditionally used to remain legal minors throughout their lives. This particularly limited a woman's rights to enter into a contract, to rent a house in a township, to own or inherit property, to maintain child custody, even to open a bank account or belong to a savings club (Ncube, 1987). This situation was officially reversed in December 1982, with the enactment of the Legal Age of Majority Act, which stipulated that anyone who reaches the age of 18 is legally considered an adult. This is gradually becoming the norm, despite initial problems of acceptance and implementation (Kazembe, 1986).

In agriculture, the generally deteriorating position of women under the semi-proletarian system of colonial capitalist development has been well documented. One legacy of the institutionalised migrant labour system in Zimbabwe is the prevalence of split families, in which women remain behind, dependent on irregular and generally insufficient remittances from their 'temporary migrant worker' husbands, as has occurred elsewhere in Southern Africa (Cliffe, 1978; First, 1983; Bryceson, 1985). Women operate as de facto (but rarely de jure) heads of farming households, without formal access to extension services, credit, transportation or marketing channels (Mutuma et al., 1987). Few have access to land in their own right. Even the resettlement programme introduced immediately after independence designates usufructuary rights almost exclusively to men (Pankhurst and Jacobs, 1988). Irrigation schemes are principally controlled by men (Kachingwe, 1986, p. 30).

As throughout Africa, when the peasant sector is incorporated into the nexus of commercial crop production, women in Zimbabwe are often displaced when it comes to making decisions about cash crops and new technology for agricultural production and food-processing (Cutrufelli, 1983, pp. 120–123; ILO, 1984, pp. 12–13; Kachingwe, 1986, pp. 27–28). Related changes result in simultaneously increasing women's overall agricultural workload and strengthening their traditional obligations to grow vegetables and process food in order to feed the household. Moreover, a fundamental contradiction is revealed when it is considered that 'the introduction of private property and consequent allotment of land [to cash crops], by forcing women to spend more time in moving from one field to another and often far-away fields, have made it impossible for them to attend literacy or refresher courses on farming' (Cutrufelli, 1983, p. 120).

Analyses of women's activities and status in the communal, family resettlement, co-operative and small-scale freehold areas were undertaken by Cheater (1981), Muchena (1982c) and Mazur (1986). In the communal areas, women engage in ground-breaking, ploughing, planting, weeding, harvesting, gardening and cattle-herding; they are occasionally assisted by men. In the family resettlement areas, both women and men engage in all types of agricultural activity, though men are sometimes exclusively responsible for ground-breaking and ploughing – noteworthy is the use of tractors for this! Men operate tractors in the co-operatives also, and share the harvesting and cattle-tending, while women are primarily responsible for planting and weeding. As in the family resettlement and co-operative subsectors, male heads of households in the small-scale freehold subsector almost never become migrants; this is often legally proscribed. In contrast to the other areas, women in the freehold areas do control at least some of the proceeds of their agricultural labour. This occurs whether women are direct producers, managers with hired labourers, or outright owners; it is most extensive in the latter situation.

While recognising the wide variety of activities engaged in by women to supplement their agricultural income (such as selling fruit and vegetables, cooking, brewing beer, sewing, knitting, homecraft projects, and raising small livestock for sale), programmes to improve women's position in rural areas should place more emphasis on supporting women's activities in agricultural production (Muchena, 1982c, p. 15; Kachingwe, 1986, pp. 30–33). To date, the great variety of locally initiated informal co-operatives that exist among Zimbabwe's rural population (see GOZ, 1983b, p. 3; Bratton, 1986) have received little or no support from the government (Zimbabwe Women's Bureau, 1981). Providing initial financial support for these co-operatives while they retain local autonomy, flexibility and accountability is increasingly crucial.

Studies of urban women by May (1979) and Muchena (1980) revealed that women characteristically find themselves in a precarious economic position with great demands placed upon them. Few women know their husbands' actual earnings, and most are only given allowances, and yet women are responsible for most types of domestic expense (usually excluding rent). Women are often caught in the contradictory position of facing such restrictions while at the same time their husbands encourage, or even require, them to engage in extra-domestic economic activities to increase the family income. Discrimination against women in wage employment by employers is reinforced by husbands, who fear that women with independent sources of income will become uncontrollable. Further, their access to trading and commercial activities is restricted, they are exploited in industry and the 'global assembly line' (Made and Lagerstrom, 1985), they are relegated to predominantly low-status, poorly paying 'women's occupations' (Kazembe, 1986, p. 385), and their overall opportunities are limited because child-care services are almost never provided (Kazembe, 1986, p. 399).

Relegation of women to household activities and self-employment in petty trade in vegetables, clothing, or sewn, knitted and crocheted items amounts to little more than a labour-intensive method of subsidising the capitalist sector through maintenance of the semi-proletarian household, rather than genuine income generation. More than one-quarter of formally employed women are in domestic service and larger numbers balance their opportunities and commitments by engaging in informal sector activities (small-scale production, repairs and petty trading), though the work is usually hard and requires long hours.

Urban women's informal sector activities are extremely diverse, including crocheting, knitting, dressmaking, embroidery, selling vegetables and fruit, and selling prepared food at industrial sites, beer halls and 'shabeens' (GOZ, 1983b, p. 3). Yet they generally lack an organised structure to represent their interest (Brand, 1986, p. 73), they are exploited by middlemen, and the 'lack of credit facilities also hampers the development of this sector. Financial institutions do not entertain loans to women even when they organised' (GOZ, 1983b, p. 5). Finally, as Gaidzanwa (1984, p. 22) notes,

[much] petty commodity production depends on inputs from the large capitalist producers
. . . vegetable vendors order their vegetables from commercial farmers who grow them on
a large scale and highly capitalised basis. The same applies to the women who make and
sell knitted and crocheted goods when it comes to yarn and other inputs necessary for their
small scale production. This kind of relationship can hardly be termed 'informal'.

With structural links developed to multinational firms as regards inputs and, frequently, export markets, 'women's activities' often represent super-exploitation of
women and their families, who work in relatively unregulated, unsupported and
insecure conditions (Gaidzanwa, 1984, pp. 23–25).

Women readily cite the 'culturally' institutionalised discrimination at early phases
of the life cycle that denies them the necessary educational qualifications to compete
equally in the urban formal economy. The difficulties inherent in transforming their
economic position are easier to understand when it is recognised that in 1982, for
example, approximately equal numbers of girls and boys were enrolled in Grade 1
but girls constitute only 43 per cent of those in Grade 7 and 33 per cent of those
in Form 6 (GOZ, 1985a, p. 39). The latter figures clearly represent the effects of pre-
independence limitations on enrolments. However, the removal of discriminatory
educational policies at independence in 1980 resulted in a tremendous expansion of
education, which has benefited women. Primary school enrolment more than doubled
between 1979 and 1984 while primary and secondary schools increased by 173 per
cent and 638 per cent, respectively. The proportion of women who had not attended
school decreased from 18 per cent in 1984 to 14 per cent in 1988 (Mhloyi, 1992).
A greater proportion of women in rural areas do not attend school. However, the proportion of women with no formal schooling in rural areas decreased from 23 per cent
to 17 per cent while that in urban areas declined from 9 per cent to 6 per cent. Educational attainment is negatively associated with age, with the 15–24-year age cohort
experiencing a 50 per cent reduction in the proportion that had not attended school
(Mhloyi, 1992). Urban areas benefited more than rural areas. For instance, the proportion of women aged 15–24 years who had at least secondary education increased
twice as much in urban areas as in rural areas. Unfortunately the bias against girls
having a chance to attain higher levels of education is likely to be reinforced to some
extent with the reintroduction of school fees in 1992 as part of Zimbabwe's 1991–96
Structural Adjustment Programme. Another consequence of this is the reduction in
public spending.

Women are highly represented relative to men in certain aspects of the formal
economy's occupational structure: in 1982 they constituted 52 per cent of all sales
workers and 40 per cent of professional and technical workers, many of the latter
being teachers and nurses (GOZ, 1985a, p. 126). They were moderately represented
among clerical workers (34 per cent) and service workers (32 per cent), but constituted
relatively few of administrative and managerial workers (15 per cent) or production
workers (14 per cent). When women's employment is considered according to occupational group and racial classification (GOZ, 1983a, p. 76), African women are highly
represented among female production workers (74 per cent), salesworkers (66 per
cent) and professional and technical workers (59 per cent), the latter again consisting
primarily of teachers and nurses. In contrast, they constitute only 38 per cent of
salesworkers, 24 per cent of clerical workers, and 12 per cent of female administrative
and managerial workers.

Prior to independence, women in formal employment could be discharged when they became pregnant. Use of family planning clinics at the industrial sites where they worked was common, reflecting these coercive conditions. We now turn to an assessment of the current demographic situation, particularly concerning fertility, and how it relates to the issues outlined.

Demographic Situation and Trends

Population size, growth and distribution

Zimbabwe's population was enumerated as 7.55 million in August 1982, and is now estimated to be over 10 million, growing by 3 per cent annually with a high age-dependency ratio of 101 (GOZ, 1985a, pp. 11, 32). The population density of 19.3 persons per square kilometre is not high by world standards, but as only 36 per cent of the country's total area is suitable for regular cultivation (designated as Natural Regions I, II and III), this requires a realistic upward revision of the overall density ratio by a factor of three. The arable land is divided so that the approximately 5000 large-scale commercial farms (1 per cent of all farms) have 52 per cent of this land, the 8000 medium-scale freehold farms (1 per cent of all farms) have 6 per cent, the 36,000 household resettlement farms (5 per cent of all farms) have 9 per cent, and the 675,000 communal farms (93 per cent of all farms) have 33 per cent (Weiner et al., 1985, p. 259; Palmer, 1990, p. 169). The population is concentrated in these higher-quality agricultural zones, along the principal transport lines, and in the major urban areas. The urban population represented 26 per cent of the 1982 total and was growing by 5.6 per cent per year, with at least several cities and towns in every size class growing even more rapidly (GOZ, 1984, pp. 9, 29–30).

Mortality

It is difficult to know precisely the extent of infant, child and adult mortality since the vital registration system is only partially established. Thus, the estimates of infant mortality as ranging from 60 to 95 per thousand live births and life expectancy as 56 years for males and 59 years for females are necessarily based on methods of indirect estimation (GOZ, 1985a, pp. 171–173, 178–179, 1985b, p. 73).

Fertility

The principal sources of fertility estimates are the 1982 Census of Population (GOZ, 1985a, pp. 131–165), the 1984 Zimbabwe Reproductive Health Survey (RHS) (GOZ, 1985b), and the Demographic and Health Survey (DHS) of 1987–88 (GOZ, 1989). Total fertility rates estimated from these data are 5.6, 6.5 and 5.7, respectively. The apparent increase in fertility between 1982 and 1984 is largely an artefact of variations in the quality of data according to their respective sources: census data tend to underestimate fertility. Indirect estimations produce a total fertility rate slightly higher than 6.5 for 1982. Thus, a fertility decline is under way in Zimbabwe. Cumulative fertility has also declined. For instance, fertility for women aged 45–49 declined from 7.5 in 1984 to 5.0 in 1988 (Table 9.1).

Fertility policy and family planning

Consistent with the political peripheralisation of the Africans, the demography of the African population was left to speculation from the first census in 1901 until the 1962

Table 9.1 Current and cumulative fertility by woman's age, Zimbabwe, 1969–88

Age of woman	Age-specific fertility rate					Mean number of children ever born			
	1988	1984	1982	1981		1988	1984	1982	1969
10–14	–	–	0.001	–		–	–	–	–
15–19	0.103	0.131	0.091	0.073		0.2	0.3	0.2	0.3
20–24	0.247	0.289	0.258	0.247		1.3	1.6	1.5	1.7
25–29	0.347	0.299	0.253	0.262		2.9	3.2	3.1	3.4
30–34	0.219	0.263	0.225	0.235		4.1	4.6	4.7	4.9
35–39	0.160	0.220	0.165	0.183		4.8	6.2	5.9	5.9
40–44	0.086	0.092	0.093	0.110		4.9	7.0	6.8	6.6
45–49	0.036	0.011	0.038	0.050		5.0	7.5	7.2	6.9
TFR	5.49	6.52	5.62	5.80	CEB	5.0	7.5	7.2	6.9

Sources: 1988 data are from GOZ, 1989.
1984 data are from GOZ, 1985b, Tables 4.6 and 4.10.
1982, 1981 and 1969 data are from GOZ, 1985a.

and 1969 censuses, which provided the most detailed African demographic data so far – crude estimates of total population size and some other characteristics (GOZ, 1985a, p. 7). There was no formal 'population policy' during this period other than the notorious pre-independence migration laws, nor was there a sound database for any such policy. Yet attempts were made to affect one of the most important population factors: fertility. Family planning services were introduced in Zimbabwe (then Southern Rhodesia) in 1953. In 1965, the various uncoordinated family planning activities were consolidated into a single welfare organisation – the Family Planning Association of Rhodesia. The provision of family planning services was not viewed, initially, as a vehicle to reduce population growth. This is evidenced by the provision of services that were limited only to the white population, which comprised a very insignificant proportion (never more than 5 per cent) of the total population. In 1966, the Minister of Health approved the distribution of contraceptives from government hospitals, thereby making family planning services available to some segments of the African population.

In 1970, field educators were deployed and women were trained to distribute contraceptives. This was essential preparation for an expanded family planning programme. However, it is important to note that, while provision of family planning services, particularly to the African communities, could have been timely from a demographic point of view, the political situation negated such efforts, which were viewed simply as colonial genocidal policies (Clarke, 1972, p. 46). Further, the socio-economic environment was not conducive to deliberate use of modern contraception, particularly for limiting family size. Thus the Zimbabwean government in 1980 faced not only the problem of a lack of data for the formulation of an explicit and implementable policy, but also the need to avoid an outcry of neo-colonial genocide from the general public, while at the same time launching programmes to affect population growth.

In view of these and other planning problems, the government carried out the first comprehensive population census in 1982. At the same time, reference to the nation's high level of population growth was intricately woven into every section of the government's Transitional National Development Plan (GOZ, 1982, 1986). The latter facilitated a more direct influence over the existing Family Planning Association by the government. Thus, the Government of Zimbabwe took control of the Family Planning Association in September 1981, subsequently changing its name to the 'Child Spacing and Fertility Association' and then to the 'Zimbabwe National Family Planning Council' (ZNFPC). Since child spacing is deeply rooted in Zimbabwean culture this name change made a previously foreign-imposed practice seem more acceptable (Mhloyi, 1988). As communities changed, it began to be perceived as one of those inevitable changes brought by modernisation which becomes gradually more attractive with the erosion of traditional practices. Increasingly the President's statements in various addresses to the nation have become more explicit concerning support for the government's family planning programme. Consider this portion of his address at the 1985 Conservation Conference:

> We need also increasingly to focus on an issue that has tended to be given cursory attention in the last five years of our independence and that is the issue of population growth. The pressure on the land and its resources is partly, perhaps, a pressure of people. And whilst we do not propose in some crude arbitrary manner to limit population growth, we must nonetheless seek to achieve a definable relationship between population growth and the capacity of our country progressively to provide our growing population with their material requirements and other essential services at an adequate level.
>
> There is, quite simply, no point in having more people whose fate it will be to go without adequate food, shelter, health care or education. Hence the varied work of the Zimbabwe Child Spacing and Family Planning Council must be given every support possible by the public and Government Ministers alike. The Council, in conjunction with all relevant authorities and interested parties, should assist us in achieving a rate of population growth – for growth there must be – that is commensurate with our capacity to provide our people in their entirety with the means to live a better life all round. (Mugabe, 1985)

With the government's support, the Family Planning Council has intensified its activities in the country. Thus, the 28 family planning clinics, along with 200 other active institutions under the Ministry of Health, deliver family planning services throughout the country (GOZ, 1985b). Approximately 400 community-based distributors are deployed in rural areas to educate, motivate, and supply pills and condoms to clients. Family planning services are now provided not only for health reasons but also for demographic reasons, with the aim of limiting the country's rapid population growth. In addition, there is continuous emphasis by the Maternal and Child Health (MCH) programme on the importance of breast-feeding to enhance child health. Government has complemented such efforts by introducing a statutory breast-feeding hour for working mothers.

Women's Socio-Economic Status and Fertility

In this section, we examine the available evidence concerning the relationship between women's socio-economic status and fertility, both directly and as it operates through the proximate determinants. It is both important and revealing to consider the implications of these data, despite the limitations of census data. In an attempt to overcome some of the shortcomings of the official sources, preliminary results from two small-scale surveys that were conducted by Mazur – one rural in 1984 and the other urban in 1985 – are included in this analysis. The 1984 RHS and 1987–88 DHS survey data are utilised to assess the relationships between fertility and some of the socio-economic variables. Interpretation of such data is enhanced by use of qualitative information from an in-depth survey on 'Couples' perceptions of family formation' conducted by Mhloyi in 1984.

Proximate determinants of fertility
Previous research on fertility has demonstrated in both theoretical and empirical terms the efficacy of explicitly addressing the 'black box', the proximate determinants, as the immediate determinants of fertility (Bongaarts, 1984). Some have an involuntary effect on fertility, that is, post-partum amenorrhoea, primary sterility and secondary sterility. All these operate to diminish or prevent fertility. More directly relevant to our discussion are the proximate determinants that reflect voluntary limitation of fertility. Abstinence, due to either separation during a 'marital' union or observance of cultural taboos following a pregnancy, obviously has a primary impact. Contraception has a marked impact as well, with efficacy varying according to the particular method used. Finally, breast-feeding stimulates production of the prolactin hormone, which, to a certain extent, inhibits ovulation, thereby effectively reducing fertility both in an immediate sense, as regards the probability of a further pregnancy, and, *ceteris paribus*, over one's lifetime.

Involuntary limitation of fertility
Reporting of post-partum amenorrhoea is suspect. This may be partly explained by the fact that termination of the post-partum amenorrhoeic period is non-volitional and is therefore more susceptible to memory lapse than, say, breast-feeding (Mhloyi, 1987). This is also accentuated by the fact that little cultural or biological significance is attached to this variable by couples. The mean duration of post-partum amenorrhoea, according to Mhloyi's 1984 in-depth survey, was approximately 12 months. While the estimate of duration may not be precise, it is, however, consistent with that of breast-feeding, and also suggests the significance of the variable as a fertility depressant.

Breast-feeding is practised principally for its nutritional and immunological qualities. None the less, a modest proportion of women in the in-depth study, approximately 15 per cent, reported that they breast-fed their infants for long durations as a contraceptive method (Mhloyi, 1987). However, most women are not aware of the biological link between breast-feeding and post-partum amenorrhoea. Because of the perceived benefits of breast-feeding, this variable is more resistant to erosion than others. The reported mean duration of breast-feeding, according to the in-depth survey, is approximately 18 months, with 19.5 months noted for the older generation and 17 for the younger generation (Mhloyi, 1987). These estimates are consistent with those based on the RHS and DHS data. The duration of breast-feeding increased slightly between 1984 and 1988. It is also higher in rural than in urban areas. Breast-feeding also declines with education; however, there has been a larger than proportionate increase in the duration of breast-feeding among more educated women. This may be partly explained by the fact that it is the most educated working mothers who benefit from the statutory feeding time. Generally the emphasis by the Maternal and Child Health programme on the importance of breast-feeding may account for the overall sustenance of breast-feeding at such high levels.

Primary sterility is very low. Only 1–2 per cent of women aged 40–49 were reported as primarily sterile (GOZ, 1985b, p. 51). However, secondary sterility seems to affect women in certain zones of the country. While less than 1 per cent of women of reproductive age reported secondary sterility in one of the study areas covered by Mhloyi (1987), approximately 7 per cent reported it in the other. While sterility has a direct depressant effect on fertility, it also has an indirect positive effect on fertility as sterility is among the many side-effects of contraception dreaded by most women. Although no data are available to assess the association between regional and individual development conditions and sterility in Zimbabwe, the perceived indifference of the family planning programme to the problem of sterility, whether real or unfounded, creates a scepticism reminiscent of pre-colonial perceptions (Mhloyi, 1988).

In addition to the non-susceptible (to pregnancy) period conferred by breast-feeding, a small percentage (5 per cent) of women reported that they experienced 'temporary' separation from their husbands who were working in the urban areas. The reported rates of partner's absence were much higher in the RHS survey, as 39 per cent of rural women's partners were absent, with 23 per cent of urban women thus characterised (GOZ, 1985a, p. 47). However, for both rural and urban women, more than half of temporary separations were for periods of less than one month. Women generally do not perceive this experience as lost exposure to the risk of getting pregnant, since they claim that visits by either spouse are arranged to overlap with the period after termination of breast-feeding, at which point the couple attempts to achieve a further pregnancy. Yet one should not underestimate the latent negative effect of such temporary but common separations on cumulative fertility.

In the in-depth study, couples explained that exposure is also lost when an infant becomes ill, particularly with measles. It is believed that coitus when the child is having measles will stop the rash from developing. This, in turn, is believed to result in measles affecting the child's internal organs, consequently increasing the chances of death. Lost exposure due to such taboos is minimal, however, and rarely reported.

Voluntary limitation of fertility
Overall levels of contraceptive use in Zimbabwe are high, and more so in urban areas and among currently married women (Mhloyi, 1991). Ever-use of contraception increased from 53 per cent in 1984 to 60 per cent in 1988. The proportionate increase in ever-use is, however, larger in rural than in urban areas, 10 and 2 per cent, respectively (Mhloyi, 1991). It is also larger among the uneducated than the educated. Current contraceptive use increased slightly, from 31 to 32 per cent (after standardising for age distribution and excluding abstinence). Contraception within marriage increased by four percentage points. Current contraception declined slightly in urban areas and increased in rural areas, where there was a substantial increase among women aged 25–34, largely among the uneducated. A combination of a substantial increase in ever-use and a minimal change in current use suggests short durations of use and an increase in accepters.

The most obvious change in contraceptive patterns is in the methods used. There was a 36 per cent reduction in the use of traditional methods (Mhloyi, 1991) and a 19 per cent increase in the use of modern methods between 1984 and 1988. The pill remains the dominant method. The overall level of use of modern methods is higher in the rural areas, as is the increase in the proportion using modern methods, especially among uneducated rural women (Mhloyi, 1991). The relative gains as regards adoption and quality of contraception are thus greatest for uneducated rural women.

It seems that the socio-economic nexus within which decision-making as regards fertility takes place is generally conducive to the adoption of fertility control for limiting the total number of children. This can be attributed to the liberalising of attitudes towards contraception and abortion during the armed struggle and the changing socio-economic context during the post-independence era, which has greatly increased the cost of raising children (Mhloyi, 1987).

The impact of socio-economic status
The tremendous importance attached to, or even dependence on, large families in Zimbabwe has been specifically linked to the nature of rural underdevelopment and differentiation associated with the institutionalisation of the migrant labour system and selective development of capitalist relations of production in rural and urban areas. Clarke (1972, p. 40) asserts that, as economic conditions in the labour reserves deteriorated from the mid-1950s onwards, the average rural household was 'encouraged to protect itself, on the basis of maximising security and minimising risk, by maintaining or increasing its size'. The links with the migrant labour system are made clear in the following passage: 'not only does the existence of additional children increase aggregate family income and the expectation that one of the migrants in the family will be fortunate in securing a high earning job, but a large number of children would also increase the expectation and continuity of cash remittances' (Clarke, 1972, p. 39). As observed elsewhere in Africa, the value of this 'logic' would not necessarily be diminished by rising urban unemployment and the growth of the informal sector, as the striving to have at least one child who is successful may even increase, thereby maintaining high fertility levels. During the last three decades, wage employment has not been expanding rapidly enough to transform the economy effectively or, more specifically, its 'traditional' sex-stratified division of labour, both within the family and in the wider society (Clarke, 1972, pp. 42–43; GOZ, 1986, pp. 6, 48).

It has been widely asserted that socio-economic status has an important impact on fertility – both directly and indirectly via its influence on the proximate determinants of fertility. Later age at marriage is generally believed to lead to lower fertility by restricting exposure to pregnancy. In turn, higher levels of education generally have a negative impact on fertility, partly through delaying age at marriage while pursuing higher levels of education and developing a work commitment prior to marriage (United Nations, 1985, p. 51), and partly through affecting people's perspective on the costs (financial and opportunity) and benefits of having many children and beginning child-bearing early (Cochrane, 1983). Further, actual work, or economic activity, is affected (but not determined) by education.

In Zimbabwe, although early marriage remains the norm its practice is diminishing. Official estimates from the 1982 census indicate that 26 per cent of women aged 15–19 were married, with 77 per cent of those aged 20–24 and 91 per cent of those aged 25–29 having married; about 3 per cent never married (GOZ, 1985a, pp. 38–39). The concept of marriage was broadened to include consensual unions in the 1984 Reproductive Health Survey. The corresponding rates were 48 per cent for women aged 15–19, 92 per cent for those aged 20–24, and 99 per cent for women aged 25–29 (GOZ, 1985b, p. 44), and 18 per cent, 61 per cent and 82 per cent for the respective age groups in 1988 (Mhloyi, 1991). Thus, entry into consensual unions and marriage remains nearly universal, but early marriage in particular is decreasing.

Table 9.2 classifies rural and urban women according to education, work status and

Table 9.2 Percentage distribution of socio-economic characteristics of women by residence, Zimbabwe, 1984 and 1988

	1984		1988	
	Rural	Urban	Rural	Urban
Education				
No. education	23.0	8.9	17.0	6.4
Primary	66.2	58.0	62.6	42.6
Secondary +	10.7	33.1	20.4	51.0
Work status				
Not working	67.8	59.6	69.9	59.5
Working	32.2	40.4	30.1	40.5
Education of partner				
No education	12.3	3.6	15.5	4.8
Primary	68.3	50.5	61.8	39.4
Secondary +	19.4	45.8	22.7	55.9

Sources: GOZ, 1985b, 1989.

education of partner, as indicated by the 1984 RHS and 1988 DHS surveys. As noted earlier, the post-independence expansion in education benefited women. Although the differentials between rural and urban areas remain, they are declining. For instance, while overall illiteracy rates declined in both rural and urban areas, the differential between rural and urban areas declined from 14 to 11 per cent. However, the proportion of women who had completed secondary or higher education increased by only 10 per cent in rural areas compared with 18 per cent in urban areas. The partners of women who are currently in a union also tend to be more highly educated in urban than in rural areas. However, men remain more educated than their female counterparts, despite relative gains in education being lower among males than among females.

Working for remuneration, either for cash or for payment in kind, was higher among urban (40 per cent) than rural (32 per cent) women in 1984. There was almost no change in labour force participation between 1984 and 1988. Although this may be partly explained by the differences in definition, it is also partly a reflection of the fact that there has been no significant change in labour force participation. Among those working, rural women are predominantly engaged in agricultural, service, craft, and skilled or unskilled labour activities. In comparison, urban women are more highly represented in professional, technical and managerial positions, clerical jobs, and skilled or unskilled labour activities.

It is possible, however, that the almost universal omission of a more explicit treatment of a woman's social class, both independent of and in conjunction with her partner, leads to conclusions which are either spurious or irrelevant. It may be, as Kabeer (1985) has asserted, that a woman's social class is the essential determinant of her education, her labour force and occupational status, and the value – or even almost total reliance – that she places on ensuring her survival in the uncertain future by producing many children, especially sons, early in the life cycle. The contradictions inherent in the position of poor women needing assistance from their children who are themselves unlikely to achieve socio-economic mobility can be noted but not easily reconciled with their actual fertility. The overall evidence linking women's work to lower fertility is therefore substantial, but detailed specification and consistent interpretation remain inconclusive (Standing, 1983).

The 'role incompatibility' assumed to exist among working women who are also raising young children is less than overwhelmingly supported by the evidence. In the United Republic of Tanzania, for example, it was observed that 'there was no substantial difference between the average number of children per women in the waged and self-employed groups, and there were no signs of women withdrawing from the labour force during peak reproductive years' (Bryceson, 1985, p. 146). In developing countries, the constraints on fulfilling both roles are shaped by the nature of the economic activity (i.e. the type and amount of activity, flexibility of scheduling, seasonality, substitutability) and the relative availability of child-care (Standing, 1983; United Nations, 1985, p. 6). Expansion of the idea of women's roles by Oppong (1983) to include maternal, conjugal, domestic, occupational, kin, community and individual roles is conceptually useful in understanding the myriad possibilities for role conflict and, thus, the multidimensional opportunity costs associated with fertility and raising children for working women. This resolves some of the methodological and theoretical concerns about measuring 'women's work' and assessing its relation to fertility, but the lack of systematic data sets incorporating the required information has to date hindered the full utilisation of this approach.

Perhaps the most complete and thoroughly analysed appropriate data source currently available is the mid-1970s Malaysian Family Life Survey. DaVanzo and Lee (1983) have drawn from their analysis of these data several important findings: production and sales occupations are more compatible with on-the-job care of young children (under age 5) than professional, managerial, clerical and even agricultural activities; availability (and, by implication, affordability) of alternative child-care and/or a work substitute seems principally to determine these patterns; as the number of hours a mother works outside the home increases, some of the child-care responsibilities are assumed by husbands, older children and others (including non-household members); and, overall, working mothers primarily reduce their leisure time rather than the time they spend on child-care and domestic responsibilities. Finally, it may be, as Lewis (1982, p. 237) has observed, that working women's achievement of 'balance' between their economic activities and child-care is less a mechanical problem – as the role incompatibility idea is too often articulated – than a social process; stress between multiple desirable and necessary roles is perhaps the most appropriate focus of understanding.

Ultimately, it has been asserted that when the influence of age, education, place of residence and social class has been statistically controlled, the strength of the relationship between women's work and fertility may be significantly reduced (United Nations, 1985, pp. 23–52). It is important to note, however, that such background variables may help us understand who works and in what types of activity, but do not necessarily diminish the meaning of the relationship between work and fertility. Indeed, it underscores the need for more detailed investigation into the nature of this complex relationship.

The relationship between socio-economic characteristics and fertility, with the latter measured by the number of children ever born alive (CEB), is depicted in Table 9.3. The data presented here are the observed values, which have been standardised to eliminate the influence of underlying age differences. The first important observation is that fertility is lower among urban than rural women, across all socio-economic characteristics. Moreover, women's education has a significant depressant effect on

Table 9.3 Mean number of children ever born to women classified by socio-economic characteristics and residence, Zimbabwe, 1984 and 1988

	Residence			
	1984		1988	
	Rural	Urban	Rural	Urban
Education				
No education	4.2	3.3	4.2	3.7
Primary	3.3	2.8	3.1	2.9
Secondary +	1.4	0.8	0.8	1.3
Work status				
Not working	2.9	2.2	2.6	1.9
Working	3.8	2.8	3.2	2.5
Education of partner				
No education	4.2	3.3	4.2	3.5
Primary	3.3	2.8	4.1	3.6
Secondary +	2.8	2.2	2.4	2.7

Sources: GOZ, 1985b, 1989.

fertility, more dramatically so among rural women. The most significant difference is that between women who have completed primary education and those with at least some secondary education. Similar educational differences were observed in the 1982 census, as women with no education had 3.6 CEB, those with some or completed primary education had 2.8, and those with at least some secondary education had 1.2 (GOZ, 1985a, p. 162). Although fertility was negatively associated with education in both 1984 and 1988, the fertility of women with higher education increased slightly while that of uneducated women declined. While partner's education is also negatively related to fertility, the differentials between the educated and the uneducated are not as large as with women. In 1984, for instance, uneducated women had 3.2 more CEB than their educated counterparts; the corresponding figure for men is 2.0 CEB. In 1988, the corresponding figures were 3.0 CEB and 1.6 CEB for women and men, respectively.

The only measure of women's work available to assess fertility differentials was whether or not a woman was working for remuneration. From these highly aggregated figures (Table 9.3), it can be seen that women working has a positive relationship with fertility in both rural and urban areas and in both 1984 and 1988. This may suggest that high fertility often leads women to seek paid employment. Again, these data need to be interpreted with caution since the measurement of work is inconsistent and of questionable accuracy. An assessment of the association between fertility and several dimensions of women's socio-economic status is provided by the data from Mazur's 1984 rural survey and 1985 urban survey, contained in Tables 9.4 and 9.5, respectively. It is important to note that occasional deviations from meaningful patterns are perhaps more likely to be due to the small sample size and the effects of bivariate cross-classification than to substantive differences.

Among rural women (see Table 9.4), education is associated with lower fertility, with the effect being strongest for those aged 15–29. Fertility is lowest among never-married women, as expected, and consistently highest for women in monogamous unions, though women who are divorced, separated or widowed have the highest

Table 9.4 Number of children ever born among rural women surveyed by age and socio-economic characteristics, Zimbabwe, 1984

Socio-economic characteristics	N	Age of woman						
		15–19	20–24	25–29	30–39	40–49	50+	Total
Education								
No schooling	240	0.81	1.94	3.30	5.66	6.83	8.51	5.30
Some primary	245	0.03	1.81	2.86	5.75	7.32	7.81	3.38
Completed primary	30	0.20	0.67	2.17	5.10	7.67	–	3.07
Secondary and more	30	0.00	0.00	4.00	–	–	–	0.13
Marital status								
Married monogamous	233	0.91	2.10	3.19	6.02	7.38	9.03	5.33
Married polygamous	150	0.57	1.90	3.56	5.40	6.51	7.50	4.94
Div./sep./widowed	32	–	2.00	2.00	4.86	7.50	7.76	6.38
Never married	130	0.03	0.13	0.50	0.00	–	–	0.06
Occupation								
Clearing land	337	0.09	1.50	3.21	5.99	7.76	8.86	3.97
Not clearing	208	0.24	1.88	2.79	5.10	6.13	7.71	4.12
Ploughing	340	0.09	1.47	3.16	5.99	7.70	8.67	3.97
Not ploughing	205	0.23	1.96	2.85	5.10	6.21	7.88	4.12
Planting	500	0.13	1.63	3.13	5.77	6.95	8.43	3.94
Not planting	45	0.25	1.67	1.75	4.13	8.50	7.94	4.98
Weeding	498	0.13	1.63	3.17	5.78	6.95	8.38	3.94
Not weeding	47	0.29	1.75	1.40	4.30	8.50	8.06	4.89
Harvesting	490	0.11	1.64	3.18	5.74	6.95	8.58	3.96
Not harvesting	55	0.44	1.50	2.00	4.82	8.50	7.53	4.66
Marketing	145	0.13	1.73	3.57	6.09	7.24	8.30	4.83
Not marketing	400	0.14	1.61	2.83	5.45	6.91	8.31	3.74
Gardening	283	0.17	1.81	3.40	6.02	7.24	8.54	4.11
Not gardening	262	0.10	1.39	2.62	5.29	6.71	8.16	3.94
Tending cattle	130	0.16	1.60	3.47	6.22	8.13	8.53	4.08
Not tending	415	0.13	1.64	2.95	5.43	6.78	8.25	4.01
Work group	22	0.00	1.00	4.57	5.60	7.60	11.00	5.05
Not in group	523	0.14	1.65	2.90	5.65	6.99	8.27	3.98
Non-agric. work	20	0.00	2.33	4.00	4.25	5.33	4.00	3.65
No non-agric.	525	0.14	1.59	3.01	5.70	7.15	8.37	4.04
Subsector								
Freehold	97	0.13	0.70	3.00	6.18	6.29	8.62	4.79
Resettlement	178	0.10	1.61	2.87	5.95	7.95	8.65	3.74
Training farm	144	0.28	2.21	3.13	5.30	5.76	7.31	3.79
Communal	126	0.06	1.27	3.06	5.32	7.96	7.69	3.93

Source: Preliminary results of small-scale rural survey carried out in 1984 by R.E. Mazur.

overall fertility, given their concentration at the older ages where cumulative fertility is highest. Women aged 25 and over, and even those aged 20 and over, who are engaged in the wide variety of agricultural activities recorded have consistently higher fertility than those not doing such work. In a complementary manner, those engaged in non-agricultural income-earning activities have somewhat lower fertility. Viewed from another perspective, it appears that women with more children engage in agricultural activities, and those with fewer children are more likely to have non-agricultural sources of income. Which agriculture subsector a woman belongs to has no clear influence on fertility.

Table 9.5 Number of children ever born among urban women surveyed by age and socio-economic characteristics, Zimbabwe, 1985

Socio-economic characteristics	N	Age of woman					
		15–19	20–24	25–29	30–39	40+	Total
Education							
No schooling	23	0.00	2.00	3.60	4.63	4.50	3.91
Some primary	115	0.63	1.74	2.90	5.25	4.77	3.10
Completed primary	64	1.00	1.67	3.06	3.27	3.50	2.41
Secondary and more	59	0.18	1.06	2.11	6.75	0.00	1.17
Marital status							
Married	185	1.18	1.68	3.05	5.52	6.17	3.24
Div./sep./widowed	34	1.00	1.00	1.33	1.67	2.42	1.74
Never married	42	0.14	1.00	–	–	–	0.26
Occupation							
Unemployed	146	0.31	1.50	2.56	4.18	4.22	1.88
Selling food	23	1.00	1.55	4.00	5.78	5.50	4.26
Selling clothes	34	1.50	2.00	2.50	4.91	5.00	3.29
Sewing, making dresses	25	0.00	1.75	4.14	4.75	1.50	3.36
Unskilled labour	20	0.50	1.60	3.75	5.40	3.25	3.20
Semi-skilled/prof.	13	0.00	1.33	2.50	5.00	6.00	2.69
Occupational status							
Self-employed	88	1.00	1.85	3.32	5.19	4.00	3.55
Employee	21	1.00	1.63	3.00	5.40	5.67	3.33
Employment status							
Part-time/casual	61	1.25	1.93	3.39	4.89	5.71	3.62
Full-time	47	0.00	1.64	3.09	5.77	3.13	3.34
Work location							
At home	55	0.33	1.88	3.64	5.75	5.50	3.76
In township	18	2.00	1.67	2.17	5.17	4.50	3.33
In city	31	2.00	1.71	3.43	4.11	3.29	3.16

Source: Preliminary results of small-scale urban survey carried out by R.E. Mazur in 1985.

Several different measures, including participation in the informal sector, reveal the importance of socio-economic status in relation to fertility among urban women (see Table 9.5). Education is clearly related to lower fertility, particularly for those women with at least some secondary education. Married women also have the highest fertility and never married women the lowest; divorced, separated or widowed women have moderate fertility levels. Among women who are working, those with lower status occupations (especially women selling vegetables, fruits and prepared foods) have higher fertility. Unemployed women have relatively moderate fertility levels. Finally, several dimensions of informal sector activities are instructive to consider. It is only self-employed women between the ages of 20 and 29 that have higher fertility than women employees, which suggests that the incompatibility between formal employment and fertility applies only for women who have achieved formal employment since new, higher-status occupations have been 'opened up' for African women. That formally employed women aged 30 and over have more children than their self-employed counterparts also suggests the greater burdens on formally employed women prior to independence. In a related way, women who work on a part-time or casual basis, or who work at home or in their township away from the central city, have higher fertility. Thus, from these data, it appears that all dimensions of women's higher socio-economic status considered here, in both urban and rural areas, are at least moderately associated with lower fertility, though this is not apparent from the two national surveys.

Women's work might also be linked to contraceptive use and breast-feeding practices. It is commonly asserted that differences in fertility between women in different occupations are at least partly due to differences in contraceptive use. International comparisons show that contraceptive use is highest in more 'modern' occupations. Some of this variation has been explained by differences in age, education, duration of marriage, place of residence, husband's occupation, and parity (United Nations, 1985, pp. 77–78). Yet occupation also has an independent effect on contraceptive use and, in turn, both occupation and contraception have a significant influence on fertility.

The prevalence, intensity and duration of breast-feeding have been observed to be lower among women who work away from home (Nag, 1983), though again such factors as education, income and place of residence are also important in explaining variations in breast-feeding practices. However, the loss of breast-feeding's fertility-inhibiting effect (via post-partum amenorrhoea) is 'outweighed by the deliberate limitation of fertility through contraceptive use by women who work in the modern sector of the economy' (United Nations, 1985, p. 82). No discernible relationship between women's work and fecundity has been consistently demonstrated as an explanation for fertility differentials.

In Zimbabwe, the duration of breast-feeding is lower only among women with at least some secondary education, about 16 months compared with the 19-month average (GOZ, 1985b, p. 76). In addition, the duration of breast-feeding increased proportionately more among more educated women between 1984 and 1988 (Mhloyi, 1991). This may partly reflect the effect of the legislated breast-feeding hour, which is likely to benefit most those educated women who have a chance to work in the formal sector. It is significant that women's working does not affect the duration of breast-feeding.

Finally, data pertaining to the relationship between socio-economic characteristics and contraceptive knowledge and use are presented in Table 9.6. The mean number of methods known increases with the respondent's and partner's education. However, partner's education is more strongly associated with knowledge of contraception than the respondent's. Similarly, current use increases with education, though the relationship is not monotonic when only the woman's education is considered. Women who have completed high school have the highest level of contraceptive use. Again, partner's education is associated with significantly higher levels of use than the woman's education. This may be partly explained by the fact that women who can report on their partner's education are themselves more educated, and possibly have more intimate relationships with and/or more influence on their husbands. It is also likely that husband's education is more important because men are assumed to be the decision-makers on household issues including fertility. Use of modern methods increases with education, while use of traditional methods is negatively related to education.

Table 9.6 Knowledge and practice of contraception among women according to socio-economic characteristics, Zimbabwe, 1984 and 1988

| | Socio-economic characteristics | | | | | | | |
| | Education | | | Work status | | Partner's education | | |
	No education	Primary	Secondary+	Not working	Working	No education	Primary	Secondary+
1984								
Number of methods known	1.1	1.6	1.9	1.4	1.9	1.2	1.7	2.2
Current use	22.9	33.5	29.8	25.9	40.2	23.6	34.8	45.0
Use modern	16.1	23.6	26.6	17.7	32.2	14.0	23.8	37.1
Use traditional	6.8	9.9	3.2	8.2	8.0	9.6	11.0	7.9
1988								
Number of methods known	1.3	1.8	2.2	1.7	2.2	1.5	2.0	2.6
Current use	30.0	33.7	30.4	28.8	38.8	32.6	40.5	50.5
Use modern	23.5	27.8	27.7	24.4	32.6	27.9	32.2	46.1
Use traditional	6.5	5.9	2.7	4.4	6.2	4.7	8.3	4.1

Source: Mhloyi, 1991.

Finally, knowledge of modern methods is positively related to work status. Contraceptive use is greater among women who are working; this difference is much greater for modern methods than traditional methods. It appears that work status differentiates women's knowledge and use of contraceptives more than education. The differentials as regards contraceptive use between uneducated and educated, working and non-working women, were reduced between 1984 and 1988. The difference in contraceptive use between the educated and uneducated was reduced from 7 per cent to less than 1 per cent. Among workers and non-workers the difference was reduced from 14 per cent to 10 per cent.

The Prospects for Change

Changes in the institutionalised patterns of discrimination and stereotyping made possible by women's vital role in the liberation struggle are yet to be fully realised (see Ngwenya, 1983; Weiss, 1986). It has been suggested that:

> Independence sharpened the divisions: between urban and rural life, between the educated and the uneducated, between the old and the young. *The young women who had fought returned to the cheers of the multitude and the silent disapproval of the family, particularly the male members.* Older women, too, resented the younger generation. They had been taught that submissiveness and obedience, coupled with the bearing of many children, was the road to respect. The new young woman, having grown up in a military camp and mixed on equal terms with young men, was often ignorant of village customs and did not fit into traditional society. (Weiss, 1986, pp. 104–105; emphasis added)

Rather than requiring individual solutions designed to aid reintegration of these women, these conflicts represent a unique opportunity to initiate and sustain the social transformation that will enable all women to share in the benefits of Zimbabwe's hard-won independence.

Widespread recognition of these problems, particularly during the United Nations Decade for Women (1975–85), has produced some increase in consciousness, the impact of which started to bear some fruit after 1985. However, the solution proposed for women's inability to control the earnings from their work in producing the principal marketed crops is most often the introduction of relatively unrewarding and burdensome 'income-generating projects', while 'employment opportunities' remain the distinct preserve of men (ILO, 1984, p. 7). What needs to be recognised is that 'There is need to support both formal and informal activities, those based on traditional sectors and also non-traditional, in services as well as production. It is not enough to wait until men move out of an activity into something more remunerative, for women to acquire a new skill or trade' (ILO, 1984, p. 34). These views are echoed by others (Muchena, 1982b; GOZ, 1983b). It remains open to debate whether the plethora of externally funded short-term, piecemeal 'women's projects' is ultimately deleterious, as governments become dependent on foreign assistance and fail to plan women's projects carefully themselves (ILO, 1984, p. 37).

In order to improve their social and economic situation women have initiated collective efforts since independence, though some were initiated even earlier. These include a variety of women's clubs concerned with adult literacy and other training, income-generating and an assortment of traditional 'home economics' activities (Muchena, 1982b). Further, a large number of women's co-operatives have been established

(Smith, 1987). Finally, nationwide organisations, such as the Zimbabwe Women's Bureau, the women's branches of the major political parties, and the newly created Ministry of Community Development and Women's Affairs (Mugabe, 1985; Kazembe, 1986), have established forums that are used to articulate women's social, economic and political problems and to devise solutions for these problems.

It is clear that there exist difficulties to be overcome. It is imperative that women continue their efforts to educate themselves and increase their own consciousness, to educate men who persist in 'traditional' attitudes and practices, and to organise themselves to generate resources and obtain new types of resources from government and donors that will be used in a manner consistent with their own goals. Government is complementing these efforts by making funds available to women who are interested in starting businesses. It appears that a new generation of businesswomen may appear during the 1990s.

It is important to highlight education as the one aspect of women's status that will ultimately affect their ability to compete in the modern labour market. Given the lag between education and training, on the one hand, and labour force participation, on the other, it is expected that there will be an increased level of female labour force participation in the 1990s. While the impact of education on fertility was via delayed entry into marriage during the 1984–88 period, during the 1990s it is expected that education will also have an impact on fertility via work status and lower demand for children. Mhloyi (1992) noted that in 1984 contraception was the most important of the proximate determinants in depressing fertility, followed by post-partum infertility and then marriage. However, the relative importance of the variables differed with women's educational level. For uneducated women the most important was post-partum infertility, followed by contraception and marriage. For women who had completed at least secondary school, on the other hand, the most important determinant was contraception, followed by marriage and finally post-partum infertility. The pattern for the most educated group is typical of a transitional society. Thus, educated women are leading the fertility transition via use of contraception and lower levels of marriage.

The relative impact of the variables changed between 1984 and 1988. The impact of post-partum infertility remained constant while that of contraception and marriage increased by five and eight percentage points, respectively (Mhloyi, 1992). The increased relative importance of contraception is largely due to a shift towards modern methods, which was greater among uneducated than educated women and also among non-working compared with working women. The increase in use in these groups can partly be explained by the increased cost of raising children (an aspect not covered in detail here but discussed in the 'Couple's Perceptions' study). The increase in the relative importance of marriage is, however, attributed largely to delayed age at marriage, which is due to an increase in education.

Conclusion

In this chapter, we have attempted to show the importance of taking explicitly into account the nature of 'underdevelopment' as institutionalised in Zimbabwe, in both quantitative and qualitative terms. The structure of economic and social development, in turn, has distinct effects on the demographic characteristics of Zimbabwe. The direct consequences of underdevelopment are initially manifest in the uneven distribution and movement of the population – with different patterns of migration associated with the respective subsectors in the rural economy (Mazur, 1986). Similar findings characterise the nature of health, morbidity and mortality (Gilmurray *et al.*, 1978; Davies and Sanders, 1987). Patterns of fertility differentials have also been demonstrated to reflect the nature of underdevelopment.

Zimbabwe is currently undergoing significant social change, which is in large part a response to the oppressive pre-independence conditions and the nature of the liberation struggle. The post-independence expansion of educational and health services to the previously excluded majority of the population is impressive (GOZ, 1986). However, the limits imposed on substantial transformation of the economy are equally noteworthy. The very real consequences of the inferior positions in which women find themselves have been well articulated (Zimbabwe Women's Bureau, 1981), which also reflects an awareness of the existing limits for transforming women's status.

It is important to mention that the disadvantaged position of women depicted here must not be erroneously perceived as comprising personal antagonism between men and women; rather, it consists of co-ordinated social systems deeply entrenched in the culture, systems which cannot be mechanically and expeditiously changed (Mhloyi, 1990). Thus, long-term changes in the status of women will entail fundamental and sustained social change such as changes in education, another form of socialisation. Unfortunately, the Structural Adjustment Programme which was initiated in 1992 may represent a setback for the education of women, largely because of the reintroduction of school fees. In the face of limited funds, parents may again favour sons over daughters in schooling. In most instances such decisions are made by both marriage partners. Because of their socialisation, girls themselves often volunteer to stay out of school to enable their brothers to go. Thus, long-term improvements in the status of women are expected to the extent that the overall economic situation improves.

It has been observed that age at marriage is rising somewhat. In turn, age at marriage and women's socio-economic status, as manifested in education, working for remuneration, and partner's education, are all associated with lower fertility. The impact of education on fertility is clearly demonstrated by the fact that the fertility pattern of women with at least secondary school education is typical of a transitional fertility situation, while women with no education have a pre-transitional pattern. Several dimensions of informal sector economic activity can also be seen to be related to higher fertility. It must be noted, however, that, while the impact on fertility of improvements in women's education is quite evident, any impact on fertility of changes in work status, or of evolving structural changes in the economy, must await the availability of more detailed and longitudinal data.

It remains for future studies to establish further links between case-studies of fertility and the issues of world system, status and dependency identified by Ward (1984). It is hoped that the quantitative and qualitative depiction of Zimbabwe's socio-economic structure in this chapter has contributed to that process. More research is needed to assess the actual improvements to women's status, both in general and in country-specific implementation of the recommendations made at the

1984 International Conference on Population (Boohene, 1985). Operationalisation in studies of the significant variables of role incompatibility and stress and changes in them, often produced through specific programmes and legislation designed to improve women's status, will also be of great value. Finally, new research methods need to be devised to begin assessing the diffuse impact on fertility of such fundamental processes as those initiated by the United Nations Decade for Women and the struggles for national liberation in Zimbabwe and elsewhere.

10 Women, Work & Fertility in Swaziland

ADERANTI ADEPOJU

Swaziland is one of Africa's smallest countries in both population and land area. The 1986 census enumerated 712,131 people (a resident population of 681,059 and 31,072 Swazi absentees temporarily working or living outside Swaziland). The estimate for 1990 was about 772,500, based on the 1976–86 growth rate of 3.2 per cent per year. In 1976, 479,685 *de facto* residents were enumerated. The Swazi people are a remarkably homogeneous group: in 1986 about 96 per cent of the population was Swazi, and only 4.4 per cent belonged to other ethnic groups. This is in sharp contrast to other countries in Africa, which are marked by ethnic diversity. In effect, an overwhelming majority of the population are ethnically Swazi, speak Swazi, and are subject to the same traditional laws and customs.

The population of Swaziland is predominantly rural: in 1976, 85 per cent of the population lived in rural areas, a small drop from the 1966 figure of 87 per cent. By 1986, 77 per cent of the population was so classified. Population distribution is remarkably uneven, varying significantly by ecological zone and type of land tenure. In 1976, the population of the Swazi Nation Land constituted 66 per cent of the total and was spread over 52 per cent of the total land area, with a population density of 36 people per square kilometre. Individual tenure farms occupied 47 per cent of the total land area, but only 19 per cent of the total population lived on them. Urban areas occupied the remaining 1 per cent of the land area, and 15 per cent of the population lived in them (Adepoju, 1991b).

Overall, the level of urbanisation is low: 13 per cent in 1966, 15 per cent in 1976 and 23 per cent in 1986. During this period, however, the country experienced rapid urban growth. While the population of towns, excluding industrial housing estates known as 'company towns', grew at an average annual rate of 4.5 per cent between 1966 and 1976 and 4.3 per cent in the 1976–86 period, the urban corridor in the western Middleveld grew at an annual rate of over 5 per cent, especially the country's two major towns, Manzini and Mbabane, which gained the lion's share of migrants. These towns are the country's major commercial and administrative centres, and accounted for 63 per cent of the urban population in 1966. By 1976, that proportion had increased to 69 per cent, but it had declined to 60 per cent by 1986. These

157

two towns accounted for 8 per cent and 10.5 per cent of the total population of the country in 1966 and 1976, respectively.

Traditionally, Swazis live in family units referred to as homesteads – collections of related people living and working together. The family is the basic unit of the social system in Swaziland. Although they belong to kinship groups and clans, families normally live in scattered homesteads. These homesteads are neither households nor villages in the conventional sense. The household is an integral part of the homestead and is not a separate residential unit. Traditionally, the family unit may acquire land, but neither the man nor the woman may hold land individually. The head of the homestead represents its members in all dealings with the chief and the king. Daughters are regarded as transient members of the homestead: they are expected to leave the homestead to marry and bear children in other lineages (Kuper, 1963; Matsebula, 1972).

In 1986, 63.7 per cent of the population (64.5 per cent of males and 63 per cent of females) aged 5 and over were classified as literate, a marked improvement from less than 50 per cent in 1976. The highest literacy rate was observed for the Manzini district (71 per cent), followed by the Hhohho and Shiselweni district (64 per cent each), with the Lubombo district trailing far behind (54 per cent). Except in the Shiselweni district, males led females in literacy status by a clear two percentage points. The reverse situation in the Shiselweni district (64 per cent for females; 63 per cent for males) is explained by the high rate of migration of young educated men to South Africa.

Information on external migration is based on census figures, but these are incapable of tapping clandestine migration. Migration, mainly to South Africa, is male-dominated: men constituted 66.7 per cent of the absentee population in 1966, 74.6 per cent in 1976, and 76.2 per cent in 1986 (Maro, 1990). The sex ratio in towns was 100 males for every 106 females in 1986. The districts with scarce resources topped the list: 42 per cent of the total absentee population originated from the Shiselweni district, followed by Hhohho district (23 per cent), Manzini district (20 per cent) and Lumbombo district (15 per cent).

Up to 1946 very few Swazi women participated in labour migration. The year 1966 was the peak when a full one-third of all absentees were women, up from 10 per cent a decade earlier. Since then, the proportion of female absentees has remained more or less stable at one-quarter (Table 10.1). Since 1911, absentees have constituted 5 per cent or more of the resident population. The female absentees recorded in the 1986 census are concentrated in the working group 15–44 years, as is the case with men.

Fertility and Mortality

Since the 1960s, the population of Swaziland has experienced a high level of fertility and slowly declining mortality. While the crude death rate declined only slightly, from 20 per thousand in 1966 to 18.5 in 1976 and 15 in 1986, the crude birth rate increased from 49 per thousand in 1966 to 52.5 in 1976, dropping to 47 per thousand in 1986 – reflecting the combined effect of early child-bearing and the desire for large families that is dominant in Swaziland (Government of Swaziland, 1978).

All this has resulted in a high rate of natural increase of the population: 2.8 per cent in 1966 and 3.4 per cent in 1976. The current annual population growth rate

Table 10.1 External migration from Swaziland, 1911–86

Year	De jure African population	Absentees	Absentees				Absentees as % of population
			Male		Female		
			N	%	N	%	
1911	104 533	5 800	5 700	98.3	100	1.7	5.60
1921	110 295	5 990	5 839	97.5	151	2.5	5.43
1936	153 270	9 561	9 451	97.6	235	2.4	6.23
1946	181 269	8 677	8 254	95.1	423	4.9	4.78
1956	229 744	11 728	10 569	90.1	1 159	9.9	5.10
1966	381 687	19 219	12 817	66.7	6 402	33.3	5.03
1976	520 184	25 650	18 903	74.6	6 447	25.4	4.93
1986	681 059	31 072	23 682	76.2	7 390	23.8	5.00

Source: Maro, 1990.

is estimated at 3.2 per cent. The high rate of population growth is reflected in the very young population. With some 47 per cent of the population less than 15 years of age in 1986 and 3 per cent or less aged 65 years and over, the dependency burden is high.

The high level of fertility is explained by a complex of inter-related factors: the significant contribution of children to agricultural activities in the predominantly rural country, the practice of polygyny, the absence of a modern social security system, the prevailing high level of infant mortality, the strong cultural preference for large families, the early start of child-bearing for women in spite of late marriage, and the low level of contraceptive use (Government of Swaziland, 1985).

Teenage pregnancies have increased dramatically in recent years, probably as a result of high school drop-outs and the social acquiescence as regards illegitimate births. The most urbanised regions tend to have the highest rates – a trend that is in general likely to increase as modernisation intensifies. It is thus age of entry into sexual union – and not necessarily age at first marriage – that indicates the onset of child-bearing and that is closely related to a woman's completed fertility (Adepoju, 1991a).

There are also observed variations in the level of fertility. Fertility varies inversely with the level of education. Education tends to postpone the start of family formation and to influence the number and spacing of births. As in other African countries, it is not education *per se* but a minimum number of years' schooling that has a negative impact on fertility. Thus, in 1976, Swazi women without any formal education had, on average, 6.27 children and those with one or two years of schooling had 7.12 children, while women with secondary education or higher had an average of 5.47 children.

Studies of the female labour force in developed countries indicate a negative relationship between female labour force status and fertility, with education as the intervening variable. The limited empirical evidence suggests that in developing countries, too, education is a crucial factor in female labour force participation. It is expected that, as the education level of Swazi women increases, so will their participation in wage employment, and that this will result in a probable reduction in completed family size.

The level of fertility also varies by occupation, residence, and related socio-economic indicators such as availability of piped water. On average, women in the homesteads had a higher level of fertility (5.7 children) than women in the towns (5.0 children). Women in homes with a piped water supply had a lower fertility level (5.05 children) than those with outside tap water (5.92) or other sources of water supply (6.48) (Government of Swaziland, 1978; World Bank, 1985). As far as district differentials are concerned, Lubombo district had the lowest fertility level – 6.13 children – compared with 6.54 for the Highveld area, the highest among the districts – reflecting in part differences in social, economic and ecological conditions.

Infant mortality in Swaziland is also high – 168 per thousand in 1966, with a slow decline to 156 per thousand in 1976 and an estimated 107 per thousand in 1986. At most, 30 per cent of all births occurred in hospital in 1984. Early childhood mortality is also high: currently nearly one-fifth of children die by the age of 5. The underlying causes of high childhood morbidity and mortality are inadequate water and sanitation facilities, poor nutrition, the introduction of inadequate bottle-feeding, and a lack of understanding of and means of preventing illness. The direct causes are mainly infectious diseases such as gastro-enteritis, pneumonia, measles and tetanus (UNFPA, 1981). These factors have resulted in very limited gains in life expectancy from 44 years in 1966 to 46.5 in 1976 and 53 in 1986. The estimate for 1990 is 57 years. In general, life expectancy is higher for women: in 1976, it was 49 years compared with 43 for men.

A striking feature of mortality patterns in Swaziland is the high level of mortality among adult men, compared with that for children and adult women. World Bank (1985) estimates show that in 1970 life expectancy after the age of 10 was five years shorter for men than for women, a difference explained largely by the health hazards of mine work in South Africa and at home.

The National Nutrition Survey of 1983 showed that 24 per cent of all infant deaths occurred during the neonatal period (one month after birth) and 76 per cent during the next 11 months, signifying that the risks to the survival of children are traceable largely to environmental factors (UNICEF, 1990). The high rate of home deliveries – approximately 50 per cent in 1989 – is a major factor in high perinatal mortality related to obstetric problems, such as prolonged labour, prematurity, and the lack of neonatal care in the critical first day of life.

Maternal mortality, too, is believed to be high, although there are no reliable etimates. UNICEF (1990) estimates the maternal mortality rate at 107 per 100,000 births. It is not clear, however, if this estimate is based on hospital data. The risks from pregnancy are increased in women with underlying illnesses, short intervals between births, or a large number of children (UNFPA, 1981).

The three most serious health problems in Swaziland are poor maternal and child health (including the lack of family planning), the prevalence of communicable and environmental disease, and malnutrition. According to a recent UNICEF (1990) report, these problems reflect 'practices in the home, especially as related to breast-feeding, food choices, sanitation and hygiene and the treatment and prevention of ill-health. They also reflect access to health care and potable water, and household insecurity.' In 1986, only 43 per cent of the population had access to a piped water supply.

At the district level, Hhohho district had the lowest mortality level in 1970, and Lubombo district the highest. These differences reflect variations in work opportunities, coverage of social services and urbanisation, all of which are more favourable in Hhohho district. This is also true of Manzini district, which trails Hhohho in mortality. Above all, differing mortality rates, epecially childhood mortality, reflect differences in socio-economic status. In particular, the education status of mothers has a positive effect in reducing mortality among children. This positive effect is reinforced by enhanced living conditions, especially the availability of piped water for middle-class people.

Women in Swazi Society

Swaziland is characterised by its duality in all spheres of life. Customary law (which applies to the ethnic Swazis) and the general law (imposed by the colonial regime and applying to everyone in the country) exist side by side. The economy, too, is dualistic in nature, with a subsistence agricultural sector and a modern export sector. The government, characterised by a strong traditional monarchy, coexists with a parliamentary system fashioned on the Westminster model. Even the way people dress reinforces this dualism: while many observe the traditional mode of dress, Western attire is increasingly conspicuous in the towns. All this has a great influence on the position of women – their fertility, their access to jobs, and even the availability of contraceptives (Adepoju, 1991a).

A distinct demographic feature of Swaziland is the excess of females in the population, a situation that has profound effects on the social structure, the economic organisation, and the status and roles of women. The low sex ratio of 88 males to 100 females for the *de facto* population in 1976 has been sustained over the years for which data are available, especially for the resident African population – a situation that can be partly explained by the highly selective male out-migration. But, even when the absentee population is taken into account, the predominance of females over males persists. The reason for this peculiar phenomenon is not clear and cannot simply be explained in terms of higher mortality among males. Whatever the reason, the effect on social organisation, marriage, and labour utilisation in the homestead is profound. One obvious consequence is the incidence of female-headed households, estimated at about 25 per cent in the homesteads in the late 1970s and early 1980s (de Vletter, 1983), and at up to 40 per cent by 1990 (UNICEF, 1990).

The rural population is markedly female: almost three females to every two males. This situation is explained partly by higher male mortality but more importantly by male predominance both among absentees outside the country and among those working in the company towns. Overall, 82 per cent of all homesteads (in rural areas) have absentee members in wage employment. When the husband dies, his widow becomes the *de facto* head of the homestead until his eldest son – the heir – assumes headship; widow-headed homesteads are therefore transitory. Prolonged female headship signifies marital separation or premature death of the male head, leaving no male heir or only a young boy.

The kinship system is a cornerstone of Swazi society; under Swazi law and custom, marriage is regarded as a union between two groups. Since the *raison d'être* of Swazi marriage is primarily procreation, the payment of *lobola* (bride price) guarantees that the man's family acquires rights over the woman's reproductive capacity. In fact, Swazi culture views fertility as the most important human endowment (UNFPA, 1981). In the same vein, the traditional values of the Swazi woman include obedience, submissiveness and humility; a woman is expected to perform the roles of wife, mother, child-bearer, food producer and household manager. Women's lives – what clothes they wear, the kinds of friends they make, where they work, where they go – are subject to constant and close scrutiny by their husbands, and both their own and their husbands' relatives. Thus, in effect, a woman is regarded as a 'ward under guardianship' (Armstrong and Nhlapo, 1985).

Women are required to respect and obey men, just as children are required to respect and obey their elders: Swazi tradition teaches submission on the part of both women and young children. A woman is required to provide the signed permission of a male relative before the Ministry of the Interior will issue her a passport for travel abroad for training or study. Nor will the town council allow her to buy land without proof of her husband's authorisation. Above all, her husband's permission is required for her to obtain a loan from the Swaziland Development and Savings Bank (Armstrong, 1987).

In the homesteads, women have the prime responsibility for rearing the children, caring for the sick, providing meals and cultivating the fields, which are tilled principally by wives and unmarried children. They are expected to provide maize and vegetables for themselves, and at least part of the husband's food needs (de Vletter, 1983; Kabagambe, 1991).

Yet women are important in their own right in the political context. The monarch, a man, normally rules with his mother, the queen mother. When a king dies, the queen mother acts as the monarch until a new king succeeds the throne. Traditionally, the new king is a minor and, when he comes of age and is crowned king, he rules with his mother, each having certain exclusive powers and the responsibility to check and balance each other's prerogatives. Although historically the balance of power sometimes shifts towards the queen mother, the king normally rules supreme (Matsebula, 1972).

There are at least five major development groups where women are strongly active: the women-in-development programme; the People's Participation Project; Lutsango Lwaka Ngwane; Zenzele; and women's informal credit and savings schemes.

The women-in-development programme became operational in 1978, initially within the context of the Northern Rural Development Area Programme, but it later expanded to other regions. Over a four-month period, female participants are trained in a wide range of skills: weaving, leather work, food catering, batik, tie-and-dye techniques, etc. Over the period 1978–84, over 900 participants benefited from such training.

The People's Participation Project, an income-generating programme executed by the FAO, targets women: in 1988, 86 per cent of participants were women, and special efforts are made to involve female heads of households. Collateral-free loans are granted to groups of women who engage in pig-rearing, cotton farming, poultry-keeping, sewing, etc. Women are accepted as farmers in their own right (UNICEF, 1990).

Lutsango Lwaka Ngwane, a loose, all-embracing organisation, engages in education and income-generating projects (day care centres, vocational training and community centres, piggery projects). The organisation has become more active recently with the participation of educated, urban-based women. Another group – the 'do-it-yourself' Zenzele association – is spread throughout the country; each of the 200 groups has 20 members. Rural health motivators regard these groups – which are primarily concerned with nutrition, community sanitation, disease prevention, child-care, family planning and income-generating activities – as important channels for health education at the community level. There are now about 60 women's informal credit and savings groups in the country.

Gender differences are fundamental to the traditional social organisation in Swaziland. As Armstrong and Russell (1985) conclude, many of the attitudes that constrain women in their domestic, economic and social roles are firmly grounded in traditional society, and efforts to change the situation of Swazi women would imply major changes in society as a whole.

The laws that affect a woman's health and control over her fertility and her employment opportunities and remuneration are extremely important for both the roles and the status of women. Generally, a woman is required to provide proof that she has the permission of her husband or another male relative before she can receive treatment in a hospital or clinic. Such consent is also required for general medical care. Many clinics in Swaziland insist that a woman must obtain permission from her husband before being given contraceptives. In Swaziland, the basic minimum age at marriage is 18 years for boys and 16 for girls. However, the customary law does not stipulate a minimum age of marriage; it does not frown on early marriage or early procreation. It should not restrict (young) married women's access to contraception – and yet it does (Amoah *et al.*, 1982).

Access to education
The root causes of many inequalities in Swazi society are traceable to the unequal access to education for boys and girls. In 1966, 55 per cent of Swaziland's male population had no schooling of any kind, 21 per cent was still at school and 24 per cent had left school. Corresponding percentages for females were 55 per cent, 19 per cent and 26 per cent. Taking the African resident population in 1966, 56.2 per cent of males and 56.4 per cent of females had no schooling of any kind. By 1976, the proportions were 42 per cent for males and 43 per cent for females, which indicates a substantial improvement in school attendance. In 1982, 81 per cent of primary school age children were enrolled in primary schools, of which 78 per cent attended grant-aided schools. This figure includes under- and over-aged students. For Forms 4 and 5, only 22 per cent of the 16–17 age group was enrolled in 1982, which constituted 22 per cent of the actual students in those forms (Sentongo, 1991).

Data from the school-mapping project confirm that the social demand for education in Swaziland is in fact a major consideration in the increasing educational opportunities throughout the country. The expansion of educational facilities has been dramatic from the late nineteenth century, when the first formal schools were established by the missionaries, to 1985, when there were at least 484 primary schools and 102 secondary schools in Swaziland.

Gender differences in access to education have narrowed in recent years. In 1985 an almost equal proportion of boys (50.3 per cent) and girls (49.7 per cent) was enrolled in primary school. At the junior and high (secondary) level, 49.3 per cent of the pupils were girls. However, two-thirds (66 per cent) of drop-outs at the secondary school level were girls (Sentongo, 1991). This is partly due to pregnancy-related factors, but that is not all. A UNICEF (1990) report notes: 'Boys are supported with greater persistence to obtain educational qualifications despite their later entry and initially poor performance.' At the primary level, more boys than girls were enrolled consistently from 1968 to 1985. Although the gap is closing, the number of boys continues to be swelled by higher repetition rates. Girls tend to be younger than boys, the latter often spending their early years herding cattle.

Parents view the education of boys as a direct long-term investment which will yield dividends: male children are expected to support their parents financially whereas a girl's reproductive and productive capacity becomes the effective possession of her husband's kin upon marriage, and she is under no obligation to support her parents. This tradition is recognised to act as a brake on parents' spending on girls' education. Consequently, while almost all girls go to school, they receive less support than boys to enable them to stay on to the highest level.

Women constitute 40 per cent of local university graduates and 30 per cent of technical college graduates. Women's share of tertiary education – 36 per cent – is lower than the other Southern African countries.

Women's Economic Activities

The size of the female labour force in Swaziland as reflected in official statistics appears relatively small. The majority of family workers in the home and on the farm, especially in the homesteads, are women, who also engage in unpaid household chores. The small proportion of women engaged in wage employment reflects the high drop-out rate of girls from school, as well as early and closely spaced pregnancies. It is often argued that female drop-outs easily find unskilled jobs; it is perhaps the case that they are employed in unskilled jobs because they are drop-outs.

In recent years, women have participated increasingly in wage employment. It is estimated that in the early 1980s more than one-quarter of workers in wage employment in Swaziland were women (Armstrong and Nhlapo, 1985), mainly in unskilled and clerical jobs. In the private sector, women on average earn less than men at all levels of skill, the average female wage being about 65 per cent of the male. This discrimination persists in spite of government affirmation of the right of women to equal pay for equal work: the Employment Act of 1980 guarantees equal pay for men and women of the same skill. However, the same Act prohibits women from working night shifts or working underground, for example, as miners (Appiah, 1991).

In 1982, 24 per cent of all employees in the private sector were women, mostly unskilled workers. In the public sector, which absorbs 30 per cent of all formal sector workers, 27 per cent were women. In 1987, 29 per cent of formal sector jobs (35 per cent of the public sector and 26 per cent of the private sector) were held by women. There has thus been a marked increase in women's employment in the public sector, but the situation has remained more or less static in the private sector. The ratio of female employment in the private relative to the public sector is 1.8 to 1.

Structurally, skilled employment is dominated by workers with lower-level skills. About two-thirds of all skilled workers are clerical and manual workers, while professionals and subprofessionals, respectively, form about 13.5 and 18 per cent of the total skilled workforce. The government employs 70 and 84 per cent of all professionals and subprofessionals, respectively, mostly as secondary and primary school teachers, who form the bulk of workers in these groups. When secondary school teachers are excluded, however, the private sector's share of professional employment is larger than the government's. Moreover, the private sector employs nearly 60 per cent of professionals with technical and scientific skills. On the other hand, the government sector employs the majority of all subprofessionals, even when primary school teachers are excluded from consideration. Nearly three-quarters of all clerical and manual workers are employed in the private and parastatal sectors.

Men predominate in all sectors and in all but one occupational group (non-technical subprofessionals) (Table 10.2). However, the government sector employs more female skilled workers than the private and parastatal sectors, both absolutely and relatively. The predominance of women among primary school teachers largely accounts for the clustering of skilled women in the government sector and their majority share of non-technical subprofessional employment. Women also predominate in the professional cadres of the civil service.

Wage employment in Swaziland as a whole is dominated by men: nearly 75 per cent of the total number of people in unskilled employment are men. Female representation is higher in skilled employment, however, with women holding about one-third of skilled jobs. Most skilled female workers (about 57 per cent) are employed by the government (Table 10.3). The next largest concentrations of skilled female workers are in trade and hotels and the finance sector (19 per cent and 7 per cent, respectively). Skilled expatriate women comprise about 4 per cent of total skilled workers (Table 10.3).

In primary schools, 81 per cent of the teachers were women in 1985. At the secondary school level, 46.3 per cent of the teachers were women; this proportion had increased to 49 per cent by 1990 (Sentongo, 1991). Of the 35 per cent of teachers who were university graduates, 41 per cent were women.

Wage differentials for men and women vary between the private and public sectors. The average earnings of women in the public sector have exceeded men's since 1982 (Table 10.4). Over 60 per cent of all public service professionals are women; wages are relatively high for the professional and technical levels. Men, on the other hand, are concentrated in the unskilled manual jobs (78 per cent) where wages are relatively low. In reality, however, women are generally paid less than men doing the same job in the public sector (except in the clerical grade). The better-paid administrative and managerial jobs are also the domain of the men (Armstrong and Russell, 1985).

In the private sector, average earnings for women have been consistently lower than men's since 1981. In fact, the private sector pays women in professional and administrative jobs less than half the rates paid to men (UNICEF, 1990), although the private sector pays women more than the public sector for similar skills.

When earnings in the public sector are compared with those in the private sector, in general the private sector pays higher wages for both men and women. The exception is female manual workers, who are better paid in the public sector. There is, nevertheless, a little-observed concentration of unskilled women in the private sector, most of them poorly paid. Women in white-collar jobs are more visible and are relatively well paid (Armstrong and Russell, 1985).

Women have become active in informal sector activities; by selling handicrafts and vegetables and other homestead-based activities they acquire additional cash incomes to boost their economic independence. Matsebula (1988) estimated that 76 per cent of those engaged in urban informal sector activities are women. In addition, 30 per cent of women in the wage sector are simultaneously engaged in other part-time informal sector activities (Armstrong, 1985). These activities include sewing, knitting, making traditional attire, repairing shoes, etc. Brewing alcohol and traditional healing are

Table 10.2 Distribution of skilled workers by occupational category, citizenship and sex, Swaziland, 1986

Skill category	Government sector				Private sector				All sectors			
	Citizens		Non-citizens		Citizens		Non-citizens		Citizens		Non-citizens	
	Males (%)	Females (%)	Males (%)	Females (%)	Males (%)	Females (%)	Males (%)	Females (%)	Males (%)	Females (%)	Males (%)	Females (%)
Professionals in technical occupations	1.6	0.5	13.3	1.3	0.6	0.3	10.4	–	1.0	0.4	10.1	0.5
Other professional occupations	17.5	19.9	77.0	54.1	3.4	1.3	30.0	16.0	8.8	12.0	33.3	32.0
Subprofessionals in technical occupations	6.6	7.7	3.6	0.6	2.3	5.6	7.4	10.2	4.0	6.8	6.3	6.6
Other subprofessional occupations	15.7	45.0	1.9	43.4	1.5	0.3	3.5	4.6	6.9	25.9	3.0	20.9
Skilled clerical and manual occupations	25.2	25.8	3.9	0.6	40.9	57.0	31.5	46.1	34.8	39.1	21.9	27.0
Semi-skilled clerical and manual occupations	33.5	1.1	0.3	–	51.3	35.5	19.2	22.4	44.5	15.8	22.4	13.0
Total	100.0	100.0	100.0	100.0	100.0	100.0	100.0	100.0	100.0	100.0	100.0	100.0
Number	7 101	5 750	360	159	11 372	4 279	1 829	219	18 473	10 028	1 289	378

Source: Swaziland: Manpower, Education and Training (ILO, 1986b).

Table 10.3 Structure of skilled employment by sector, citizenship and sex, Swaziland, 1986

| | Citizens | | | | Non-citizens | | | |
| | Males | | Females | | Males | | Females | |
Sector	N	%	N	%	N	%	N	%
Agriculture and forestry	2 273	12.3	126	1.3	326	14.9	16	4.2
Mining	248	1.3	40	0.4	117	5.3	6	1.6
Manufacturing	2 584	14.0	682	6.8	471	21.5	43	11.4
Electricity	96	0.5	41	0.4	3	0.1	–	–
Construction	424	2.3	48	0.5	217	9.9	10	2.6
Trade and hotels	2 604	14.1	1 877	18.7	248	11.3	47	12.4
Transport	1 202	6.5	114	1.1	48	2.2	–	–
Finance	801	4.3	613	6.1	37	1.7	5	1.3
Insurance, real estate and other business services	642	3.5	299	3.0	264	12.1	62	16.4
Other services	7 101	38.5	5 750	57.3	360	16.5	159	42.2
Total	18 473	100.0	10 028	100.0	2 189	100.0	378	100.0

Source: *Swaziland: Manpower, Education and Training* (ILO, 1986b).

Table 10.4 Women's average monthly earnings as a percentage of men's earnings, public and private sectors, Swaziland, 1981–87

Year	Private sector (%)	Public sector (%)
1981	48.6	95.1
1982	65.4	104.0
1983	72.3	127.4
1984	71.3	118.7
1985	63.1	130.3
1986	67.2	117.8
1987	93.3	109.8

Source: *Swaziland: Employment and Wages, 1987* (Central Statistical Office, 1989).

also the domain of women. In the rural areas, de Vletter (1983) found that 63 per cent of all homesteads earn cash from non-agricultural, non-wage sources. Earnings are low, however, averaging SZL18 per month, compared with SZL117 from wages and SZL50 from crops and livestock.

In Swaziland most agricultural tasks are now performed by women, as about 60 per cent of male homestead members are absentees, working either in the urban labour market or in the South African mines. Traditionally, men performed the more arduous tasks of clearing the fields, ploughing, fencing and preparing the land, while women planted, weeded, sowed, harvested and preserved the farm produce, in addition to their routine duties. The men also hunted, looked after the cattle, built houses and served national and local chiefs as members of regiments. The long absences of men, however, imply that women must now take on an additional work burden if output is to be maintained. Children supplement the efforts of their mothers. It has been estimated that about 70 per cent of labour devoted to cattle husbandry is contributed by children under 15 years of age. Crop production is essentially a female task, however: adult women normally contribute about half the labour hours, compared with 22 per cent by men and 27 per cent by children (Armstrong and Russell, 1985).

There is beginning to be an overlap between the sexes with regard to agricultural activities. Applying manure is becoming a man's activity because fertiliser, which is now used instead of manure, is applied mechanically. Weeding is being taken up by men because of the introduction of mechanical weeders. Part of the explanation for these changes relates to the widespread use of the tractor for agricultural tasks both in individual homesteads and in Swaziland as a whole. That has led to a higher degree of mechanised farming, so that a homestead might be using a tractor, a planter, a harrow and a weeder. Women in rural Swaziland do not normally drive tractors. With increased mechanisation, it is therefore likely that men will participate in what have traditionally been regarded as female agricultural activities (Kabagambe, 1991).

The ability of women to contribute positively to agricultural output is, however, severely constrained by their frequent exclusion from the making of relevant decisions affecting patterns of agricultural management practice, procurement of agricultural inputs and access to loans. These cultural and legal constraints inhibit the productivity of women in agriculture. The dominant involvement of women in agricultural and domestic chores in the rural areas obfuscates an assessment of the extent of involvement of women in national development. It is, however, clear from the limited evidence available that women have played a subservient role in social change and development.

Marriage, Reproduction and Contraception

Marriage in Swaziland is a rather complex institution because a combination of traditional (or customary), civil and religious marriages can occur. Traditional marriages can also become civil marriages, and couples married by means of civil registration can also – and, in fact, frequently do – undergo traditional marriage.

Neither the 1966 nor the 1976 census included questions on marital status. The results of the 1986 census show that marriage in Swaziland is mainly of the traditional form, and that polygynous marriages are common. In 1986, only 7.8 per cent of marriages in Swaziland were celebrated civilly under Roman–Dutch law. Civil marriage is monogamous, and essentially involves a contract between two individuals. Customary marriages outnumber civil marriages by four to one.

Traditionally, child-bearing is the primary aim of Swazi marriage; if a woman is infertile, her husband is normally entitled to a refund of his bride price (*lobola*) or to a substitute wife (usually the wife's sister) to bear him children.

In Swaziland, it is also traditional for child-bearing to precede marriage, since early conception and late marriage are both common among girls and women. The 1986 census showed that, even though 43.5 per cent of women over 20 were unmarried, only 10 per cent of these were childless (Table 10.5). Marriage thus comes late for many women, and a high proportion never marry. Even by the age of 50, 20 per cent are unmarried but have children (UNICEF, 1990).

Yet child-bearing does not necessarily interrupt women's employment in the formal sector; indeed, participation is highest at the peak of reproduction (Armstrong, 1985).

Table 10.5 Marital status of women in Swaziland, 1986 (%)

	Age of women	
Marital status	14 or over	20 or over
Married by Swazi custom	32.8	40.1
Unmarried with children	30.3	33.4
Unmarried, childless	23.8	10.1
Married by civil rites	7.8	9.7
Widowed	4.5	5.8
Divorced, separated	0.8	1.0
All	100.0	100.0

Source: UNICEF, 1990.

At one extreme is the situation of unmarried workers whose situation compels them to work.

Female employees, irrespective of marital status, who have been in continuous employment for one year or more are entitled to maternity leave of not less than 12 weeks, but employers are not obliged to pay them during this period. This practice has profound effects on women's health. Most women, especially unmarried ones, return to work soon after confinement to ensure continuity of income. In the process, breast-feeding is stopped too early, the infant is placed in the care of a proxy mother, and the limited resources are inadequate to buy food supplements for the infant. Even in government service, women, who constitute 69 per cent of all teachers, are handicapped: if unmarried, they are entitled to paid leave only for the first child. Subsequent leaves are not paid for, yet about 60 per cent of mothers in the peri-urban areas of Swaziland are single (Armstrong and Nhlapo, 1985).

However, motherhood need not imply mothering: there is a well-developed institution in Swaziland whereby somebody else, a grandmother, looks after the child – a situation that minimises role conflicts for nursing working mothers and inadvertently supports high fertility (Armstrong and Russell, 1985).

The major characteristics of a Swazi traditional marriage are: the production of as many children as possible in order to perpetuate kin groups (this being the primary aim); the union of two kin groups rather than two individuals; the payment of *lobola* as a form of compensation to the bride's kin for the loss of a daughter and her procreative capacities; the practice of the levirate, whereby a widow marries her husband's brother so that women remain married; minimal divorce (this being a very lengthy and tedious process involving the two kin groups); patrilineal descent: children are the property of the husband; a patrilocal residence pattern: the married couple resides at the homestead of the husband's father; and an abhorrence of childlessness, which encourages the practice of a sororate system, whereby a barren woman's sister is given in marriage to the husband to procreate 'on her behalf' (Lule, 1991).

Polygyny is a legitimate and desirable form of marriage in Swaziland, and is deeply rooted in the socio-economic and religious way of life of the Swazi. Children are highly valued, being considered as economic assets and as providing old-age insurance. Through polygyny, a man can produce many sons to avoid extinction of his name and many daughters who will enrich him through *lobola* payments; this will enable him to pay *lobola* for his sons and even to acquire more wives. The additional children and wives elevate his social status (Ferraro, 1980). Polygyny also serves as a socially accepted alternative to post-partum abstinence.

Traditionally, women were eligible to marry in their mid- to late teens. Men, on the other hand, were prohibited by the age regiment organisation from marrying young. According to Kuper, an age regiment, usually inaugurated every five to seven years, was liberated to marry somewhere between the ages of 25 and 35. Any man marrying before being liberated to do so would be committing an offence against the king and was fined a beast (Kuper, 1963).

A man attains adult status – and a degree of authority and self-determination – upon marriage. A woman, upon marriage, exchanges the authority of her parents for that of her husband and his parents, particularly her mother-in-law. This is especially the case with customary marriage. A woman, through marriage, transfers her labour capacity, as much as her reproductive capacity, from her kin group to her husband's kin group and must seek permission to work: her labour is no longer her own to dispose of at her will but is at the service of the kin group. When she works, her wages accrue to her husband's kin group (UNICEF, 1990). She may be barred from allocating part of her earnings to her parental kin, except when earnings come from subsidiary activities which provide personal sources of additional income.

Divorce is very rare and extremely difficult to obtain under Swazi law and custom (Kuper, 1963). One good ground for divorce is when a woman is barren or when she has artificially induced barrenness through the use of contraceptives (Nhlapo, 1983). The changes that have occurred recently in the structure of Swazi society are, however, likely to increase marital instability. Ferraro (1980) cites several reasons for such an increase: greater geographical mobility, with a high proportion of absentee husbands engaging in labour migration; the education of women; an increase in female labour force participation; the improved status of women; and the diminishing role of the extended family in solving marital disharmony. The report of the 1986 census shows that only 1 per cent of women aged 20 years and over were divorced or separated.

The multiplicity of marital categories in Swaziland makes it very difficult to relate fertility behaviour to any particular marital category (Lule, 1991). Study of the institution of polygyny, its functions within the socio-economic and cultural context, and its consequences for marital fertility is of importance in the many African countries where polygyny exists. It has been postulated that the transition from polygynous to monogamous types of union may have the effect of increasing age at marriage and thereby reducing the rate of population growth.

Lule (1991) found no significant difference between the fertility of women in polygynous unions (CEB of 5.24) and monogamous unions (CEB of 4.66). This result to some extent reflects the somewhat greater average age of women in polygynous unions, who were more advanced in their reproductive life. When controlled for age and marriage duration, however, the fertility of the two groups is still very similar. All husbands had an average of ten children, with husbands in polygynous unions having a greater number.

The National Family Planning Programme was launched by the Ministry of Health in 1973, and yet contraceptive use is low, being constrained by fear, resistance and antagonism from men. Above all it is considered 'unSwazi' – a catch-phrase of the largely traditionalist group who argue strongly that contraceptives, *per se*, are forbidden by Swazi culture, even when it is obvious that child-spacing practices, such as abstinence during breast-feeding and periods of mourning (*ukujuma*), are not unknown. It is also customary for a woman to stop bearing children when her eldest child reaches maturity, sometimes when she is in her early thirties (given the early age of child-bearing) (Armstrong, 1987).

Results from the 1988 Family Health Survey indicate that 16.6 per cent of women were currently using contraception and 30.7 per cent had used contraception at some time; 2.4 per cent had been sterilised while 14 per cent had given up contraception because of side-effects. The proportion of women who practised contraception after the first birth, 14.6 per cent, increased sharply to 23.3 per cent after the birth of the second child. The most active contraceptive users were women aged 30–34 years (UNICEF, 1990).

Nearly three-quarters of the women interviewed (73 per cent) reported having heard of some method of contraception. Younger women were more aware, and the level of awareness increased with age, and then declined among women aged 30 years or over. Wives in monogamous unions reported slightly more awareness than those in polygynous unions, possibly because they were younger and had a higher level of education. Of those who reported having heard of contraceptive methods, one-quarter knew of a modern method, 61 per cent reported knowledge of traditional methods, and 15 per cent knew of both methods.

These findings are similar to the results of Lule's survey (1991) where one-quarter of the women interviewed reported having used some method, modern or traditional, and 15 per cent were currently using some method. Lule found no significant difference in ever-use between women in polygynous and monogamous unions, when age and level of education were controlled for. When those practising abstinence or using other traditional methods were excluded, the proportion dropped to 11 per cent. Nearly three-quarters of the current users were on the pill – a finding supported by the Family Health Survey, according to which the pill was closely followed by injectables as the most popular method among women. A larger proportion of monogamously married women were current users of contraception than of those in polygynous unions. Current use of contraception was positively related to wife's education and husband's occupation, especially with professional or clerical workers. Clinics and hospitals were the main sources of information on family planning, followed by friends. Reasons for non-use of contraception varied, with husband's disapproval accounting for 11 per cent; health reasons for 8 per cent; lack of knowledge for 11 per cent; and religion for 49 per cent.

Nearly half the women Lule interviewed had breast-fed, 40 per cent had breast-fed and bottle-fed, and 12 per cent had bottle-fed only. A higher percentage of polygynously married women had breast-fed only, while more monogamously married women had bottle-fed (17 as opposed to 6 per cent). Women in polygynous unions had longer birth intervals – on average 26.2 months, compared with 18.9 months for monogamously married women. Women in monogamous unions were more likely to practise family planning than those in polygynous unions, mostly because of higher education levels, and polygynously married women were less likely to use abstinence in the post-partum period. Lule concluded that the two groups of women would end up with approximately the same number of children, a result of the compensation between education effects and other child-spacing behaviour.

Summary

Swazi society is highly homogeneous in its ethnic composition. It is, however, characterised by a distinct dualism in all aspects of life – the economy, law, culture and government. All these have a great influence on the position of women and issues relating to family formation, fertility and women's productive activities.

The population of Swaziland, like its land area, is small. The population growth rate is high, because of the high level of fertility. Infant, childhood and maternal mortality remain high.

The position of women in Swaziland is circumscribed in a number of ways: what a woman does, where she works, how she disposes of her income – indeed, the key aspects of her life – are traditionally sanctioned by men.

The high fertility level is explained by these constraints as much as by the early start of child-bearing. As in most African countries, contraceptive use is low. Male resistance to the use of contraception by women is strong. Abortion is illegal, and in the absence of strict adherence to the traditional forms of contraception (abstinence and breast-feeding), the ability of women to control their fertility consciously is severely restricted. Consequently, teenage pregnancy is rampant, resulting in high drop-out rates in schools. Again, boys receive stronger support than girls to help them remain in school up to the tertiary levels.

In spite of all this, women contribute the lion's share of agricultural labour. They also dominate the informal sector, using their earnings there to supplement their incomes, which are otherwise strictly controlled by their husbands. Wage employment is dominated by men, while women in wage employment face a series of discriminatory practices relating to wages, paid maternity leave, etc. Nevertheless, women are increasingly visible in skilled professions, where earnings are relatively high.

11 Breast-feeding & Birth Spacing: Erosion of West African Traditions

YAW OFOSU

There is considerable evidence that behaviour relating to breast-feeding and female post-partum sexual abstinence is changing in much of sub-Saharan Africa.[1] The tradition of long spaces between births found among most ethnic groups is being eroded as a result of socio-economic change associated with factors such as education, urbanisation, employment in non-traditional economic activities and the spread of imported religions. Given the important role played by prolonged breast-feeding and post-partum abstinence in traditional birth spacing, the ongoing changes could have grave consequences if appropriate policies are not put in place in good time.

The main function of prolonged breast-feeding and abstinence is to safeguard maternal and child health by postponing a further pregnancy until weaning can safely take place and, at the same time, giving the mother a reasonable length of time to recover from the effects of the last pregnancy (see, for example, Lorimer, 1954, pp. 86–88; Caldwell and Caldwell, 1977; Lesthaeghe et al., 1981).[2] This generally long period of 'maternity leave', as Abu calls it (see Chapter 12), also has fertility regulation effects, although the main purpose of traditional birth spacing is not to reduce fertility, but rather to maximise the number of surviving children. Thus, apart from a possible increase in maternal and child morbidity and mortality, the erosion of traditional post-partum behaviour will result in shorter birth intervals and increased fertility, if the contraceptive effects of prolonged breast-feeding and abstinence are not adequately compensated for. Indeed, in sub-Saharan societies which have not in the past suffered from high levels of infertility and subfecundity and for which recent fertility increases have been reported, inadequate compensation is often the main explanation for such increases (see, for example, Bongaarts et al., 1984; Caldwell and Caldwell, 1987; Page, 1988; Schoenmaeckers, 1988).

Shorter birth intervals and the state of maternal and child health are, of course, directly related. In many instances it is the occurrence of an earlier than desired pregnancy which leads to the shortening of breast-feeding and the mother's recovery time. Shorter birth intervals will also increase the pressure on the household's often inadequate resources. At a time when, in addition to falling real incomes, households are being made to bear increasingly high proportions of health and education costs

173

under structural adjustment programmes, shorter birth intervals will thus lead to poorer levels of health and education.

In this chapter, the changes in post-partum behaviour and some of its consequences are examined, using information from a number of recent fertility surveys undertaken in the West African subregion. In addition, an exploratory analysis of the relationships between the two post-partum variables and a number of 'explanatory' variables is undertaken, with a view to obtaining an indication of the pattern of change. The object of this exercise is to identify the subpopulations most likely to experience the greatest changes in traditional post-partum behaviour.

Differentials in Post-Partum Variables

Reliable data with which to measure trends in post-partum variables in the West African subregion (or indeed elsewhere in sub-Saharan Africa) are not easily available. Most of the current information at our disposal is from the large-scale fertility surveys of the 1970s and 1980s, namely the World Fertility Surveys (WFS) and the Demographic and Health Surveys (DHS), which, because of their retrospective nature, are subject to recall lapses and similar dating errors to which the analysis of trends is rather sensitive. In the absence of prospective studies across a number of countries, there is nevertheless little alternative to these single-round surveys for studying changes in post-partum behaviour at the national and regional levels. In the present study post-partum differentials, estimated according to such presumed factors of social change as education, type of residence and occupation, are used to indicate the extent and direction of change.

While cross-sectional differentials do not, in themselves, signify that change is taking place, they do corroborate the evidence gathered by other researchers to this effect (see references cited in note 1). In using these differentials in this manner, I have assumed that the behaviour of the 'least modernised' subpopulations (for instance rural residents, those with no formal education, adherents of traditional religion) is closest to the traditional models of birth spacing, and that increasing levels of modernisation are associated with increasing deviation from tradition. Consequently, the differentials in mean durations of breast-feeding, post-partum amenorrhoea and female post-partum sexual abstinence reported in Table 11.1, which are based on births occurring in the 36 months preceding DHS surveys in six West African countries, are indicative of the changes that are taking place: the durations of breast-feeding and abstinence are being reduced as more women become educated and/or move into urban areas. Moreover, because the traditional values and institutions of society are themselves affected by social change, in societies undergoing social and cultural change (as in West Africa) recently observed post-partum behaviour considered to be 'traditional' is only so in relative terms, that is, by comparison with contemporary practices characterised by various degrees of 'modernity'. It can therefore be assumed that erosion of traditional behaviour is occurring among all sections of society, albeit at different speeds.

Unfortunately, none of the DHS country reports cited in Table 11.1 provides estimates of mean durations of breast-feeding and abstinence according to respondent's occupation. The Ghana DHS data set has a section on women's employment history, but it is not clear whether the information can be used to study relationships

Table 11.1 Estimated mean durations of breast-feeding, post-partum amenorrhoea and post-partum sexual abstinence according to place of residence and level of education, selected West African DHS surveys

Country	Subgroup	Breast-feeding	Amenorrhoea	Abstinence	No. of births
Ghana (1988)					
Residence:	Urban	17.5	11.4	12.2	713
	Rural	21.4	15.0	14.1	1 875
Education:	None	22.8	16.4	17.1	1 114
	Primary	20.1	13.9	13.2	420
	Middle	18.1	12.0	10.0	922
	Secondary +	16.1	9.0	9.0	132
Total sample		20.4	14.0	13.5	2 588
Liberia (1986)					
Residence:	Urban	14.1	9.2	12.1	2 212
	Rural	18.9	12.6	13.4	1 055
Education:	None	18.6	12.4	14.1	2 150
	Primary	17.1	11.1	13.7	598
	Secondary +	10.0	6.4	9.0	519
Total sample		17.0	11.2	13.2	3 267
Mali (1987)					
Residence:	Urban	20.2	12.1	4.7	512
	Rural	22.0	16.4	7.7	1 630
Education:	None	21.7	15.6	7.2	1 843
	Primary	21.5	14.1	5.9	279
	Secondary +	a	a	a	16
Total sample		21.6	15.3	7.0	2 141
Nigeria (Ondo State, 1986)					
Residence:	Urban	16.3	12.5	20.2	841
	Rural	19.8	15.1	25.8	932
	Riverine	19.4	15.4	18.5	152
Education:	None	20.4	16.3	26.7	803
	Primary	18.4	13.6	21.4	657
	Secondary +	14.4	10.6	18.0	466
Total sample		18.2	14.0	22.8	1 925
Senegal (1986)					
Residence:	Urban	16.2	12.4	6.7	
	Rural	20.2	18.1	8.4	
Education:	None	19.4	17.2	8.1	
	Primary	16.6	12.2	7.3	
	Secondary +	14.1	9.1	5.3	
Total sample		18.8	16.2	7.9	
Togo (1988)					
Residence:	Urban	18.6	10.6	13.5	512
	Rural	24.1	15.8	21.5	1 416
Education:	None	24.2	16.3	19.0	1 237
	Primary	19.5	11.6	15.4	526
	Secondary +	20.7	9.4	12.9	165
Total sample		22.6	14.4	17.5	1 928

Notes: [a] Fewer than 20 cases.

1 Estimates are based on births occurring within 36 months of the interview. Durations are in months.

2 'None' stands for 'No formal schooling'.

3 Respondents whose level of education is equivalent to that of Ghana's middle school are classified under 'Secondary +' in other countries.

4 Totals may not add up because of missing cases on background variables.

Sources: Ghana Statistical Service, 1989a, Table 2.6; Liberia, Bureau of Statistics, 1988, Table 2.9; Mali, 1989, Table 2.6; Ondo State, Nigeria, 1989, Table 2.6; Sénégal, 1988, Table 2.7; Togo, 1989, Table 2.7.

between type of employment and post-partum behaviour. In general, the DHS appear to have paid less attention to women's employment than did the WFS, perhaps in part because the latter's attempt in this direction produced less than satisfactory results (Lloyd, 1990). Nevertheless, given the often strong association between level of education and occupation, differentials between occupational categories are expected to reflect those of education at least to some extent.

Implications of Observed Trends in Post-Partum Behaviour

Both prolonged breast-feeding and prolonged sexual abstinence have contributed to the maintenance of adequate birth intervals in much of the subregion in the past. The contraceptive function of prolonged breast-feeding is derived from its effect in delaying the return of full ovulatory activity in the mother. Table 11.1 shows evidence of this, in the form of a positive association between mean duration of breast-feeding and of post-partum amenorrhoea (see, for example, Tietze, 1963; Perez et al., 1971, 1972). Although both infecundity arising from continued breast-feeding beyond the time of the first post-partum menses and conception during amenorrhoea do occur (van Ginneken, 1977, pp. 44–45; Brown et al., 1985; see also Tietze, 1963), on the whole the duration of post-partum amenorrhoea may be taken as an approximate indicator of the contribution of breast-feeding to the inter-birth interval, provided, of course, that the duration of abstinence does not exceed that of amenorrhoea. Table 11.1 does, in fact, indicate that lactational amenorrhoea makes an important contribution to the length of the birth interval among a large proportion of the respondents, the notable exceptions being from Liberia, Togo and, most notably, Ondo State, Nigeria. The case of Ondo State is particularly significant in that, unlike the others, the estimated mean duration of abstinence far exceeds that of breast-feeding. Among the Yoruba, who occupy much of the south-west, including Ondo State, abstinence is known to have been observed until at least six months after weaning (Caldwell and Caldwell, 1977). Here breast-feeding's contribution to the inter-birth interval is largely indirect, through its influence on the duration of abstinence. WFS results indicate, however, that this distinction is not representative of Nigeria as a whole (Ofosu, 1989).

Traditionally, the duration of sexual abstinence has been largely determined by norms relating to breast-feeding. This point is supported by the positive association between mean durations of breast-feeding and abstinence in Table 11.1 (cf. Lorimer, 1954, pp. 87–88; Caldwell and Caldwell, 1977, 1981; Orubuloye, 1977; Schoenmaeckers et al., 1981; Lesthaeghe, 1984; Ofosu, 1989, p. 230). However, it is possible, in view of the fact that the duration of abstinence was mostly, on average, shorter than that of breast-feeding and in many cases even than that of amenorrhoea, that in some instances weaning was occasioned by the start of a new pregnancy. Caldwell and Thompson (1975, pp. 522–523), for instance, report a study in rural Gambia in which about half of the mothers were found to have become pregnant during the period of lactation. Similar reports relating to the Luo of western Kenya (Cosminsky, 1985) and to western Zaïre (Sala-Diakanda et al., 1981) have also been reported; similar findings have been reported for Central Java (Bracher and Santow, 1982), an area where the durations of breast-feeding and post-partum abstinence are comparable to those of much of sub-Saharan Africa. The duration of breast-feeding may thus

Table 11.2 Estimated infant and child mortality rates according to length of preceding birth interval, selected West African DHS surveys

Country and period	Previous birth interval	$_1q_0$	$_4q_1$	$_5q_0$
Ghana (1978–87)	<2 years	0.115	0.087	0.192
	2–3 years	0.068	0.080	0.142
	4+ years	0.052	0.059	0.107
	Total sample	0.081	0.079	0.154
Liberia (1976–86)	<2 years	0.203	0.092	0.277
	2–3 years	0.124	0.095	0.207
	4+ years	0.072	0.058	0.126
	Total sample	0.153	0.091	0.230
Mali (1977–86)	<2 years	0.202	0.239	0.393
	2–3 years	0.081	0.147	0.216
	4+ years	0.045	0.087	0.129
	Total sample	0.131	0.170	0.279
Nigeria (Ondo State, 1981–86)	<2 years	0.080	(0.035)	(0.112)
	2–3 years	0.047	0.060	0.105
	4+ years	0.045	(0.068)	(0.110)
	Total sample	0.056	0.055	0.108
Senegal (1976–85)	<2 years	0.115	0.139	0.138
	2–3 years	0.072	0.133	0.196
	4+ years	0.058	(0.097)	(0.149)
	Total sample	0.091	0.130	0.210
Togo (1978–88)	<2 years	0.121	0.085	0.195
	2–3 years	0.071	0.080	0.146
	4+ years	0.057	0.081	0.134
	Total sample	0.083	0.082	0.159

Notes: 1 Figures in parentheses were calculated from fewer than 500 person years of exposure.
2 $_1q_0$ represents the probability of dying within the first year of life (between birth and age 1), $_4q_1$ represents the probability of dying between age 1 and age 5, and $_5q_0$ that of dying within the first five years of life.
Sources: Ghana Statistical Service, 1989a, Tables 6.4 and 6.5; Liberia, Bureau of Statistics, 1988, Table 6.3; Mali, 1989, Table 6.3; Ondo State, Nigeria, 1989, Table 6.2; Sénégal, 1988, Tables 6.4 and 6.5; Togo, 1989, Tables 6.3 and 6.4.

depend both on the return of the menses and on the resumption of normal sexual relations (Hull and Simpson, 1985, p. 9; Santow, 1987). Indeed, it is likely that the erosion of prolonged breast-feeding is often the result, rather than the justification, of reduced durations of abstinence. Moreover, behaviour relating to abstinence appears to change more easily than that relating to breast-feeding (Ofosu, 1989; see also Caldwell and Caldwell, 1981, p. 79); hence, apart from cases where employment or some other factor makes prolonged breast-feeding difficult or impossible, most mothers would probably be disposed to observe the traditional norm about duration of breast-feeding unless a new pregnancy occurred.

Where a shorter period of breast-feeding is adopted because a woman's labour force participation makes it difficult to do otherwise, the consequences might not be serious if there are sufficient resources to ensure good nutrition for the child, and especially if the contraceptive effects of traditional birth-spacing practices are adequately compensated for. In contrast, the consequences of breast-feeding being cut short by a new pregnancy, or more generally by inadequately compensated-for erosion of traditional post-partum sexual abstinence, may be quite grave for both mother and child. Table 11.2 shows DHS estimates of infant and child mortality rates according to the length of the preceding birth interval. Some of the estimates, especially those from Ondo State, might have been severely biased. Nevertheless, any omissions of infant and child deaths are more likely to affect cases where the preceding inter-birth interval was short, as long intervals usually attract further probing by the interviewers. The differentials shown are thus probably conservative. That long inter-birth intervals have beneficial effects on child survival is quite evident. This holds true for the preceding child as well: according to a study by the Populations Reference Bureau based on WFS data (Impact, 1986), the death rate for Ghanaian children aged between 1 and 4 years whose younger sibling was born less than two years after his or her own birth was 99 per thousand, compared with 54 per thousand if the younger sibling was born two or more years later. Comparative figures for Kenya were 80 and 68 per thousand, respectively. The study concluded that longer birth spacing could reduce infant deaths by 17 per cent in Ghana and 20 per cent in Kenya. Arguably, maternal deaths could be similarly reduced.

Although prolonged breast-feeding should be encouraged whenever possible, the greatest need is to increase the use of contraception to ensure adequate inter-birth intervals. Table 11.3 provides a comparison of median breast-feeding and abstinence durations with median birth intervals, based on births occurring in the five years preceding the Ghana WFS survey of 1979–80. The most interesting result is that, while the more 'modernised' subpopulations exhibited the highest degree of erosion of traditional post-partum behaviour, they also had the longest inter-birth intervals (see also Gaisie, 1984, pp. 19–20). The explanation seems to be found in the last column, in their comparatively high levels of contraceptive use. Further analysis suggests, in fact, that contraception was being used for both birth spacing and fertility limitation among these subpopulations (Ofosu, 1992). Overall levels of use of modern contraceptives are, however, still quite low in Ghana, and even lower elsewhere in the region, as Table 11.4 indicates.

The Most Vulnerable Groups: Exploratory Analysis of Patterns of Differentials

While all subpopulations should be targeted both to maintain sufficient breast-feeding durations and to compensate for erosion of traditional birth-spacing practices, especially abstinence, certain groups are more likely to experience rapid changes in post-partum behaviour than others. They would thus require special attention. In this section, the automatic interaction detector (AID) technique (Sonquist and Morgan, 1964; Sonquist, 1970; Sonquist et al., 1973; Blalock, 1981, pp. 538–540) is applied to WFS data from Cameroon, Côte d'Ivoire, Ghana and Nigeria to explore the pattern of relationships between background characteristics of respondents and durations of breast-feeding and post-partum sexual abstinence in an attempt to identify the most vulnerable (and least vulnerable) groupings.[3]

WFS information about durations of breast-feeding and abstinence relates to either

Table 11.3 Estimates of birth spacing and fertility measures for the five-year period preceding the 1979–80 Ghana WFS survey for categories of selected background variables

Variable	Median breast-feeding duration	Median abstinence duration	Median birth interval	Total fertility rate	% Currently using contraception[a]
Ethnic grouping					
Akan	13.2	6.4	38.1	6.4	15
Ga-Adangbe	12.9	6.5	38.8	6.7	24
Ewe	15.2	10.2	40.2	6.5	16
Northern	21.8	18.1	44.2	6.5	2
Education					
No schooling	17.2	9.1	40.7	6.8	6
Primary	13.8	6.9	37.2	6.9	16
Middle	13.0	7.0	38.6	5.8	23
Secondary +	10.5	5.8	47.8	4.2	52
Occupation					
None	15.7	10.6	41.3	5.8	4
Prof./Admin.[b]	11.4	6.2	47.0	4.5	51
Sales	13.9	7.7	39.3	7.0	15
Agriculture	16.3	7.5	39.1	7.0	8
Other[c]	13.6	7.9	42.2	6.1	20
Residence					
Rural	16.3	8.1	39.4	6.8	9
Small urban	13.4	7.3	39.7	6.2	18
Large urban	12.5	6.8	42.1	5.5	26
Religion					
Catholic	14.5	7.5	40.0	6.0	15
Other Christian	13.1	6.5	38.3	6.3	19
Muslim	17.1	11.8	41.7	6.9	6
Traditional	20.8	14.7	42.9	6.8	3
'No religion'	14.9	7.4	38.2	6.9	9

Notes: For each background variable, estimates of medians and trimeans were obtained from a life table regression model (hazards model) involving, in addition to that variable, birth order and age at reference event. Estimates have therefore been adjusted for the effects of these two variables. Medians are in months.
[a] Respondents using a method of contraception other than sexual abstinence in the open or the last closed pregnancy interval.
[b] Including clerical staff.
[c] Service industries, skilled and unskilled production, private household work.
Source: Computed from the Ghana World Fertility Survey data set (standard recode, version 3).

the last birth (open birth interval) or the last-but-one birth (last closed interval).[4] Current residence, level of education, religion, region or ethnic grouping,[5] and occupation were used as explanatory variables. Age at last-but-one confinement, in quinquennial groupings, was included in the analysis as a control variable.

The proportion of variation in the reported durations of breast-feeding accounted for by the five background variables (that is, the sum of the proportion of variance 'explained' by each of the five variables) ranges from 0.11 for Côte d'Ivoire to 0.48 for Ghana. Total explained variation is, in fact, higher than 0.25 in all cases except Côte d'Ivoire. For sexual abstinence, total variation explained ranges from 0.09 for Côte d'Ivoire and Nigeria to 0.5 for Ghana, being generally low in all cases except Ghana. The amounts of variation explained are, however, not as important in

Table 11.4 Percentage of currently married women reported as current users of contraception, selected West African DHS surveys

Country	Subgroup	Any method	Any modern method	Traditional method	N
Ghana (1988)					
Residence:	Urban	19.6	8.1	11.4	961
	Rural	9.9	3.9	6.1	2 195
Education:	None	8.5	3.2	5.3	1 467
	Primary	12.1	6.1	6.1	512
	Middle	16.8	6.7	10.1	999
	Secondary +	28.7	10.1	18.5	178
Total sample		12.9	5.2	7.7	3 156
Liberia (1986)					
Residence:	Urban	11.6	9.7	1.9	
	Rural	3.4	3.1	0.3	
Education:	None	2.8	2.5	0.3	
	Primary	7.3	6.6	0.7	
	Secondary +	26.8	22.1	4.7	
Total sample		6.4	5.5	0.9	
Mali (1987)					
Residence:	Urban	11.4	4.7	6.6	745
	Rural	2.3	0.1	2.3	2 203
Education:	None	2.8	0.3	2.5	2 539
	Primary	12.6	5.5	7.1	375
	Secondary +	52.7	20.3	32.3	34
Total sample		4.7	1.3	3.4	2 948
Nigeria (Ondo State, 1986)					
Residence:	Urban	8.9	5.5	3.4	1 144
	Rural	4.5	2.9	1.6	1 471
	Riverine	0.9	0.4	0.5	217
Education:	None	2.9	1.8	1.1	1 454
	Primary	5.5	3.6	1.9	825
	Secondary +	15.0	9.0	6.0	553
Total sample		6.0	3.7	2.3	2 832
Senegal (1986)					
Residence:	Urban	14.2	6.7	7.5	
	Rural	9.9	0.3	9.6	
Education:	None	9.8	1.0	8.8	
	Primary	14.9	5.9	9.0	
	Secondary +	32.9	22.2	10.7	
Total sample		12.3	2.4	9.9	
Togo (1988)					
Residence:	Urban	32.3	6.5	25.5	705
	Rural	34.5	1.7	32.8	1 749
Education:	None	33.5	1.7	31.8	1 664
	Primary	32.0	3.9	28.0	593
	Secondary +	42.1	12.2	29.4	197
Total sample		33.9	3.1	30.7	2 454

Notes: 1 'None' stands for 'No formal schooling'.
2 Respondents whose level of education is equivalent to that of Ghana's middle school are classified under 'Secondary +' in the other countries.
Source: Ghana Statistical Service, 1989a, Table 4.8; Liberia, Bureau of Statistics, 1988, Table 4.6; Mali, 1989, Table 4.8; Ondo State, Nigeria, 1989, Table 4.7; Sénégal, 1988, Table 4.8; Togo, 1989, Table 4.9.

themselves as are the indications they give of the relative importance of individual background variables as 'explanatory' factors. Thus, for breast-feeding, ethnic grouping was by far the most important factor in the Ghanaian data set; it came a close second to religion in the Nigerian data, and a weak second to education in the data for Cameroon. It is only in Côte d'Ivoire data that ethnic grouping was relatively unimportant, ranking only fourth after religion, education and occupation; even there, and in Nigeria as well, ethnic grouping may be more important than these results suggest, since it is highly correlated with religion. With the exception of Cameroon, education did not appear to be a particularly strong factor although, as noted below, this may be partly due to the selection of shorter durations by the last closed birth interval (see note 4). The same reason may partly explain the relative unimportance of type of current residence and, perhaps to a lesser extent, occupation.[6]

The dominant position of ethnic grouping among the five background variables is even more evident in the data on post-partum sexual abstinence: it accounts for well over half of the total explained variation in each of the data sets. In fact, with the exception of religion in the Ghanaian data, no other variable can be considered of any importance.[7]

Proportions of total variation explained do not, however, reflect the way in which the background variables are associated with subsets of the sample: a variable may not be important over the whole sample and yet may have substantial importance in certain subgroups. Trees drawn from the results of the splitting process performed by AID give an idea of how important each variable is in the various subgroups. These are discussed below.

Structure of relationships in breast-feeding data
Figure 11.1 shows AID trees obtained from the splitting process for the breast-feeding data. Group mean durations have been presented in their raw form, with no adjustments made for age at confinement, so that the actual magnitudes of durations and of group differentials are preserved; results not presented here indicate, however, that the effects of such adjustments are minimal in nearly all cases. Figures provided against 'proportions explained' are based on a one-way analysis of co-variance, in which the final subgroups shown in the tree diagrams constitute factor categories. Note that these are not the same as the explained variations discussed above.

None of the background variables has a consistent pattern of relationships across the four samples. In the Cameroon data, strong associations with ethnicity were indicated only among respondents with no formal education. If we assume that such respondents adhere more closely to traditional norms, then the results suggest, as far as breast-feeding is concerned, that education was strongly associated with a considerable decline in the influence of traditional practices. Whereas Bantus with no formal education constituted one fairly homogeneous subgroup within which none of the other background variables available showed significant differentials, among Semi-Bantus and Northerners from the same educational category religion appeared to be an important factor, with adherence to a non-traditional religion being associated with a shorter duration of breast-feeding. This point is noteworthy, for the duration of breast-feeding was shorter among Bantus than among the other two ethnic groupings.

Two main groupings are indicated in the the Côte d'Ivoire breast-feeding data.

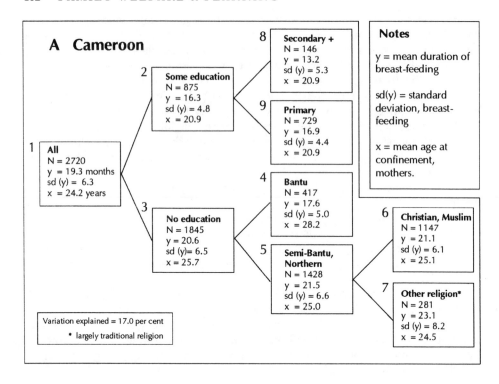

A Cameroon

1 All
N = 2720
y = 19.3 months
sd (y) = 6.3
x = 24.2 years

2 Some education
N = 875
y = 16.3
sd (y) = 4.8
x = 20.9

8 Secondary +
N = 146
y = 13.2
sd (y) = 5.3
x = 20.9

9 Primary
N = 729
y = 16.9
sd (y) = 4.4
x = 20.9

3 No education
N = 1845
y = 20.6
sd (y)= 6.5
x = 25.7

4 Bantu
N = 417
y = 17.6
sd (y) = 5.0
x = 28.2

5 Semi-Bantu, Northern
N = 1428
y = 21.5
sd (y) = 6.6
x = 25.0

6 Christian, Muslim
N = 1147
y = 21.1
sd (y) = 6.1
x = 25.1

7 Other religion*
N = 281
y = 23.1
sd (y) = 8.2
x = 24.5

Notes

y = mean duration of breast-feeding

sd(y) = standard deviation, breast-feeding

x = mean age at confinement, mothers.

Variation explained = 17.0 per cent
* largely traditional religion

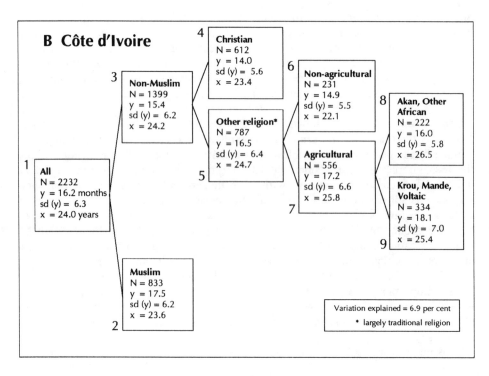

B Côte d'Ivoire

1 All
N = 2232
y = 16.2 months
sd (y) = 6.3
x = 24.0 years

3 Non-Muslim
N = 1399
y = 15.4
sd (y) = 6.2
x = 24.2

2 Muslim
N = 833
y = 17.5
sd (y) = 6.2
x = 23.6

4 Christian
N = 612
y = 14.0
sd (y) = 5.6
x = 23.4

5 Other religion*
N = 787
y = 16.5
sd (y) = 6.4
x = 24.7

6 Non-agricultural
N = 231
y = 14.9
sd (y) = 5.5
x = 22.1

7 Agricultural
N = 556
y = 17.2
sd (y) = 6.6
x = 25.8

8 Akan, Other African
N = 222
y = 16.0
sd (y) = 5.8
x = 26.5

9 Krou, Mande, Voltaic
N = 334
y = 18.1
sd (y) = 7.0
x = 25.4

Variation explained = 6.9 per cent
* largely traditional religion

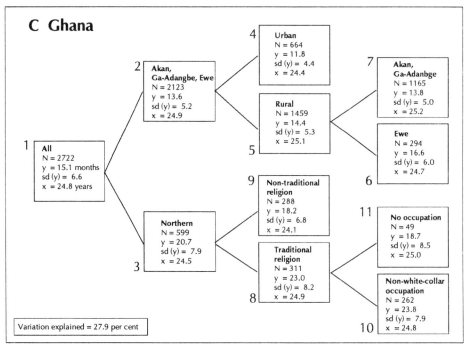

C Ghana

1 — All
N = 2722
y = 15.1 months
sd (y) = 6.6
x = 24.8 years

2 — Akan,
Ga-Adangbe, Ewe
N = 2123
y = 13.6
sd (y) = 5.2
x = 24.9

3 — Northern
N = 599
y = 20.7
sd (y) = 7.9
x = 24.5

4 — Urban
N = 664
y = 11.8
sd (y) = 4.4
x = 24.4

5 — Rural
N = 1459
y = 14.4
sd (y) = 5.3
x = 25.1

7 — Akan,
Ga-Adanbge
N = 1165
y = 13.8
sd (y) = 5.0
x = 25.2

6 — Ewe
N = 294
y = 16.6
sd (y) = 6.0
x = 24.7

9 — Non-traditional
religion
N = 288
y = 18.2
sd (y) = 6.8
x = 24.1

8 — Traditional
religion
N = 311
y = 23.0
sd (y) = 8.2
x = 24.9

11 — No occupation
N = 49
y = 18.7
sd (y) = 8.5
x = 25.0

10 — Non-white-collar
occupation
N = 262
y = 23.8
sd (y) = 7.9
x = 24.8

Variation explained = 27.9 per cent

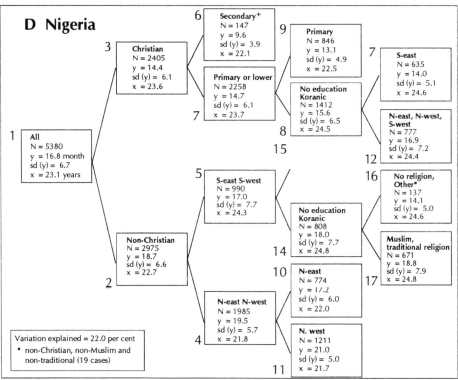

D Nigeria

1 — All
N = 5380
y = 16.8 month
sd (y) = 6.7
x = 23.1 years

2 — Non-Christian
N = 2975
y = 18.7
sd (y) = 6.6
x = 22.7

3 — Christian
N = 2405
y = 14.4
sd (y) = 6.1
x = 23.6

6 — Secondary+
N = 147
y = 9.6
sd (y) = 3.9
x = 22.1

7 — Primary or lower
N = 2258
y = 14.7
sd (y) = 6.1
x = 23.7

9 — Primary
N = 846
y = 13.1
sd (y) = 4.9
x = 22.5

8 — No education
Koranic
N = 1412
y = 15.6
sd (y) = 6.5
x = 24.5

7 — S-east
N = 635
y = 14.0
sd (y) = 5.1
x = 24.6

12 — N-east, N-west,
S-west
N = 777
y = 16.9
sd (y) = 7.2
x = 24.4

5 — S-east S-west
N = 990
y = 17.0
sd (y) = 7.7
x = 24.3

4 — N-east N-west
N = 1985
y = 19.5
sd (y) = 5.7
x = 21.8

14 — No education
Koranic
N = 808
y = 18.0
sd (y) = 7.7
x = 24.8

10 — N-east
N = 774
y = 17.2
sd (y) = 6.0
x = 22.0

11 — N. west
N = 1211
y = 21.0
sd (y) = 5.0
x = 21.7

16 — No religion,
Other*
N = 137
y = 14.1
sd (y) = 5.0
x = 24.6

17 — Muslim,
traditional religion
N = 671
y = 18.8
sd (y) = 7.9
x = 24.8

Variation explained = 22.0 per cent
* non-Christian, non-Muslim and
non-traditional (19 cases)

Muslims, whatever their ethnic background, ended up in one not-too-heterogeneous subgroup.[8] Since these ethnicity differentials are not important, we are not looking at important deviations from what may be regarded as antecedent influences. Non-Muslims (largely Christians and Traditionals) tended to have shorter durations, especially Christians and Traditionals with non-agricultural occupations. Again, the relationship between education and breast-feeding does not appear to be strong, although the former was the most important variable among Christians (group 4). As with ethnic grouping, differentials between educational categories, though in the expected direction, are not important. It is also interesting that, as in Cameroon (and in southern Ghana, see below), ethnic factors remained important within the most traditional subgroup (group 7).

Two principal groupings are also indicated in the Ghanaian breast-feeding data: the three southern ethnic groupings, with generally shorter durations, and the longer-duration Northern grouping. Among the southern groupings urban residence was associated with untraditionally short durations of breast-feeding, while the persistence of traditional practices in the rural areas was indicated by the partition of group 5 along ethnic lines, a result similar to the one obtained for Cameroonian respondents with no formal education. This relatively marked differentiation by residence was not reproduced in the Northern grouping, partly because religion substituted for type of residence, the correlation between these two variables among Northern respondents being fairly high. A similar substitution may have occurred in the case of education, which was partly replaced by ethnic grouping in the national sample.[9] The explanatory power of occupation was even lower than that of education, and its use in splitting group 8 may have been largely the result of the substitutions mentioned earlier.

In the Nigerian data Christians and non-Christians showed different factor associations. Among Christians, formal education was associated with fairly homogeneous subgroups having shorter mean durations of breast-feeding. For respondents with no formal education, however, region of residence, our proxy for ethnicity, remained an important factor. Among non-Christians the results indicate greater sophistication in the economically more modernised south than in the north. With respect to the remaining variables, type of residence was the second most important factor in groups 2 and 5 but was otherwise generally unimportant. Occupation was second in group 3, but was partly substituted for by education.

The absence of symmetry in the tree diagrams is indicative of the strength of interactions between background variables. Much of the above discussion, of course, concerns these interaction effects. Their significance is highlighted in the concluding section.

Structure of relationships in the data on post-partum sexual abstinence
AID trees for the abstinence data are shown in Figure 11.2. The picture is, on the whole, much simpler than for breast-feeding. Among ethnic groupings with mean durations of no more than 12 months (Bantu and Northerners for Cameroon, the three southern groupings for Ghana, Akan and Other Africans for Côte d'Ivoire), no socio-economic factor (that is, factors other than ethnic grouping) was useful enough for splitting; in fact, differentials between subgroups defined according to socio-economic factors tended to be small.[10] Differentials between residence categories were even smaller, and so were occupational differentials, which, to some extent, reflect those of education.

The relative simplicity of the structure of relationships in the abstinence data is further reflected by the fact that in the groupings in Cameroon and Ghana where splitting did take place it was done on only one variable in each case. The only complex structures were from the Côte d'Ivoire, where significant three-factor interactions involving ethnic grouping, religion and occupation are indicated, and from Nigeria, where the same order of interactions was observed between region, religion and residence, and between region, education and religion. Significant two-factor interactions also exist in all four data sets. Note that, in the largely Yoruba South-west region of Nigeria, Catholics, Traditionals and respondents professing no religion have mean durations that are well below those of Muslims and non-Catholic Christians. This rather unexpected result contrasts with results obtained elsewhere showing longer durations for adherents of traditional religion, and is probably due to a severe selection bias involving Traditionals, Catholics and those professing no religion.

In general, a positive relationship exists between group means and their standard deviations for both breast-feeding and abstinence. For subgroups defined according to ethnicity, the greater relative homogeneity implies there is little incentive for deviation. This might be the case, for instance, with abstinence among the Akans and Ga-Adangbes of Ghana. For subgroups defined according to factors such as education, relative homogeneity may imply the existence of substantial peer-group effects. This appears to be particularly so with breast-feeding in Cameroon (education), southern Ghana (urbanisation) and Côte d'Ivoire (Christianity) and among Nigerian Christians (education).

Conclusion

It is clear from the results of the preceding exploratory analysis that ethnicity remains an important determinant of the durations of breast-feeding and post-partum sexual abstinence. Not only are important ethnicity differentials indicated, but in addition most of the observed statistical interactions involve ethnic grouping. Although change is, in general, in the direction of shorter durations of breast-feeding and abstinence, the presence of interactions indicates ethnic (or geographical) differences in the pace of change. In effect, changes in post-partum behaviour do not depend only on the extent to which a group has undergone the kind of social change associated with factors such as education, urbanisation and employment in a non-traditional occupation; they also depend on how long people are expected to breast-feed or to abstain sexually under the traditional birth-spacing model. Where the traditional durations are long, modernisation tends to be associated with substantial deviations from the traditional model. In contrast, differentials among ethnic groupings with a tradition of relatively short durations are not important. This suggests a movement towards national homogeneity as regards breast-feeding and abstinence. Given that the majority of West African societies have traditionally long durations of breast-feeding and post partum abstinence (the major exceptions being the Akans and Ga-Adangbes of Ghana and, to a lesser degree, the Akans of Côte d'Ivoire, together with long-Islamised societies in the Sahel, as indicated by the data from Mali and Senegal shown in Table 11.1), this implies further major erosions of traditional birth-spacing practices all over the subregion in the short to medium term.

Women's participation in the 'formal' sector of the economy will probably result

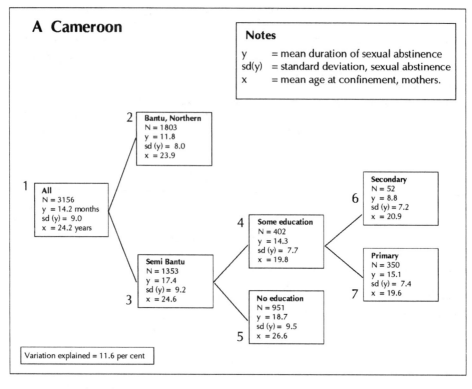

A Cameroon

Notes

y = mean duration of sexual abstinence
sd(y) = standard deviation, sexual abstinence
x = mean age at confinement, mothers.

1 All
N = 3156
y = 14.2 months
sd (y) = 9.0
x = 24.2 years

2 Bantu, Northern
N = 1803
y = 11.8
sd (y) = 8.0
x = 23.9

3 Semi Bantu
N = 1353
y = 17.4
sd (y) = 9.2
x = 24.6

4 Some education
N = 402
y = 14.3
sd (y) = 7.7
x = 19.8

5 No education
N = 951
y = 18.7
sd (y) = 9.5
x = 26.6

6 Secondary
N = 52
y = 8.8
sd (y) = 7.2
x = 20.9

7 Primary
N = 350
y = 15.1
sd (y) = 7.4
x = 19.6

Variation explained = 11.6 per cent

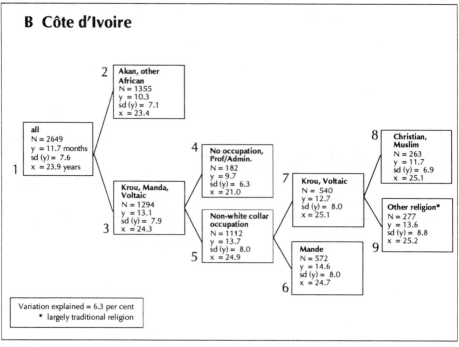

B Côte d'Ivoire

1 all
N = 2649
y = 11.7 months
sd (y) = 7.6
x = 23.9 years

2 Akan, other African
N = 1355
y = 10.3
sd (y) = 7.1
x = 23.4

3 Krou, Manda, Voltaic
N = 1294
y = 13.1
sd (y) = 7.9
x = 24.3

4 No occupation, Prof/Admin.
N = 182
y = 9.7
sd (y) = 6.3
x = 21.0

5 Non-white collar occupation
N = 1112
y = 13.7
sd (y) = 8.0
x = 24.9

6 Mande
N = 572
y = 14.6
sd (y) = 8.0
x = 24.7

7 Krou, Voltaic
N = 540
y = 12.7
sd (y) = 8.0
x = 25.1

8 Christian, Muslim
N = 263
y = 11.7
sd (y) = 6.9
x = 25.1

9 Other religion*
N = 277
y = 13.6
sd (y) = 8.8
x = 25.2

Variation explained = 6.3 per cent
* largely traditional religion

C Ghana

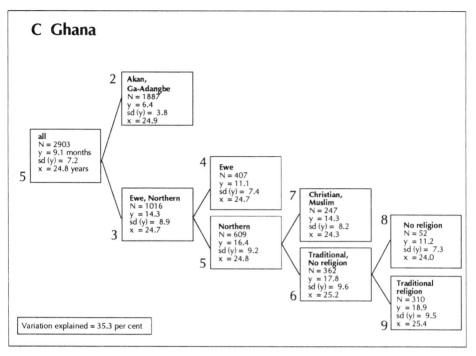

Variation explained = 35.3 per cent

D Nigeria

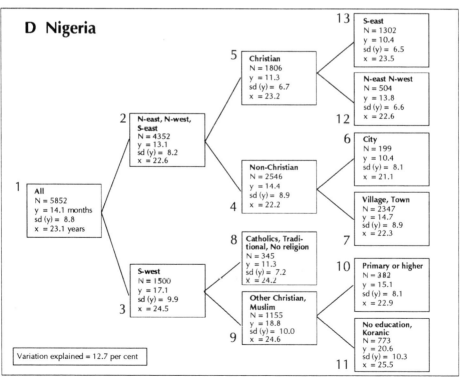

Variation explained = 12.7 per cent

in substantial declines in the duration of breast-feeding. In order to ensure adequate nutrition for their children and sufficient recovery time for themselves, as well as time for their (non-reproductive) careers, it will be essential for women in this position to be provided with the knowledge and means to postpone further pregnancy. Given that job opportunities in the formal sector are quite limited, however, only a minority of women will find themselves in this position. For the vast majority, the flexibility of informal sector employment will probably dispose them favourably to current campaigns aimed at ensuring adequate breast-feeding. At the same time, it will be difficult to promote continued prolonged post-partum sexual abstinence, particularly as traditionally this post-partum sexual abstinence has been biased against women, as men are not required to abstain. It could even be argued that, by providing an excuse for men to enter into extra-marital and polygynous relationships, prolonged abstinence leads to changes in the distribution of household income that are detrimental to women and children. Indeed, for a possibly increasing proportion of couples, shorter periods of post-partum abstinence might be perceived as essential for healthy family life. It would, therefore, be hard to stop the already established trend towards erosion of this practice. Other forms of contraception will therefore have to be promoted if adequate breast-feeding durations and inter-birth intervals are to be ensured.

Apart from the beneficial effects that increasing use of modern contraception will have on maternal and child health, it will at least prevent fertility from rising. Moreover, the widespread practise of modern contraception, once introduced in this way, will facilitate other efforts aimed at reducing fertility and the rapid growth of population in the subregion. In this connection, the interactions observed between traditional birth spacing and socio-economic change point to the evolution of new cultural models of birth spacing which ought to be harnessed and consolidated to help discourage traditional high-fertility aspirations and establish the small family size as the norm. Changes in this direction are indeed taking place, as the Ghanaian example given in Table 11.3 illustrates. However, real fertility change has yet to begin for a large majority of West Africans. One point arising from the above results which is worthy of consideration is that, to be effective, programmes aimed at influencing birth-spacing behaviour and the level of fertility ought to be tailored to suit specific subpopulations. A second but unrelated point is that the perception of burden is likely to be an important catalyst for change (cf. Oppong, 1977). It would appear, for instance, that declines in the duration of sexual abstinence occur when individuals perceive the traditionally sanctioned duration as being unnessarily long and a shorter one as being both desirable and legitimate for their social grouping, especially if they have other means of ensuring adequate inter-birth intervals. Similarly, it is unlikely that substantial changes in fertility will occur unless individuals and couples perceive high fertility as unnecessarily burdensome and smaller families as desirable and legitimate for their social grouping.

Part of this burden, of course, arises from the fact that frequent confinements deprive women of opportunities for income generation and career development. Planners and policy-makers interested in harnessing the considerable potential of women to contribute to the national development effort should give a high priority to providing women with the means to control their reproduction so as to devote more of their talents and energies to the satisfaction of economic needs.

Acknowledgements

Most of the research upon which this paper is based was carried out at the Australian National University, Canberra. The financial support of the University and the Population Council, New York, is hereby gratefully acknowledged. Thanks are also due to the International Statistical Institute and the national statistical agencies of Cameroon, Côte d'Ivoire, Ghana and Nigeria for permission to use the WFS data sets, and to Christine Oppong for helpful comments on an earlier draft.

Notes

1. Most of the contributions in Page and Lesthaeghe (1981) deal with this subject; see also Lesthaeghe (1984) and van de Walle and van de Walle (1988).
2. Lesthaeghe (1980) and Caldwell and Caldewell (1981) posit additional roles for prolonged abstinence relating to the preservation of existing social structures. However, any such function is likely to be secondary to that of enhancing maternal and child health; see, for example, Chapter 12 in this volume.
3. By partitioning the sample into subgroups that are more or less homogeneous in terms of the response variable, the AID technique provides a picture of the relative importance of the explanatory variables as predictors of the response variable, and indicates the nature and extent of any interactions existing among the explanatory variables. The algorithm performs a series of binary splits on the data such that, after each partition, differences between subgroup means are maximised relative to within-group variation. At each stage of the partitioning process the subgroup which has the largest total sum of squares around its own mean is selected for splitting. After comparing all possible binary splits on all background variables and the splits that would be performed on each of the possible subgroups one step down that branch of the tree (a 'look-ahead'), the one resulting in the largest reduction in the error sum of squares is selected for the actual partition. The look-ahead technique is designed to handle possible offsetting interactions between background variables so as to enhance each variable's chances of being used for splitting. The process comes to an end when splits can no longer be performed usefully because there is little variation within existing subgroups, subgroup numbers are too small, there are no 'useful' background variables for splitting, or the number of currently unsplit subgroups exceeds a pre-specified value. The technique does not work satisfactorily if the response variable is highly skewed on any predictor variable, or if predictor variables are highly correlated. For this study, AID runs were made on square root transformations of the response variables to verify that skewedness would not be a serious problem.
4. Information relating to the last-but-one closed birth interval was also provided in the case of Nigeria. The original information in the data sets from Cameroon, Côte d'Ivoire and Ghana actually relates to pregnancy intervals. I have transformed the pregnancy intervals into birth intervals for the purposes of the present analysis. (See Brass (1981) and Page *et al.* (1982) for discussions of some of the potential problems associated with the use of data from differentially truncated birth histories.) Because of the presence of censored observations in the post-partum data relating to the open birth interval, the AID analysis was limited to data from the last closed birth interval. Preliminary investigations indicated, however, that the patterns of reporting in the two birth intervals were similar, although data from the last closed birth interval suffered from considerable selection bias when compared with those from the open birth interval. On the whole, the two sets of data should yield fairly similar results in terms of underlying relationships, although less so in terms of the magnitude of estimated averages and differentials. That this is largely so was ascertained comparing AID results with those obtained by a hazard models analysis of Ghanaian data from the open interval, in which terms representing first-order interactions were included in the model (Ofosu, 1989, pp. 231–236).
5. Many ethnic groups were merged on the basis of common cultural, linguistic and historical affinities to form larger groupings. For Cameroon, Bakosi-Mbo, Bakundu-Balundu, Douala, East and South Bafia, Bassa, Batanga, Boulou, Fang, Maka, Sanaga and Yaounde were grouped as 'Bantu'; Baya, Kaka, Bamenda, Bamileke, Bamoun, Mbembe and Widekun as 'Semi-Bantu'; and Toupouri-Guiziga-Mou,

North and South Logone, Fringe and North and South Mandara, Adamawa, Arabs, Benue, Chari, Hausa, Fulani and Wandala as 'Northerners'; about 5 per cent of the sample, made up largely of Efik, Ekoi and Pygmies, could not be classified under any of the three groupings and were thus excluded. For Côte d'Ivoire, in addition to the Akan, Krou, Mande and Voltaic groupings, a group consisting of respondents from other African countries (mainly Burkina Faso, Mali and Guinea), who constituted a quarter of the total sample, was retained. For Ghana, the Southern Guans were added to the Akans, all the groups from the Volta region were combined as 'Ewe', and all the northern groups were put together as 'Northern'. Because of restrictions imposed by the Nigerian authorities on the use of information relating to ethnicity in their data set, I have used region of residence (North-east, North-west, South-east and South-west) as a proxy for ethnic group for Nigeria.

6. Hazard models analysis of the data relating to the open birth interval (Ofosu, 1989, pp. 231–236) does, in fact, show that these factors were more important than they appear here, although the overall results were quite consistent with those presented here.

7. It must be noted, however, that these results are dependent to some extent on the way the background variables were categorised initially.

8. The adjusted mean durations of breast-feeding were as follows: 19.1 months for Akan ($N = 31$), 14.3 for Krou ($N = 6$), 18.0 for Mande ($N = 314$), 17.0 for Voltaic ($N = 97$) and 17.0 for Other Africans ($N = 385$).

9. Although education accounted for 4.9 per cent of the total variation in the national sample, this percentage dropped to only 1.2 in group 2 and nil in group 3. Education was, however, the most important variable in the southern urban group (group 4). The adjusted mean durations for educational categories in group 4 are as follows: No education 12.8 months ($N = 291$), Primary 12.0 ($N = 79$), Middle 11.1 ($N = 234$), and Secondary+ 9.1 ($N = 60$). In comparison, the corresponding means for group 3 (Northern) are 21.0 ($N = 560$), 16.8 ($N = 15$), 18.2 ($N = 20$; the unadjusted mean for this category is 15.6) and 12.2 ($N = 4$) months respectively.

10. For example, adjusted mean durations for educational categories are, for the Bantu and Northerners of Cameroon: No education 12.2 months ($N = 1226$), Primary 11.6 ($N = 470$) and Secondary+ 8.7 ($N = 107$); for the Akan and Ga-Adangbe of Ghana: No education 6.5 ($N = 1108$), Primary 6.4 ($N = 223$), Middle 5.9 ($N = 483$) and Secondary+ 5.4 ($N = 73$); the corresponding figures for Ghana's Ewe are 11.6 ($N = 216$), 10.4 ($N = 65$), 10.7 ($N = 117$), and 6.9 ($N = 9$) months, respectively; and for the Akan and Other Africans of Côte d'Ivoire: No education 10.6 months ($N = 1148$), Primary 8.8 ($N = 154$), and Secondary+ 7.9 ($N = 53$).

12

Family Planning & Welfare in Northern Ghana

KATHARINE ABU

This chapter draws upon a body of qualitative data on reproductive issues collected in the town of Tamale over the past decade. Using both focused biographies and focus groups, data have been collected from women and men, literate and non-literate, of the major ethnic groups of northern Ghana. Findings are analysed in the light of the published data available from the Ghana Fertility Survey (GFS). The chapter also examines the different ways in which reproductive issues affect the women and men of two of the main ethnic groupings of northern Ghana, and the effects of socio-economic status on reproductive perspectives and attitudes to contraceptive use. Finally, the influence of research method on findings is examined, and the views of local family planning workers are given.

Social and Economic Characteristics of Northern Ghana

There is a major ethno-geographic divide between the north and south of Ghana. The north is economically weaker with virtually no industry, mining or major export crop and low rates of schooling. Patterns of religious adherence are also very different. According to the GFS, 70.5 per cent of northern women practise traditional religion, 18.5 per cent are Muslim and 10.9 per cent are Christian, in contrast to the south where over 70 per cent are Christian (Singh *et al.*, 1985, Table 1.16).

Tamale is the administrative capital of the Northern Region and the only major urban area in the geographical north. Many of the indigenous Dagomba in the city still depend heavily on farming activities for a survival that is increasingly precarious as the city swallows up their farm lands. Many of the men in these studies combine small-scale farming and livestock-raising with unskilled labouring, or traditional occupations such as drummer, butcher or Islamic teacher. The younger ones form part of the pool of 'by day' agricultural labour that is hired in the town and taken out to perform the manual tasks that still remain to be done on the mechanised farms. The non-literate Frafra men in Tamale have very limited access to land and are forced to take on the most unpopular and menial jobs such as watchman, cleaner and night-soil carrier.

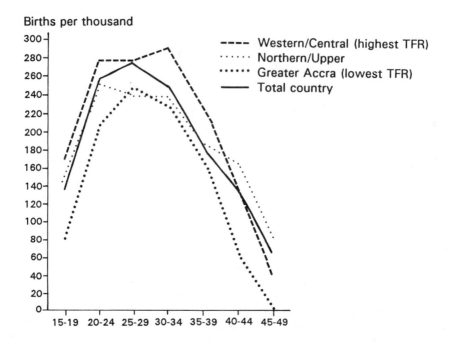

Births per thousand

Fig. 12.1 *Age-specific fertility rates for whole of Ghana, Northern/Upper, Greater Accra and Western/Central Regions, 1975–79.* **Source**: Based on Singh *et al.*, 1985.

Non-literate Dagomba women in Tamale are mostly engaged in food-processing and selling foodstuffs. Milling rice and flour, extracting oil, trading in foodstuffs and cooking food for sale are the activities that sustain most urban women, while a few of the more prosperous trade in imported goods. Frafra women, especially the more recent migrants to the city, usually lack the capital and contacts for trade. They are more dependent on their husbands than the Dagomba women, with a far greater long-term commitment to and economic integration with their husbands' lineage (see below). Some of the Frafra women come for a year or so at a time to be with their husbands and then return to their home area to farm for his family. Many husbands with more than one wife rotate their duties in this way.

Demographic characteristics
The contrast between northern and southern Ghana is manifested in their demographic characteristics.[1] Although at 6.52, the total fertility rate (TFR) for the north is very close to that for the whole country, the age-specific fertility rate curve for the north differs interestingly from that of the whole country and other regions (Fig. 12.1). Instead of peaking at 25–29 years, northern women's fertility maintains a plateau of medium-to-high fertility right through from the 20–24 to the 30–34 age groups, and it drops off less sharply after 35 than in the country as a whole. This flatter age-specific fertility curve is reflected in the birth spacing. Birth intervals in

Table 12.1 Mean birth interval in months and percentage reaching parity by 60 months since previous parity (quintum) by interval and region, Ghana

Region	Order of interval						
	1st[a]	2nd	3rd	4th	5th	6th	7th
Western/Central	19.2	30.5	30.4	31.8	31.3	29.8	29.7
	(88.8)[b]	(88.2)	(83.8)	(85.6)	(83.4)	(84.4)	(84.1)
Greater Accra	20.9	33.3	32.0	31.2	32.4	31.2	–[c]
	(90.5)	(81.6)	(77.9)	(76.2)	(77.7)	(70.4)	–
Eastern	20.5	31.3	31.5	32.1	30.5	31.0	31.5
	(92.0)	(84.3)	(83.8)	(84.0)	(84.8)	(82.9)	(79.3)
Volta	17.9	31.5	32.4	32.6	32.6	33.7	33.8
	(93.4)	(83.6)	(85.2)	(85.4)	(85.7)	(89.1)	(79.9)
Ashanti/Brong-Ahafo	20.6	32.3	32.5	32.5	31.9	32.1	32.6
	(93.1)	(89.2)	(88.1)	(84.9)	(84.0)	(77.8)	(77.5)
Northern/Upper	26.0	34.0	34.8	34.5	33.1	34.0	33.6
	(71.8)	(86.5)	(82.8)	(80.9)	(81.0)	(78.3)	(77.1)

Notes: [a] 1st interval is from marriage to birth.
[b] Quintum is given in brackets.
[c] Numbers too small for analysis.
Source: Shah and Singh, in Singh *et al.*, 1985, pp. 79–80, Table 3.21.

Table 12.2 Percentage distribution of women aged 15–49 by current marital status and by dissolution status of first marriage, showing total country and Northern/Upper Region, Ghana

	Marital status					First marriage	
	Single	First union	Later union	Separated	Widowed	Dissolved	Undissolved
All women	19.3	58.3	14.1	6.8	1.5	72.2	27.8
Northern/Upper	7.3	80.7	9.6	1.1	1.3	87.1	12.9

Source: Aryee, in Singh *et al.*, 1985, Table 2.8.

Northern/Upper Region arc longer at every interval than in any other region, averaging about two and a half months longer than in the country as a whole (Table 12.1).

Northern women spend more of their child-bearing years in the married state than southern women (Table 12.2). Mean age at first marriage in Northern/Upper Region is 17.5, at least two years younger than in the south, and, unlike all other regions except Western Region, mean age at marriage shows a slight fall rather than a substantial rise over the last decade.

It is this combination of a high marriage rate and low marital fertility that produces the north's close to national average TFR. 'The level of marital fertility in Northern/Upper Region is higher than that for Greater Accra, but lower than levels for the other regions, after adjusting for other variables' (Shah and Singh, in Singh *et al.*, 1985, p. 86b).

In short, northern women marry younger, have longer spaces between births, and continue child-bearing slightly longer to produce about the same number of births as women in the south. Despite the longer birth intervals, however, infant mortality is far higher in the north, on both adjusted and unadjusted measures. Although neonatal mortality is not particularly high, mortality in infancy and early childhood is at least double that of the rest of the country (Fig. 12.2).

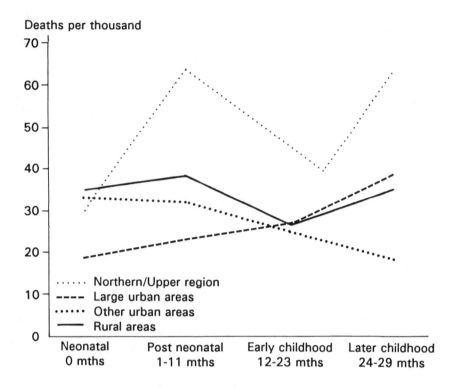

Deaths per thousand

...... Northern/Upper region
---- Large urban areas
•••••• Other urban areas
—— Rural areas

| Neonatal | Post neonatal | Early childhood | Later childhood |
| 0 mths | 1-11 mths | 12-23 mths | 24-29 mths |

Fig. 12.2 *Adjusted infant and child mortality by place of residence, Ghana.* **Source**: Based on Adansi-Pipim, in Singh *et al.*, 1985.

Ethnicity and social organisation – Dagomba and Frafra

The ethnic groups of northern Ghana are many, but they fall into two main types as regards their social organisation – a division which cuts across linguistic affinities, both Dagomba and Frafra belonging to the Mole-dagbani group. There are the centralised traditional peoples, represented in this study by the Dagomba, and the acephalous peoples, represented here by the Frafra or Tallensi, whose settlement in the area predates that of the Dagomba-type societies. These two ethnic groupings differ not only in political organisation but also in kinship and family structure in ways that ultimately affect the readiness with which contraception is accepted.

The Frafra present the classical picture of segmentary clans and exogamous patrilineal descent groups described by Fortes (1949). Bride price is high, widow inheritance is customary, and marriage increases in stability with the birth of successive children. Ancestral shrines are the focus of traditional religion but many educated and some non-literate people are now Christians. The Dagomba, on the other hand, have descending kindreds or ambilineal descent groups, and ties among bilaterally reckoned kin are maintained by extensive kin marriage and the practice of child fostering. For three centuries there has been an Islamic presence in the Dagomba state; in the latter half of this century it has become Islamised to such an extent that practically all urban and many rural Dagomba are now practising Muslims.

In the Frafra- or Tallensi-type society, wives are much more permanently attached to their husband's kin groups and homestead than among the Dagomba. At their husband's death, even if not inherited by a younger brother, they stay on in their marital home, gaining seniority with time and status as mothers-in-law and mothers of household heads. Divorce is more common and less disruptive amongst the Dagomba, since no significant bride price is involved. Moreover, widows of fertile age are expected to return to their own kin and from there to remarry rapidly into another family. In fact, many older Dagomba women, even if not widowed, retire from marriage to spend their declining days in the more congenial company of their own kin. Dagomba women also traditionally return to their own kin for the entire period of lactation and sexual abstinence after the first three births. Another significant contrast is that Dagomba husbands may bring women they are flirting with or courting to the house, but there are spiritual sanctions against a Frafra man so doing. Thus Frafra marriage is institutionally stronger than Dagomba marriage. These differences are the background to our finding that there is greater scope for conjugal co-operation over contraception among the Frafra than among the Dagomba.

Birth Spacing

The long spaces between births in the north reflected in the GFS data are part of a traditional pattern of long lactation combined with post-partum sexual abstinence, typically reinforced by removal of the young mother to her own kin in the case of the Dagomba and to her mother-in-law's room in the case of the Frafra (Gaisie, 1984). The findings of our focus groups and biographies show a continuing preoccupation with birth spacing among Tamale-dwelling women of both groups.

Women's attitudes to birth spacing and contraception
Dagomba women reported a growing reluctance on the part of husbands to let them go back to their kinsfolk after giving birth, and pressure to shorten the duration of abstinence. Weaning of the infant and resumption of sexual relations is supposed to depend on the health and development status of the child (cf. Adeokun, 1983). When the child 'walks' weaning is deemed safe, and it is on the interpretation of 'walking' that wives and husbands in Tamale today differ. Traditionally it was not enough for a child to take its first steps to be weaned; it had to be well established in walking and around 2 years old before the mother became pregnant again. Dagomba men did not admit to finding the observance of post-partum abstinence difficult. They cited the availability of other wives or girlfriends or the strength of custom as facilitating factors. Dagomba women produced eloquent evidence to the contrary.

> 'Dagomba men marry to get children but they don't take care of them. When the child is about one year three months old whether it is walking or not the man is troubling you for sex.'

> 'Look at my case. I delivered with a one year one month interval each time. Now I have three children. I suffered too much because people insulted me. Now I will wait four years. Some people don't realise our husbands force us to sleep with them. They say you were jealous and that was why you gave yourself to him to stop him doing that.'

The right of a wife to go to her own people after the first three births is also beginning to be eroded. Husbands miss the domestic services and may experience financial strain, since they are expected to provide some things, such as soap and paraffin, for a wife staying with her kin, and also do not benefit from her usual contribution to buying food for the home. To women who are able to go on 'maternity leave' in this way for a sufficient length of time, contraception as an alternative means of birth spacing has no attraction, since a break from the work of wifehood and a chance to enjoy the company of their kin is appreciated.

Contraception appeals chiefly to women who experience difficulties in achieving the desired birth spacing by traditional means. One of the immediate benefits of contraception was perceived to be less quarrelling with the husband over refusing him sexual access.

> 'Our marriages will last longer because our husbands will get all the sex they want.'

> 'As my husband has been harassing me for sex all this time and I have been refusing him, I will go to the drugstore and get the medicine and entertain my husband very well.'

The chief motivation for maintaining or extending birth intervals is promotion of the health and welfare of the children in the face of growing economic stress.

> 'It is good to limit births to five or six so that the little strength you have you can use to care for your children. Now our trading is too hard and you may get no more than a hundred cedis profit a day and each wants money for school, and by afternoon when they come back they have to eat and where is the money? You don't have it and the child will be running after you saying he is hungry and you will be weeping. If he sees something to steal he will do so because he is hungry.'

The need for a regular cash income to support children is a relatively recent urban phenomenon.

Before presenting the Tamale husband's view of birth spacing and contraceptive use, we shall give a brief analysis of the shifts in the respective responsibilities of mothers and fathers as providers that have taken place with adaptation to living in a large urban area.

The mother's role in providing for her children

The traditional mode of domestic provision is that the man provides the starchy staples and the woman provides soup ingredients from her own gathering, gardening and income-earning activities. Wives would cook in rotation for the whole household. Many Tamale women now report that their husbands are unable to provide the staples all the year round. A related development is that the range of meals catered for in bulk for the whole household has contracted and the provision of breakfast and lunch has now become one of the grey areas of responsibility, with individual mothers to varying extents providing for their own children. This shift towards greater maternal economic responsibility is attributable both to the growth in female spheres of economic activity and to the greater constraints faced by men in meeting their obligations to 'feed the house'. In the urban setting much of the expanded range of consumer goods such as children's clothes, cooking utensils and new foods falls into categories of trade traditionally considered female. Moreover, at the consumption level these goods mainly fall within the female sphere of domestic purchasing. Not only do the starchy staples which husbands provide constitute a smaller proportion of household consumption, but the husbands' ability to provide them is less assured than in a farming community. Wives in Tamale are increasingly dependent on their own efforts for their daily food and that of their children. This is particularly true of the

Dagomba. Frafra migrant women are not well established in trade, and, when their husbands' incomes are not sufficient to support them, they are more likely to be sent to the home area to farm.

The incomes on which poor urban women depend in order to feed themselves and their children are precarious. The poorer women, who retail local foodstuffs, engage in food-processing or sell cooked food on a very small scale, use this tiny daily income for their day-to-day survival. Their capital is so small and their ability to reinvest so limited that they often risk being pushed out of business when prices rise and they cannot replace their stock or raw materials. Even better-established traders, wholesalers or sellers of manufactured goods are susceptible to all sorts of market fluctuations.

Widowhood, divorce, the arrival of co-wives and the fluctuating fortunes of the husbands, as well as the precarious nature of their own incomes, make it impossible for mothers to predict their capacity to maintain their children in the long term. Given their fundamentally pro-natalist outlook, however, it is evident that these non-literate urban women need extremely flexible family planning strategies. As well as postponing births in response to immediate difficulties in feeding their children, they want to be able to increase their fertility should their fortunes improve. The economic constraints which motivate them to limit family size are experienced in an immediate short-term form, and do not produce a long-term perspective on the availability of resources for raising children.

Demographers debate as to whether maternal depletion syndrome or competition between close-spaced siblings for food and parental care is the prime cause of the relationship between birth spacing and infant mortality (Adansi-Pipim in Singh *et al.*, 1985, p. 221b). In the eyes of poor women in Tamale these factors are themselves inter-related. They perceive a direct relationship between length of birth interval and their ability to spend time on income-generating activities. When mothers talk of resting between pregnancies, they are talking only in part of their own physical health and mainly in terms of having enough energy to generate the income to provide for their children's immediate needs.

> 'If I use contraception then the money I would have used for the baby I can use to look after myself and the children.'

> 'I want five years between each of the next so that in between I can be looking for money to take care of them.'

Just as women in northern Ghana use abstinence for spacing, final limitation of family size is achieved through terminal abstinence. The reason given for stopping is 'tiredness'. When a woman says that she is tired of giving birth she is referring only in part to the strain of pregnancy, delivery and child-care, and mainly to the continual struggle to provide for the children. Given that the 'tiredness' that prompts older Dagomba women to cease bearing children is often related to dissatisfaction with the husband, it is not surprising that such women show little interest in contraception and prefer abstinence. If an older woman's husband is supporting her adequately, she is not tired and continues having children. Similarly a successful trader carries on in marriage and child-bearing long after others have given up and retired. Her large family size is a sign of her success and everybody knows that it is she, from her own income, who is responsible for her children, and the credit for raising a large family accrues to her.

Older Frafra women do not retire from marriage. They rather talk of using contraception for a while and then having 'just one more' before stopping altogether. This reflects a reluctance to cease child-bearing finally. Women prefer to delay births indefinitely rather than admit that they have stopped.

Men's attitudes to contraception

The shifts in the respective responsibilities of mothers and fathers as providers that have taken place with adaptation to living in a large urban area have had a considerable impact on women's and men's approaches to family planning. With mothers taking considerable responsibility for providing for their children's material needs, many men continue to be able to 'afford' several wives. This situation has important implications for decision-making about fertility. First, it is mothers who experience stress in providing for children and who therefore care most about birth spacing. Second, having more than one wife, or even the possibility of acquiring an additional wife in the future, makes it difficult for men to be involved in decisions about limiting family size.

An underlying assumption of polygyny is that a man can support all the children that each wife bears, and to suggest that any wife limit her fertility when she is not the only sexual partner would be very difficult. Moreover, a man cannot be party to a decision to limit births with one wife and then marry an additional one later. Participating in a decision to use contraception within marriage would limit a man's options. Men therefore prefer not to know when their wives are using contraception and publicly express disapproval of married women using contraception.

For a man, the acquisition of the first wife and birth of the first child mark important transitional stages in his life, almost to the same extent that marriage and motherhood do for a woman. The addition of subsequent wives and the growing number of his offspring are the substance of his growing status and seniority within kin groups and community. The interminable topic of young men's conversation is the difficulty of getting a wife, with all the attendant costs of bride price or ceremonial gifts and the wedding feast. The acquisition of a second wife can also mark a significant stage in the domestic cycle, since it is on marrying a second wife that a Dagomba man typically moves out of his elders' compound and sets up on his own, thereby achieving the status of household head. The birth of a child is welcomed as swelling the numbers of dependants and descendants, for in traditional society seniority is enhanced when offspring are numerous.

> 'So as I am seated here today what makes me happy about my three wives is that I am a young man and I will give birth to children early in my life and as we are all young we will struggle to survive and one day if you see my son you won't think that he is my child, because at present my first-born is already seven years old and reaches my waist. At present I have two boys and two girls and only two of my wives have delivered. By the grace of God and by his will in five years' time I may have eight children. If I get at least eight I can take care of them because by then the first-born will be old enough to help me take care of the brothers and sisters. So long as I have long life I can manage. Without health your enemy will get you. Hunger will come in because you won't have strength to work.'

This statement by a man of about 30 illustrates the sense in which a man's life is almost a race against time and numbers to head a family.

Being the only child of the father or mother is considered a great disadvantage.

Siblings are much valued and a small family is seen as a misfortune. Within the wider kin group, only children are at a disadvantage compared with larger groups of cousins. At funerals they make a less impressive showing; their claims to titles in the paternal line are harder to assert. Worst of all, there is a risk of their father's line dying out. It is thus that a high fertility dynamic inheres in societies in which the kin group is a major mediating institution between the individual and the wider society.

Although they express disapproval publicly, Dagomba husbands in Tamale are often ready to turn a blind eye to a wife's using contraception because they themselves cannot provide for many children. Besides, it gives them more status to have several wives with a limited number of children each than one wife with as many children as she can produce.

Frafra men in Tamale appear much readier to accept contraception within marriage than Dagomba men. This was evident both from their own statements and from the fact that when Frafra wives are interested in contraception they expect to discuss family size and contraceptive method with their husbands rather than hiding what they are doing.

'We men will allow our wives to take the pill. Why not?'

'Some say that the condom can be re-used, but if not, then it is too expensive and it is more economical to let your wife be on the pill and remind her to take it.'

Frafra women do not report the pressure from husbands to reduce post-partum abstinence periods that Dagomba women do. This may be because they have traditionally maintained abstinence without residential separation. Nor do Frafra husbands express fears that wives who use contraception will be adulterous, as Dagomba husbands do. When a Dagomba woman is discovered to have committed adultery, she is most likely to be summarily divorced and the stigma of paternity in doubt hangs over all her children. When a Frafra woman is found to have committed adultery, or confesses it, when there is bad luck or sickness in the home, she goes through a ritual of purification, the public nature of which is a strong deterrent to adultery, but she is not divorced. It is believed by the Frafra that a woman can never commit adultery with impunity, because even if it is not discovered her transgression will carry such spiritual consequences, manifested in misfortune, that she is bound to confess eventually. The spiritual sanctions are considered to be effective, even in present-day urban settings, and are widely held to account for the reputation of Frafra women for fidelity. Dagomba women face more disruptive consequences in that they are cast out of the marital home if they are discovered committing adultery, but if they are not caught, and especially if there is no child from the adulterous union, they may commit adultery with impunity. It is even said that in the large urban areas some husbands overlook their wives' transgressions out of a desire to avoid the disruption of divorce and the expense and difficulty of getting another wife.

Real data on the adultery rate among women are of course hard to obtain, but ethnic reputation in this respect is reflected in husbands' attitudes to their wives' contraceptive behaviour.

Table 12.3 TFR by education, percentage change in TFR by calendar period, and TMFR by education, Ghana

| Education | TFR | Percentage changes | | TMFR |
		1970/74–1975/79	1965/69–1970/74	
No schooling	6.88	−6.8	+0.7	8.01
Primary	6.91	−0.4	−0.3	
				8.58 (primary and incomplete middle)
Incomplete middle	5.98	−10.6	−3.7	
Complete middle and secondary or higher	5.64	−0.9	−6.7	
				8.08 (complete middle only)
Secondary or higher only	–	–	–	7.25

Source: Shah and Singh, in Singh *et al.*, 1985, Tables 3.12 and 3.14.

Influence of Education and Occupation on Fertility

The level of female education in the north is far lower than in the south: 90 per cent of northern women had never been to school as compared with 50 per cent for the whole country. Only 0.3 per cent had had any secondary schooling as compared with 4.3 per cent for the whole country.

GFS findings for the whole country indicate that the decline in total fertility rates for those with incomplete or completed middle school (Table 12.3) is attributable chiefly to reduced exposure due to later age at first marriage. Substantial declines in marital fertility rates (TMFR) are only observable in the tiny category of those with secondary education or higher.

The configuration of responsibilities of educated mothers and fathers as regards physical care, social training and material provision differs from that of traditional rural-derived, non-literate families. Educated men take a lot more financial responsibility for their children and show more interest in their welfare than non-literate fathers do, and they therefore experience economic strain in proportion to the number of children that they have. They realise that, given the standard of living and educational opportunities they want for their children, they cannot leave such a large proportion of child-rearing responsibility to the children's mothers as is traditionally done. They are critical of non-literate fathers.

'An illiterate sees a child as not productive and therefore not worth spending on.'

'An illiterate doesn't care about a child until he can be of use. If he happens to be a bad boy when he grows up the blame goes to the mother. While we think of their future the illiterates just let them grow and be anything and leave everything to the mother, including medicine.'

Educated fathers perceive their offspring as needing certain material and social training advantages, if they are to compete effectively for jobs and specialised training. All these requirements entail parental inputs in terms of time and money, and the educated man, looking at his and his wife's respective material resources, perceives that she is not in a position to take on as large a proportion of these responsibilities as mothers in traditional and non-literate contexts. Educated men tend to marry women with a somewhat lower level of education and income than themselves. It is firstly in the sphere of material provision and secondly in the sphere of school and career guidance that educated fathers perceive their parental responsibilities.

In discussing the duties of fathers and mothers, respondents of both sexes with a medium level of education (no post-secondary training) concentrated on the responsibilities of a father to provide materially and of a mother to take time in providing physical care, regular meals, baths, clean clothes and so on. This does not mean that these mothers are not also expected to contribute substantially to providing for the material needs of the children, but that they should not have to shoulder almost the entire expense of raising them, as many urban non-literate women do.

With secondary education and higher, parents also express increasing concern about the need to spend time supervising, teaching and sharing leisure with them (Oppong and Abu, 1987). Although some educated fathers are prepared to spend a little time with their children, the response of most to the perceived need of children for more parental time is that the mothers should provide this. Educated fathers are often critical of their wives for burdening the children with too many domestic tasks or not paying sufficient attention to their emotional and disciplinary needs.

'The mother should instil confidence in the children, have time for them and not think that they are a bother – persist with training. The father should give them lessons if the mother is not willing. I have to do it as their mother is not all that interested.'

'A father should not only provide financially but also show interest in the child. Let him see that he cares about his general level and school work. A woman's duty is to give most attention to the children because time is not a problem for them. I'm the breadwinner.'

'The father should have more time for the children because the mothers are always busy and they don't care much. Sometimes as we are here together I take more care than my wife. Sometimes I have to ask her to supervise them more carefully (such as not letting them climb on dangerous things). She doesn't have time to read books with them and I do a bit.'

The contrast between the parental behaviour of wealthy non-literate men and the relatively impoverished educated fathers highlights the impact of education on attitudes to parenthood.

'An illiterate may have a car but not think of using it to drop the children at school. An educated man can put his child on the crossbar of his bicycle and take him to school.'

One educated Dagomba respondent who held a managerial post, but whose parental behaviour rather reflected his traditional princely background, suffered considerable criticism from his occupational peers. Unlike them, his response to the financial strains of child-rearing did not include any limitation of family size.

'In the last two years there have been some financial problems in caring for the children – school fees, etc. Also they had been used to taking things like tea and bread when they were hungry. That had to stop. I don't like family planning. If the children and their mothers are hard-working they should be able to cope. I may be a chief one day and then the villagers will farm for us.'

While not quite as family size conscious as their wives, most educated Tamale men favour some degree of family size limitation for economic reasons.

'In the African life we don't have a limit, but now things are different. An individual has his way of thinking. If things improve I'll have five, but if not, stop at two or three. If I am in a position to take care of the house, she [wife] is ready to bring forth more children.'

'Some of our mates are wretched, though the parents were wealthy. Most of my half-brothers and sisters aren't making ends meet. That's why I don't want plenty children.'

Among the Muslims the option of polygyny is always open. It is rare to meet a Muslim man, however highly educated and however long-standing his marriage to one woman, who has entirely ruled out the possibility of an additional wife in the future.

'I can't tell if I will marry another wife or not, but my children shouldn't go into double figures.'

Educated women, like non-literate women, feel more acutely than their husbands the need to limit family size. Like non-literate women, they experience the strains of child-rearing more than the fathers do, even though the latter contribute substantially to child-rearing expenses. With higher standards of nutrition and hygiene, educated women spend a greater proportion of their time on domestic tasks as opposed to income generation than urban non-literate women, and yet it is still considerations of finance rather than time that influence their fertility decisions.

'He jokingly said that Musa needs a brother. I didn't say anything but I feel that four is enough. Look at all the children [kin] that he is bringing into the house. He says he doesn't want to discriminate between his children and his brothers' children but he forgets that ours are much younger. They need more nutritious food. But since Musa was born has he bought even one pair of shorts for him? Yet the boy dresses. Last night when I had fever so many thoughts were going through my mind. I thought that if Alhaji dies I will have to take care of the children alone. I can't have another one.'

Husband: 'I never thought about family size except the cost of living is so high now. I'd like one more boy and then stop.'
Wife: 'I think my four is enough but my husband insists we try for another boy. If that is a girl too I'll definitely stop.'

Educated women generally have a long-term perspective as regards the number of children they can afford, given their likely future resources and the costs of child-rearing. They are ready to specify preferred numbers of children even though their plans are often modified in practice. GFS data on fertility by education level within regions or ethnic groups are not at present available, but small-scale studies show that family size among educated Dagomba women conforms fairly closely to the national pattern (Oppong and Abu, 1987). Since birth-spacing intervals among the overwhelmingly non-literate northern female population are longer than for Ghana as a whole, we can deduce that in the north non-literate women space their births at least as much as literate women, although the latter achieve smaller family sizes by marrying later and finishing having children sooner.

The variation in TFR by occupational category is far more striking than that by education level. Fertility declines markedly with increasing modernity of occupation (Table 12.4). Occupation and education level are of course linked, but the expansion in schooling opportunities of the last two decades has not been matched by an expansion in occupational opportunities, and it is an important finding that modernity of occupation rather than education *per se* depresses fertility. After multi-variate analysis

Table 12.4 TFR by most recent occupation, showing changes by calendar period, Ghana

		Percentage changes	
Occupation	TFR	1970/74–1975/79	1965/69–1970/74
Not working	5.91	−5.3	+12.0
Sales and service	6.85	−4.5	+6.9
Agriculture	7.08	−2.5	−1.8
Manual	6.32	−6.8	−3.8
Professional and clerical	4.62	−0.6	−16.2

Source: Based on Shah and Singh, in Singh *et al.*, 1985, Table A.1.

of socio-economic factors, GFS authors found that marital fertility does not show much variation by education and that such differentials as do exist are primarily due to age at marriage (Shah and Singh, in Singh *et al.*, 1985, p. 87a).

The more traditional urban occupations for women, such as trading and food-processing, permit them to combine work and child-rearing with relative ease. They can have their infants with them as they work and then older children either care for younger ones or work in the trade itself. Women employees, in contrast, are obliged to separate income generation and motherhood in terms of time and place. Arrangements must therefore be made for young children to be cared for during the mother's working hours. Older children have to be at school and moreover cannot assist their mothers in their work.

Maternity leave and daily breast-feeding breaks are the right of female employees in Ghana, but often it is not practical in terms of time and transport costs. Not all employees are aware of their rights and many managers, including those in government service, are unwilling to grant them. In practice either the baby or the job suffers. The following two excerpts from biographies illustrate how with lower-grade, poorer employees it tends to be the baby who suffers, while more advantaged women are able to mark time or accept a set-back in their careers.

'My daughter has just got a job in the education office and doesn't qualify for maternity leave. It is a problem with the baby. We sacrificed and bought powdered milk for the day-time feeds and now the baby won't take the breast at all. We tried to force and let him be hungry enough so that he would take it but the neighbours came and asked why we were letting him cry so long. To carry on buying so much milk powder will be difficult.'

'I am interested in that job with the *x* company. It's better paid than my work for the administration, but the baby is still very small and even if I'm not paid well in my present job at least I can take time off as I need. If I were to work for a private company I'd really have to work, and to get a baby nurse to meet my standards would not be easy, so I think I will stay where I am for now.'

These two cases in different ways show how the formal employment context imposes strains when a woman attempts the traditional combination of income-earning and motherhood. Some public sector organisations require women to accept frequent repostings, causing great disruption in their home life and necessitating complicated arrangements for the care or schooling of their children.

It is not uncommon for educated mothers to plan births to fit in with career developments. Even though they marry later than non-literate women, first-generation educated northern girls in particular are under great pressure from kin to marry young, and as they are often given too little support during their education they tend not to progress through the school system quickly. Having married and had one or two children, they plan to acquire further qualifications before going on to achieve their fertility goals. These strategies for combining maternal and career roles require both a high level of motivation and careful planning and juggling of domestic arrangements. They are also made easier when mothers live in their home area, where kin or in-laws are available to take care of the children. The great pressures and supports to high fertility that educated mothers in their home area experience compared with migrants is reflected in their fertility achievements. A study that compared the maternal and occupational roles of static and migrant educated mothers amongst a southern (Ga) and northern (Dagomba) group found the Dagomba educated mothers living in their home area, Tamale, had the highest fertility, though family size preferences were the same for all groups (Oppong and Abu, 1987).

It is thus increasingly apparent that the respective responsibilities of mothers and fathers in the urban north of Ghana differ from their recently rural-derived traditional patterns. Non-literate mothers, especially amongst the poor, are increasingly providing for the greater part of their children's material needs. Amongst the more educated, fathers perceive their children as having material needs that the mothers cannot be expected to meet alone.

Amongst non-literate fathers the Dagomba are unwilling to involve themselves in family planning other than the traditional abstinence, while the Frafra with their stronger marriage institutions are willing to replace abstinence with modern contraception. Among both literate and non-literate people of both groups it was the mothers who felt most acutely the need to limit family size by some means.

The most striking difference in the approaches of educated and non-literate women to family planning is in the time-scale of the planning. Non-literate women are primarily interested in ensuring that they can raise each child to at least three years before having another one. They need this interval in order to promote child survival and allow themselves time and energy to earn enough to feed the children. Their planning is *ad hoc* in the sense that it does not go beyond the timing of the next birth. When and whether to have subsequent children will be influenced by the mother's economic strength at the time. Good fortune in trade will encourage her to go on and have more children, set-backs will motivate her to 'postpone' the next birth indefinitely. The incomes of the urban poor are precarious and the extended spacing approach to contraception is ideally suited to people who are pro-natalist but constrained by limited resources and in particular by unpredictable incomes. Educated mothers, in contrast, typically employees in the public sector, feel they have a fair idea of their likely resources in relation to child-rearing expenses over their reproductive and income-earning careers. This enables them to plan in the long term and to set goals or limits on family size from the start.

Just as non-literate women experience material constraints in rearing children in an immediate form, so the time aspect of combining income-earning and child-rearing is dealt with continuously and requires only day-to-day planning. In contrast, an educated woman's combining of occupational activities and motherhood involves long daily mother–child separations which require advance planning for regular delegation of child-care.

Influence of Research Methods on Findings

Data were collected from non-literate people by three qualitative methods: focus groups, focused biographies and interviews with opinion leaders.

Dagomba men appeared very anti-contraception in focus groups but more amenable to the idea when approached individually in the course of biographical data collection. The reverse was the case with the Dagomba women, from whose biographies emerged a very conservative picture of women's attitudes to reproductive issues. It seems that, when interviewed in or near their homes and pinpointed individually, women were afraid to express views that were deviant from the dominant and accepted norm. In focus groups, in contrast, women showed themselves highly enthusiastic about contraception. Ensuring sufficient privacy for the focus groups was important. Insufficient privacy proved a problem in the biographical data collection. As a group, women were ready to challenge the norms of a male-dominated society which places them under increasing pressure to provide for their children. In the company of other women who were facing similar problems, each readily justified her deviant behaviour, thereby taking part in the process of generating a female subculture.

Men, as already mentioned, appeared more receptive to the idea of family planning when interviewed separately. Men, as husbands and fathers, are the holders of authority and the articulators of the traditional ideology that legitimates that authority. In a group before their peers, they did not wish to be seen to compromise on issues that are held to be fundamental to family life. Interviewed individually, however, some of the same men indicated that contraception could be acceptable to them.

With Frafra respondents, findings did not vary according to data collection method or even by sex. This is a reflection of the greater community of interest between spouses and also the lack of inhibition the Frafra have in discussing sexual matters. Even the unplanned participation of old men and women at a men's focus group did not restrain respondents in their habitual ribaldry.

Interviews with opinion leaders all produced views significantly more negative towards modern contraceptive methods than were found amongst other participants. This was perhaps to be expected. For the same reason that Dagomba men do not want to be heard approving of contraception, opinion leaders of both sexes and ethnic groups, identified through their seniority and wealth or religious status, are public articulators of traditional values.

Literate respondents were altogether more at ease than non-literate respondents, especially when discussing reproductive issues. There were still some differences by sex, but in the opposite direction from that experienced with non-literates. Educated women appeared to feel that domestic and reproductive issues were their sphere of concern and expertise and that they had much of interest to communicate, while the men showed less interest in such issues, often stating that these were more the wife's concern.

Given the divergent findings presented by the different data collection methods employed, it might be asked which presented the correct picture (if any of them did), and by implication which is the best method to use? The contention here is that each method is of value in its different way. Much was learned from the men's focus groups and the women's biographies that clarified the specific nature of pro-natalist desires, and the forces working against the use of contraception even when lengthy birth intervals are wanted. Biographical data collection from all groups showed, as focus groups did not, how women's and men's reproductive roles figure in family, kin group and domestic organisation.

The women's focus groups revealed the motives of would-be contraceptive users. They brought out the reasoning with which these women justify deviation from dominant norms. The very arguments they brought forward can accordingly be used to develop family planning messages. These centre upon the economic arguments mentioned above but also include concern about delinquency amongst children and young people who are inadequately fed and supervised.

Given that these data collection methods did tap divergent trends in attitudes to contraception, and that non-literate women did seem constrained in individual interview situations, one is prompted to question the reliability of the 'attitude' and, even more, the 'practice' elements of knowledge, attitude and practice (KAP)-style surveys. It was noted in the focus groups that although some knowledge and approval of contraception was evidenced nobody personally admitted to using it, and it seems likely, among the Dagomba at least, that few non-literate women would admit to being contraceptive users.

The Views of Local Family Planning Workers

When interviewed, five Tamale family planning workers of both the main northern ethnic groupings, some with the Planned Parenthood Association of Ghana (PPAG) and others with the Ministry of Health, all indicated that they were well aware of the general differences in attitude to contraception and reproductive issues amongst members of the two main ethnic groupings, though they attributed these to differences in religion rather than ethnicity. The one difference that is held to be of ethnic significance is the greater fear amongst Dagomba husbands that wives who use contraceptives will commit adultery. Several family planning workers mentioned the deterrent purification rite for adulterous wives in the Frafra type of society.

Since conversion to Islam and Christianity has for historical reasons taken place along ethnic lines, the attribution of cultural differences to religion is understandable, especially since Islam is the religion of the Dagomba, whose men are more resistant to family planning. It is generally considered by non-literate orthodox Muslims themselves as well as by non-Muslim observers in northern Ghana that the religion opposes contraception. Christianity, in contrast, is viewed as more modern and therefore more predisposed to accept contraception as part of Christian marriage – despite the fact that the Roman Catholic Church figures prominently amongst the groups under consideration. Monogamy rather than natural reproduction is the key family-life issue in all the Christian churches.

Family planning workers' understanding of cultural differences that affect attitudes to reproductive issues are reflected in their observations on clients' behaviour.

'I would say that at least 90 per cent of the Muslim women who come to us do so without their husband's knowledge.'

'The women from Upper East and Upper West [Regions], they don't hide what they are doing from their husbands. Occasionally a Christian man may bring his wife for family planning, especially if he has been to school and she has not.'

At the same time family planning workers consider ethnic or religious differences to be of minor significance as regards acceptance of contraception:

'Things these days are so hard that everyone is beginning to see the sense in family planning.'

Economic pressures on parents in the urban north are now so great that attitudes to family planning, even amongst the most conservative sections of society, are undergoing change. Moreover, whether women use contraception with or without their husband's consent, at the level of converting interest into action among the married, women have to be the main targets, since male methods are disliked, especially for use within marriage.

Family planning workers know what themes most attract listeners to the idea of using contraception. Male PPAG workers addressing Muslim leaders in Tamale have found that concern about adolescent delinquency, because of parents' producing more children than they can maintain or supervise properly, is the most effective issue. Nurses addressing women in Dagomba villages near Tamale report that they get a good hearing when they address the tensions that arise over maintaining traditional post-partum abstinence.

Conclusion

Research findings indicate, and family planning workers concur, that the level of demand for information and potential demand for services is not at present being adequately met by the family planning agencies' outreach programmes. At times, too, supplies of preferred contraceptives, including certain brands of the pill and foam tablets, run out. There are women in Tamale and the surrounding villages who have heard something of contraception and are interested but who do not know where the services are provided.

Two main directions for improvement in outreach approaches to non-literate women are suggested. First, information on contraceptive methods needs to be accompanied by very specific information on where to get contraceptives. In the urban and semi-urban areas groups of women who are given information about family planning need also to be taken to the nearest clinic so that they become familiar with the place and personnel. Such women would then also act as resource persons capable of introducing others to the services. Bringing interested women to the clinic without pressurising them to become clients could be an important step in bridging the gap between interest in contraceptive use and action. Many villages have health posts that are used by visiting health personnel. Markets move from one town or village to another on different days of the week, and family planning personnel could 'follow the market' just as full-time traders do, making their services available to the full range of women that frequent each market.

The second area for suggested improvement is the development of a more interactive communication style. Experience with focus groups has shown that, although these are designed to inform the researcher, in practice participants also learn a lot about contraception from them. The non-directive and interactive style of the focus group encourages participants to ask for clarification of the information being offered.

Young men who participated in focus groups in Tamale became contraceptive information resource persons amongst their peers. One, who had been vocal against contraception in the focus group, approached the researcher a year later with a request to take his wife to a family planning clinic. Research by its nature seeks not to convince people but to elicit their views, and yet our experience has been that research interactions stimulate demand for information and services. The indications are that person-to-person communication with informed personnel is most effective in doing this. Meetings designed to promote two-way communication, in which the recipients' views are sought and respected, may well be more successful than overt and direct attempts to convince and recruit. In other words, sounding out the subjects' views needs to precede the giving of information, which ideally then takes place as a response to demand.

Notes

1. The GFS groups the administrative regions of the north (at the time of the survey two, and now three) together as Northern/Upper Region.

13 The Grandmother & Household Viability in Botswana

BENEDICTE INGSTAD

This chapter focuses on the part that the grandmother frequently plays in Tswana households and the influence she has on economic and demographic strategies, including family planning and child-rearing, in a rapidly changing society stressed by drought.

In discussing family policies and their implications for demographic change in developing countries, attention has mostly been given to the choices made by the couples actually producing children, and little to the part played by other family members, in spite of an apparently increased awareness among policy-makers, programme managers and social scientists of the importance of the 'extended family' in household decision-making and as a social support system in many developing societies. In doing so one may easily overlook factors that have an important impact on the process of demographic increase (or decrease). Such factors may not be identifiable at the macro level but only through an accumulated understanding of the choices that individuals make as they play their several roles, including those of kin, within their particular social and cultural frameworks (Oppong, 1985).

By focusing on the role of the grandmother, I do not aim to give a complete picture of family planning, child-care and child survival among the Batswana.[1] I rather seek to demonstrate how, by shifting the angle of vision slightly away from the immediate child-producing couple – the biological mother and father – one may accumulate added information which might be of value for a deeper understanding of the issues as well as for practical policy-making and the implementation of relevant programmes to promote household viability and ultimately child survival.

The data on which this analysis is based were gathered over a period of two years (1984–85) in Kweneng district, Botswana. A follow-up study of 94 households was carried out in connection with an evaluation of a Government/World Health Organisation (WHO)/Red Cross-initiated programme for community-based rehabilitation. Semi-structured interviews, conducted with an interval of one year, covered a whole range of questions on household composition, economic activities, child-care, health and rehabilitation. Additional data were gathered by participant observation and informal interviews (Ingstad, 1984).

The sample was selected on the basis of having a disabled family member, but has

209

proved to be representative of rural Tswana households judging by important criteria such as household composition, household headship, ownership of livestock and lands, income-earning activities, etc. It may therefore, for our purposes of qualitative analysis, be considered a fairly random sample of rural households.

The Setting

Kweneng district

Kweneng district is located in the south-western part of the country. Towards the east it borders on the capital Gaborone, and the villages are strongly influenced by urbanisation. Towards the west it stretches into the Kalahari Desert with small, scattered and sometimes very remote settlements not much touched by modern society. The main village of Molepolole is the tribal as well as the district administration centre. It has a population of approximately 25,000, most of whom live in traditional dwellings and are members of the Bakwena tribe.

Like most other districts in Botswana, Kweneng has been affected by a drought that lasted from 1981 until 1987. This seriously affected the mixed pastoral/agricultural based-economy. By the time of the field work for this study, a large number of the households had lost many or all of their cattle and had not ploughed their fields or had any crops for some years. This caused considerable hardship for many people, a situation which would have been even worse had it not been for the free food rations given through the government drought-relief programme. Drought in Botswana is not an exceptional situation, but rather a condition which occurs at fairly regular intervals (Hinchey, 1978); thus it has to some extent been prepared for.

Unemployment is high all over the district, and openings for unskilled labour are few and poorly paid. Kweneng has always been one of the districts in Botswana that has ranked high as regards contributing young men as labourers to the mines in South Africa. Although such work is increasingly difficult to obtain due to the changing employment policies of the mining companies, it is still important for the economy of many rural households. More than one-third of the households surveyed had a father or brother in the mines. There is also considerable migration of both men and women from rural areas to urban centres within Botswana.

The drought-relief programme also has a labour-based component, creating openings locally for both male and female unskilled workers, but such jobs are scarce and usually available for only two weeks of the month with very low pay.

Thus we see a diminished contribution from the traditional farming and cattle-breeding economy, and an increasing dependency on cash income and/or relief.

Health care and demographic changes

Since 1973 the emphasis in Botswana's health policies has been on primary health care (PHC). A network of clinics, health posts and mobile stops has been built all over the country, serving around 80 per cent of the population within 15 kilometres' walking distance of their homes.

The primary health care system is largely nurse-based, with one regional medical officer supervising the clinics at two- to four-week intervals. The daily responsibility for preventive health care as well as normal deliveries and simple curative work thus rests on the registered nurse-midwife, assisted by family welfare educators, who are the link between the village and the health care system. Family welfare educators are (usually) elected by the villagers and given a 16-week training course.

About 60 per cent of all babies are delivered in a hospital or clinic. The rest are delivered at home by traditional birth attendants. Recently attempts have been made to create a dialogue with these birth attendants in order to teach them simple hygiene measures and make them refer difficult cases to the modern health care system in time (Anderson and Staugard, 1987).

It has been estimated that 96 per cent of expectant mothers attend antenatal clinics and that 80 per cent of children are fully immunised (Government of Botswana and UNICEF, 1986). The improved health care has of course had an influence on the child survival rate. Infant mortality has gone down from 119 per thousand live births in 1960 to 68 in 1987 (UNICEF, 1989). Life expectancy at birth has, however, only increased from 56 in 1971 to 58 in 1986. The population grew by nearly 85 per cent in the period 1964–81 and has now passed 1 million (Brunborg, 1987).[2]

This almost explosive population growth has important implications for the development of the country. In 1981, 47 per cent of the population was below 15 years of age. Such a high proportion of dependants has implications for economic development as well as for services such as health care and education. 'Development' becomes not simply a question of making progress as regards providing new or increased opportunities, better standards of living, etc., but is to a large extent a struggle to prevent conditions from becoming worse for the rapidly increasing population. Fortunately Botswana's national economy has been fairly prosperous during the last 20 years due to the discovery of large diamond deposits. However, the income from these is managed rather restrictively and has only benefited the rural population to a limited extent.

Although it is claimed that no deaths were reported during the drought years from hunger alone, the main health problem for children under 5 is malnutrition, which makes them more vulnerable to infections and thus may cause death, in spite of free drought-relief food rations for all children under 5. Kweneng district rated among the highest in the country as regards child malnutrition in 1984 (27 per cent of all under-5s registered at the clinic), with only a slight improvement towards the end of 1985.

Children registered as malnourished or otherwise at risk were given daily rations of extra nutritious foods. For this they had to be brought to the clinic and fed in the presence of health personnel, a task which might easily conflict with the main care person's other duties.

In addition to children under 5 and those who were malnourished, drought-relief food rations were given to children under 10 who were not at school, primary school children, pregnant and lactating mothers, TB patients and destitutes. It has been estimated that around 60 per cent of the population received such rations during the drought years.[3] In the sample from Kweneng discussed here, such rations were the main source of subsistence in around one-third of households.

Another major killer of small children is diarrhoea. To fight this problem mothers are taught how to mix a sugar and salt solution, and rehydration salts are distributed. Major programmes for clean water and sanitation have also been launched and 'health talks' constitute a major part of the preventive work done by health workers.

Family planning policies

Family planning programmes have been on the agenda since the establishment of a primary health care system. Recent studies showed that 28 per cent of married women aged 15–29 years (including women living in consensual unions) practised contraception, 26 per cent approved of family planning, and 80 per cent knew of a contraceptive method; 70 per cent of the users lived within 30 minutes of a place where they could get contraception. Thus, in theory at least, contraception is quite easily available and widely accepted, although its use is still not very widespread.

Family planning advice and contraceptives are given mainly to women coming to child welfare clinics with their babies, but may also be given at other consultations. All contraceptives are free. Information on family planning is given in health talks, and posters are distributed.

The responsibility for family planning programmes has thus been placed mainly with the health care system. Sex education in schools has only taken place with the consent of parents. There are strong contradictory views on this, mostly resulting from the general lack of information about family planning issues. Prominent church people, even from churches that are not officially opposed to family planning, argue strongly against giving young people such information, and yet teenage pregnancies are today the main reason for the high drop-out rate of girls from secondary schools.

Women have been the primary target of family planning campaigns, with the emphasis more on the spacing of children for the sake of the health of the mother and child(ren) than on limiting the number of children born to each woman. Although the campaign apparently has had some success as far as spacing is concerned, the average number of children born to each woman during her lifetime is still considered too high from the point of view both of the mother's health and of the further development of the country. A shift in emphasis towards advocating smaller families is thus occurring.

Another change in policies currently taking place is due to the recent campaign for AIDS prevention. More responsibility is being placed on men by advocating the use and distribution of condoms. Radio and press are being used to disseminate information, together with slogans such as 'stick to one partner', and the campaign is also reaching the school curriculum. To what extent this will influence sexual behaviour and family planning practices in the long run remains to be seen.

Household composition and changes

The Bakwena, like other Tswana tribes, trace descent through their fathers. The custom is for the man at marriage to settle in the near vicinity of, or even within, his parents' compound with the new wife. If he is the child of a polygynous marriage he will settle in or near his mother's compound (since each of the wives in such a union is supposed to occupy a separate compound).[4] The daughters-in-law thus become the main supporters of the old lady in her daily tasks and are expected to show her respect and obedience.

The traditional marriage is a process over time, starting with negotiations between the family elders and ending with the transfer of the bride-wealth (*bogadi*) to the wife's family (usually eight head of cattle) and the removal of the bride to her new home. Between the first negotiations and the final event there may be a period of several years, in which the couple is allowed to meet and even to have sexual intercourse.

Thus by the time the new bride arrives at her mother-in-law's compound she might bring one or even two grandchildren with her.[5]

Unmarried children traditionally remain attached to their parents' household after reaching adolescence, the girls being closely guarded by their mothers and the boys often going away to the cattle posts or the mines. In this context to have a child without being (or in the process of getting) married is not common and is considered shameful.[6]

With this pattern of marriage and cohabitation a Tswana household will most often consist of an 'extended family'.[7]

The traditional marriage has been supplemented, and in some cases replaced, by a modern marriage conducted by the district commissioner or some other authorised person (church minister or administrative officer). Such a marriage requires neither the consent of the parents or guardians for people over 21 years nor the payment of bride-wealth (unless a traditional marriage is conducted simultaneously). This gives young people an opportunity to establish legal unions without the involvement of parents and other relatives. In fact, it is becoming more and more common to establish unions without any sort of formalisation.

When couples get married today it is no longer taken for granted that they will establish themselves near, or even in the same village as, the man's parents. Jobs, as well as the desire to establish a modern household based on the nuclear family, may lead them to different places, although the social and emotional bonds usually remain strong.

The most marked changes in family and household patterns are seen in the large number of children born to unmarried mothers and the significant number of households headed by women. While children were accepted and even to some extent expected during the 'betrothal period' in the old days, we see today an increasing number of women having children without any officially recognised father and often without even trying to claim support for the child (which is possible through both the traditional and the modern court system) (Comaroff and Roberts, 1977). For some educated women with the ability to support a child themselves, who choose not to be under the jurisdiction of a man, staying single is a conscious choice. But in most cases the woman would have preferred to marry but for a number of reasons has not succeeded in doing so. Out of the 94 households in this sample, 64 (68 per cent) include one or more children born out of wedlock, the maximum being 14 in one household.

With situations like this occurring more frequently, unmarried women are obviously suffering less social stigma. However, a clear distinction is made between respectable girls who 'just happen' to have a child (or children), or even chose to have one, and promiscuous women (*seaka*) who are suspected of sleeping with many men within a short period, which is considered very shameful.[8] One important reason why many girls and their families do not try to claim support for their children is the fear that the boy will claim she has been with other men who might just as well be the father of the child (Ingstad and Saugestad, 1984).

According to the 1981 population census, only 29.8 per cent of women in the 20–24 age group were married and around 50 per cent in the 25–29 age group. In total 60 per cent of all women between 15 and 49 years of age had ever been married, but only 10 per cent of those between the ages of 55 and 64 had failed to marry. This shows a tendency for women in Botswana to marry late in life, but may also be interpreted as indicating a growing tendency for women to go through life unmarried in spite of having children. Seventy-five per cent of all births to mothers between 15 and 19 and 57 per cent of all births to mothers between 20 and 24 were to single mothers.

According to the 1981 census 45 per cent of all households had a female head; however, it has been suggested that the figure may be as high as 75 per cent in some villages.[9] Female heads of households may be widows, unmarried mothers, divorced or separated women, or women whose husbands are temporarily away (for instance as labour migrants to South Africa). In the cross-section of Kweneng households included in this study 53 per cent were permanently or temporarily female-headed.

In consequence we see another type of household composition emerging and becoming more frequent: a middle-aged woman living with her unmarried daughters and their children. Unmarried sons are also considered part of such a household but they are often away working or looking for jobs. Sometimes the unmarried daughters go away to work and the older woman will be left alone to care for the grandchildren.

The Value of Children

In discussing social changes and population growth in general and the role of the grandmother in particular, it is important to consider how children are regarded in the context of the Tswana household – how they are 'valued'.

Children as contributors to the household
Children not only consume household resources such as food and clothes. They also contribute to the household in various ways.

Traditionally the boys play an important part in looking after cattle and other livestock. This might start from a fairly early age, depending on the number of boys in the household and the number and type of livestock. Small boys would stay near the home looking after goats and sheep while older boys would go further away with the men to look after cattle. The importance of these tasks has diminished somewhat in recent years, partly as a result of the drought, which killed off much of the livestock, but mainly as a result of increased school attendance (85 per cent of all children of primary school age). Some families still keep at least one of their sons away from school (which is not compulsory), or let them drop out early to look after cattle.

Girls traditionally start to look after their younger siblings at a very early age and help their mothers with household chores such as cooking and carrying wood and water (which may also be done by younger boys). This pattern still prevails but the chores are to a large extent combined with school and done during the lunch hour and free time; there are actually more girls than boys attending primary school. The fact that most rural households consist of more than one grown woman and that unskilled jobs are hard to get makes the presence of the daughters during the day less imperative. Some teenage girls drop out of school to help in the house, but most such drop-outs are due to pregnancy.

Both girls and boys played a very important part in traditional agricultural production, and still do to the extent that the climate allows any yield at all. They watch the fields to keep livestock and birds away, and help with weeding and harvesting.

Since these are very time- and labour-consuming tasks, households with a limited amount of manpower may take their children out of school for months at a time.

Another type of contribution that children make to the household is in the form of food rations, given through the drought-relief programme. As previously mentioned, all children under 5 years of age and children under 10 not attending school get monthly rations of mealie meal, powdered milk and cooking oil. Babies also contribute through their mothers, who receive similar rations while they are pregnant or lactating. Households with an 'advantageous' household composition may thus receive enough monthly rations to make up a basic (although very meagre) diet for all members, since the food is shared by everyone. Occasionally children under 10 are kept away from school so that their rations can be shared between all household members (instead of the child being fed daily at school).

Children as security
In a longer-term perspective Botswana parents clearly see their children as an 'investment' in security for themselves and other dependent household members. This emphasis on the obligations of the family members towards each other has roots deep in Tswana culture, but has also been cemented in modern law and is an assumption which underlies the social policies of the modern state (Molokomme, 1985).

'Even if I do not get married I want at least one child to take care of me when I get old' is an often encountered statement among unmarried young women. It reflects the basic insecurity that many people feel towards the future and their own inability to make secure their old age. It also reflects the official social policies in which old age as such is no criterion for support from the government but only the very strict criterion of being classified as destitute (meaning someone with absolutely no resources or family members to lean on).

Parents express clearly their expectations that the children will help them to lead a better life than they have now. A new avenue has opened up for girls in terms of education, making it possible for them to contribute in other ways as well as through the traditional bride-wealth (*bogadi*). Fathers often want their sons to continue the old pattern of going to the mines as soon as possible and sending money home, while mothers are more likely to see a better future for them in education.

When asked about their feelings regarding a disabled child, parents often say, 'I feel sorry because now he will not be able to take care of me in the future.'

Traditional expectations are of greater support from boys than girls. The fact that these days educated rural girls seem as likely as boys to obtain moderately well-paid jobs (as teachers, nurses, clerks) and the fact that they are often more likely to continue to contribute to their parents' household (because they often remain unmarried and leave their children with their parents) is not yet reflected in common attitudes.

Children as replacements
Child mortality is still high in Botswana and consequently most families have experienced the loss of one or more children.[10] The attitude that a lost child should, or will, be replaced by another one is reflected in the naming practices.

According to Tswana tradition a child is given a name which is meaningful for the situation into which it is born, or a name which reflects the feelings or expectations surrounding it. Thus there are special names for a child who replaces another child and even for one who replaces one that was itself a replacement, for a girl replacing another girl, a boy replacing a girl and so on. On the loss of a child the expectation that it will (and should) soon be replaced is clearly expressed to the parents, and approval and understanding is voiced when a new one arrives.

It seems quite probable that the experience of losing children makes people actually strive for more children beyond the replacement factor (Bergstrom, 1985). Moreover, since children are prestigious benefits and effective contraception is often not practised, subsequent births are likely to occur whether expected or not.

Children to be loved and cared for
An important motive for people to have children, in Botswana as elsewhere, is the joy and pride of having them. Although sometimes expressed in purely practical terms, the level of appreciation of children for themselves is high. In Botswana children are seen as a necessary part of a satisfactory life, and the cultural standard for a proper family size usually sets four or five as a minimum. This may, however, be changing slowly as people become more urbanised, with households being based more on the nuclear family and depending more on two incomes.

The Botswana joy in children is most clearly expressed in the case of the very young ones. Infants are cuddled and played with and passed from arm to arm to the extent that they hardly have a chance to cry when not sleeping or suckling. Visiting women coming into the yard will pick up a baby to play with, as soon as the formal greetings have been exchanged, and men do the same. This type of attention is reduced gradually as the child grows and is able to walk around on its own, and gradually the feeling for it is expressed more in terms of future expectations for it than in what it represents as a child. This, however, should not be misinterpreted as meaning that the family cares less about it or is less interested in its well-being.

The Role of The Paternal Grandmother

In discussing the role of the grandmother in matters such as family planning and child-care, it is vital to distinguish between the role of the paternal and the maternal grandmother, as these are very different.

The grandmother of the children of married sons
Since married sons these days tend not to settle close to their mothers, it is difficult for the mothers to retain their traditional control over their daughters-in-law, including the control of money sent home by sons working as migrant labourers. In earlier days this was left to the son's parents or mother to allocate according to need. One old lady living alone under very poor conditions with four working and married sons settled elsewhere put it like this: 'Before, the daughter-in-law listened more to the mother-in-law than to her husband, but now she wants the money all for herself.'

It seems quite possible that the desire of young wives to escape this type of control plays an important part in the decision to settle elsewhere. The obligation of the son to help his parents still remains but is often not fulfilled, although it is considered very shameful to neglect it.

The reduced contact with and increased physical distance from the son's household also have important implications for the grandmother's relationship with his children.

Although sons are still considered the heirs to their fathers'/grandfathers' estate (mainly cattle) and girls may increase the estate through bride-wealth, they are much less to be counted on for daily chores in their grandmothers' (grandparents') household. However, if a married son divorces (which is not very common), he has the customary claim to the children and will bring them to his mother to care for. In rare cases this may also happen if he has been living in a steady relationship without marriage.

> A man who had lived with a woman for many years without being married left her and their seven children. After a long time without being provided for, the woman brought the case before the chief in the traditional court (*kgotla*). The verdict was that the man should bring the four oldest children to live with his mother and provide for the remaining three with their mother. Thus the economic and practical burden for the mother of his children was reduced. She was satisfied and saw this as a confirmation that their relationship had been equivalent to a formal marriage.

In the old days it would often be the paternal grandmother who delivered the babies and helped to take care of the new mother and child. Due to an increase in hospital deliveries and the change in residence patterns this function has been reduced, although the paternal grandmother may still come to her son's household to help and supervise.

The grandmother of the children of unmarried sons

Unmarried grown-up sons living in the parents' home are expected to contribute to the household from whatever income they may have, whether it is earned in the village or away from home. Upon their son's marriage the parents can only hope for future support, but there are few possibilities for sanctions. Households thus often face a gradual decline in their standard of living as the grown-up sons get married. The need to keep working sons in the household increases if unmarried daughters bring children to the home, and especially if the mother is widowed or single.

There are thus two mutually reinforcing trends at work in the present situation. The more unmarried mothers there are, the more the son/brother's assistance is needed in the household and the less willing families in rural households are to induce the father to take on responsibility for children born to 'other' families. This may lead to more permanent changes in household composition in years to come, with matrifocal households becoming a more established pattern and an increasing number of women never marrying.

While it is quite unlikely that the mother will have any influence over the procreative behaviour of her son, she may both directly and indirectly influence whether he takes up economic responsibility for a child or not. When unmarried mothers were asked why they had not tried to bring pressure upon the father of their child to make him support it, they would often answer, 'Because I like the child more than money.'[11] The meaning of this is that if a man was forced to pay, or even if he did so voluntarily, they would be afraid of his mother or sisters practising witchcraft upon the child to kill it, to prevent their own household economy being drained of resources.

Fathers of children born out of wedlock have no legal claims to their offspring, although they have a duty to support them. An 'illegitimate' child has, however, no duty to support the father or his parents when it grows up. Even if compensation or support is paid, fathers usually have little or no contact with these children, unless they are the product of a union which eventually results in marriage.

We can see from this that the paternal grandmother has little chance of becoming emotionally attached to the children of her unmarried sons, nor does she have any prospect of obtaining practical help or economic support from them as they grow up. These children thus come mainly to represent a threat to the viability of the household and as such a responsibility to be avoided if possible.

> Neo is young and unmarried. She is living with two sisters in a family headed by her mother, who makes a little money by cooking food and selling it to people during lunch hours. Neo became pregnant by a miner who was home on leave, the son of a widow from one of the powerful families in the village. Neo's mother went to the man's family to ask for marriage or economic compensation and support, but they rejected any responsibility for the pregnancy. No further attempts were made by Neo's mother, though the case could have been taken to the customary court (*kgotla*) for the chief to consider.

The Role of the Maternal Grandmother

The grandmother of the children of married daughters
Since married daughters often settle quite far away from their parents, distance may limit the contact between the children and their maternal grandmother. On the other hand, ties between mothers and daughters are expected to remain strong after marriage, with frequent visits by the daughter and her children to her parents' home. If the grandmother is alone in her old age and without any daughters-in-law or unmarried daughters to take care of her, she will expect to move in with a married daughter.

Although married women are expected to have their babies at their new home, or to return there shortly after hospital delivery, it has been quite a common and accepted practice for a young wife to go home to her own mother to have the first child because 'she will care for it better than the mother-in-law'. It has also been quite common for this first child, especially if it is a girl, to return to the mother's parents at a young age, and to stay and help them with the daily tasks. Several women actually claimed that their mothers would have taken it as an offence if they had not sent them a child for fostering. The children of married daughters thus often come to have a close relationship with their maternal grandmothers and may be useful to them in many ways.

> A young nurse had grown up with her maternal grandparents and felt that her grandmother was closer to her than her own mother. When she herself bore a son without being married she sent him to be fostered by her own grandmother (who was by then a widow), because this was where she visited most frequently, and this way she could also send money to her grandmother without her own parents becoming jealous.

The grandmother of the children of unmarried daughters
The present pattern of households providing for the children of unmarried daughters may be seen as an extension of the traditional practice of sending children to grandmothers for fostering. The number of children living with maternal grandmothers seems to be increasing rapidly, however, with a maximum of 14 in one of the households in this study. Even if the mother eventually marries and moves away, these children are often left behind.

Middle-aged or elderly women living in rural areas have very few opportunities for wage employment. If they make any money at all it is mainly in the informal sector, where the brewing and sale of traditional beer is the most common activity. This is done in the home with a limited input of physical labour and the care of small children thus creates no major hindrance.

For analytical purposes we may distinguish between households where unmarried mothers are living with their children in their parents' home, and households where the children have been left with the maternal grandmother (and grandfather) while the mother is away working. In reality, of course, we most often find a combination of the two, with some daughters at home and some away.

In the first type of household there is a surplus of female working capacity due to the shortage of local employment opportunities. Thus all the women of the household, including older children, co-operate in taking care of the little ones and doing the household chores. Everyone then has time for other activities such as visiting friends and neighbours some time during the day. During ploughing and harvest seasons, when most household members go to 'the lands', it is usually possible to spare someone to look after the small children if necessary, while others may remain in the village with the school children.

In the second type of household, where the mothers are away working, the child-care may strain the working capacity of the grandmother, especially as she grows older, and she may have to cut down on other valued activities (such as visiting friends and neighbours) and limit the household chores (by not engaging in agricultural activities) in order to manage.

For children growing up in both types of setting, the maternal grandmother usually becomes the main female figure, the one who organises the daily life of the household, the one who makes the decisions (if there is no male head), the one to be looked up to and respected. Unmarried women living at home never really have the status of grown-up, independent people. If they go away to work they have more autonomy, but they are still subordinate to their mother/parents when they are at home visiting. With this type of relationship the grandmother (grandparents) may also have good reason to hope that one or more of the children of the unmarried daughters, if they succeed in life, will eventually support them. Thus an investment in care for these grandchildren also becomes an investment in (possible) future security for themselves.

Children, of course, represent an immediate economic strain on a rural household, especially in times of drought, when subsistence production is minimal and most foodstuffs have to be bought. The other main costs involved are connected with clothes and schooling. Although primary and secondary education as such is free, uniforms and shoes have to be bought and a small yearly sum paid for the cooking of the (free) food at school. Outside school, children inherit clothes from each other and wear them until they literally fall apart. Small children wear little or nothing.

As already mentioned, however, children of the right age may also bring food rations into the household in times of drought, thus considerably reducing the costs involved, even to the extent of making them an economic asset. In cases where fathers actually support their illegitimate children, this is of course a valuable contribution to the household economy, but this was the case in less than one-quarter of the households in the sample with children born out of wedlock. When caring for the children of working mothers, the household may also expect to have a share in their salary, which it might otherwise not have. The problem, however, is that uneducated

Table 13.1 Percentage distribution of households by number of illegitimate children and type of headship, Botswana ($N = 94$)

Head of household	0	1	2	3	4	5 or more	Total
Female-headed	16	16	6	12	12	38	100(32)
Male head absent	50	11	11	16	6	6	100(18)
Male-headed	39	18	14	9	14	7	101(44)
Total	32(30)	17(16)	11(10)	12(11)	12(11)	17(16)	101(94)

girls often earn such low wages that there is little or nothing left to send home after their own living expenses have been met.

We can see from this that the opportunity costs involved in raising children, defined as the time spent in caring for children and the value of special goods and services used in child-rearing, may be kept at a fairly low level in rural Botswana. Large numbers of 'fatherless' children can be absorbed by the household of the maternal grandmother/grandparents and even to some extent become assets.

Table 13.1 indicates the tendency for female-headed households to have a larger number of 'illegitimate' children than those headed by a male or with a male head who is temporarily away (*de facto* female-headed). For this there may be at least two different explanations. First, it is quite likely, as in the example of Neo above, that households without a male head will be in a much weaker bargaining position *vis-à-vis* the man's family; the pregnant daughters may therefore more frequently remain unmarried and the children not provided for. Second, female heads of households, seeing their sons getting married or drifting away, are actually quite keen to have children from their daughters, both as short-term contributors of food rations (for as long as the drought lasts) and as a long-term 'investment' in labour power and security. We shall return to this below.

These two explanations are not of course mutually exclusive; rather, they operate at the same time to create a pattern which makes women very vulnerable in rural Botswana today. It has been well documented that female-headed households are to be counted among the disadvantaged groups in Botswana (although there are of course exceptions). They are clearly poorer than the average, as manifested in smaller herd sizes and draught-power problems that decrease the opportunities for agricultural production (Gulbrandsen, 1980; Government of Botswana and UNICEF, 1986).

It is difficult to work out what is the optimal number of children in such a household. What might seem like a good 'investment' in the short term may easily turn out to be disastrous as time goes by.

An elderly woman had for several years been taking care of her unmarried daughter's children. The daughter worked as a maid in Gaborone and regularly sent home what little extra she had, which, together with the food rations of the children, made up the living of the rural household. When the daughter gave birth to child number five and found it was disabled, she realised that her mother was now too old to manage this extra task and she quit her job to stay with the children. By now only two children were eligible for rations and she was not able to get a job locally. All they could hope for was some help from an unmarried brother/son, who had proved to be rather elusive in the previous years.

Influence on the family planning practices of unmarried daughters
According to the traditional moral code a young unmarried girl should stay at home after sunset, and her mother is responsible for seeing that this happens. Mothers now in their thirties and forties may say, 'Nice girls don't go out at night, but when I was young I sometimes sneaked out after my mother had fallen asleep.' This was, however, explicitly in breach of a manifest norm and imposed upon the girl a strong obligation to be careful and to look after herself.

The wisdom of grown-up life used to be given to boys and girls separately as part of their initiation to new age-sets (Schapera, 1978; Tlou and Campbell, 1984). This instruction was given by elders, and it was therefore considered an insult for children to ask their own parents questions of a sexual nature. Parents would also avoid discussing such topics with their children. The 'initiation schools' were abandoned decades ago among the Bakwena, but many older people today regret this and feel that the modern school system has not succeeded in teaching the youngsters traditional values and moral standards.

Nowadays things are changing. The most marked changes are in the increased opportunities for young men and women to be together away from their parents' supervision. It happens in secondary school, where most youngsters are boarders, and where the large number of girls who drop out due to pregnancy shows that the teachers are not keeping a very close watch over them. It happens when the family go to 'the lands' for months at a time and teenage girls remain in the village to go to school and look after younger school children. And it happens in the evenings when youngsters meet at discos and bars, with plenty of opportunity to go off into the bushes if they feel like it. Since young girls would mostly be much too shy to line up with the married women at the clinic for 'family planning', especially without their mothers' consent, and young men do not bother to get condoms (which are now freely available following the recognition of AIDS), pregnancies are quite likely to be the outcome of the resulting unions.[12]

To protect young girls from the dangers of modern life takes a discipline and control which not all parents are able to enforce, especially women who bear the responsibility alone. It is still difficult for mothers and daughters to discuss sexual topics. The following example shows, however, that some of these household heads may be more in control of their daughters' fertility than one might be led to think, by observing a large number of 'fatherless' children in a family.

> A middle-aged woman, herself head of the household, had five unmarried daughters in their twenties. Each daughter had two small children, because as one said: 'Mother allows us to have two and then she sends us for family planning.' The household had no support from sons/brothers and lived mainly from the children's rations and what could be earned from occasional beer brewing. In spite of this the household members were well dressed and well equipped with utensils. There is reason to believe that contributions from boyfriends were an important part of the household economy and might even be encouraged by the mother.

The increasing number of children born out of wedlock cannot be sufficiently explained by the changing moral standards or the growing opportunities for young people to be together. It must be seen in a total household perspective, where the apparent lack of maternal control over the daughters may sometimes be a strategic choice. Often a suitable marriage (for instance to a miner with the ability to pay bride-wealth) is the hoped-for outcome of a sexual union, but parents are not unaware of the difficulties that may be involved in achieving this and have also to be prepared for other eventualities. The knowledge and availability of 'family planning' even makes it possible to plan for families of 'illegitimate' children, if the maternal grand-mother is supportive.

Influence on breast-feeding and nutrition

According to tradition a woman who has given birth to a child should stay in confine-ment for a three-month period. During this time she and the child should stay inside the room, resting and eating, so that both mother and baby become fat, and only com-ing out when absolutely necessary. An elderly woman, usually her mother-in-law or mother, was put in charge to see that no one entered without permission – especially a man, even the father – for the first week. The belief was that, if the father (or any other man) were to have intercourse with the mother during this period, he would bring pollution to the mother from any other woman he had slept with during this period. The pollution would enter the mother's blood and from there pass into the milk and affect the child with *Mopakwane* – severe physical and mental retardation. Moreover, strangers might bring the dangers associated with witchcraft into the room.

Confinement after birth is still practised quite extensively, although it has to be reduced somewhat for working women.[13] The belief in *Mopakwane* is still strong – strong enough to make women who do not observe the full three-month period, and even those who have other boyfriends than the father of the child after confinement, seriously consider terminating breast-feeding.[14]

With the diminishing practical importance of the mother-in-law, the maternal grandmother has come to play the main part in the organisation of confinement in many families, as the following example illustrates:

> A young girl, diagnosed by traditional healers as *Mopakwane*, was living with her maternal grandmother while her mother was working in Gaborone and her elder sister was away at secondary school. When the sister became pregnant it was decided that the confinement period should be extended to four months to be on the safe side. She was sent before delivery to her maternal grandmother, who was considered to be the one best able to supervise it properly.

The confinement period is obviously an important time for the passing on of know-ledge about breast-feeding and child-care in general. The baby is massaged several times a day for stimulation and relaxation, while the mother is prohibited from any type of work other than baby care and is encouraged to rest and eat plenty of nutritious food (if available). So far, breast-feeding is widely practised and most women seem to enjoy the confinement as a period of leisure. However, some younger educated women tend to resent being under the control of an older woman and use their limited maternity leave as an excuse to get away as soon as possible. This may be an increasing trend in the future and may also come to influence breast-feeding practices.

We can see from this that mothers/grandmothers may play an important part in ensuring that breast-feeding is given a successful start, thus influencing infant nutri-tion and also – in an indirect way – child spacing. However, they may also play a part in ending the breast-feeding too early by taking over the care of the baby so that the mother can go away to (seek) work. Although done with the best intentions and out of consideration for the household economy, such taking over of care probably accounts for a major part of childhood malnutrition and infant mortality. No major study has yet been done on this, but a survey of malnourished children from the Kweneng district may give some answers when published (Mokganedi, forthcoming).

Influence on child survival and quality of care
The quality of care given to a child fostered by the maternal grandmother will depend on the economic situation of the household as well as on the motivation of the grandmother. If the household is very poor it will be difficult to maintain the standards of hygiene and nutrition necessary for the child's development and good health. This may become critical if the mother goes away soon after birth and the child has to rely on substitute milk.

Poverty tends to be part of a vicious circle in which the desire to give good care may itself be worn down in the long run. A special problem here is alcoholism, which may of course hit rich and poor alike but which is often part of the same vicious circle. Left behind with a grandmother who drinks, a small child gets a poor start in life.

> A 2-year-old boy was staying with his maternal grandmother and two young aunts while his unmarried mother was away working. Their house was close to the busy main road going into the village. There have been several occasions of neighbours picking up the boy, who was wandering along the road during the day, while the aunts were at school and the grandmother somewhere drinking.[15] The child was malnourished and was also somewhat mentally retarded.

It is equally important to realise, however, that many grandmothers do an excellent job in taking care of their daughters' children. In some cases they insist on fostering the child, because they see themselves as better able to look after it than their daughters. These women have preserved the best of the traditional baby-care practices but are also able to adopt new knowledge obtained from the clinic.

> A 5-year-old girl was living with her younger brother at their maternal grandmother's house while the mother was away working. During her first year of life it became clear that she was developing very slowly, probably due to brain damage. Guided by a local health worker, who was inspired by the community-based rehabilitation programme, the grandmother put in an enormous effort in training the girl. The techniques they used were a combination of old and new practices adapted by themselves to the surroundings and circumstances, and at 5 the girl walked almost normally and played happily with the older children. When it transpired that the little brother was malnourished, due to a general shortage of food in the household, the grandmother followed up the daily feeding programme very faithfully in spite of having to carry him for long distances to and from the clinic.

Although the child welfare clinics are mainly centred around the unit of the mother and child, there is nothing to prevent a grandmother bringing her grandchild, and she would be expected to do so if she takes over the fostering completely. However, since these older women do not have the same tradition of utilising modern health care as the young ones, it may easily happen that attendance becomes irregular or is even discontinued when the mother goes away.

Finally, the quality of care and consequently the chances of survival and proper development for the child depend on the working capacity of the main care person and the supportive network around her. A well-founded economy and proper motivation may not be sufficient if the grandmother is overburdened due to a large workload (for instance, many grandchildren to look after) or her own frail health.

Household viability, defined as a proper balance between resources, labour capacity and needs (Stenning, 1962; Rudie, 1984), thus becomes a critical issue. Improving child-care is largely a question of helping households to cope with multiple responsibilities and activities and to restore viability once it is threatened.

Conclusion and Policy Implications

The grandmother plays an important part in Tswana households, and the consequences (mostly unintended) of modern development have to some extent placed even more responsibility on her than before. She may be a family head with the main responsibility for the economic dispositions and daily running of the household. She may also be the main care person for a number of her daughters' children, with or without support from their mothers. She may be the preserver of the old values (such as moral standards and child-care customs), but also the one who decides to leave them behind for practical and other reasons. And she is often the one responsible for decisions such as whether to utilise the opportunities of modern society (such as health care and education) on behalf of the child.

Seen in this light, it seems that grandmothers are often as important a target for counselling about child-care and family planning as the younger women themselves. It may be difficult to involve them directly, since young health workers often find it difficult to instruct older women on such topics, but their voice may be heard indirectly through the village health committees and information disseminated to them through women's organisations and the Red Cross. In any case, grandmothers should be seen as key figures – which they often are in rural households – when policies and projects to promote family planning and child welfare are being developed and implemented.

Acknowledgements

The field work on which this article is based was made possible by grants from the following sources: Royal Norwegian Ministry of Development Co-operation, World Health Organisation, Carl Lumholtz Fund, Scandinavian Institute of African Studies, Uppsala, and the University of Oslo, Norway.

Edwin Sandberg, Sidsel Saugestad and Axel Sommerfelt have made valuable comments.

Notes

1. Botswana – the country/nation.
   Batswana – the people of Botswana.
   Setswana – the language.
   Tswana – the term most commonly used in anthropological literature meaning both the culture and the people.
2. One National Census carried out in 1991 has come out with the preliminary figure of 1.3 million inhabitants.
3. The drought-relief feeding programmes were discontinued after the onset of good rains in 1989, leading to an increase in malnutrition in several districts. The feeding of malnourished children continues, however.

4. Polygyny has largely been abandoned, although some older people are still polygynously married and younger men may settle with mistresses in polygynous-like unions.
5. For further discussion of traditional Tswana marriages, see Ingstad and Saugestad (1984), Gulbrandsen (1986) and Schapera (1987).
6. For further details on unmarried mothers, see Ingstad and Saugestad (1984).
7. The term 'family' here stresses the links established by kinship and marriage and the rights and obligations connected with such links. The term 'household' stresses the actual co-residential domestic group and the people who in effect contribute to the household livelihood.
8. The concept of 'prostitution' is not attached to the practice of obtaining money or gifts through sexual relations but to having a large number of partners within a short period. A boy is expected to give money presents to a girlfriend to show his gratitude. Since young men home on leave from the mines have quite a bit of money to spend (in village terms), such gifts may play an important part in the household economy.
9. Personal communication from researcher Ulla Kann, 1987, National Institute of Development Research and Documentation, Botswana.
10. It is estimated that about one out of ten children dies before reaching adolescence and that 70 out of every thousand babies die before the age of 1 (Government of Botswana and UNICEF, 1986).
11. A one-off compensation for 'damages' (loss of virginity) may be claimed through the traditional court system. It usually amounts to eight head of cattle or an equivalent sum of money. Regular monthly support may be claimed for all children born out of wedlock through the modern court system. The demand for this must be brought forward within one year of the birth of the child (Molokomme, 1985).
12. Abortion is illegal (except under specified conditions) and punishable by up to seven years in prison.
13. Maternity leave is six weeks prior to delivery and six weeks after delivery on half salary. Subsequently 30 minutes' leave may be taken twice a day for six months to suckle the baby.
14. This might cause a milder form of illness for the child, *Malwetsana*. To illustrate this we may mention that the bus which returns to the village every Friday with miners from South Africa goes under the nickname 'kwisang ngwana', meaning literally 'take the child away from your breast', thus leaving the mother free to receive her partner without harming the child.
15. Home-brew is easily available every day in most neighbourhoods and may be obtained more or less free by going from place to place taking it 'on credit'.

Bibliography

Abu, K. 1983. 'The separateness of spouses: conjugal resources in an Ashanti town', in C. Oppong (ed.), *Female and male in West Africa*. London, George Allen and Unwin.

Acharya, M.; Bennett, L. 1981. *The rural women of Nepal: an aggregate analysis and summary of eight village studies. The Status of Women in Nepal*, Vol. II, Part 9. Kathmandu, Tribuvan University, Centre for Economic Development and Administration.

Adeokun, L.A. 1983. 'Marital sexuality and birth spacing among the Yoruba', in C. Oppong (ed.), *Female and male in West Africa*. London, George Allen and Unwin.

Adepoju, A. 1983. 'Patterns of migration by sex in West Africa', in C. Oppong (ed.), *Female and male in West Africa*. London, George Allen and Unwin.

——. 1984. 'Migration and female employment in South West Nigeria', *African Urban Studies*, Vol. 8, Spring.

——. 1988. 'An overview of rural migration and agricultural labour force structure in Africa', *African Population Studies*, No. 1, pp. 5–25.

——; Clarke, J.I. 1985. 'The demographic background to development in Africa', in J.I. Clarke, M. Khogali and L.A. Kosinski (eds), *Population and development projects in Africa*. Cambridge, Cambridge University Press.

Adepoju, A. 1989. 'The consequences of influx of refugees for countries of asylum in Africa' in R. Appleyard (ed.) *The impact of International migration on developing countries*. Paris, OECD.

Adepoju, A. (ed.) 1991a. *Swaziland: population, economy, society*. New York, UNFPA.

Adepoju, A. 1991b. *Demography of Swaziland: training manual series 3*. New York, UNFPA.

Adepoju, A. 1991c. 'Africa's Population Crisis: Formulating Effective Policies' *African Recovery Briefing Paper No. 3*. United Nations, New York.

Africa Confidential. 1991a. 'Zimbabwe: the land at stake', *Africa Confidential*, Vol. 32, No. 2, 25 Jan., pp. 4–5.

——. 1991b. 'Zimbabwe: a test case', *Africa Confidential*, Vol. 32, No. 6, 22 March, pp. 5–6.

——. 1991c. 'Zimbabwe: pluralism in a one-party state', *Africa Confidential*, Vol. 32, No. 17, 30 Aug., pp. 6–7.

Ainsworth, M. 1989. *Economic aspects of child fosterage in Côte d'Ivoire*. Paper to Conference on the Family, Gender Differences and Development, Yale University, Economic Growth Center, 4–6 Sept.

Alauddin, T. 1980. 'Contribution of housewives to GNP: a case study of Pakistan'. MS thesis, Vanderbilt University, Nashville, Tennessee.

Allsopp, D. 1982. *World Fertility Survey standard background variables: definitions, warnings, marginals and cross tabulations*. London, WFS; mimeo.

Amoah, M.; Nhlapo, R.J.; Similane, T. and Takirumbudde, N. 1982. *Law, population and development in Swaziland*. Kwaluseni, University of Swaziland.

Anderson, S.; Staugard, F. 1987. *Traditional midwives*. Gaborone, Ipelegeng Publishers.

Anker, R. 1983. 'Female labour force participation in developing countries: a critique of current definitions and data collection methods', *International Labour Review* (Geneva, ILO), Vol. 122, No. 6, Nov. – Dec.

——. 1990. 'Methodological considerations in measuring women's labour force activity in developing countries: the case of Egypt', in *Research in Human and Capital Development*, Vol. 6. Greenwich, Conn., JAI Press, pp. 27–58.

——; Anker, M. 1988. *Improving the measurement of women's participation in the Egyptian labour force: results of a methodological study*. World Employment Programme Research Working Paper No. 163. Geneva, ILO.

——; ——. 1989. 'Measuring the female labour force in Egypt', *International Labour Review* (Geneva, ILO), Vol. 128, No. 2.

——; Khan, M.E.; Gupta, R.B. 1987. 'Biases in measuring the labour force: results of a methods test survey in Uttar Pradesh, India', *International Labour Review* (Geneva, ILO), Vol. 126, No. 2.

——; ——; ——. 1988. *Women's participation in the labour force: a methods test in India for improving its measurement*. Women, Work and Development Series No. 16. Geneva, ILO.

Appiah, K. 1991. 'Manpower and employment in Swaziland' in Adepoju, A. (ed.) *Swaziland: population economy, society*. New York, UNFPA.

Ardayfio-Schandorf, E.; Kwafo-Akoto, K. 1990. *Women in Ghana – an annotated bibliography*. Accra, Woeli Publishing Services.

Armstrong, A. 1985. *A sample survey of women in Swaziland*. Research Paper No. 15. Kwaluseni, University of Swaziland, Social Science Research Unit.

——. 1987. 'Access to health care and family planning in Swaziland: land and practice', *Studies in Family Planning*, Vol. 18, No. 6, pp. 371–382.

——; Nhlapo, R.T. 1985. *Law and the other sex: the legal position of women in Swaziland*. Kwaluseni, University of Swaziland.

——; Russell, M. 1985. *A situation analysis of women in Swaziland*. Kwaluseni, United Nations Children's Fund (UNICEF)/University of Swaziland, Social Science Research Unit.

Arnold, F.; Blanc, A.K. 1990. *Fertility levels and trends*. Demographic and Health Surveys Comparative Studies No. 2. Columbia, Md., Institute for Resource Development/Macro Systems Inc.

Arrighi, G. 1973. 'Labour supplies in historical perspective: a study of the proletarianization of the African peasantry in Rhodesia', in G. Arrighi and J. Saul (eds), *Essays on the political economy of Africa*. New York, Monthly Review Press, pp. 180–234.

Awusabo-Asare, K. 1988. 'Interpretation of demographic concepts: the case of Ghana', *Population and Development Review*, Vol. 14, No. 4, pp. 675–686.

Azefor, M.N.A. 1981. 'Counteracting forces in the continued decline of mortality in Africa', in *International Population Conference Manila, 1981, Solicited Papers*, Vol. 2. Liège, IUSSP.

Batezat, E.; Mwalo, M.; Truscott, K. 1988. 'Women and independence: the heritage and the struggle', in C. Stoneman (ed.), *Zimbabwe's prospects: issues of race, class, state and capital in Southern Africa*, London, Macmillan, pp. 153–173.

Benería, L. 1981. 'Conceptualizing the labour force: the underestimation of women's economic activities', *Journal of Development Studies*, Vol. 17, No. 3, April.

——. 1982. 'Accounting for women's work', in L. Benería (ed.), *Women and development: the sexual division of labour in rural societies*. New York, Praeger.

Berger, I.; Robertson, C. 1986. *Women and class in Africa*. New York, Africana.

Bergstrom, A. 1985. *Familieplanering i U-land. Om barns värde, barnbegränsning och barnloshet i tredje världen*. Stockholm, S. Bergstrom.

Berry, S. 1984. 'The food crisis and agrarian change in Africa: a review essay', *African Studies Review*, Vol. 27, No. 2, June.

Blacker, J.G.C. 1978. 'A critique of the international definition of economic activity and employment status and their applicability in population censuses in Africa and the Middle East', *Population Bulletin* of the United Nations Economic Commission for Western Asia, Beirut, Vol. 14, June.

——; Hill, A.G.; Timaeus, I. 1985. 'Age patterns of mortality in Africa: an examination of recent evidence', in *International Population Conference, Florence*, Vol. 2. Liège, IUSSP.

Blades, D.W. 1975. *Non-monetary (subsistence) activities in the national accounts of developing countries*. Paris, OECD.

Blalock, H.M. 1981. *Social statistics*. Singapore, McGraw-Hill.

Blanc, A.K.; Lloyd, C.B. 1990. *Women's childrearing strategies in relation to fertility and employment in Ghana*. Population Council Research Division Working Paper No. 16. New York, Population Council.

Bledsoe, C.; Isiugo-Abanihe, U. 1989. 'Strategies of child-fosterage among Mende grannies in Sierra Leone', in R.J. Lesthaeghe (ed.), *Reproduction and social organization in Sub-Saharan Africa*. Berkeley, Calif., University of California Press.

Boateng, E.O.; Ewusi, K.; Kanbur, R.; McKay, A. 1990. *A poverty profile for Ghana 1987–88*. SDA Working Paper No. 5, Policy Analysis. Washington, DC, World Bank.

Bongaarts, J. 1984. 'A simple method for estimating the contraceptive prevalence required to reach a fertility target', *Studies in Family Planning*, Vol. 15, No. 4, pp. 184–190.

——. 1990. *The measurement of wanted family*. Population Council Research Division Working Paper No. 10. New York, Population Council.

——; Frank, O.; Lesthaeghe, R. 1984. 'The proximate determinants of fertility in sub-Saharan Africa', *Population and Development Review*, Vol. 10, No. 3, pp. 511–537.

Boohene, E.S. 1985. 'Promoting women's status', *Populi*, Vol. 12, No. 1, pp. 29–35.

Boserup, E. 1970. *Women's role in economic development*. New York, St Martins Press.

Botswana, Central Statistics Office. 1989. *Botswana: Family Health Survey II 1988*. Columbia, Md., Institute for Resource Development/Macro Systems Inc.

——; Ministry of Finance and Development Planning. 1976. *The rural income distribution survey in Botswana, 1974–75*. Gaborone, Government Printer.

Boulding, E. 1983. 'Measures on women's work in the Third World', in M. Buvinic, M.A. Lycette and W.P. McGreevey (eds), *Women and poverty in the Third World*. Baltimore, Johns Hopkins University Press, pp. 286–299.

Bracher, M.D.; Santow, G. 1982. 'Breastfeeding in Central Java', *Population Studies*, Vol. 36, No. 3, pp. 413–429.

Brand, V. 1986. 'One dollar workplaces: a study of informal sector activities in Magaba, Harare', *Journal of Social Development in Africa*, Vol. 1, No. 2, pp. 53–74.

Brass, W. 1981. 'Birth history analysis' (with discussion), in *World Fertility Survey Conference 1980: Record of Proceedings*, Vol. 3, Voorburg, International Statistical Institute, pp. 143–181.

Bratton, M. 1986. 'Farmer organizations and food production in Zimbabwe', *World Development*, Vol. 13, No. 3, pp. 367–384.

Brown, J.B.; Harrison, P.; Smith, M.A. 1985. 'A study of returning fertility after childbirth and during lactation by measurement of urinary oestrogen and pregnanediol excretion and cervical mucus production', in M. Potts, S. Thapa and M.A. Herbertson (eds), *Breast-feeding and fertility*. *Journal of Biosocial Science* supplement, No. 9. Cambridge, Galton Foundation, pp. 5–23.

Brunborg, H. 1989. 'The population of Botswana' in R. Hasse and E. Zeil-Fahlbusch (eds), *Botswana – Entwicklung am Rande Apartheid*. Hamburg: Arbeiten aus dem Institut für Afrikakunde, Nr 61, pp. 211–227.

Bryceson, D.F. 1985. 'Women's proletarianization and the family wage in Tanzania', in H. Afshar (ed.), *Women, work and ideology in the Third World*. London, Tavistock, pp. 128–152.

Bryson, J.C. 1980. 'The development implications of female involvement in agriculture: the case of Cameroon'. MA dissertation, University of Manchester.

——. 1981. 'Women and agriculture in Sub-Saharan Africa: implications for development', *Journal of Development Studies*, Vol. 17, No. 2. Apr., pp. 29–46.

Bujra, J. 1986. 'Urging women to redouble their efforts: class, gender and capitalist transformation in Africa', in I. Berger and C. Robertson (eds), *Women and class in Africa*. New York, Africana.

Bukh, J. 1979. *The village woman in Ghana*. Uppsala University, Scandinavian Institute of African Studies.

Burfisher, M.E.; Horenstein, N. 1985. *Sex roles in the Nigerian Tiv farm household*. West Hartford, USA, Kumarian Press.

Cabanero, T.A. 1978. 'The "shadow" price of children in Laguna households', *Philippine Economic Journal* (Quezon City), Vol. 17, No. 1–2, pp. 62–87.

Caldwell, J.C.; Caldwell, P. 1977. 'The role of marital sexual abstinence in determining fertility: a study of the Yoruba in Nigeria', *Population Studies*, Vol. 31, No. 2, pp. 193–217.

——; ——. 1987. 'The religious and cultural context of high fertility in sub-Saharan Africa', *Population and Development Review*, Vol. 13, No. 3, pp. 409–437.

Caldwell, P.; Caldwell, J.C. 1981. 'The function of child-spacing in traditional societies and the direction of change', in H. Page and R. Lesthaeghe (eds), *Child-spacing in tropical Africa: traditions and change*. London, Academic Press, pp. 73–92.

——; Thompson, B. 1975. 'Gambia', in J.C. Caldwell, N.O. Addo, S.K. Gaisie, A. Igun and P.O. Olusanya (eds), *Population growth and socioeconomic change in West Africa*. New York and London, Columbia University Press, pp. 493–526.

Caplan, A.P. 1984. 'Cognatic descent, Islamic law and women's property on the East African Coast', in R. Hirschon (ed.), *Women and property and women as property*. London, Croom Helm.

Cardoso, F.H.; Faletto, E. 1979. *Dependency and development in Latin America*. Berkeley, Calif., University of California Press.

Carloni, A.S. 1987. *Women in development: A.I.D.'s experience, 1973–1985*. Washington, DC, US Agency for International Development.

Carney, J.A. 1988. 'Struggles over crop rights and labour within contract farming households in a Gambian irrigated rice project', *Journal of Peasant Studies*, Vol. 15, No. 3, April.

Central Bureau of Statistics. 1981. *The Integrated Rural Surveys, 1976–79.* Nairobi, Central Bureau of Statistics.

Central Statistical Office. 1989. *Swaziland: employment and wages, 1987.* Mbabane.

Chabala, C.; Nguiru, R.G. 1986. *Intra-household dynamics and farming systems research/evaluation in Zambia: a case study of traditional recommendation domain 3 in Central Province.* Urbana-Champaign, University of Illinois.

Cheater, A. 1981. 'Women and their participation in commercial agricultural production: the case of medium-scale freehold in Zimbabwe', *Development and Change*, Vol. 12, No. 3, July, pp. 349–377.

Clark, C.M. 1981. 'Land and food, women and power in nineteenth century Kikuyu', *Africa*, Vol. 50.

Clarke, D.G. 1972. 'Problems of family planning amongst Africans in Rhodesia', *Rhodesian Journal of Economics*, Vol. 6, No. 2, pp. 36–48.

——. 1980. *Foreign companies and international investment in Zimbabwe.* Gweru (Gwelo), Mambo Press.

Cliffe, L. 1976. 'Rural class formation in East Africa', *Journal of Peasant Studies*, Vol. 4, No. 2.

——. 1978. 'Labour migration and peasant differentiation: Zambian experiences', *Journal of Peasant Studies*, Vol. 5, No. 3, pp. 326–346.

Cloud, K. 1976. *Report of fact finding trip to Niger, Mali, Senegal and Upper Volta.* Washington, DC, Office of the Sahel Francophone, West African Affairs, USAID.

Cochrane, S. 1983. 'Effects of education and urbanization on fertility', in R.A. Bulatao and R.D. Lee (eds), *Determinants of fertility in developing countries.* New York, Academic Press, pp. 587–626.

Comaroff, J.; Roberts. A. 1977. 'Marriage and extramarital sexuality, the dialectics of legal change among the Kjatla', *Journal of African Law*, Bd. 21, pp. 97–123.

Conti, A. 1979. 'Capitalist organisation of production through non-capitalist relations: women's role in a pilot settlement in Upper Volta', *Review of African Political Economy*, Vol. 15/16.

Cosminsky, S. 1985. 'Infant feeding practices in rural Kenya', in V.J. Hull and M. Simpson (eds), *Breastfeeding, child health and child spacing: cross-cultural perspectives.* London and Dover, Croom Helm, pp. 35–54.

Cutrufelli, M.R. 1983. *Women in Africa: roots of oppression.* London, Zed Press.

Dahl, H.E. 1979. *Rural production in Botswana 1974–75: a national accounts analysis of the Rural Incomes Distribution Survey.* Economic Papers No. 17. Bergen, University of Bergen, June.

Date-Bah, E. 1986. 'Sex segregation and discrimination in Accra-Tema: causes and consequences', in R. Anker and C. Hein (eds), *Sex inequalities in urban employment in the Third World.* London, Macmillan.

DaVanzo, J.; Lee, D.L.P. 1983. 'The compatibility of child care with market and nonmarket activities: preliminary evidence from Malaysia', in M. Buvinic, M.A. Lycette and W.P. McGreevey (eds), *Women and poverty in the Third World.* Baltimore, Johns Hopkins University Press, pp. 62–91.

Davies, R.; Sanders, D. 1987. 'Adjustment policies and the welfare of children: Zimbabwe 1980–85', in A. Cornia, R. Jolly and F. Stewart (eds), *Adjustment with a human face: country case studies.* New York, UNICEF.

Demographic and Health Surveys. 1990. Demographic and Health Survey Newsletter. DHS/Macro Systems. Columbia.

de Vletter, F. 1983. *The Swazi rural homestead survey.* Kwaluseni, University of Swaziland, Social Science Research Unit.

——. 1985. *Recent trends and prospects of black migration to South Africa.* International Migration for Employment Working Paper No. 2. Geneva, ILO.

Dey, J. 1981. 'Gambian women: unequal partners in rice development projects?', in N. Nelson (ed.), *African women in the development process.* London, Frank Cass.

——. 1982. 'Development planning in the Gambia: the gap between planners' and farmers' perceptions, expectations and objectives', *World Development*, Vol. 10, No. 5, May.

Dixon, R. 1980. *Assessing the impact of development projects on women.* AID Program Evaluation Discussion Paper No. 8. Washington, DC, US Agency for International Development.

——. 1982. 'Women in agriculture: counting the labour force in developing countries', *Population and Development Review*, Sept.

Dixon-Mueller, R. 1985. *Women's work in Third World agriculture: concepts and indicators.* Women, Work and Development Series No. 9, Geneva, ILO.

——. 1989. 'Patriarchy, fertility, and women's work in rural societies', in *Proceedings of the IUSSP General Conference.* New Delhi, International Union for the Scientific Study of Population (IUSSP).

——; Anker, R. 1988. *Assessing women's contributions to development.* Population, Human Resources and Development Planning Training Paper No. 6. Geneva, ILO.

Durand. 1975. *The labour force in economic development: an international comparison of census statistics.* Princeton, NJ, Princeton University Press.

Dwyer, D. 1983. *Women and income in the Third World: implications for policy.* Population Council Working Paper No. 18. New York, Population Council.

Evans, A.; Young, K. 1988. 'Gender issues in household labour allocation: the transformation of a farming system in Northern Province, Zambia'. Report submitted to Overseas Development Agency.

Evers, H.-D. 1981a. 'The contribution of urban subsistence production to incomes in Jakarta', *Bulletin of Indonesian Economic Studies* (Canberra), Vol. 17, No. 2, July, pp. 89–96.

——. 1981b. *Subsistence production and wage labour in Jakarta*. Working Paper No. 8. Bielefeld (Federal Republic of Germany), University of Bielefeld, Sociology of Development Centre; mimeo.

Ewusi, K. 1978. *Women in occupation in Ghana*. Paper presented at the Seminar on Women and Development held by the Council on Women, Legon, Ghana, 4–8 Sept.

Facts and Reports. 1991a. '1,2 Million Homeless in Zimbabwe', in *Facts and Reports*, Vol. 21, No. L, p. 10. (Original source: *Namibian*, 27 May 1991, no page number cited). (14 June).

Facts and Reports. 1991b. 'Growth', in *Facts and Reports*, Vol. 21, No. R, pp. 16–17. (Original source: *Financial Times*, Britain, 30 August 1991, no page number cited).

Facts and Reports. 1991c. 'Remodelling the economy', in *Facts and Reports*, Vol. 21, No. R, p. 16. (Original source: *Financial Times*, Britain, 30 August 1991, no page number cited).

Feachem, Richard G.A.; Burns, Elizabeth; Cairncross, Sandy; Cronin, Aron; Cross, Piers; Curtis, Donald; Khalid Khan M.; Lamb, Douglas; Southall, Hilary. 1978. *Water, health and development: an interdisciplinary evaluation*. London, Tri-med Books.

Feldman, R. 1981. 'Employment problems of rural women in Kenya'. Unpublished paper prepared for the ILO.

Ferraro, G. 1980. 'Swazi marital patterns and conjugal roles: an analysis and policy implications'. Kwaluseni, University of Swaziland; unpublished.

Fiawoo, D.K. 1976. 'Some patterns of foster care in Ghana', in C. Oppong; G. Adaba; M. Bekombo-Priso and J. Mogey (eds), *Marriage, fertility and parenthood in West Africa*. Canberra, Australian National University Press.

Findley, S.E.; Williams, L. 1990. *Women who go and women who stay: reflections of family migration processes in a changing world*. Working Paper Series. Geneva, ILO.

First, R. 1983. *Black gold: the Mozambican miner, proletarian and peasant*. New York, St Martin's Press.

Folbre, N. 1986. 'Hearts and spades: paradigms of household economics', *World Development*, Vol. 14, No. 2.

Fortes, M. 1949. *The web of kinship among the Tallensi*. Oxford, Oxford University Press.

Frank, O. 1983. 'Infertility in Sub-Saharan Africa: estimates and implications', *Population and Development Review*, No. 9.

Freund, B. 1984. *The making of contemporary Africa*. London, Macmillan.

Gaidzanwa, R.B. 1984. 'The policy implications of women's involvement in the informal sector in Zimbabwe', *Manpower Information Services*, Vol. 3, No. 3, pp. 22–25.

Gaisie, S.K. 1984. *The proximate determinants of fertility in Ghana*. WFS Scientific Reports No. 53. Voorburg, Netherlands; International Statistical Institute.

Garbett, G.K. 1975. 'Circulatory migration in Rhodesia: towards a decision model', in D. Parkin (ed.), *Town and country in Central Eastern Africa*. Oxford, International African Institute.

Ghana, Central Bureau of Statistics. 1983. *Ghana Fertility Survey 1979–1980: first report*. Accra, Central Bureau of Statistics.

Ghana Statistical Service. 1987a. *1984 Population Census of Ghana: Demographic and Economic Characteristics* (11 volumes: Total Country, Western, Central, Greater Accra, Eastern, Volta, Ashanti, Brong Ahafo, Northern, Upper West and Upper East Regions). Accra, Ghana Statistical Service.

——. 1987b. *1984 Population Census of Ghana*. The Gazetteer (comprising two volumes – The Gazetteer 1 and The Gazetteer 2). Accra, Ghana Statistical Service.

——. 1989a. *Ghana Demographic and Health Survey 1988*. Accra, Ghana Statistical Service, and Columbia, Md., Institute for Resource Development/Macro Systems Inc.

——. 1989b. *1984 Population Census of Ghana: Special Report on Localities by Local Authorities* (10 volumes, one for each region of the country). Accra, Ghana Statistical Service.

——. 1989c. *Ghana Directory of Industrial Establishments: Analysis of 1984 Population Census Data*. Accra, Ghana Statistical Service.

——. 1989d. *Ghana Living Standards Survey: first year report: September 1987 – August 1988*. Accra, Ghana Statistical Service.

Gill, D.S. 1987. *Effectiveness of agricultural extension services in reaching rural women: a synthesis of studies from five African countries*. Rome, Food and Agriculture Organisation.

Gilmurray, J.; Riddell, R.; Sanders, D. 1978. *The struggle for health*. From Rhodesia to Zimbabwe Series No. 7. Gweru (Gwelo), Mambo Press.

Giorgis, B.W. 1988. 'The status of women and population policy in Africa', in *African Population Conference, Dakar*. Liège, IUSSP.

Glewwe, P.; Twum-Baah, K. 1989. 'The distribution of welfare in Ghana'. World Bank; draft.

Goldschmidt-Clermont, L. 1982. *Unpaid work in the household: a review of economic evaluation methods.* Women, Work and Development Series No. 1. Geneva, ILO.

——. 1983. 'Does housework pay? A product-related microeconomic approach', *Signs* (Chicago), Vol. 9, No. 1, Autumn, pp. 108–119.

——. 1987. *Economic evaluations of unpaid household work: Africa, Asia, Latin America and Oceania.* Women, Work and Development Series No. 14. Geneva, ILO.

——. 1990. 'Economic measurement of non-market household activities: Is it useful and feasible?', *International Labour Review* (Geneva, ILO), Vol. 129, No. 3, pp. 279–299.

——. 1992. 'Measuring household non-monetory production', in P. Ekins and M. Max-Neef (eds), *Real-life economics: understanding wealth-creation.* London and New York, Routledge, pp. 265–282.

Goody, E. 1976. 'Some theoretical and empirical aspects of parenthood in West Africa', in C. Oppong; G. Adaba; M. Bekombo-Priso and J. Mogey (eds), *Marriage, fertility and parenthood in West Africa.* Canberra, Australian National University Press.

Gordon, E. 1981. 'An analysis of the impact of labour migration on the lives of women in Lesotho', *Journal of Development Studies*, Vol. 17, pp. 59–76.

Government of Botswana; UNICEF. 1986. *The situation of children and women in Botswana*, Gaborone.

Government of Ghana. 1969. *Population planning for national progress and prosperity: Ghana Population Policy.* Accra-Tema, Ghana Publishing Corporation.

Government of Swaziland. 1978. *Report on the 1976 Swaziland Population Census.* Mbabane.

——. 1985. *Fourth National Development Plan 1983–88.* Mbabane.

Government of Zimbabwe (GOZ). 1982. *Transitional National Development Plan, 1982/83–1984/85*, Vol. I. Ministry of Finance, Economic Planning and Development. Harare, Government Printer.

——. 1983a. *National Manpower Survey 1981*, Vols. I and III. Ministry of Manpower and Development. Harare, Government Printer.

——. 1983b. *The role of women in the informal sector.* Paper number 3, draft paper presented at the informal sector study seminar, 27–30 Sept., Harare. Ministry of Community Development and Women's Affairs. Harare, Government Printer.

——. 1984. *1982 Population Census: a preliminary assessment.* Central Statistical Office. Harare, Government Printer.

——. 1985a. *Main demographic features of the population of Zimbabwe: an advance report based on a ten per cent sample (of the 1982 Population Census).* Central Statistical Office. Harare, Government Printer.

——. 1985b. *Zimbabwe Reproductive Health Survey 1984.* Zimbabwe National Family Planning Council. Harare, Government Printer.

——. 1986. *First Five-Year National Development Plan, 1986–1990*, Vol. I. Ministry of Finance, Economic Planning and Development. Harare, Government Printer.

——. 1989. *Demographic and Health Survey 1988.* Central Statistical Office. Harare, Government Printer.

Gulbrandsen, O. 1980. *Agro-pastoral production and communal land use, a socio-economic study of the Bangwaketse.* Norway, University of Bergen and Rural Sociology Unit, Botswana.

——. 1986. 'To marry – or not to marry: marital strategies and sexual relations in Tswana society', *Ethnos*, Vol. 51, pp. 7–28.

Guyer, J. 1980a. *Household budgets and women's incomes.* African Studies Centre Working Paper No. 28. Boston, University of Boston.

——. 1980b. 'Food, cocoa and the division of labour by sex in two West African societies', *Comparative Studies in Society and History*, Vol. 22.

——. 1981. 'Household and community in Africa', *African Studies Review*, Vol. 24, No. 2/3.

——. 1983. *Anthropological models of African production: the naturalisation problem.* African Studies Centre Working Paper No. 78. Boston, University of Boston.

——. 1984a. 'Women in African rural economies: contemporary variations', in S. Strichter and E. Hay (eds), *African women south of the Sahara.* London, Longman.

——. 1984b. *Family and farm.* African Studies Centre Working Paper No. 15. Boston, University of Boston.

Hagan, G.P. 1983. 'Marriage, divorce and polygyny in Winneba', in C. Oppong (ed.), *Female and male in West Africa.* London, George Allen and Unwin.

Hanger, J.; Moris, J. 1973. 'Women and the household economy', in R. Chambers and J. Moris (eds), *Mwea: an irrigated rice settlement in Kenya.* Afrika-Studienstelle 83. Munich, Weltforum Verlag.

Harris, O. 1981. 'Households as natural units', in K. Young (ed.). *Of marriage and the market: women's subordination in international perspective.* London, CSE Books.

Harrison, P. 1987. *The greening of Africa: breaking through in the battle for land and food.* London, Paladin Grafton Books.

Hay, M.J. 1976. 'Luo women and economic change during the colonial period', in N. Hafkin and E.G. Bay (eds), *Women in Africa: studies in social and economic change*. Stanford, Calif., Stanford University Press.

Henn, J.K. 1978. 'Peasants, workers and capital: the political economy of labor and incomes in Cameroon'. Ph.D. dissertation, Harvard University, Cambridge, Mass.

——. 1983. 'Feeding the cities and feeding the peasants: what role for Africa's women farmers?', *World Development*, Vol. 11, No. 12, pp. 1043–1055.

Hill, A.G. (ed.). 1990. *Determinants of health and mortality in Africa*. Demographic and Health Surveys Further Analysis Series No. 10. New York, Population Council/Institutes Systems.

Hill, P. 1963. *The migrant cocoa farmers of Southern Ghana*. Cambridge, Cambridge University Press.

Hinchey, M.T. 1978. *Proceedings of the symposium on drought in Botswana*. The Botswana Society, Gaborone and University Press, Clare, New England.

Hull, V.J.; Simpson, M. (eds). 1985. *Breastfeeding, child health and child spacing: cross-cultural perspectives*. London and Dover, Croom Helm.

Hussmans, R.; Mehran, F.; Verma, V. 1990. *Surveys of economically active population, employment, unemployment and underemployment: an ILO manual on concepts and methods*. Geneva. ILO.

IBRD. 1979. *Recognising the invisible in development: the World Bank experience*. Washington, DC, IBRD.

ICRW. 1980. *The productivity of women in developing countries: measurement issues and recommendations*. Washington, DC, Agency for International Development.

IDS Bulletin. 1985. 'Sub-Saharan Africa: getting the facts straight', *IDS Bulletin*, Vol. 16, No. 3.

ILO. Various years. *Yearbook of Labour Statistics*. Geneva, ILO.

——. 1973. *Labour force projection 1965–1985: methodological supplement*. Geneva, ILO.

——. 1977. *Labour force estimates and projections, 1950–2000* (2nd edn). Geneva, ILO.

——. 1979. *Options for a dependent economy*. Addis Ababa, International Labour Office, Jobs and Skills Programme for Africa. (JASPA).

——. 1982. Thirteenth International Conference of Labour Statisticians, amended draft resolution concerning statistics of the economically active population, employment, unemployment and underemployment. Geneva, ILO; mimeo.

——. 1984. *Rural development and women in Africa*. Geneva, ILO.

——. 1985. *Report on equal opportunities and treatment for women and men in employment*. Geneva, ILO.

——. 1986a. *Economically active population, estimates and projections, 1950–2025* (3rd edn). Geneva, ILO.

——. 1986b. *Swaziland: manpower, education and training*. Geneva, ILO.

——. 1991. *African employment report*. Addis Ababa, ILO, JASPA.

Impact. 1986. *Family planning saves lives: a strategy for maternal and child survival*. Washington, DC, Population Reference Bureau, Inc.

Ingstad, B. 1984. 'An evaluation of community based rehabilitation in Kweneng District, Botswana', a halfway report from a research project. University of Oslo, Institute of Social Medicine; mimeo.

——; Saugestad, A. 1984. *Unmarried mothers in changing Tswana society – implications for household form and viability*. Oslo, Forum for Utviklingsstudier Nr. 4, Norsk Unterikspolitisk Institutt.

International Fund for Agricultural Development. 1986. *Zambia agricultural rehabilitation project*. Rome, Project Preparation Mission.

International Research and Training Institute for the Advancement of Women (INSTRAW). 1985. *The importance of research and training to the integration of women in development*. Research Study No. 2. Santo Domingo, INSTRAW.

——. 1990. *Statistics on women*. INSTRAW/SER.A/22. Santo Domingo.

Isiugo-Abanihe, U.C. 1985. 'Child fosterage in West Africa', *Population and Development Review*, Vol. 11, No. 1, pp. 53–73.

Jabara, C.L. 1984. *Agricultural pricing policy in Kenya*. Discussion Paper 185. Cambridge, Mass., Harvard Institute for International Development.

Jackson, C. 1985. *The Kano River irrigation project*. Women's Roles and Gender Differences in Development, Cases for Planners. West Hartford, USA, Kumarian Press.

Joekes, S. 1983. 'Women's work and social support for child care in the Third World', in J. Leslie and M. Paolisso (eds), *Women, work, and child welfare in the Third World*. AAAS Selected Symposium. Westview Press, Boulder, Colorado.

Johnson, S. 1988. 'Intra household relations and agricultural development in Sub-Saharan Africa'. Unpublished manuscript submitted as part of M.Sc. for Department of Agricultural Economics, University of Reading.

Jones, C.W. 1986. 'Intra-household bargaining in response to the introduction of new crops: a case study from Northern Cameroons', in J. Moock (ed.), *Understanding Africa's rural households and farming systems*. Westview Press, Boulder, Colorado.

Kabagambe, J.C. 1991. 'Labour utilization in the Swazi homestead', in A. Adepoju (ed.), *Swaziland population, economy and society*. New York, UNFPA.

Kabeer, N. 1985. 'Do women gain from high fertility?' in H. Afshar (ed.), *Women, work, and ideology in the Third World*. London, Tavistock, pp. 83–108.

Kachingwe, S.K. 1986. 'Zimbabwean women: a neglected factor in social development', *Journal of Social Development in Africa*, Vol. 1, No. 1, pp. 27–33.

Karefa-Smart, J. 1986. 'Health and family planning in Africa', *Populi*, Vol. 13, No. 2, pp. 20–29.

Karimu, J.; Richards, P. 1980. *The northern area integrated development project: the social and economic impact of planning for rural change in northern Sierra Leone*. Freetown and London, Inter-University Council for Higher Education Overseas.

Kazembe, J.L. 1986. 'The women issue', in I. Mandaza (ed.), *Zimbabwe: the political economy of transition, 1980–86*. Dakar, Codesria.

Kenya, National Council for Population and Development. 1989. *Uganda: Demographic and Health Survey 1988/89*. Columbia, Md., Institute for Resource Development/Macro Systems Inc.

Kitching, G. 1980. *Class and economic change in Kenya: the making of an African petite-bourgeoisie*. New Haven, Conn., Yale University Press.

Knight, V.C. 1990. 'Zimbabwe a decade after independence', *Current History*, Vol. 89, No. 547, pp. 201–227.

Kossoudji, S.; Mueller, E. 1983. 'The economic and demographic status of female headed households in rural Botswana', *Economic Development and Cultural Change*, Vol. 31, No. 4.

Kuper, H. 1963. *The Swazi: a South African kingdom*. New York, Holt Rinehart and Winston.

Kusnic, M.W.; Da Vanzo, J. 1980. *Income inequality and the definition of income: the case of Malaysia*. Santa Monica, Calif., Rand Corporation.

Lesthaeghe, R. 1980. 'On the social control of human reproduction', *Population and Development Review*, Vol. 6, No. 4, pp. 527–548.

——. 1984. *Fertility and its proximate determinants in sub-Saharan Africa: the record of the 1960s and 70s*. Working Paper No. 1984–2. Brussels, Inter-University Programme in Demography, Vrije Universiteit Brussel.

——. (ed.). 1989. *Reproduction and social organization in sub-Saharan Africa*. Berkeley, Calif., University of California Press.

——; Ohadike, P.O.; Kocher, J.; Page, J. 1981. 'Child-spacing and fertility in sub-Saharan Africa: an overview of issues', in H. Page and R. Lesthaeghe (eds), *Child-spacing in tropical Africa: traditions and change*. London, Academic Press, pp. 3–23.

Lewis, B. 1982. 'Fertility and employment: an assessment of role incompatibility among African urban women', in E.G. Bay (ed.), *Women and work in Africa*. Boulder, Col., Westview Press, pp. 249–276.

Liberia, Bureau of Statistics. 1988. *Liberia: Demographic and Health Survey 1986*. Columbia, Md., Institute for Resource Development/Macro Systems, Inc.

Lim, L.L. 1988. 'Effects of women's position on migration', in *Conference on Women's Position and Demographic Change in the Course of Development, Oslo, Solicited Papers*. Liège, IUSSP.

Lloyd, C.B. 1990. *Understanding the relationship between women's work and fertility: the contribution of the World Fertility Surveys*. Working paper No. 9. New York, Research Division, Population Council.

Lochfie, M.F. 1975. 'Political and economic origins of African hunger', *Journal of Modern African Studies*, Vol. 13, No. 4.

Longhurst, R. 1977. 'The provision of basic needs for women: a case study of a Hausa village in Nigeria'. Draft report for the ILO.

——. 1982. 'Resource allocation and the sexual division of labour: a case study of a Moslem Hausa Village', in L. Benería (ed.), *Women and development: the sexual division of labour in rural societies*. New York, Praeger.

Lorimer, F. 1954. *Culture and human fertility*. Paris, UNESCO.

Low, A. 1986. *Agricultural development in Southern Africa: farm household economics and the food crisis*. London, James Currey.

Lule, E.L. 1991. 'Marriage and marital fertility in rural Swaziland', in A. Adepoju (ed.), *Swaziland population, economy and society*. New York, UNFPA.

Lycette, M.; Self, J. 1984. *A preliminary evaluation of A.I.D. income generation and employment projects*. Washington, DC, International Center for Research on Women.

Mabogunje, A.L. 1981. 'The policy implications of child-spacing practices in tropical Africa', in H. Page and R. Lesthaeghe (eds) *Child-spacing in tropical Africa*.

Made, P.; Lagerstrom, B. 1985. *Zimbabwean women in industry*. Harare, Zimbabwe Publishing House.

Makinwa-Adebusoye, P. 1988. 'Labour migration and female-headed households', in *Conference on Women's Position and Demographic Change in the Course of Development, Oslo, Solicited Papers*. Liège, IUSSP.

——. 1990. 'Female migration in Africa: an overview', in Union of African Population Studies, *Migration and development in Africa: issues and policies for the 90s*. Dakar, IUSSP.

Mali. 1989. *Enquête démographique et de santé au Mali 1987*. Bamako, Centre d'Etudes et de Recherches sur la Population pour le Développement, Institut du Sahel, and Columbia, Md., Institute for Resource Development/Westinghouse.

Maro, P.S. 1990. 'The effects of labour migration to South Africa on Swaziland demography and economy'. Paper presented at Conference on the Changing Flows in Eastern and Southern Africa, Nairobi.

Mason, K.O. 1984. *The status of women: a review of its relationships to fertility and mortality*. New York, Rockefeller Foundation.

——; Blanc, A.K. 1985. 'Demographic and Health Surveys proposed module on women's employment'. Unpublished manuscript.

——; Palan, V.T. 1981. 'Female employment and fertility in Peninsular Malaysia: the maternal role incompatibility hypothesis reconsidered', *Demography*, Vol. 18, No. 4, pp. 549–575.

Matsebula, J.S.M. 1972. *A history of Swaziland* (2nd edn). Capetown, Longman.

——. 1988. 'Swaziland's urban informal sector: its characteristics, constraints and production from an aggregate viewpoint', in H. Tieleman (ed.), *Scenes of change: visions on developments in Swaziland*. Research Reports No. 33. Leiden, African Studies Centre.

May, J. 1979. *African women in urban employment: factors influencing their employment in Zimbabwe*. Mambo Occasional Papers – Socio-Economic Series No. 12. Gweru (Gwelo), Mambo Press.

Mazur, R.E. 1986. 'Reversal of migration in the labor reserves of Zimbabwe? Prospects for change', *Studies in Comparative International Development*, Vol. 19, No. 4, pp. 55–87.

Mehran, F. 1986. *Surveys of the economically active population*. Geneva, ILO; mimeo.

Mhloyi, M. 1987. *The proximate determinants and their socio-cultural determinants: the case of two rural settings in Zimbabwe*. Paper presented at the Conference on True Determinants of Fertility in Africa, University of Ife, Ile-Ife, Nigeria.

——. 1988. 'The determinants of fertility in Africa under modernization', in E. van de Walle (ed.), *The state of African demography*. Liège, IUSSP.

——. 1990. 'Perception on communication and sexuality in marriage in Zimbabwe', *Women and Therapy*, Vol. 10, No. 3, pp. 61–73.

——. 1991. *Fertility transition in Zimbabwe*. Paper presented at Conference on the Course of Fertility Transition in Sub-Saharan Africa, Harare.

——. 1992. *Status of women and fertility in Zimbabwe*. Paper presented to the Population Division, United Nations, New York.

Mitchell, J.C. 1969. 'Structural plurality, urbanization and labour circulation in Southern Rhodesia', in J.A. Jackson (ed.), *Migration*. Cambridge, Cambridge University Press, pp. 156–180.

Mokganedi, F. forthcoming. *A survey of malnourished children in Kweneng District*. Kweneng District Health Team.

Molokomme, A. 1985. *The woman's guide to the law: an outline of how the law affects every woman and her family in Botswana*. Gaborone, Women's Affairs Unit, Ministry of Home Affairs.

Monsted, M. 1976. *The changing division of labour within rural families in Kenya*. Project Paper A.77.4. Copenhagen, Centre for Development Research.

Morna, C.L. 1990. 'Swords into plowshares', *Africa Report*, Vol. 35, No. 2, pp. 61–64.

Muchena, O.N. 1980. *Women in town: a socio-economic survey of African women in Highfield Township, Salisbury*. Harare, University of Zimbabwe, Women in Development Research Unit, Centre for Applied Social Sciences.

——. 1982a. *A socio-economic overview: Zimbabwean women*. Addis Ababa, UN Economic Commission for Africa, African Training and Research Centre for Women.

——. 1982b. 'Women's organizations in Zimbabwe and assessment of their needs, achievements and potential', in K. Jorgensen (ed.), *Women's programmes in Zimbabwe*. Copenhagen, KULU and Women in Development.

——. 1982c. *Women's participation in the rural labour force in Zimbabwe*. Working paper on Southern African Team for Employment Promotion, World Employment Programme. Lusaka, ILO.

——. 1984. *Women and development in Zimbabwe: an annotated bibliography*. Bibliography Series No. 9. African Training and Research Centre for Women. Addis Ababa, UN Economic Commission for Africa.

Mueller, E. 1984. 'The value and allocation of time in rural Botswana', *Journal of Development Economics* (Amsterdam), Vol. 15, No. 1–3, pp. 329–360.

Mugabe, R.G. 1985. 'Zimbabwe', in UNFPA, *Population perspectives: statements by world leaders* (2nd edn). New York, UNFPA.

Munslow, B. 1985. 'Prospects for the socialist transition of agriculture in Zimbabwe', *World Development*, Vol. 13, No. 1, pp. 41–58.

Muntemba, M.S. 1982. 'Women as food producers and suppliers in the twentieth century: the case of Zambia', *Development Dialogue*, Vol. 1, No. 2.

Mutuma, P.M.; Magonya, S.; Moyo, S. 1987. *An evaluation of agricultural extension services support to women farmers in Zimbabwe with special reference to Makonde District*. Consultancy report to FAO. Harare, Zimbabwe Institute of Development Studies.

Nag, M. 1983. 'The impact of sociocultural factors on breastfeeding and sexual behavior', in R.A. Bulatao and R.D. Lee (eds), *Determinants of fertility in developing countries*, Vol. 1. New York, Academic Press, pp. 163–198.

——; White, B.N.F.; Peet, R.C. 1978. 'An anthropological approach to the study of the economic value of children in Java and Nepal', *Current Anthropology* (Chicago), Vol. 19, No. 2, pp. xxxi–xxxv.

Ncube, W. 1987. 'Underprivilege and inequality: the matrimonial property rights of women in Zimbabwe', in A. Armstrong (ed.), *Women and law in Southern Africa*. Harare, Zimbabwe Publishing House.

Newman, J.S. 1984. *Women of the world: sub-Saharan Africa*. Washington, DC, United States Department of Commerce, Bureau of Census.

Ngwenya, J. 1983. 'Women and liberation in Zimbabwe', in M. Davies (ed.), *Third World – second sex*. London, Zed Press, pp. 78–83.

Nhlapo, R.J. (ed.). 1983. *Women and the law in Swaziland*. Kwaluseni, University of Swaziland.

Nissell, M. n.d. *Women and government statistics – basic concepts and assumptions*. London, Policy Studies Institute.

Oakley, A.; Oakley, R. 1978. *Demystifying social statistics*. London, Pluto Press.

Ofosu, D.Y. 1989. 'Hazard models analysis of birth intervals: a study based on West African data'. Ph.D. thesis, Demography Department, Australian National University, Canberra.

——. 1992. 'Socio-economic change and the evolution of cultural models of reproduction in Ghana: implications for population policy'. Working Paper No. 184. ILO, Geneva.

Omran, A.R.; Martin, J.; Hamza, B. (eds). 1987. *High risk mothers and newborns: detection, management and prevention*. Ott Verlag AG, Thun, Switzerland.

Ondo State, Nigeria. 1989. *Ondo State, Nigeria, Demographic and Health Survey 1986*. Akure, Nigeria, Medical/Preventive Health Division, Ministry of Health, and Columbia, Md., Institute for Resource Development/Macro Systems Inc.

Oppong, C. 1973. *Growing up in Dagbon*. Accra, Ghana Publishing Corporation.

——. 1977. 'The crumbling of high fertility supports: data from a study of Ghanaian primary school teachers', in J.C. Caldwell (ed.), *The persistence of high fertility*, Vol. 1. Canberra, Demography Department, Australian National University, pp. 331–359.

——. 1982a. 'Family structure and women's reproductive and productive roles', in R. Anker, M. Buvinic and N. Youssef (eds), *Women's roles and population trends in the Third World*. London, Croom Helm 1982 (repr. 1988 Routledge).

——. 1982b. *Middle-class African marriage*. London, George Allen and Unwin.

——. 1983. 'Women's roles, opportunity costs, and fertility', in R.A. Bulatao and R.D. Lee (eds), *Determinants of fertility in developing countries*, Vol. 1. New York, Academic Press, pp. 547–589.

——. 1985. 'Some aspects of anthropological contributions', in G. Farooq and G. Simmons (eds), *Fertility in developing countries: an economic perspective on research and policy issues*. London, Macmillan.

——. 1987a. *African mothers, workers and wives: inequality and segregation*. Working Paper No. 2, Population, Human Resources and Development Planning in Sub-Saharan Africa. Geneva, ILO.

——. (ed.) 1987b. *Sex roles, population and development in West Africa: policy-related studies on work and demographic issues*. Portsmouth, Heinemann, and London, James Currey.

——. 1991. *Relationships between women's work and demographic behaviour: some research evidence in West Africa*. ILO WEP 2-21, Working Paper No. 175. Geneva, ILO.

——. 1992a. 'Traditional family systems in rural settings in Africa', in E. Berquo and P. Xenos (eds), *Family systems and cultural change*. Oxford, Clarendon Press, for IUSSP.

——. 1992b. *African family systems in the context of socio-economic change*. Paper presented at the Third African Regional Population Conference, Dakar, Dec.

——; Abu, K. 1987. *Seven roles of women: impact of education, migration and employment on Ghanaian mothers*. Women, Work and Development Series No. 13. Geneva, ILO.

Orubuloye, I.O. 1977. 'Fertility, sexual abstinence and contraception among the Yoruba of Western Nigeria: a study of selected rural communities in Ekiti and Ibadan divisions'. Ph.D. thesis, Demography Department, Australian National University, Canberra.

Page, H. 1988. 'Fertility and family planning in Africa', in E. van de Walle, P.O. Ohadike and M.D. Sala-Diakanda (eds), *The state of African demography*. Liège, IUSSP, pp. 29–45.

——. 1989. 'Child rearing versus childbearing: co-residence of mother and child in sub-Saharan Africa', in R.J. Lesthaeghe (ed.), *Reproduction and social organization in Sub-Saharan Africa*. Berkeley, Calif., University of California Press.

——; Lesthaeghe, R. (eds). 1981. *Child-spacing in tropical Africa: traditions and change*. London, Academic Press.

——; Lesthaeghe, R.; Shah, I.H. 1982. *Illustrative analysis: breastfeeding in Pakistan*. WFS Scientific Reports No. 7. Voorburg, International Statistical Institute.

Pala, A.O. 1978. *Women's access to land and their role in agriculture and decision making on the farm: experience of the Joluo of Kenya*. Discussion Paper No. 263. Nairobi, IDS.

——. 1979. 'Daughters of the lakes and rivers', in M. Etienne and E. Leacock (eds), *Women and colonialisation: anthropological perspectives*. New York, Praeger.

Palmer, I. 1981. 'Seasonal dimensions of women's roles', in R. Chambers, R. Longhurst and A. Pacey (eds), *Seasonal dimensions to rural poverty*. London, Frances Pinter (Publishers) Ltd.

——. 1985a. *The impact of agrarian reform on women*. Women's Roles and Gender Differences in Development: Cases for Planners. West Hartford, USA, Kumarian Press.

——. 1985b. *The impact of male out-migration on women in farming*. West Hartford, USA, Kumarian Press.

——. 1991. *Gender and population in the adjustment of African economies: planning for change*. Women, Work and Development Series No. 19. Geneva, ILO.

Palmer, R. 1977. 'The agricultural history of Rhodesia', in R. Palmer and N. Parsons (eds), *The roots of rural poverty in Central and Southern Africa*. Berkeley, Calif., University of California Press, pp. 221–254.

——. 1990. 'Land reform in Zimbabwe, 1980–1990', *African Affairs*, Vol. 89, No. 355, pp. 163–181.

Pankhurst, D.; Jacobs, S. 1988. 'Land tenure, gender relations and agricultural production: the case of Zimbabwe's peasantry', in J. Davidson (ed.), *Agriculture, women and land: the African experience*, pp. 202–227.

Perez, A.; Vela, P.; Masnick, G.S.; Potter, R.G. 1971. 'Timing and sequence of resuming ovulation and menstruation after childbirth', *Population Studies*, Vol. 25, pp. 491–503.

——; Vela, P.; Masnick, G.S.; Potter, R.G. 1972. 'First ovulation after childbirth: the effect of breastfeeding', *American Journal of Obstetrics and Gynecology*, Vol. 114, No. 8, pp. 1041–1047.

Phillips, A. 1953. *Survey of African marriage and family life*. London, IAI and Oxford University Press.

Pittin, R. 1984. 'Migration of women in Nigeria: the Hausa case', *International Migration Review*, Special Issue: Women in Migration, Vol. 18, Winter.

——. 1985. *Deconstructing the household: relations of production and reproduction in rural Nigeria*. Paper presented to the WIN Annual Conference, Ilorin.

Poewe, K.O. 1981. *Matrilineal ideology: male female dynamics in Luapula, Zambia*. London, Academic Press, International African Institute.

Population Crisis Committee. 1988. *Population: Briefing Paper No. 20 – Country rankings of the status of women: poor, powerless and pregnant*. Washington, DC, Population Crisis Committee.

Pottier, J. 1985a. 'Introduction', in J. Pottier (ed.), *Food systems in Central and Southern Africa*. London, School of Oriental and African Studies.

——. 1985b. 'Reciprocity and the beer pot: the changing pattern of Mambwe food production', in J. Pottier (ed.), *Food systems in Central and Southern Africa*. London, School of Oriental and African Studies.

Prest, A.R.; Stewart, I.G. 1953. *The national income of Nigeria 1950–51*. Colonial Research Studies No. 11. London, HMSO.

Rapp, R.; Ross, E; Bridenthal, R. 1977. 'Examining family history', *Feminist Studies*, Vol. 5, No. 1.

Richards, P. 1983. 'Ecological change and the politics of African land use', *African Studies Review*, Vol. 26, No. 2.

Roberts, P. 1979. 'The integration of women into the development process: some conceptual problems', *IDS Bulletin*, Vol. 10, No. 3.

——. 1983. 'Femininism in Africa', *Review of African Political Economy*, No. 27/28.

——. 1984. *The sexual politics of labour: notes towards the history of women's labour within the household, with special reference to Ghana*. Paper given at the Workshop on Conceptualising the Household in Africa, Harvard University.

——. 1985. *Rural women's access to labour*. Paper given to BSA/DSA Study Group Workshop on Class and Gender in the Third World.

Rose, T. 1985. *Crisis and recovery in sub-Saharan Africa: realities and complexities*. Paris, OECD.

Rudie, I. 1984. 'Fra kjernefamilie til kollektiv. En modell for analyse av hushold', in *Myk start – hard hard landing. Kvinners levekar og livslop*. Oslo, Universitetsforlaget, pp. 141–160.

Rukandema, M. 1980. 'Determinants of crop yields on smallholder farms in Kenya', *Eastern Africa Journal of Rural Development*, Vol. 13, Nos. 1 and 2, pp. 49–62.

——; Mavua, J.K.; Audi, P.O. 1981. *The farming system of lowland Machakos District, Kenya*. Report on Farm Survey Results from Mwala Location, Technical Report No. 1. Nairobi, UNDP/FAO/GK Dryland Farming Research and Development Project.

Sadik, N. 1989. *The state of world population 1988*. New York, UNFPA.

——. 1990a. *The state of world population 1989, investing in women: the focus of the 90s*. New York, UNFPA.

——. 1990b. *The state of world population 1990*. New York, UNFPA.

——. 1991a. *The state of world population 1991*. New York, UNFPA.

—— (ed.). 1991b. *Population policies and programmes: lessons learned from two decades of experience*. New York and London, New York University Press.

Safilios-Rothschild, C. 1982. 'A class and sex stratification theoretical model and its relevance for fertility trends in the developing world', in C. Hohn and R. Mackensen (eds), *Determinants of fertility trends: theories re-examined*. Liège, Ordina Editions.

——. 1983. *The state of statistics on women in agriculture*. ESA/STAT/AC/17/7. New York, Statistical Division of the United Nations.

——. 1985a. 'The persistence of women's invisibility in agriculture: theoretical and policy lessons from Lesotho and Sierra Leone', *Economic Development and Cultural Change*, Vol. 33, No. 2, pp. 299–317.

——. 1985b. *The implications of the roles of women in agriculture in Zambia*. New York, Population Council.

——. 1987. 'Conclusions and recommendations of the CIDA sponsored seminar on agricultural development, population status of women', held in Nyeri, Kenya, on 2–3 Sept.

——. 1988a. 'The agricultural production and income of wives left in charge of farming in Nyeri, Kenya', in *Proceedings of the African Population Conference, Dakar, Senegal, November 7–12, 1988*. Liège, IUSSP.

——. 1988b. *A typology of farming systems of men and women in Kenya*. The Hague, Ministry of Agriculture and Fisheries.

——. 1990. 'Women as a motor in agricultural development: lessons learned from Eastern and Southern sub-Saharan Africa', in *Beyond adjustment, sub-Saharan Africa*. Maastricht, Ministry of Foreign Affairs, Directorate General for International Cooperation.

——. forthcoming. 'The impact of structural adjustment policies on men and women smallholders in sub-Saharan African countries', in *Debt crisis in developing countries: who is footing the bill?* Amsterdam, Free University of Amsterdam.

Sala-Diakanda, M.; Pitshandenge, N.A.; Tabutin, D.; Vilquin, E. 1981. 'Fertility and child-spacing in western Zaire', in H. Page and R. Lesthaeghe (eds), *Child-spacing in tropical Africa: traditions and change*. London, Academic Press, pp. 287–299.

Santow, M.G. 1987. 'Reassessing the contraceptive effect of breastfeeding', *Population Studies*, Vol. 41, No. 1, pp. 147–160.

Savane, M.A. 1984. 'Women as industrial wage-earners and changing family structures in Africa', in UNESCO. *Women on the move: contemporary changes in family and society*. Paris, UNESCO.

Schapera, I. 1978. *Bogwera: Kjatla initiation*. Mochudi, Phuthadikobo Museum.

——. 1987. *Married life in an African tribe*. London, Faber and Faber.

Schoenmaeckers, R. 1988. 'Les Niveaux et tendances de la fécondité', in D. Tabutin (ed.), *Population et sociétés en Afrique au sud du Sahara*. Paris; Editions L'Harmattan, pp. 111–139.

——; Shah, I.H.; Lesthaeghe, R.; Tambashe, O. 1981. 'The child-spacing tradition and the postpartum taboo in tropical Africa: anthropological evidence', in H. Page and R. Lesthaeghe (eds), *Child-spacing in tropical Africa: traditions and change*. London, Academic Press, pp. 25–71.

SEDES. 1966. *Le Niveau de vie des populations de la zone cacaoière du Centre-Sud Cameroun*. Paris, Secrétariat d'Etat aux Affaires Etrangères, Chargé de la Coopération.

Seidman, A. 1981. 'Women and the development of "underdevelopment": the African experience', in R. Dauber and M.L. Cain (eds), *Women and technological change in developing countries*. Boulder, Col., Westview Press, pp. 109–126.

Selassie, S.G. 1986. 'Patterns of women's employment in Africa', in JASPA, *The challenge of employment and basic needs in Africa*. Nairobi, Oxford University Press.

Sender, J.; Smith, S. 1987. 'A report to ODA's economic and social committee for research on small holder tea production in the West Usambaras'. Manuscript.

Sénégal. 1988. *Enquête démographique et de santé au Sénégal 1986*. Dakar, Ministère de l'Economie et des Finances, Direction de la Statistique, Division des Enquêtes et de la Démographie, and Columbia, Md., Institute for Resource Development/Westinghouse.

Sentongo, C. 1991. 'School mapping and micro-planning of education in Swaziland', in A. Adepoju (ed.), *Swaziland: population, economy and society*. New York, UNFPA.

Shopo, T.D. 1985. *The political economy of hunger in Zimbabwe*. Working Paper No. 2. Harare, Zimbabwe Institute of Development Studies.

Singh, S.; Owusu, J.Y.; Shah, I.H. (eds). 1985. *Demographic patterns in Ghana: evidence from the Ghana fertility survey 1979–80*. Voorburg, International Statistical Institute.

Smith, S. 1987. 'Zimbabwean women in co-operatives', *Journal of Social Development in Africa*, Vol. 2, No. 1, pp. 29–47.

Sonquist, J. 1970. *Multivariate model building: the validation of a search strategy*. Ann Arbor, Mich., Institute for Social Research, University of Michigan.

——; Morgan, J.N. 1964. *The detection of interaction effects: a report on a computer program for the selection of optimal combinations of explanatory variables*. Ann Arbor, Mich., Institute for Social Research, University of Michigan.

——; Baker, E.L.; Morgan, J.N. 1973. *Searching for structure*. Ann Arbor, Mich., Institute for Social Research, University of Michigan.

Spiro, H. 1984. *Agricultural development strategies: the experience at Ilora*. Paper given at Workshop on Women in Agriculture, IITA, Ibadan, Nigeria.

——. 1985. *The Ilora farm settlement in Nigeria*. Women's Roles and Gender Differences in Development. West Hartford, USA, Kumarian Press.

Stamp, P. 1989. *Technology, gender and power in Africa*. Technical Study 63e. Ottawa, Canada, International Development Research Centre.

Standing, G. 1978. *Labour force participation and development*. Geneva, ILO.

——. 1983. 'Women's work activity and fertility', in R.A. Bulatao and R.D. Lee (eds), *Determinants of fertility in developing countries*, Vol. 1. New York, Academic Press, pp. 517–545.

Stenning, B.J. 1962. 'Household viability among the pastoral Fulani', in J. Goody (ed.), *The developmental cycle in domestic groups*. Cambridge, Cambridge University Press, pp. 92–119.

Stichter, S. 1985. *Migrant laborers*. Cambridge, Cambridge University Press.

Sudarkasa, N. 1974–75. 'Commercial migration in West Africa with special reference to the Yoruba in Ghana', *African Urban Notes*, Series B-No. 1.

Tabatabai, H. 1986. *Economic decline, access to food and structural adjustment in Ghana*. World Employment Programme Research Working Paper. Geneva, ILO.

Tienda, M.; Booth, K. 1988. 'Migration, gender and social change: a review and reformulation', in *Conference on Women's Position and Demographic Change in the Course of Development, Oslo, Solicited Papers*. Liège, IUSSP.

Tietze, C. 1963. 'The effect of breastfeeding on the rate of conception', in *Proceedings of the International Population Conference, New York, 1961*, Vol. 2. London, International Union for the Scientific Study of Population, pp. 129–136.

Tlou, T.; Campbell, A. 1984. *History of Botswana*. Gaborone, Macmillan Botswana Publishing Co.

Togo. 1989. *Enquête démographique et de santé au Togo 1988*. Lomé, Unité de Recherche Démographique, Direction de la Statistique and Direction Générale de la Santé, and Columbia, Md., Institute for Resource Development/Macro Systems Inc.

Trip, R.B. 1981. 'Farmers and traders: some economic determinants of nutritional status in Northern Ghana', *Journal of Tropical Pediatrics*, Vol. 27, No. 1.

Uganda, Ministry of Health. 1989. *Uganda: Demographic and Health Survey 1988/89*. Columbia, Md., Institute for Resource Development/Macro Systems Inc.

UNESCO. 1956. *Social implications of industrialization and urbanization in Africa south of the Sahara*. Paris, UNESCO.

UNFPA. 1981. *Swaziland: report of mission on needs assessment for population assistance*. Report No. 39. New York, UNFPA.

——. 1988a. *Comparative evaluation of UNFPA support to population and development planning in sub-Saharan Africa region: preliminary regional report*. Geneva, UNFPA.

——. 1988b. *Governing Council decisions on UNFPA adopted at the thirty-fifth session*. Geneva, UNFPA, June; mimeo.

——. 1988c. *Integrating a women's component into population programmes*. Report of a Training Workshop for UNFPA Field Staff in the Africa and Middle East Regions. Mombasa, UNFPA.

——. 1988d. *Report of the UNFPA Global Conference Review and Assessment of the Field of Population*. New York, UNFPA, Apr.; mimeo.

UNICEF. 1988. 'Adjustment policies and programmes to protect children and other vulnerable groups in Ghana', in G.A. Cornia, R. Jolly and F. Stewart (eds), *Adjustment with a human face: ten country case studies*. Oxford, Clarendon Press.

——. 1989. *The state of the world's children, 1989*. New York, UNICEF.

——. 1990. 'Children and women in Swaziland: a draft situation analysis'. Mbabane, UNICEF, unpublished.

United Nations. 1975. Report of the United Nations World Population Conference, Bucharest, 19–30 August 1974. New York, United Nations.

——. 1984a. *Improving concepts and methods for statistics and indicators on the situation of women*. Studies in Methods Series F, No. 33. New York, United Nations.

——. 1984b. *Compiling social indicators on the situation of women*. Studies in Methods Series F, No. 32. New York, United Nations.

——. 1985. *Women's employment and fertility: a comparative analysis of world fertility survey results for 38 developing countries*. Department of International Economic and Social Affairs, Population Studies No. 96, ST/ESA/SER.A/96. New York, United Nations.

——. 1986. *The Nairobi forward-looking strategies for the advancement of women*. As adopted by the World Conference to Review and Appraise the Achievements of the United Nations Decade for Women: Equality, Development and Peace, Nairobi, 15–26 July, 1985. New York, United Nations.

——. 1986b. *Population policy briefs: the current situation in developing countries, 1985*. Department of International Economic and Social Affairs. Population Policy Paper No. 2. New York, United Nations.

——. 1987. *Fertility behavior in the context of development: Evidence from the world fertility surveys*. Population Studies No. 100. New York, United Nations.

——. 1989. *Levels and trends in contraceptive use as assessed in 1988*. Population Studies No. 110. New York, United Nations.

——. 1990. *Handbook for national statistical data bases on women and development*. ST/ESA/STAT/SER.K16. New York, United Nations.

——. 1991. *The world's women: a statistical portrait*. New York, United Nations.

——. 1992. 'Revised system of national accounts'. Provisional ST/ESA/STAT/SER.F/2/REV.4 (Introduction). New York, United Nations.

United Nations Economic and Social Council, Commission on the Status of Women. 1987. *Report on the thirty-second session, Vienna, 14–23 March*. Vienna, United Nations.

United Nations Statistical Commission; Economic Commission for Europe. 1987. Conference of European Statisticians, *Report of the 35th Plenary Session, June 15–19*. Mimeo.

United Nations Statistical Commission; International Labour Office. 1987. *Summary of the main conclusions of the Work Session on Manpower Statistics, December 7–9*. Mimeo.

United Nations Statistical Office. 1968. *A system of national accounts*. Studies in Methods, Series F, No. 2, rev. 3. New York, United Nations Statistical Office.

Vail, L.; White, L. 1977. 'Tawani Machembero: forced cotton and rice growing on the Zambezi', *Journal of African History*, Vol. 19, No. 2.

van de Walle, E.; Foster, A.D. 1990. *Fertility decline in Africa – Assessment and prospects*. World Bank Technical Paper No. 125, Africa Technical Department Series. Washington, DC, World Bank.

——; van de Walle, F. 1988. 'Les pratiques traditionelles et modernes des couples en matière d'espacement ou d'arrêt de la fécondité', in D. Tabutin (ed.). *Population et sociétés en Afrique au sud du Sahara*. Paris, Editions l'Harmattan, pp. 141–165.

van Ginneken, J.K. 1977. 'The chance of conception during lactation', in A.S. Parkes, A.M. Thomson, M. Potts and M.A. Herbertson (eds), *Fertility regulation during human lactation: Proceedings of the Sixth Biomedical Workshop of the International Planned Parenthood Federation, London, 23 and 24 November, 1976. Journal of Biosocial Science* supplement, No. 4. Cambridge, Galton Foundation, pp. 41–54.

von Bulow, D.; Sorenson, A. 1988. *Gender dynamics in contract farming: women's role in small holder tea production in Kericho District, Kenya*. CDR Project Paper 88.1. Copenhagen, Centre for Development Research.

Wainerman, C. 1988. 'Improving censal accounting of female workers', in *African Population Conference*. Senegal, IUSSP.

——. 1991. *Improving the accounting of women workers in population censuses: lessons from Latin America*. World Employment Programme Research Working Paper No. 178. Geneva, ILO.

Ward, K.B. 1984. *Women in the world-system: its impact on status and fertility*. New York, Praeger.

Ware, H. 1988. 'The effects of fertilty, family organization, sex structure of the labour market and technology on the position of women', in *Conference on Women's Position and Demographic Change in the Course of Development – Oslo 1988*. Liège, IUSSP.

——; Lucas, D. 1988. 'Women left behind, the changing decision of labour and its effect on agricultural production', in *African Population Conference Dakar*. Liège, IUSSP.

Weiner, D.; Moyo, S.; Munslow, B.; O'Keefe, P. 1985. 'Land use and agricultural productivity in Zimbabwe', *Journal of Modern African Studies*, Vol. 23, No. 2, pp. 251–285.

Weiss, R. 1986. *The women of Zimbabwe*. London, Kesho Publishers.

Whitehead, A. 1981a. 'I'm hungry, Mum: the politics of domestic budgeting', in K. Young (ed.), *Of marriage and the market: women's subordination in international perspective*. London, CSE Books.

——. 1981b. *A conceptual framework for the analysis of the effects of technological change on rural women*. WEP Working Paper, 2–22, No. 79. Geneva, ILO.

——. 1984. *Beyond the household: gender and resource allocation in a Ghanaian domestic economy*. Paper given to Workshop on Conceptualising the Household in Africa, Harvard University.

——. 1986. *Economic transformation and the sexual division of labour in rural production*. Paper to ESRC

Conference on Economic Transformation in Tropical Africa, Centre for West African Studies, Birmingham.

WIN (Women in Nigeria Editorial Committee). 1985. *Women in Nigeria*. Codesria Book Series.

Winikoff, B.; Castle, M.A. 1988. 'The influence of maternal employment on infant feeding', in B. Winikoff; M.A. Castle and V.H. Laukaran (eds), *Feeding infants in four societies*. London, Greenwood Press.

World Bank. 1980. *Employment and income distribution in Indonesia*. East Asia and Pacific Regional Office. Washington, DC, World Bank.

——. 1981. *Accelerated development in sub-Saharan Africa: an agenda for action*. IBRD 3358. Washington, DC, World Bank.

——. 1983. *Sub-Saharan Africa: progress report on development prospects and program*. Washington, DC, World Bank.

——. 1984a. *Sénégal settlement projects in the Terres Neuves Region*. Operations Evaluation Department, Impact Evaluation Report No. 5170. Washington, DC, World Bank.

——. 1984b. *The Gambia agricultural development project*. Operations Evaluation Department, Impact Evaluation Report No. 5125. Washington, DC, World Bank.

——. 1985. *Swaziland: population and health sector review*, Washington, DC, World Bank.

——. 1989a. *Sub-Saharan Africa: from crisis to sustainable growth: a long term perspective study*. Washington, DC, World Bank.

——. 1989b. *The role of women in economic development*. A World Bank Country Study. Washington, DC, World Bank.

——. 1989c. *World development report 1989: financial systems and development, world development undicators*. Oxford University Press.

Wright, M. 1983. 'Technology, marriage and women's work in the history of maize growers in Mazabuka, Zambia: a reconnaissance', *Journal of Southern African Studies*, Vol. 10, No. 1.

Wulf, D. 1985. 'The future of family planning in sub-Saharan Africa', *International Family Planning Perspectives*, Vol. 2, No. 1, March, pp. 1–8.

Yeboah, Y. 1993. *Equal opportunities for women: the implications of adolescent pregnancy and childbirth in sub-Saharan Africa for ILO policies and programmes*. ILO World Employment Programme Working Paper No. 186. Geneva, ILO.

Young, S. 1977. 'Fertility and famine: women's agricultural history in southern Mozambique', in R. Palmer and N. Parsons (eds), *The roots of rural poverty in Central and Southern Africa*. London, Heinemann.

Youssef, N.; Hetler, C. 1984. *Rural households headed by women: a priority concern for development*. ILO World Employment Programme Research Working Paper No. 31. Geneva, ILO.

Zimbabwe, Central Statistical Office. 1989. *Zimbabwe: demographic and health survey 1988*. Columbia, Md., Institute for Resource Development/Macro Systems Inc.

Zimbabwe Women's Bureau, 1981. *We carry a heavy load: rural women in Zimbabwe speak out*. Harare, Zimbabwe Women's Bureau.

Index